THE STRUCTURE OF THE METROPOLITAN COMMUNITY

A Study of
DOMINANCE and SUBDOMINANCE

THE STRUCTURE OF THE
METROPOLITAN COMMUNITY

A Study of
DOMINANCE and SUBDOMINANCE

by

DONALD J. BOGUE

Director, Community and Family
Study Center
The University of Chicago

NEW YORK / RUSSELL & RUSSELL

UNIVERSITY OF MICHIGAN
CONTRIBUTIONS OF THE INSTITUTE FOR HUMAN ADJUSTMENT
SOCIAL SCIENCE RESEARCH PROJECT

FIRST PUBLISHED IN 1950 BY THE
HORACE H. RACKHAM SCHOOL OF GRADUATE STUDIES
UNIVERSITY OF MICHIGAN, ANN ARBOR
REISSUED, 1971, BY RUSSELL & RUSSELL
A DIVISION OF ATHENEUM PUBLISHERS, INC.
BY ARRANGEMENT WITH DONALD J. BOGUE
L. C. CATALOG CARD NO: 75-139904
PRINTED IN THE UNITED STATES OF AMERICA

CONTENTS

Part I

THE PROBLEM OF STUDY, PROCEDURES AND TECHNIQUES, SUMMARY OF FINDINGS

Part II

THE POPULATION STRUCTURE OF METROPOLITAN COMMUNITIES

Part III

THE STRUCTURE OF SUSTENANCE ACTIVITIES IN METROPOLITAN COMMUNITIES

FOREWORD

Amos H. Hawley

ONE OF the most significant social consequences of the industrialization of society is the extraordinary increase in the size and the organizational complexity of the aggregates in which men live. It has long been the practice to conceive this phenomenon in terms of the city, and an enormous literature, scientific and non-scientific, has accumulated about the city concept. But the processes of centralization and expansion unleashed by the Industrial Revolution have refused to yield to the confines of corporation limits. Every advance in the efficiency of transportation and communication has further extended the radius of convenient daily movement, thereby diffusing the urban mode of life over a greatly enlarged area. The result has been the emergence of an entirely new type of urban unit. Indeed, the city is the creature of the nineteenth century; its successor in the twentieth century is the metropolitan community. This new urban unit is an extensive community composed of numerous territorially specialized parts the functions of which are correlated and integrated through the agency of a central city.

Although the development of the metropolitan community has progressed rapidly since the turn of the century, its maturation is far from complete even yet. Manifold changes are still at work in the spatial distribution of population, industry, retailing and services of all kinds and, what is more important, in the total structure of relationships in the city and its tributary area. Because these movements have such radical and hence vital implications for the administration, financing, and functioning of collective life there is urgent need for sound knowledge of the metropolitan community.

Needless to say, the metropolitan community has received a great amount of attention from research scholars. Most of the work that has been done, however, is either of the case study variety or restricted to small problems. Not since the writings of N. S. B. Gras and R. D. McKenzie has a comprehensive analysis appeared; that is, not until the publication of the present volume. But while Gras and McKenzie dealt at length with the development phase of the metropolitan community, Dr. Bogue's study is confined to an examination of metropolitan structure as of a given moment, namely, 1940. It is just this delimitation that permitted the author to achieve a depth of analysis never before attained on so large a scale. His exhaustive treatment of the quantitative relationships among all metropolitan centers, satellite cities, and county units in the United States in respect to the distribution of population, manufacturing, wholesaling, retailing, and personal services, with size of place, distance from metropolis, direction of location relative to a metropolis, and region controlled, stands as a monumental contribution to knowledge on the subject. But this, important as it is, is regarded by Dr. Bogue as preliminary to a larger study which will repeat the analysis contained herein for 1930 and 1950 as a means of plotting the trends of change over the two decades. A reasonable forecast is that the study reported in these pages will serve as a major reference point not only for the author's future efforts but for all subsequent research into metropolitan phenomena.

The publication of this volume by the Social Science Research Project is in keeping with its program of providing graduate research training, fostering research undertakings, and disseminating the findings of research in problems of the metropolitan community. The Social Science Research Project shares the privilege of making this volume available to the public with the Scripps Foundation for Population Research. Dr. Bogue, formerly associated with the Project as a graduate Fellow, devoted almost a full year of his time as a member of the Scripps Foundation staff to the completion of the study. Without the generous assistance of that organization the outcome of so ambitious an enterprise would have been extremely dubious.

THE DISTRIBUTION OF POPULATION AS AN AREA FOR RESEARCH

A Foreword, by Warren S. Thompson

ONE OF the questions which this study aims to answer is: Does the large city have an influence in organizing the distribution of population not only in its immediate vicinity, but within a much larger area tributary to it? If it does, as I believe Dr. Bogue's work demonstrates, then it must be clear that we cannot hope to understand the general pattern of population distribution today or its probable future changes without studying the population structure of the larger metropolitan community in detail as he has done.

Dr. Bogue's study of the metropolitan community was begun without any knowledge on the part of the author of the plans of the Scripps Foundation to undertake a somewhat more ambitious study of the changes taking place in the distribution of population in the United States. His investigation fitted so well into the larger scheme for study of population distribution that he was asked to join the staff of the Scripps Foundation. It was hoped that in this way he would not only be able to expand the study he had begun at the University of Michigan but would be enabled to continue his investigation into many of its related problems.

An important assumption underlying Dr. Bogue's investigation is that the distribution of population within the metropolitan community is a consequence of the type of economy we had developed during the past century or more in Western countries — the economy of the age of steam. We commonly think of the steam-powered economy as a product of the Industrial Revolution (with capitals). Revolution is indeed a highly appropriate term because there occurred not only a wholly new system of production in industry but also a wholly new manner of life. Unfortunately, in our desire to emphasize the significance of manufacturing industry we often seem to forget that the Industrial Revolution was preceded by and accompanied by an agricultural revolution (seldom capitalized) of equal importance from the standpoint of changing man's customary manner of life. Among other effects, these two revolutions completely changed the pattern of the distribution of population. On the one hand, the steady release of labor from agriculture made a rapidly increasing proportion of all labor available for nonagricultural tasks, industry, commerce, science, and the furtherance of human welfare; on the other hand, the use of steam made possible the aggregation of the population released from agriculture in comparatively few large cities and their immediate environs. We can see now that such a pattern of distribution was the natural consequence of those economic changes, but that was not generally realized at the time.

During the steam age, as a matter of fact, there was comparatively little interest in the distribution of population. It was commonly assumed that the maintenance and the increase of the efficiency of the economy demanded such a distribution as was taking place and therefore that was the best possible distribution. Moreover, it was not widely realized that the direct use of steam as motive power and as an agent of communication was the determining factor in the growth of a large city.

Under these circumstances it is not surprising that the metropolis-centered pattern of population distribution was regarded as something inevitable, a development which could not be controlled even if there had been any good reason to attempt its control. So long as population movements contributed, or were believed to contribute, to the increased efficiency of the economy they were good and their desirability was not to be questioned. That the tendency toward concentration might have harmful effects on the economy was unthinkable and that it might have more remote social consequences unfavorable to the community as a whole and to the development of the individual personality was too fantastic to consider seriously.

Once it is fully realized, however, that the actual distribution of population is a natural phenomenon flowing from the development of the economy based on the use of steam power, the development of new power techniques and of new means of communication such as are taking place today raises the question: "What new pattern of population distribution can be expected to emerge?" The new technology associated with the increasing use of the electric motor, the internal combustion engine, the gas turbine, and the possibility in the near future of harnessing atomic energy, are certainly as revolutionary as was the direct use of steam in the latter part of the eighteenth century. Likewise the increasing use of the telephone and the airplane and the increasing likelihood of electronic devices for direct long distance communication contribute to the probability that there will soon be a reorganization of the economic structure which will in turn effect a new pattern of population distribution purely as a matter of economic adjustment.

But, in addition to the purely economic aspects of the redistribution of population likely to arise from the use of these new techniques, many people are already questioning the desirability of living in the modern large city from other standpoints. They are asking whether the city has a harmful effect on health, citing the rapid increase of heart ailments, of cancer, and of mental ills; they are asking whether man will refuse to reproduce in crowded quarters once he has any choice in the matter, citing the fact that very few if any large cities are now maintaining their own numbers; they are wondering what will be the psychological effects on children raised in environments where they are insulated from most contacts with the phenomena of nature; they are asking whether it is possible for the masses of the workers who have relatively small incomes to live comfortably and decently in the crowded areas of modern cities. It is not in the least surprising that there is an increasing interest in the study of population and a growing feeling that we should no longer trust to chance to achieve a distribution in this new age which will assure not only an efficient economy but also a larger measure of social and individual welfare.

Finally, the development of the atomic bomb and the perfecting of methods of mass destruction through biological warfare has made us think about the settlement pattern as never before. Today man's very survival may in large measure depend on an intelligent distribution of population. It is little wonder, therefore, that there is an awakening concern with how we are distributing ourselves over the land and a growing belief that we must plan our distribution if we would have a better life.

Too little is known about the details of the relationship between population distribution and the functioning of the economy to provide a basis for answering the questions listed above. As scientists we have formulated too few verified generalizations to permit us to predict what effects present technological changes will have upon future population patterns. The knowledge which we have contributed is too general to be genuinely useful to those who are interested in altering present configurations in order to gain social ends. Any workable plan or policy for population distribution will necessarily be preceded by careful and detailed research. It is to be hoped that the study of population distribution will receive considerably more attention in the immediate future than in the past. I regard research in this field as one of the outstanding opportunities for social scientists to hasten population adjustment in this age of electronics, atomic power, and concern for human welfare.

The conclusion of this study, that urban centers are now and probably will continue to be, the major focal points of economic organization and hence, determiners of the pattern of population distribution, seems to me undeniable. Thus all plans for the redistribution of population which fail to take account of that fact would seem to be doomed in advance. This does not mean, however, that the present type of big city and the present degree of "dominance" by big cities is inevitable. Economic necessity changes with the development of new techniques and only metropolitan provincialism will deny that these new techniques may possibly have as much effect on the patterns of population distribution in the next several decades as the direct use of steam did during the 19th century.

This study is to be regarded as a step, but a significant step, in acquiring a better understanding of the present pattern of metropolitan phenomena. It is taken in the hope that it will be succeeded by longer and more assured steps in the near future which will lead to a current appraisal of the factors operating to effect the redistribution of our population. To drop the metaphor, it is hoped that this study will do something to encourage other studies so that in time we shall be able to improve our manner of life by the rational control of human settlement in those types of communities which man may find most congenial to his nature.

ACKNOWLEDGMENTS

THIS STUDY of the dominance of metropolitan centers and the subdominance of hinterland cities grew out of course work in Human Ecology under Dr. A. H. Hawley and from participation in the interdepartmental Metropolitan Community Seminar of the Social Science Research Project at the University of Michigan. It was begun in 1941 under a research fellowship, as a part of the latter program, and was resumed in 1946 after the war. In February, 1947, it was merged with the larger program of research in the field of population distribution in which Scripps Foundation for Research in Population Problems is engaged. Dr. Hawley, as Chairman of the thesis committee, and Dr. Warren Thompson, as Director of the Foundation, have both given unsparingly of their insight and experience in this attempt to test a major hypothesis concerning community and intercommunity structure and functioning. I have borrowed heavily from them, a fact which will be apparent to those readers who are students of human ecology and population.

The formulation of the problem in a form which would permit factual materials to be assembled and analyzed in order to obtain scientific generalizations is largely a product of training and experience gained as graduate assistant to Mr. Clark Tibbitts, Director of the Institute for Human Adjustment, and from his seminar in Techniques of Social Research. As a member of the thesis committee, Mr. Tibbitts reviewed the entire plan of analysis and made suggestions which proved to be invaluable at later stages of the work.

To Professor Edgar M. Hoover of the Department of Economics, to Professor Robert B. Hall, of the Department of Geography, and to the other members of the Metropolitan Community Seminar at the University of Michigan I owe many fruitful hours of discussion of the metropolitan community as an area of research. To Professors Robert C. Angell and Lowell J. Carr of the Department of Sociology, as well as to Professors Hoover and Hall, I owe many thanks for a careful study and evaluation of my research plans and helpful suggestions for executing them. Professor Gardner Ackley, who replaced Professor Hoover as a member of the thesis committee, suggested several improvements in the final manuscript.

Mr. Alan D. Meacham, University of Michigan Tabulating Station, kindly placed his tabulating machines at my disposal for use outside working hours. Mr. Charles Koethen and Mr. John Ellsworth of his staff were of great assistance in solving problems of machine tabulation.

To the staff of Scripps Foundation I am indebted for many months of statistical aid. Mrs. Ruth Smith undertook the tedious job of coding the geographical units from especially prepared maps. She and Mrs. Evangelyn Minnis prepared the data for tabulation. Mrs. Smith had charge of deriving the final talbes from the machine tabulations. Her keen interest and exceptional ability are manifest throughout the pages which follow. Mrs. Jean Calhoun, Mrs. Anita Stone, and Miss Ingrid Neuhaus assisted Mrs. Smith with the statistical work. The charts and maps are the work of Mrs. Stone.

The manuscript was typed by Mrs. W. Fred Cottrell, Mrs. Minnis, and Mrs. Beverley Weed. Mrs. Jeanette Lewis edited the entire manuscript for publication. Mrs. Elizabeth J. Bogue, my wife, assisted in collecting the data and in making the machine tabulations.

The United States Bureau of the Census kindly provided me with totals for groupings of cities and counties for which the data for wholesale trade and manufactures had been withheld to avoid disclosing the operations of individual establishments.

To the Social Science Research Council I am indebted for a Demobilization Award which permitted me to resume my graduate studies after the war. To Scripps Foundation I am indebted for funds to complete the study as a part of its program of research in the field of population distribution.

Donald J. Bogue

PART I

THE PROBLEM OF STUDY,
PROCEDURES AND TECHNIQUES,
SUMMARY OF FINDINGS

CHAPTER ONE

THE HYPOTHESIS OF METROPOLITAN DOMINANCE

I

Introduction: The Goal of This Study

This study is an attempt to explore some aspects of the hypothesis that great cities, or metropolises, dominate the social and economic organization of technologically advanced societies. The hypothesis is one of long standing and one which has been propounded by students of many disciplines. Within recent years it has become a conception of human organization taken by many leading scholars of diverse fields, and for this reason it has been stated from many points of view. In essence it is an extension and attempted refinement of the more general theory of urban dominance, that is, that cities in general are the foci about which the life of modern nations is organized. The intention in these pages is not to prove or to disprove that a single great city can dominate some of its environs; it is rather to examine the much broader proposition that, collectively, great cities can and do dominate a technologically advanced industrial and commercial society.

The aspects of human organization which this study undertakes to analyze are those which pertain to the distribution over the land of human populations and of selected types of human activities involved in gaining a livelihood. Other less tangible aspects of human culture such as morals, aspirations, values, and social activities not directed toward obtaining a livelihood are not considered, although these aspects of social organization are as germane to the problem under consideration and may be as easily dominated by great cities as the more readily observed facts of human residence and labor.

As a point of departure it has been assumed that if the great city is actually the dominating force in modern social and economic organization, then great expanses of land area and the populations which inhabit them should be found to be organized with respect to, and integrated with, the activities of the central metropolis, and that this organization and integration must manifest itself in some observable pattern of population arrangement

and territorial division of labor. To determine whether there is a metropolis-centered pattern of population distribution and a conjoined pattern of industrial and commercial interdependence is the goal of this study. In brief, the aim is to determine whether, in the course of their rise to great size, cities which are considered to be metropolitan centers have also become the focal points of a much larger physical entity with a definite pattern or structure. This larger entity, for reasons to be explained later, has been called the "metropolitan community." The problem of the study may be stated in the form of a series of questions about metropolitan communities:

a. Are there observable groupings and arrangements of people and human activities which may be termed metropolitan communities?
b. If so, by what pattern are the parts of those groupings arranged with respect to the metropolis?
c. Do metropolitan communities encompass all or only a part of the land areas and peoples of a technologically advanced society?
d. What implications does the arrangement of people and activities in the metropolitan community have for the operation of the individual city, village, or farm which lies within the metropolitan community unit at a distance from the metropolis?

Since the hypothesis under study is a broad statement about the role of metropolitan centers in the organization of an entire society, its validity cannot be tested on a small segment of land area or population. For this reason one entire nation, the United States, has been taken as an example of a technologically advanced society. It has been subjected to study by subdividing its entire area into metropolitan communities, and by abstracting patterns of population distribution from various groupings of these metropolitan communities and of their parts.

In undertaking this task it has been deemed necessary to begin with the basic facts upon which a theory of dominance in human communities must rest. If a phenomenon of metropolitan dominance exists, it must not be regarded as a mysterious "essence," but as a class name for the effects of a multitude of different processes which give to metropolitan centers a unique position in the social and economic organization of the nation. After examining the concept of "dominance" and determining the precise meaning to be given it, a procedure is outlined for studying the pattern of population distribution and the distributional patterns, with respect to metropolitan centers, of manufacturing, retail trade, wholesale trade, and service establishments.

If these preliminary considerations which constitute the first two chapters appear to be unduly abstract and somewhat speculative, the reader will be reassured to find the ideas which are developed there associated later with a plentitude of factual materials; with these materials he can determine for himself the validity, applicability, and utility the ideas have in an understanding of the role which the great city plays in the far-flung organization which supports it and which it supports.

II

The Urban and the Metropolitan Interpretation
of Modern Life

A. The Influence of Cities Upon Social Organization
It would be difficult to state a principle about human organization which commands more agreement among students of many disciplines than the general observation that:

> The city has become the central feature in modern civilization and to an ever increasing extent the dominant one . . . This rural civilization, whose making engaged mankind since the dawn of history, is passing away. The city has erased the landmarks of an earlier society. Man has entered on an urban age. . . . [1]

Cities have increased in number and size so rapidly since the beginning of the nineteenth century that more knowledge about urbanism is now a prerequisite to further progress in many branches of science, and also for arrival at a solution to many current problems. The sociologist, the political scientist, the economist, the geographer, the psychologist, and the historian find it difficult, without referring to the influence of the city, to explain fully some aspects of human behavior which they study. An industrialist selecting a site for a plant, a retailer attempting to distribute goods to a maximum number of people at minimum expense, or a railroad, telephone or bus corporation expanding and extending its services must each make choices in which future success depends to a considerable extent upon a correct judgment of the future course of urbanism. The social worker, the clergyman, the educator, and the candidate for public office must take account of the influence of the city upon those they serve. The establishment of city planning commissions and the great interest which chambers of commerce, real estate associations, and leagues of urban voters have taken in programs of urban development and redevelopment attest to the fact that even the units which have administered and promoted city growth have not understood, in the past, the full implications of their actions. The rise of the city has culminated, in the twentieth century, in a widespread and growing demand for more knowledge about cities; for a comprehension of urbanism seems to be required for an understanding of our civilization. By becoming one of the principal characteristics of the political, economic, and social organization of the western world, the city has become a major area for research.

A corollary of this view — that today's urbanism must be comprehended in order to understand today's civilization — is the generally accepted opinion that a prediction of tomorrow's civilization necessitates a forecast of the form and extent of urbanism. A great variety of events whose future course we would like to predict and guide appears to be directly related to the city. What will be the population of the United States in the year 2000 A. D.? How many automobiles will be in use twenty years from now? What are the possibilities of the United States surviving an atomic or a biological war? What are the probabilities that a labor party will elect a president of the United States in 1960? What will be the future trend of crime rates? One cannot progress far in speculating upon these and similar problems without making assumptions about the cities of the future. Whether one is seeking knowledge about human events, trying to forecast the future, or trying to operate a business successfully, he inevitably encounters the necessity of attempting to predict the behavior of cities.

If the judgment of so good an authority as Charles A Beard is accepted, in times yet to come the urgency of the endeavor to understand urbanism will increase rather than decrease:

1. Frederic C. Howe, The City, the Hope of Democracy (New York: Charles Scribner Sons, 1906), p. 22.

It is from the urban centers that the national economy of the future will be controlled, whether we like it or not, and it is the culture of urbanism which dominates the future.[2]

B. Problems Encountered in Attempting an Urban Interpretation of Modern Life.

Despite the desire and the need for scientific generalizations about cities and the role which they play in our civilization, the body of knowledge in this field is far from complete, or even adequate. Many problems beset those who attempt to make a scientific study of urbanism, two of which are extraordinarily difficult. First, cities are a very heterogeneous class of phenomena and, second, cities are not events which have occurred independently of each other.

Even a casual observation of the role which they play in the life and organization of a nation quickly reveals the fact that cities are not all alike; they differ from each other in a great many respects. By definition, cities in the United States vary in size from 2500 to several million inhabitants. Some function as simple rural service centers while others are huge and complex centers of industry, commerce, finance, or government. Some are highly specialized in one activity; others perform many functions. Cities can be alike in size and function and yet be composed of populations which are very unlike in regard to such characteristics as age, sex, nationality, education, or even religious and political affiliation.

In the case of a great many of the dissimilarities between cities, there is no norm about which the majority of cities tend to cluster. In other words, there is no representative "average" city which can be taken as representative of all cities. Consider simply the size of cities, for example. If one adds together the population of all places in the United States which were considered urban in 1940 (74,423,702 people) and divides this population by the total number of urban places in 1940 (3,464) he obtains an average population of 21,485 inhabitants for cities in the United States. Yet in 1940 2,990, or 86 percent, of all of the urban places in the United States were smaller than this, and only 14 percent were larger. A city of 21,000 inhabitants can scarcely be said to be representative of New York City, or of Green River, Wyoming, (population 2,640 in 1940). If one selects one aspect of urban life and assigns an index value of that aspect to every city in the United States, he will find, in many instances, that the average index value will differ from the index values of those cities which he considers to be, on other grounds, the most important or the most typical of modern cities. Life in New York City may be more important for the study of urbanism than life in Pine Bluff, Arkansas, which, in population size, lay almost at the national average in 1940.[3] We correctly speak of the average height, weight, or intelligence of people because the distribution of each of these traits has a "central tendency," a norm about which individual values tend to cluster. One cannot speak of "the city" or of "the urban way of life" and convey that same preciseness of meaning. Cities and urban conditions of living exhibit great diversity. There is no single norm which can be used to characterize many of their aspects.

The interdependence of cities is too familiar to require detailed comment. Many cities owe their birth and growth to the presence of other cities; dormitory cities and manufacturing satellite cities are of this type. Each city has not emerged as an event which is completely independent of similar events in the past, or of the behavior of other cities in the present. The study of cities must be pursued along lines which acknowledge this basic fact.

C. The Hypothesis of Metropolitan Dominance.

Out of the attempts to understand cities and their place in the modern world has grown a generalization which may be called the "dominant city" hypothesis or the "hypothesis of metropolitan dominance." This hypothesis seeks to escape part of the aforesaid difficulties of understanding "urbanism" as a single characteristic, and attempts to solve the problem of intercity interdependence. It classifies cities on the basis of the functions which they perform and their relative ability to "dominate" other cities and the surrounding countryside. The classification made in formulating this hypothesis is a dichotomous one; cities are divided into "metropolitan centers" and "hinterland cities." The metropolis is usually the largest and most complex (the farthest removed from the "average" city) of all of the cities in the territory. Because it is able to assemble cheaply a varied array of raw materials and products from all parts of the world; because a large number of specialized components and skills are required in the production of the goods required to sustain human beings at their present level of living; because up to a

2. "The City's Place in Civilization," National Municipal Review, December, 1925.

3. For a discussion of the magnitude of some intercity differences see W. F. Ogburn, Social Characteristics of Cities (Chicago: International City Managers Association, 1937).

certain point machine production increases in efficiency with an increased scale of operations; and because certain mutual benefits appear to accrue to business enterprises from their location in proximity to each other, the large city is able to produce and distribute more varied goods and services than is a smaller city. The more specialized the goods, and the more the goods are amenable to mass production, the greater these industrial and commercial advantages of large cities seem to become. From these facts it has been concluded that the metropolis, or modern large and complex city, exercises an organizing and integrative influence on the social and economic life of a broad expanse of territory far beyond the civil boundaries, and thereby dominates all other communities within this area. The hypothesis of metropolitan dominance assumes that there is a system of interdependency among cities, and that there are considerable differences between the activities of individual cities. It maintains that the organizing agent, and one of the forces making for intercity differentiation, is the metropolis.

Sufficient evidence has been accumulated to make of this view a very plausible hypothesis. Smaller cities and villages lying in the region about great cities appear to have been drawn into a division of labor with the larger urban center. They exchange for the specialized goods and services of the metropolis such other products as can most effectively be produced from the resources in their immediate locality. Farm operators also appear to have become more dependent upon metropolitan markets, and consequently have regulated their activities to produce, if possible, those products which will yield them the greatest return in the metropolitan market. With these exchanges of material goods has also gone the exchange of ideas and human values. The metropolis appears to have become the focal point not only of our material activities, but of much of our moral and intellectual life as well. Repeatedly it has been pointed out that not only in activities such as non-agricultural production, distribution, and finance, but also in matters of government, progress in the arts and sciences, news dissemination and the formation of public opinion, changed philosophies of religion, and the emergence of new human values, the great metropolis is now the dominating center. To one who accepts such a view, progress toward understanding many economic and social problems of this century can come only from a thorough analysis of the metropolis and its relation to other communities.

Although this hypothesis frequently has been expressed in the form stated here, it has never been submitted to a fair test of verification. However, the research which has been accomplished in the field of metropolitan dominance, although highly selective, is of such high quality that to accomplish the goal of this study it has been necessary to do little more than to assemble the various conclusions drawn by others from partial data, to organize these conclusions systematically as parts of the central hypothesis of metropolitan dominance, and then to devise a procedure for determining their validity.

Because the influence of metropolitan centers has not been analyzed for one complete society, the term "hypothesis of metropolitan dominance" rather than "theory of metropolitan dominance" is used throughout this study. Previous researches in this field have either:

a. Studied only the area immediately surrounding the metropolis and have ignored the outlying territory, or

b. Studied one, or at best only a few, of the broader metropolitan areas — usually those surrounding the very largest cities. The first type of study is an extension of the urbanism theory; the second type suffers from sampling bias.

From the outset it must be emphasized that the distinction between urbanism and metropolitanism is preserved throughout this project. This is a study of metropolitan dominance, not of urban dominance; of metropolitanized society, not of urbanized society; of the structure of the metropolitan community, not of the urban community. By urban we mean "pertaining to all cities," by metropolitan we mean "pertaining to the metropolis." One can study the internal structure of either the city community or the metropolitan community. A great deal of thought and research has been devoted to the study of urbanism and urban structure in general. By comparison, much less effort has been made to trace the influence of the metropolis and the degree to which our society is patterned or structured with respect to these larger urban centers.

III

Previous Studies of Metropolitan Dominance

Two formulations of the metropolitan hypothesis are outstanding for their completeness of detail and the care with which evidence has been collected for their expression. They are N.S.B. Gras' An Introduction to Economic History[4] and R. D.

---

4. New York: Harper & Brothers, 1922.

McKenzie's The Metropolitan Community.[5] Gras and McKenzie were among the first in their respective fields to attempt to link the present urbanized way of life to pre-industrial organization via the route of community analysis. The research of both men is based upon the premise that the community is the elemental form of social organization. Aside from this common point of view, their techniques, their data, and their modes of analysis differ; yet they reach surprisingly similar conclusions. Gras arrived at the metropolitan hypothesis by an informal case study and natural history approach, using historical and anthropological information covering the entire period of man's recorded history. McKenzie's statement of the metropolitan hypothesis is derived from a more formal statistical study of urbanism in the United States since 1790.

A. N. S. B. Gras and the "Metropolitan Economy."

The basic thesis of Gras' Introduction to Economic History is that at each stage of technological development man has simultaneously developed a community organization which is suitable to the new techniques of wresting a livelihood from the resources of nature. By using existing information about the technological progress of man through the period of his recorded history, and comparable information about his economic and social organization Gras informally correlates the two. He divides the continuum of technological and communal development of Western Civilization into five major phases or periods: (a) the collectional economy, (b) the cultural nomadic economy, (c) the settled village economy, (d) the town economy, and finally (e) the metropolitan economy. Each phase is named for the type of social development dominant in that period. Throughout his history technological change has progressively released man from the necessity of sustaining himself from his immediate environment. Yet the lessening of this dependence upon the local area has been achieved only at the expense of a corresponding dependence upon a more complex system of production and exchange extending over a wider area. Such a system has invariably involved greater specialization and division of labor. In order to achieve the potential gains of each new major technological development, new and larger combinations of population and resources have been required.

Consequently, new types of social organization have emerged which have been composed of units better adapted to operate under the new economy. Each major phase of technological development has been accompanied by a major change in the size, form, and organization of the community. Thus, according to Gras' interpretation, each of the five types of community enumerated above has risen to operate a different type of economy, which in turn has been the result of the attainment of a new level of technological advance.

The modern stage of metropolitan economy Gras describes as follows:

We may think of metropolitan economy as an organization of people having a large city as nucleus. Or we may put it this way, metropolitan economy is the organization of producers and consumers mutually dependent for goods and services, wherein their wants are supplied by a system of exchange concentrated in a large city which is the focus of local trade and the center through which normal economic relations with the outside are established and maintained.

Just as villages remained when town economy prevailed, so do towns remain when metropolitan economy comes into existence. Towns remain, but in economic subordination to the metropolis. They continue to play a part, but as tributaries to a larger center. A closer examination of these dependent towns would show different types performing different functions, but all subordinate.[6]

Gras defines his metropolis in terms of function rather than size: Hence "...mere agglomeration of individuals, important as that is, does not constitute a metropolis in the sense used in this book. What counts most is commercial dominance over a wide area."[7]

The one situational factor which Gras holds to be absolutely essential for the development of a city aspirant to metropolitan status is the possession of a hinterland,[8] "a tributary adjacent territory, rich in natural resources, accompanied by a productive population and accessible by means of transportation."[9] We are warned by Gras not to overemphasize either the metropolis or the hinterland in considering the metropolitan organization.

---

5. New York: McGraw-Hill, 1933.

6. Op. cit., p. 184.

7. Ibid., p. 184.

8. A concept developed by the Geographers. See Eugene Van Cleef, "Hinterland and Umland," Geographical Review, April, 1941. pp. 308-311.

9. Gras, op. cit., p. 185.

It is true that in studying this organization we are inclined to emphasize the great metropolitan center; but to forget the large dependent district would be fatal to a correct understanding of the subject. Perhaps, indeed, it is somewhat incorrect to speak of the area as dependent upon the center, for though that is true, the center is also dependent upon the outlying area with its towns, villages, and scattered homesteads. Interdependence of parts is really the key to the whole thing.[10]

The striking element about the metropolitan hypothesis as formulated by Gras is not that great cities exist, nor even that they dominate a broad expanse of territory, but that the metropolitan economy is the characteristic and dominant type of modern social and economic organization. Thus Gras expresses the metropolitan hypothesis that ours is a "metropolitanized" culture. The metropolis and the hinterland are held to be parts of one organic whole. Our present day society operates in terms of, and is conditioned by, these metropolitan units. According to Gras, the metropolitan economy is a modern form of social organization by which man makes effective use of his advanced technology.

B. R. D. McKenzie and "The Metropolitan Community."

From its birth sociology has been an eclectic discipline. Hence it is not surprising to find that sociologists are quick to apply to their studies of human communities the principles and findings of workers in other disciplines. A most potent importation has been the application to human communities of the point of view of a group of biologists who study plant and animal communities and who term themselves "ecologists." R. D. McKenzie, one of these sociological students of bio-ecology, has become the chief proponent of the ecological approach to the study of the human community. In a series of definitive statements he has outlined this approach.[11]

Ecology, according to two of its leading students, is the "science of community populations."[12] To the ecologist, the development of organized communities appears to be a universal technique by which all living matter adapts to external life conditions. Under conditions of universal scarcity of life-supporting resources living units act upon, and react to, the behavior of other living units and to the conditions of the non-living environment. In the course of this complex process, the behavior of the living units is altered to minimize the effort to live and to maximize the livelihood obtained by a given amount of effort. Moreover, the living units modify the non-living environment to achieve this same end. The resulting integration of organism with organism is termed a "community." The non-living matter, as modified by the members of the community, is termed the "habitat."

This postulate has been applied to the human realm in a direct and almost unaltered form by the human ecologist:

The unit of ecological study is the communal organism, which is at once an aggregation of individual persons, a geographical and cultural habitat, and an interrelated and interdependent bio-social unity. The community thus conceived has many things in common with the plant and animal community. Its component units are bound together by the interdependence which arises out of specialization and division of labor.[13]

How a division of labor between unlike units can operate to form a functioning community is clearly indicated in the following statement:

As the division of labor which thus develops approaches equilibrium such that the number of organisms engaged in each of the several activities is sufficient to provide all of the needs that are represented, the aggregate of associated individuals assumes the aspect of a compact viable entity, a super organism in fact. The (biotic) community, as such a functionally or symbiotically integrated population may be called, is in

10. Ibid., p. 186-187. (Italics are mine).
11. "The Ecological Approach to the Study of the Human Community," American Journal of Sociology, November, 1924, pp. 287-361. "The Scope of Human Ecology," American Journal of Sociology, July, 1926, pp. 141-54. "Human Ecology," Encyclopedia of the Social Sciences, Vol. 5, pp. 314-15. "The Field and Problems of Demography. Human Geography, and Human Ecology," in L. L. Bernard (ed.) The Fields and Methods of Sociology, (New York: Ray Land and Richard R. Smith, Inc., 1934).
12. Frederic E. Clements and Victor E. Shelford, Bio-ecology (New York: John Wiley & Sons, Inc. 1939), p. 3.
13. R. D. McKenzie, "The Field and Problems of Demography, Human Geography, and Human Ecology," op. cit., p. 59.

effect a collective response to the habitat; it constitutes the adjustment, in the fullest sense of the term, of organism to environment.[14]

Human ecology, pursuing its study of human aggregates as an adaption to the environment, has also arrived at the metropolitan hypothesis. One of the series of monographs published under the direction of the President's Research Committee on Social Trends was McKenzie's The Metropolitan Community, a work devoted entirely to a development of this hypothesis.

By reducing the scale of local distance, the motor vehicle extended the horizon of the community and introduced a territorial division of labor among local institutions and neighboring centers which is unique in the history of settlement. The large center has been able to extend the radius of its influence; its population and many of its institutions, freed from the dominance of rail transportation, have become widely dispersed throughout surrounding territory. Moreover, formerly independent towns and villages and also rural territory have become part of this enlarged city complex. This new type of super community organized around a dominant focal point and comprising a multitude of differentiated centers of activity differs from the metropolitanism established by rail transportation in the complexity of its institutional division of labor and the mobility of its population. Its territorial scope is defined in terms of motor transportation and competition with other regions. Nor is this new type of metropolitan community confined to the great cities. It has become the communal unit of local relations throughout the entire nation.[15]

McKenzie accumulated a detailed mass of evidence which demonstrated that the metropolitan center is a true dominant among community types. After reviewing the existing population data and data for many diverse economic activities he concludes:

The super community therefore absorbs varying numbers of separate local communities into its economic and cultural organizations. In this pattern a dominant city — that

is, dominant relative to surrounding settlement, functions as the integrating unit . . . In other words, there is developing within the United States, and in fact throughout the modern world, a pattern of settlement which may be designated as city regionalism. This new city regionalism differs from the regionalism of former times in that it is a product of contact and division of labor rather than of mere geographic isolation.[16]

The ecological view of cities may be summarized as follows:

a. The human community (including city communities) is an organization one purpose of which is adaption to the environment.
b. New techniques of transportation and production (technological change) have permitted great cities to dominate smaller cities and other communities surrounding them.
c. These outlying communities are subordinate to the metropolis and are integrated with it.
d. This integration of outlying territory (hinterland) with the metropolis has become a standard form of social organization throughout the entire United States.

Gras and McKenzie therefore reached identical conclusions: not cities in general, but metropolitan cities in particular, dominate our society today. This dominance has come about as an orderly change in human organization, through the use of new techniques for supplying the necessities of life from the environment. Such an orientation of activities toward the metropolis is regarded as an epoch of community organization.

The careful reader will note that McKenzie has used the term "metropolitan region" to refer to the broader unit of metropolitan dominance and interdependence. Gras termed such a unit a "metropolitan economy." That McKenzie conceived the metropolitan region to be a community in the ecological sense is clear from his statement of the object of his study.

The object of this study is to trace the rise of this new type of regional community, to note the forces which are bringing it about and determining its form and modus operandi.[17]

---

14. Amos H. Hawley, "Ecology and Human Ecology," Social Forces, May, 1944, p. 403.
15. R. D. McKenzie, The Metropolitan Community (New York: McGraw-Hill, 1933) p. 7. (Italics are mine).
16. Ibid., p. 313.
17. Ibid., p. 7.

The term "region" has been widely used by geographers and other social scientists to denote areas of homogeneity. If the area of metropolitan dominance is organized on the basis of specialization and a division of labor, one would expect the greatest diversity of activity among its parts. Because "region" and "regionalism" do connote homogeneity, they seem inappropriate when applied to the area of metropolitan dominance. In this study the simple expedient has been adopted of terming the whole area of postulated metropolitan dominance the "metropolitan community." Although this usage of the term "community" may be unconventional from some points of view, it can be justified on several grounds.

a. It accords with standard ecological usage.
b. There is no simple division point between the urban community of the metropolis and the hinterland. One fades into the other by degrees. The boundaries which are established must inevitably refer to some index of metropolitan influence. Since metropolitan influence in its broadest sense is the subject here, the broader definition of the metropolitan community is used.
c. It is generally assumed that the largest cities are breaking up, that new metropolitan centers are arising, and that in the not too distant future the metropolitan community, as defined here, may coincide with the local community of the metropolis where (daily) "communication" and "commuting" are the chief indices.[18]

Throughout this study the term "metropolitan community" will be used to refer to the metropolis and its hinterland as a unit. In this sense it is synonymous with the area embraced by Gras' "metropolitan economy" and McKenzie's "metropolitan region." The terms "central city," "metropolitan center," or "metropolis" will be used to refer to the hypothetically dominant aggregate at the center of the metropolitan community.

IV

The Metropolitan Hypothesis as a Problem of Ecological Dominance

The term "dominance" has been used repeatedly in the foregoing discussion to characterize the relationship between the metropolis and the hinterland. McKenzie's statement of the metropolitan hypothesis from the ecological point of view seems to depend almost entirely upon the use of this term. Gras likewise stated that "commercial dominance" over a wide area is the chief characteristic of metropolitan centers. It will be remembered that, in the above quotations from the works of Frederick C. Howe and Charles A. Beard, the term "dominant" was used by both to express the present and estimated future position of the city in civilization. In signifying the relationship between urban and rural peoples, between great and small cities, some form of the word "dominant" has been found to be meaningful to many scholars. The bio-ecologists also have found this same term a most meaningful one in expressing the interrelationship between the units of plant and animal communities. The act of dominating, the process of dominance, or the status of being a dominant unit appears to occur at all levels of communal organization. In an effort to clarify and to give more specific content to the term "metropolitan dominance," the use of the term by bio-ecologists will be explored.

To the bio-ecologist, dominance has a meaning which differs somewhat from its popular connotation.

....A dominant is an organism with such definite relations to climate and such significant reactions upon the habitat....as to control the community and assign to the other species subordinate positions of varying rank.[19]

Hence dominance, in its ecological meaning, is a special kind of control over a community of inter-functioning units.

An example from the field of plant ecology will perhaps serve to clarify the meaning of the term dominance. A single hardwood tree standing alone in a field has very little control over the number and types of plants which grow in the field. Its presence changes the field very little except in its immediate vicinity. The situation would be very different if the field were populated with many hardwood trees. Whereas the leaves which fall from a single tree are quickly blown away by the wind, a forest of trees breaks the wind, permitting the leaves to fall to the ground at the base of the trees. Humus is produced; the soil is thereby enriched, and the water holding capacity of the soil is increased. The combined shade of the trees controls the amount of sunlight and modifies the temperature of the soil. Referring to the definition

18. W. S. Thompson "Urbanization" Encyclopedia of the Social Sciences, Vol. 15, pp. 189-92; Homer Hoyt, "The Structure of American Cities in the Postwar Era," American Journal of Sociology, January, 1943, pp. 475-81.
19. Clements and Shelford, op. cit., p. 239.

of dominance given above, this forest has "reacted upon the habitat" in a very definite manner in terms of the amount of available moisture, light, and soil fertility as well as in terms of temperature. Only those species which are adapted to the conditions imposed by the forest can thrive within it. Species which cannot adapt to these conditions are extinguished. The smaller species are dependent upon the dominant species for maintaining certain environmental conditions necessary for their survival. The dominant species may be dependent upon the lesser species for other functions, such as preventing erosion, aiding in maintaining fertility, or discouraging the invasion of potential threats to the dominant species by destroying the seedlings of invaders. Thus, a genuine community of interdependent units emerges, based upon the hardwood trees as dominants.

The hardwood community did not come about as a fortuitous event, however. Many other species capable of accomplishing the same or similar controls undoubtedly made a bid for the position which the hardwoods attained. These other species failed, the bio-ecologists tell us, because they were less able to cope with all of the conditions of the environment. Perhaps they froze out in the winter. The growing season might not have been long enough for them. A predator might have destroyed their seeds and thus made reproduction impossible. The ecologists assure us that this position of control which the hardwoods have achieved, in our example, is attained only because of an ability to meet and survive under the particular conditions of the environment. If this forest plot were moved to a spot 10,000 feet above sea level or to the equator, or if the annual rainfall were quartered or quadrupled, the dominance of the hardwoods would quickly disappear in favor of other species. Again referring to the above definition of dominance, it is evident that in our example the hardwoods do have such "definite relations to climate" and, as has been shown, "have reacted upon the habitat" in such a definite manner, that the entire field (community of plants) is controlled by the hardwoods. The other members of the community must accept subordinate (dependent) positions of varying rank as determined by the presence of the dominant hardwoods.

Thus, a dominant in nature exercises its control not by ordering and forbidding, not by virtue of any authority or right to command, but by controlling the conditions of life. The right to this control is earned only after a demonstration of the ability to adjust to the wide variety of conditions in the environment. The dominant species may be thought of also as a product of the struggle of all life to adapt. It is a life form which has proved conspicuously successful in surviving, first by adapting to the conditions surrounding it and, second, by reacting upon and altering the environment to benefit its own needs.

When one reflects upon the relationship between the great city and the territory surrounding it, he is impressed by the similarity of this relationship to that found by the bio-ecologist in plant and animal communities. Metropolitan centers have no legal authority to order their smaller neighbors to produce or not to produce a given type of commodity, to inhabit or not to inhabit the land with a given number of persons per square mile, or to think specific thoughts and hold specified beliefs about political, moral, or economic events. If the metropolis does dominate its environment, it does so without coercion and edict.

If the above example of the single tree and the forest is applied to the problem at hand, the applicability of the ecological concept of "dominance" becomes clearer. At the time the territory which is now the United States was first settled, human communities were forced to deal directly with the physical environment. The villages and small cities which were established were in much the position of the lone tree in the field: they drew their nurture from the immediate vicinity, and local catastrophe threatened their existence at all times. They specialized primarily in extracting the most easily obtained resources of the environment, such as fur, lumber, fish, game, and the simpler agricultural products. A considerable amount of the materials extracted or produced were removed from the area by external forces, as were the leaves from the lone tree, for the original colonies were raw material exporters. Just as the single tree derives benefit from the production of leaves, but is able to derive the secondary benefit of the complete consumption of the product only by interacting with others of its kind, so the individual colonies could realize the full benefit of their productive efforts only when they were able to establish inter-community trade and exert some control over the external forces. Beard has well documented the struggle of the colonial communities to gain for themselves the complete nourishment of their products.[20]

Gradually the interdependences of the colonial cities increased, and as they grew in number and size they achieved a greater degree of control over the environment. The cities had not only adapted

20. Charles A. Beard, An Economic Interpretation of the Constitution of the United States, (New York: The Macmillan Company, 1913.)

to the particular conditions of their environment, but had entered the phase of dominance by modifying and differentiating that environment through new types of activity. Canals, railways, and highways were cut from city to city and from cities into the wilderness. Budding manufacturing activities and new trade opportunities encouraged deforestation and the use of the land to produce raw materials and food for fabrication and exchange through urban centers. As the cities grew they became market centers for each others products and for their respective hinterlands. The value which was placed upon the products and activities of outlying areas came to be less a matter of custom and more a matter of a price established by metropolitan markets. Cities consciously strove to annex new territory to their trade areas, to gain for themselves a hinterland.[21] As the frontier advanced westward, "gateway" cities sprang up to provide the functions which earlier colonial towns had performed. Gradually the frontier areas, too, have become "forested" with metropolitan centers. As the number of these centers has multiplied and the system of interchange among them has grown more complex, control over the physical environment has been progressively extended. Presumably this process has not yet attained a climax stage in which a point of equilibrium is attained between the dominating species and the supporting environment. In the meantime, individual communities have thrived when they have adjusted themselves to the conditions imposed by metropolitan centers. When their activities have not been so adapted they have tended to become ghost towns.

Such is the interpretation which can be placed upon the dominance of the great city. Not control through ordering and forbidding, but control through the more subtle means of heightened interdependence, alteration of the physical habitat, and a modification of the conditions under which smaller communities may thrive, are the elements by which the great city may dominate its neighbors. Such is the point of view with which this study begins.

The ecological point of view concerning the dominance of great cities assumes that if the metropolis is a dominant species among all communities, then its dominance is akin to ecological dominance in nature. The problem of the study can therefore be expressed by such inquiries as:

a. Are the metropolitan centers a group of organisms which control the entire area of the United States by controlling the conditions

of life at the present stage of technological development of culture?

b. Have these metropolitan centers, collectively, altered the use of the area of the United States in such a fashion as to affect all portions of the area and, consequently, the activities of the inhabitants of smaller communities lying at even considerable distance from a metropolis?

c. If the factors of which dominance is composed do exist, do they tend to result in typical arrangements of people and activities? If so, what is the pattern of these arrangements? What are the typical distributions of population, manufacturing, retail activity, wholesale activity, and service functions with respect to the metropolis? Are all segments of the population woven into this pattern, or only some segments of it?

If it can be shown not only that this dominance exists, but that it has a definite pattern in which the various parts of the society stand in a definite relation to each other, it can be concluded that the society is organized with respect to the metropolis. Or to state it differently, the metropolis and its surrounding territory can be considered parts of one large organization, an organization with a definite structure. Thus a given society would consist of some grouping of these organized metropolitan units.

This statement of the metropolitan hypothesis in terms of the principles of general or bio-ecology is not intended as an explanation by analogy. Man, like other living forms, must live in a universe containing limited resources for maintaining life. Centuries ago he outstripped a level of life which could be based upon a subsistence by mere collection or extraction from the immediate territory. Further increases in his number in any given territory, and in his security against extinction by natural forces (including other members of his species), have been effected only by his development of new techniques for adjustment and his organization for more effective application of those techniques. Students both of human ecology and of population accept as a basic postulate the principle that the human community and basic community activities are functional responses to the continuing endeavor of the human species to perpetuate itself under conditions of maximum security and comfort in an environment containing limited resources for life.

---

21. Arthur M. Schlesinger, "The City in American History," Mississippi Valley Historical Review, June, 1940. pp. 43-66.

The application of this ecological definition of dominance to the study of the organizing effect of metropolitan centers is not made with the intent to introduce some mysterious biological explanation for human behavior or city behavior. It has been used, rather, to emphasize the fact that here, as elsewhere, the functions of direction and control emerge from interdependency and interfunctioning, and from the universal effort to gain the maximum level of life from the resources of a larger environment. Acknowledgment that the metropolis is a product of such efforts opens the problem for further research. To maintain that a metropolis is dominant "because it dominates" is to reject the influence of such a city as an object of research. The hypothesis that a metropolis is dominant because a system of interfunctioning parts are dependent upon it to preserve certain conditions necessary for their well-being creates many questions and hypotheses concerning the nature of such interdependence and the mechanisms by which it is developed and maintained. It certainly could not be contended that the mechanisms of metropolitan dominance are paralleled in plant and animal communities, or that the various parts of the metropolitan community find their analogues in plant and animal species. At the present stage of research in social science the term "dominance" must be used as a class name for many different kinds of controls, most of which have never been subjected to rigorous study. One of the greatest unexplored areas in urban research lies in the study of "urban dynamics," or the interfunctioning of parts. Until the study of metropolitan structure is paralled by studies of "metropolitan dynamics" the term dominance must remain a useful label for the broad influence which the metropolis exerts upon outlying areas. Although part III of this study yields evidence that the above ecological definition is probably a realistic view of metropolitan dominance, it is only an argument that future studies of community interfunctioning will prove to be most worth while, and that in such studies the role of the metropolis will be shown to be one of control through interdependence.

V

Summary

This study seeks to verify or to disprove the following hypothesis of metropolitan dominance derived from the writings of N.S.B. Gras and R.D. McKenzie and restated in terms of general, or bio-ecology:

1. The metropolis is a dominant, as defined by the bio-ecologists. As such it modifies and organizes its habitat, thereby establishing life conditions which set limits to the activities of the other communities and of the dispersed populations occupying the same habitat.
2. In effecting an adaption to the total world environment as well as to local environmental circumstances, the population of the United States has distributed itself in such a manner that several metropolitan dominants have emerged.
3. The number and scope of influence of these dominants has increased to the extent that at the present time the entire area has been, or is in the process of being, invaded by the metropolis and its influence. The entire area of the United States may be broken down into a series of areas, each of which is dominated by a metropolis.
4. By a process of reciprocal adjustment, the human aggregates which inhabit each such area have already evolved, or are evolving, a pattern of distribution and arrangement with respect to each other and to the metropolis.
5. The net effect of this process is to establish a number of large communities which are composed of smaller communities.
6. Within this multiple-community complex, which may be called the metropolitan community in deference to its dominant species, the individual local community must occupy a subordinate position. The activities of the local community are a function not only of its immediate locality, but also of the relative ecological position with respect to the dominant metropolis.
7. A characteristic pattern of arrangement of local communities, population, and sustenance activities can be shown to exist as an integral part of the organization of metropolitan communities. This pattern may be spoken of as the structure of the metropolitan community.

This hypothesis is necessitated by the fact that a theory of urbanism alone cannot account for all of the facts concerning the functioning of cities. Cities are not alike in composition or function. They are also interdependent. Since there is no single norm to which they tend to conform, a division of cities on some functional basis appears to be necessary. The basis selected is that of dominance, a principle which governs community relations in the realm of plants and the lower animals.

CHAPTER TWO

A PROCEDURE FOR ANALYZING METROPOLITAN DOMINANCE
AND METROPOLITAN STRUCTURE

The intention of this chapter is to acquaint the reader with the specific conditions under which the inference of dominance may be properly made, as well as with the mechanics by which statistical data have been arranged to conform to those conditions. It has been assumed that, if metropolitan centers do dominate the remainder of the nation, that fact will reveal itself, in one aspect, by the presence of a distinctive pattern of population distribution and apparent division of labor among the various parts of the hinterland. A system of community sizes, distance zones, and sector types is the framework which will be used to determine whether such a pattern exists. Each part of this system has been designed to test one aspect of the ecological formulation of the hypothesis. The discussion which follows deals individually with each of the major problems of procedure encountered; the bearing which each problem has upon the goal of the study is explained.

I

How Can the Fact of Metropolitan Dominance be Established?

The actual mechanisms by which control is exercised vary from one type of community to another. In regard to a given community, if one were to ask the questions: "How does this community operate?", "How did this community arrive at its present structure?", or "How does species 'X' dominate this community?", an intensive study of the functional interrelationships between the parts of the community would be required. The functions which each member performs for each other member would then be the subject of inquiry. If, however, one seeks only to determine whether or not dominance exists, and what the pattern of that dominance is, he may need to ask only the questions:

a. Is the functional distribution of parts about the dominant unit of a type which is not necessarily dictated by the physical environment?

b. If so, is there a pattern to this distribution; that is, is there a pattern which is nonrandom with respect to the dominant unit?

This much simpler inquiry is made possible by the shift in point of view. In a study of a distributional pattern the specific processes which create or maintain that pattern need not be the center of attention. Instead, the distribution and arrangement of the parts of which the community is composed must be taken as the central problem. If it is found that the parts have a functional arrangement with respect to the hypothetically dominant units, and if that arrangement is one which indicates dependence upon these units for broad classes of vital functions, then it may be presumed that dominance exists.

If dominance is nonexistent, one should find a random distribution and a random combination of units in those cases where the metropolitan hypothesis would lead one to anticipate a significantly nonrandom distribution. If, on the other hand, dominance is being exercised, one would expect to find significantly fewer than expected numbers of some units in certain portions of the community, and concentrations of the same types of units in other parts of the community. Moreover, the proportions in which units of each type are found should vary from one part of the community to another. If these differences in distribution are directly related to conditions which can be attributed to the influence of the metropolis, and if nothing else in the environment requires this same distribution, then it can be inferred reasonably that the metropolis is exercising dominance over the area. The following example will illustrate the procedure and the line of argument.

The farm population must have arable land before it can farm. If the farm population were subjected to no dominance, that is, if its activities were not controlled in any way by proximity to other communities, one would expect the farm population to be distributed entirely with respect to arable land. If the metropolis or other communities did not dominate the farm population in any way, one would expect metropolitan centers and other aggregates to arise with little relationship to the amount of arable land or of farm populations lying about them. Densities of farm population would, then, be distributed quite randomly with respect to metropolitan centers, and metropolitan centers themselves would be distributed quite randomly with respect to the farm population and to arable land. Suppose one finds, however, that the number and density of farm population vary distinctly with different conditions which are attributable to the metropolis. This nonrandom distribution, definitely patterned with respect to the metropolis, permits the tentative inference that:

> The distribution of the farm population is "controlled" to some extent by factors associated with the metropolis.

Suppose that not only farming, but other hinterland activities such as manufacturing, retail trade, wholesale trade, and services are also discovered to have a distinctive pattern of distribution with respect to the metropolis. The above inference now becomes:

> Since human residence, farming, manufacturing, retail trade, wholesale trade, and services are all patterned with respect to the metropolis, all of these activities are more or less "controlled" by factors associated with the metropolis.

If it can be shown that the natural environment alone does not impose these distributions, but that these distributions are related to environmental conditions, then we can conclude that the metropolis is – to quote again the ecological definition of a dominant:[1]

> ...An organism with such definite relations to climate [the external environment] and such significant reactions upon the habitat [hinterland] ... as to control the [metropolitan] community and assign to the other species [local communities] subordinate positions of varying rank.

The pattern which this subordination takes can then be described, and the structure of the metropolitan community characterized. This is the procedure which will be used in establishing the fact of metropolitan dominance.

It should be noted that at no point in the above illustration can one infer that the metropolis commands an event which is forbidden by the environment. If there is no arable land, the metropolis cannot command open field farming; if no raw materials can be made available, the metropolis cannot force manufacture. But the demonstrated fact that there is a pattern of location about the metropolis, as an adaptation to the limits imposed by

nature, is strong evidence for the support of the metropolitan hypothesis. According to the ecological interpretation of this hypothesis, the metropolis itself is influenced by external conditions, and is a product of those conditions through struggle and adaptation. Although the metropolis may modify its hinterland, adding certain conditions of life which originally were not present, it cannot be said to "cause" a given distribution any more than a forest can be said to force a nonadapted plant to live within it – and for exactly the same reason.

Another note of caution should be sounded concerning the structure or pattern which dominance takes. Since the chief interest of this project is in the arrangement of parts, observations have been taken for only a single period of time, the years 1939-40. At no point in this study should the patterns described be regarded as being inevitable, permanent, or not subject to change with changed conditions. Undoubtedly the patterns which will be described are sufficiently stable not to be subject to capricious reversal. Nevertheless, they are not predestined. The industrial and technological change which has presumably given rise to these patterns has shown few signs of having run its course. There is no basis whatsoever for assuming that a condition of equilibrium has been attained between metropolitan communities, between central cities and their hinterlands, or between the parts of the hinterland.

II

How Shall a Sample of Metropolitan Centers Be Selected?

There has been little agreement as to which cities should be considered metropolitan centers. Gras would admit to this status only the eleven largest cities in the United States.[2] The one attempt to delimit the boundaries of a set of metropolitan communities in the United States considered only Federal Reserve cities as metropolitan centers, a rough criterion of metropolitan status suggested by Gras.[3]

For this study 67 of the largest cities in the United States were selected as metropolitan centers. The manner of selection, while somewhat arbitrary, appears to have a reasonable basis for use in the present study. The requirements for being selected as a metropolis were as follows:

---

1. See Chapter One, Section IV.
2. N.S.B. Gras, An Introduction to Economic History, 1922, p. 292.
3. From a study by R. E. Park and Charles Newcomb, reported in McKenzie, The Metropolitan Community, p. 107.

Requirement 1. Every candidate for metropolitan status should contain not less than 100,000 inhabitants, either in 1930 or 1940.

The dividing line between "big cities" and "medium-sized" cities traditionally has been at this point.[4] Cities of 100,000 or more inhabitants receive special statistical treatment by the Census. This convention appears to have a good foundation in fact, for it is at about this size that the urban unit becomes widely diversified economically.[5]

Requirement 2. Each metropolis must have a sizeable hinterland.

This requirement makes it necessary to exclude those cities of 100,000 or more which lie adjacent to, or very near to, larger cities. If the large cities lying very close to cities which are still larger are taken as metropolitan centers, the hinterlands of the very largest cities in the United States are reduced to almost zero land area. Thus, if Yonkers, N. Y., and Elizabeth, Jersey City, Newark, and Patterson, N. J. (all places of more than 100,000 inhabitants in 1940), are considered to be metropolitan centers, the land area about New York City must be divided between this metropolis and these other large cities. The result would be to give to the other cities most of the land area and to leave only a very narrow zone of a few miles depth as New York City's hinterland. In other words, a metropolis must be large compared to its immediate neighbors, for only such places can be truly dominant over a broad hinterland. This problem of determining how large a hinterland should be cannot be solved by one single definition. Setting a minimum distance between centers is hardly practicable, for Washington, D. C. and Baltimore, and Dallas and Fort Worth lie close to each other and yet each has a sizeable trade territory on the side away from the other. Raising the minimum size of cities to be defined as metropolitan centers from 100,000 to 250,000 in the northeastern states gave most of the largest centers a hinterland.[6]

Davenport, Iowa, and Rock Island and Moline, Illinois were considered to be a single metropolis because of their positions with respect to each other, because their combined population was more than the minimum required, and because they appeared to be in a position to dominate a sizeable hinterland area.

The 67 metropolises selected by the application of these requirements to cities in the United States, listed in order of size, are as follows:

New York, N. Y.	Seattle, Wash.	Jacksonville, Fla.
Chicago, Ill.	Rochester, N. Y.	Miami, Fla.
Philadelphia, Pa.	Denver, Colo.	Nashville, Tenn.
Detroit, Mich.	Louisville, Ky.	Hartford, Conn.
Los Angeles, Cal.	Columbus, Ohio	Grand Rapids, Mich.
Cleveland, Ohio	Portland, Ore.	Des Moines, Ia.
Baltimore, Md.	Atlanta, Ga.	Salt Lake City, Utah
St. Louis, Mo.	Dallas, Texas	Springfield, Mass.
Boston, Mass.	Memphis, Tenn.	Norfolk, Va.
Pittsburgh, Pa.	Toledo, Ohio	Tulsa, Okla.
Washington, D. C.	Birmingham, Ala.	Scranton, Pa.
San Francisco, Cal.	San Antonio, Texas	Albany, N. Y.
Milwaukee, Wis.	Providence, R. I.	Chattanooga, Tenn.
Buffalo, N. Y.	Omaha, Neb.	Spokane, Wash.
New Orleans, La.	Dayton, Ohio	Fort Wayne, Ind.
Minneapolis, Minn.	Syracuse, N. Y.	Erie, Pa.
Cincinnati, Ohio	Oklahoma City, Okla.	Wichita, Kan.
Kansas City, Mo.	San Diego, Cal.	Knoxville, Tenn.
Indianapolis, Ind.	Richmond, Va.	Tampa, Fla.
Houston, Texas	Fort Worth, Texas	Sacramento, Cal.

4 Mark Jefferson, "Great Cities in the United States in 1930," Geographical Review, January, 1933, pp. 90-100; Karl Bucher, "Die Groszstadt," in Die Groszstadt (Dresden: Zahn and Jaensch, 1903) p. 4.

5. Grace Kneedler, "An Economic Classification of Cities," Municipal Year Book, 1945 (Chicago: The International City Managers Association, 1945) pp. 30-38, especially Table II, p. 38.

6. Neward, Oakland, Long Beach, Jersey City, and St. Paul still constituted exceptions and were arbitrarily considered to be hinterland cities because of their proximity to centers larger than they.

Peoria, Ill.

South Bend, Ind.

Duluth, Minn.

Charlotte, N. C.

Davenport, Ia; Moline
& Rock Island, Ill.

Evansville, Ind.

El Paso, Texas

To the extent that errors have been made in selecting the central cities, the tabulations which follow will tend to show random distributions instead of patterned distributions. Errors in selection resulting either from the inclusion of too many cities or the exclusion of some genuine metropolitan centers will not invalidate the study, but will tend to obscure patterns which would otherwise manifest themselves.

III

How Shall the Total Areas of the United States Be Assigned As Hinterlands of Specific Metropolitan Centers

As indicated above, only one previous attempt has been made to determine the boundaries of metropolitan dominance throughout the United States.[7] The fact that, in the above-mentioned study, Park and Newcomb used only Federal Reserve cities as metropolitan centers does not permit the use of their boundaries. Some system must be designed for subdividing the land area into smaller parcels, and for assigning each of these parcels to some metropolis as a part of its hinterland.

In the absence of any clear-cut precedent, the following hypothesis was adopted concerning location of the boundaries of metropolitan communities: Distance is the most important single factor in determining the limits of metropolitan dominance. Each metropolis claims as hinterland all of that area which lies closer to it than to any other metropolis. The following rule was formulated.

A metropolis can dominate all of the area which lies closer to it than to any other similar city, even if the other metropolis is larger. The boundaries of metropolitan areas, therefore, pass through the points bisecting the airline distance between adjacent metropolitan centers.

In effect, this definition assumes that the entire area of the United States is blanketed with metropolitan dominance and that any given area is subject to the dominance of the metropolitan center which lies nearest it.

The procedure followed in drawing the actual boundaries is as follows:

a. Draw lines from a given metropolis to each adjacent metropolis.

b. Bisect each of these lines.

c. At the midpoint of each line draw a boundary line at right angles to the original line. The area included within the intersecting boundary lines lies closer to the enclosed center than to any other center, and is taken as an estimate of the hinterland of that center.

d. Assign each county of the United States to some metropolis on the basis of the boundaries within which the greater part of its area falls.

e. Consider all cities to lie within the hinterland of the metropolis which claims the county in which they are located.

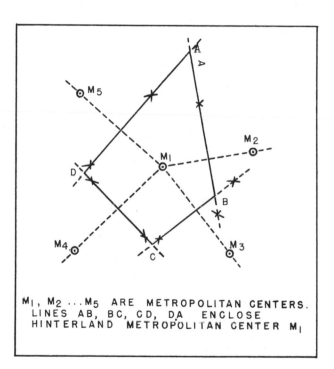

M₁, M₂ ...M₅ ARE METROPOLITAN CENTERS.
LINES AB, BC, CD, DA ENCLOSE
HINTERLAND METROPOLITAN CENTER M₁

CHART 2-1   GEOMETRIC PROCEDURE FOR DELIMITING THE BOUNDARIES OF METROPOLITAN COMMUNITIES

7. Park and Newcomb's study of Newspaper circulation, reported in McKenzie, The Metropolitan Community.

A few minor changes in the geometric procedure were made in coastal areas where bodies of water isolated a few counties from the closer metropolis but a principally traveled route connected these areas to a metropolis only slightly more distant. Although this method of delimiting boundaries is an extremely crude one, a preliminary study of the data for selected areas indicated it to be approximately correct.[8]

IV

What Units Should Be Used in Studying the Structure of Metropolitan Dominance, and How Should These Units Be Classified?

The preceding discussion has characterized the hypothetical metropolitan community as a "community of local communities." Ultimately the control exercised over the hinterland by the metropolis must consist of establishing conditions to which the activities of individual local communities located in the hinterland must be adapted. Hence, the unit of analysis must be the individual local community.

The hinterland contains a great variety of communities, ranging from cities of more than 100,000 inhabitants to small villages and local farming communities. For this reason it cannot easily be assumed that the conditions set by the metropolis force one pattern of adjustment in all areas about the metropolis. Nor can it be assumed that all hinterland communities are oriented solely toward the metropolis. It is a known fact that the hinterland centers are local shopping, manufacturing, wholesaling and general service centers for a large area surrounding them. Although these outlying centers may be under the dominance of the metropolis, they are also in active competition with the metropolis for the privilege of serving the areas in their vicinity. This general observation makes it evident that some system of classifying the hinterland communities must be adopted, and that this classification must be in terms of amount of influence exercised by the principal hinterland communities.

From the foregoing it can be concluded that dominance is not an attribute but a variable. Dominance, it appears, can take any value from high to low; it is not something which a community either possesses or does not possess (in the sense that persons either do or do not have blue eyes). It is here hypothesized that dominance is a status which every community possesses in some degree with respect to other communities with which it interacts. The proposal to classify all individual hinterland communities along a scale of dominance is therefore consistent with the aim of the study. The ecologists have provided us with a very useful scale for classifying degrees of dominance. This scale is as follows:[9]

> Dominants
> Subdominants
> Influents
> Subinfluents

The hinterland communities may be divided into four major groups corresponding to these four steps in the dominance continuum:

Metropolitan centers. . . . . Dominants
Hinterland cities . . . . Subdominants
Rural-nonfarm populations[10] . . . Influents
Rural-farm populations[10]. . . . . . Subinfluents

From the ecological point of view, decreasing values along this scale refer to two types of change in dominance: (1) decreasing range or area of dominance, and (2) decreasing number of functions over which dominance is exercised. A rural-nonfarm village may conceivably exert an intense control in the single function of education, but only over a small area. By way of contrast, a large hinterland city may dominate a broad territory and control the conduct of several different types of human activities. In this study the degree of control exercised by the rural-nonfarm and the rural-farm populations will not be a subject of inquiry, but the amount of control exercised by the hinterland cities will be one of the major lines of investigation. For this reason the ecological meaning of the term "subdominance" and its relationship to the concept of "dominance" should be amplified.

A subdominant has been defined as a species that exhibits a secondary dominance within the area controlled by a dominant. . . . Subdominants are the successful competitors among the species that accept the conditions imposed by the dominants.[11]

---

8. Although the tabulations of this study indicate that the rough guesses made concerning centers and boundaries of dominance are fairly realistic, there is urgent need for detailed studies of both of these problems.

9. F. E. Clements and V. E. Shelford, Bio-ecology, 1939. p. 234-250.

10. As defined by the United States Census.

11. Clements and Shelford, op. cit., pp. 239-240.

A great mass of evidence that cities lying in the hinterland exercise a considerable degree of influence over the area immediately surrounding them has been collected by students of market research and city trading areas. To the extent that it can be shown that all hinterland cities are patterned with respect to the metropolis, even while dominating a smaller area, we are justified in terming such cities "subdominants." For under such circumstances they would truly be the units which "accept the conditions imposed by the dominants" and under these conditions "exhibit a secondary dominance within the area controlled by a dominant."

Setting 2,500 inhabitants as the lower limit of subdominance is somewhat arbitrary, as is true of all divisions of a continuum. Investigations of retail trade activities and of other economic functions have shown that cities smaller than this in size possess relatively few specialized service institutions and that they serve an area of only a few square miles. Perhaps even more important than a lack of specialized retail and other service establishments in village centers is the lack of specialized wholesale and manufacturing facilities, the presence of both of which connote exchange and distribution over a wide area and consequently some dominance in these activities. Only under unusual conditions do places of less than urban status perform extensive manufacturing or wholesaling functions.[12]

V

What Subclassification of Units Should Be Used in Studying the Structure of Dominance?

A. Dominant Metropolitan Centers.

Since size of city has been a major element in selecting metropolitan centers, and since dominance is postulated as being a variable rather than a fixed attribute, one cannot easily assume that all of the 67 metropolitan centers dominate their hinterlands with equal intensity. The dominance of New York or Chicago over its hinterland should differ considerably from that of Spokane or El Paso. In order to study degrees of dominance, all metropolitan communities have been divided into four major classes on the basis of the size of their metropolitan centers:

Class of Metropolitan Community	Size of Metropolitan Center, 1940
A	1,000,000 or more inhabitants
B	500,000-999,999 inhabitants
C	250,000-499,999 inhabitants
D	100,000-249,999 inhabitants

In the subsequent analysis a separate inquiry will be made for each of these size classes of metropolitan communities.

B. Subdominant Hinterland Cities.

In 1940 there were in the United States 3,464 urban places, of which only 69 have been defined as metropolitan centers for the purposes of this study.[13] The remaining 3,395 urban places, which have been classed as centers of subdominance, range in size from 2,500 to 430,000 inhabitants.[14] If size alone is an indication of subdominance, then the larger hinterland cities must exercise a great deal more subdominance over the immediate hinterland than do the smaller ones. In other words, within the group of hinterland cities one could expect a great deal of variation in degree of subdominance, ranging from "near-dominance" of the largest hinterland cities to "near-influence" of the cities of 2,500 inhabitants. In recognition of this fact, not all cities in the hinterland should be treated as one single class, but should be ranked in a scale. Size of city is the only index available. In this study hinterland cities are classified by size into the following groups:

Size of Hinterland City, 1940	Number in the U. S. in 1940
50,000-over	132
25,000-49,999	211
10,000-24,999	665
5,000- 9,999	965
2,500- 4,999	1,422
Total	3,395

It is assumed that the average amount of subdominance exercised by the members of any one group

---

12. The term "subdominants" will be used throughout this study to refer to the hinterland cities. Since the rural populations will be studied only for the control which dominants and subdominants exercise over them, the ecological definitions of "influence" and "subinfluence" are not presented here, and the terms "rural-nonfarm" and "rural-farm" population will be used in referring to them. A discussion of the applicability of these terms to the rural populations will be found on pages 51-52 of the original thesis manuscript.

13. Rock Island, Moline, Davenport constitute one central city in this study.

14. Including 28 cities of 100,000 or more inhabitants which were excluded from status as metropolises.

is greater than that exercised by the group below it, and less than that exercised by the group above it.

C. The Influential and Subinfluential Rural Populations.

According to the hypothesis set up, the pattern of distribution of the rural-nonfarm population should be related both to the dominance of the metropolis and the subdominance of the hinterland cities. To determine whether or not this is true, the rural-nonfarm and rural-farm populations are studied in terms of the amount of subdominance exercised over them. The county is taken as the unit for this study. There were 3,098 counties in the United States in 1940, of which 36 were also cities, or were composed entirely of urban places. Each of the remaining 3,062 counties were located in the hinterland of some metropolis and were potential places of residence for both rural-farm and rural-nonfarm populations. The problem of classifying these rural populations is one of classifying the hinterland county units along some scale analogous to that of subdominance. It would be very difficult to devise a scale which would be even as approximate as the comparable scale for subdominance of hinterland cities which was constructed above. Theoretically, the greater the subdominance of the hinterland city, the greater its influence upon the rural populations should be. Using this as a premise, a very rough scale of influence is used in this study, namely, size of largest hinterland city contained in the county. The validity of this classification depends upon three assumptions, in addition to those made for the subdominance classification of hinterland cities, viz., that:

a. As the degree of subdominance in a local area increases, the degree of rural control decreases. It is assumed that in the vicinity of large cities the individual units of rural-nonfarm and rural-farm population have smaller and less diversified spheres of control than such populations would have in areas containing only small cities.

b. The rural population of a county is under the subdominance of only those cities contained in that county; or, at least, no other city outside the county exerts a greater control than the largest city within the county.

c. The degree of subdominance exercised is measured by the size of the largest city rather than by the composite of all cities in the county. To the extent that counties containing the larger cities are more urbanized and contain a full complement of smaller cities, this assumption appears to be justified. To the extent that some counties contain numerous cities of the same size class in lieu of one or fewer large cities, this assumption is less valid.

The county units of rural-farm and rural-nonfarm population are therefor classified in a scale of subdominance as follows:

Size of Largest City Contained in County	Number of Counties in U. S. in 1940
50,000-over	97
25,000-49,999	135
10,000-24,999	370
5,000- 9,999	509
2,500- 4,999	634
No city	1,255
Other-and counties containing central city	98

VI

How Should the Hinterland Be Subdivided in Order to Study the Pattern of Metropolitan Dominance ?

In order to determine whether there is a pattern to metropolitan dominance, it is necessary to divide the hinterland into subareas which are more or less homogeneous. Just as cities were classified by a scale of their expected subdominance, rather than according to the functions which they perform, so must the hinterland be subdivided into homogeneous dominance areas, rather than into areas of homogeneous activity. The question: "What areas of the hinterland may be expected to be subjected to a like amount of metropolitan dominance?" must be answered, and its answer used to classify every unit in the hinterland. The tentative answer which has been developed and applied in this study was derived in part from the theory of metropolitan dominance itself, and in part borrowed from the work of those who have studied the internal structure of cities.

A. Accessibility is everywhere and at all times a most basic element in metropolitan organization. Scholars of several generations have linked city growth and development to mobility. The location of the principal metropolitan centers of the world have been shown to have been determined in a large part by factors associated with movement. Great cities have arisen at points where streams of movement converge or at points where such streams are broken by a shift from one form of transportation to another. Without movement the vast and complicated system of production and exchange upon which the metropolis lives could not exist.

The site of the metropolis is inevitably an accessible one, either by natural endowment or as a result of the efforts of men. In terms of time, cost, and expenditure of energy the entire area can enter most easily into a division of labor with a city located at a highly accessible point. Exchange and interaction with a city located at the most inaccessible point could be achieved only at a maximum expenditure of time, cost, and energy. Since time, cost, and energy are all elements of life which must be conserved in order to ensure most economical survival, it can be reasoned that, since these elements vary with accessibility, the following assumption can be made:

Varying degrees of accessibility must represent varying degrees of interaction with the metropolitan center.

According to such a view, the metropolis is a metropolis because of its superior ability to serve, and be served by, the hinterland. With this assumption, the problem of delimiting areas of like degree of dominance becomes a problem of delimiting areas of like degree of accessibility. Accessibility is taken to be a variable which will co-vary with dominance.

B. Distance. "Accessibility" obviously contains more than one element. The distance to be traveled, the availability of a route, and the relative ease of traversing a route, are only some of the factors which limit opportunity to transport goods, services, and persons to or from a metropolis. One permanent requirement for changing the location of any object is the necessity of overcoming distance. Time and cost may be reduced and more direct and more numerous routes may be built, but under any given system, or combination of systems, of transportation the element of mileage distance remains. Although in any given area cost rates and time rates do not stand in a fixed ratio to mileage, it is nevertheless true that they do have a functional relationship to mileage.

McKenzie holds that the metropolitan community has been made possible by the superimposition of motor vehicle transportation upon the established waterway and railway pattern.[15] Almost every part of the hinterland is now available to the metropolis via motor vehicle transport. In this study actual mileage distance from the metropolis via most direct highway route has been taken as the chief index of hinterland accessibility.[16] After

coding each city and county unit with its actual highway mileage, the frequency distribution of these mileages was studied, class limits were set, and a series of accessibility zones was established about each metropolitan center.[17]

It is not contended that overland distance is an absolute measure of accessibility. It is assumed, however, that each zone outward from the metropolis is, on the average, less accessible than the one lying immediately inside it, and that there is a considerable degree of homogeniety in this respect among the units lying within each zone.

On the basis of the frequency distribution of all distances from all metropolitan centers, the following zones were established for the analysis which is to follow:

Distance from the nearest metropolis (miles)

0-14	65-114
15-24	115-164
25-34	165-264
35-44	265-464
45-64	465-over

C. Direction from the metropolis.

The circular pattern of accessibility can be distorted by several factors. Two of these factors are of sufficient importance to warrant the introduction of a new variable into the process of delimiting areas of like degrees of dominance.

1. Accessibility and the Presence of Large Hinterland Cities.

According to the hypotheses of this study the larger hinterland cities can be expected to play a more dominant role than the other smaller communities. Through these outlying centers the metropolis can "come to the country" to distribute its goods and services, and to collect other goods and services from the hinterland. Thus, a very highly developed organization can arise between the metropolis and a hinterland city to effect an exchange of goods between the metropolis and a broad area of the hinterland. Not only can the hinterland city stock a wide variety of goods produced in the metropolis, but this close interdependence also can produce more frequent and better transportation service between the metropolis and the subdominant city. This advantage may be even greater due to the existence of competitive freight and other transportation rates along such routes of travel. Hence there is reason to suspect that those hinterland areas lying in the general direction of a major

15. R. D. McKenzie, The Metropolitan Community, 1933, p. 143.
16. The task of classifying units on this basis was greatly facilitated by use of Standard Highway Mileage Guide (Chicago: Rand McNally & Co., 1946)
17. See Section VII-B of this chapter for details of the coding procedure.

subdominant city are more accessible to, and hence more dominated by, the metropolis than are other hinterland areas. This consideration, of course, modifies considerably the purely zonal pattern of accessibility outlined above.

2. Accessibility and Intermetropolitan Division of Labor.

A second modification of the zonal pattern of accessibility arises from the fact that metropolitan communities are not self-subsistent entities. The metropolis carries on a lively exchange with other centers throughout the world. Gras recognized two distinct types of trade carried on by the metropolis, a "hinterland trade" and an "extended trade" with other urban centers outside the immediate hinterland.[18] This fact is important for an analysis of metropolitan structure, because <u>under present modes of transportation, intermetropolitan exchange requires the movement of goods through some sector of the hinterland.</u>

Movement of goods, services, or persons is inevitably a channelized affair, for movement must follow definite land routes. The areas containing main thoroughfares into or out of a city exhibit many characteristics of the city center by virtue of the fact that, being more accessible in terms of time and cost, they are more highly developed than are other areas lying away from the thoroughfare. There is considerable scattered evidence which, when assembled, indicates that this same phenomenon extends far into the hinterland. The evidence which gives rise to this view may be reviewed briefly:

a. Outlying cities and towns appear to be located in strings along principal routes of travel.

b. A so-called "ribbon" development tends to extend from central cities into the rural areas along main highway, rail, and water routes like spokes from a hub.[19]

c. The trade of a small country town frequently "dies" when a major thoroughfare passes close to but not through it. The town commerce tends to go to the highway, or disappears as its residents join the stream flowing on toward a larger shopping center.[20]

The evidence cited leads to the hypothesis that outlying parts of a metropolitan area are differentiated not only in terms of distance from the metropolis, but also in terms of direction from the metropolis. Directionality appears to be particularly important in terms of two types of channels of movement:

a. Portions of the hinterland lying in the direction of a major hinterland city.

b. Portions of the hinterland lying along a main channel of intermetropolitan travel.

The present study attempts to express this directional aspect of metropolitan pattern by a division of the hinterland into sectors, or wedge-shaped segments, the vertices of which are at the metropolitan center and the bodies of which extend outward toward the periphery of the metropolitan community. All sectors are of 30° arc. In the completely circular hinterland, therefore, the direction of any unit can be expressed as lying within one of twelve sectors. Three types of sectors are recognized by this study: "Intermetropolitan," "Subdominant," and "Local."

VII

A System of Sectors

A. <u>The Method of Drawing and Classifying the Sectors.</u>

The sectors were drawn as follows:

1. The major intermetropolitan highway routes from each metropolis to its neighboring metropolises were determined. A transparent circular template, divided into twelve 30° sectors, was placed over the map of the metropolitan community. Through rotation of the template, an attempt was made to get each route to fall within a single sector. Each route was "centered" as nearly as possible in its sector. Since, in effect, all twelve of the sectors for one metropolitan community were "linked together" into one circle, rotation of one sector required the rotation of the remaining eleven sectors. An effort was made to get all intermetropolitan routes to lie as near to the center of a sector as possible. When this condition had been approximated, the ends of the 12 sectors were plotted on the map and lines were drawn to the center of the central city.

In selecting the major intermetropolitan routes the following procedure was used:

a. Only U. S. highway and principal state routes were considered.

18. <u>Op. Cit.</u>, p. 194.

19. <u>Interregional Highways</u> (Washington, D.C.: Government Printing Office, 1944), pp. 83-88.

20. See C. R. Hoffer, <u>Changes in the Retail and Service Facilities of Rural Trade Centers in Michigan 1900 and 1930</u>. Michigan State College Special Bulletin, No. 261 (East Lansing, 1935).

b. By reference to highway maps, the apparent closest route from the given center to each adjacent center was recorded.

c. This was checked by reference to a traffic flow map of the United States, prepared by the Bureau of Public Roads, showing the average daily volume of traffic on all principal U. S. and state highways.21

d. A further check was made with the interregional system of 78,800 road miles (a system, prepared by the Bureau of Public Roads, which includes only the most-traveled routes between major centers).22

2. Those sectors which contained an intermetropolitan highway were then coded as "intermetropolitan" sectors.

3. Of the remaining sectors, those which contained a city of 25,000 or more inhabitants located at a distance of 10 miles or more from the central city, were designated as "subdominant" sectors 23

4. The remaining sectors were classed as "local" sectors, for there was no evidence of intermetropolitan or major metropolis-hinterland city activity in their direction.24 Table I in the Appendix lists the number of sectors of each type for each central city.

B. Coding Hinterland Areas by Sectors and Distance Zones.

For the analysis in the chapters which follow several different sets of data are distributed by the classifications of area which have been established. The data to be used, however, are available only for political units of area, that is, for individual cities and counties. In order to perform the analysis, it is necessary to assign these political units, and hence the data, to specific sectors and zones.

Cities may be assigned directly to the sectors and distance zones into which they fall. Counties, on the other hand, exceed the breadth of the sectors in many cases, and in all cases the sectors as drawn cut across county lines in quite a random fashion. The geographic center of each county was determined, and the entire county was assigned to that sector and distance zone in which this center

lies. Every city and every county unit in the entire United States was coded by its most approximate distance zone and sector type. Maps 2-1 and 2-2 illustrate the manner in which county units were assigned to specific distance zones and sector types in each of the metropolitan communities.

VIII

What Functions Should Be Used to Measure the Influence of the Metropolis Over the Hinterland?

In the foregoing discussion of metropolitan organization, the general terms "function," "division of labor," and "interdependence" have been used to refer to the activities involved in the relation of the metropolis to its hinterland. The all-inclusive nature of the hypothesis under consideration has permitted the discussion to proceed under the assumption that any community activity whatsoever is influenced by the metropolis. It would appear reasonable to anticipate that, if a metropolis-centered control exists among human communities, such dominance would be clearly manifest in human sustenance activities. This does not deny that dominance of an equally intense or identical pattern might operate in other human activities which are less clearly related to human sustenance. In this study the functions of retail trade, of wholesale trade, of services, and of manufacturing have been selected for study because of their basic sustenance nature, and because of the availability of data for them. The United States Census provides general information on all of these activities for individual city and county units and for the entire nation. A more reliable and more comparable set of data does not exist concerning community activities for the entire nation. Many other elements of community sustenance, such as marketing and financial controls, also would have been useful in studying dominance. Lack of sufficiently detailed data prevented their inclusion.

The following data were selected for the analysis of metropolitan dominance:

---

21. Map showing the average daily volume of traffic in 1941 on major routes of the federal system of the United States Highways, Bureau of Public Roads, 1945.

22. Interregional Highways, p. 142.

23. In a few cases, if a large hinterland city lay just outside the metropolitan community boundary, and if there was evidence of considerable traffic between the metropolis and this city, the sector in that direction was coded as "subdominant" also.

24. Local sectors may contain a city of 25,000 inhabitants or more only in the 0-10 mile zone.

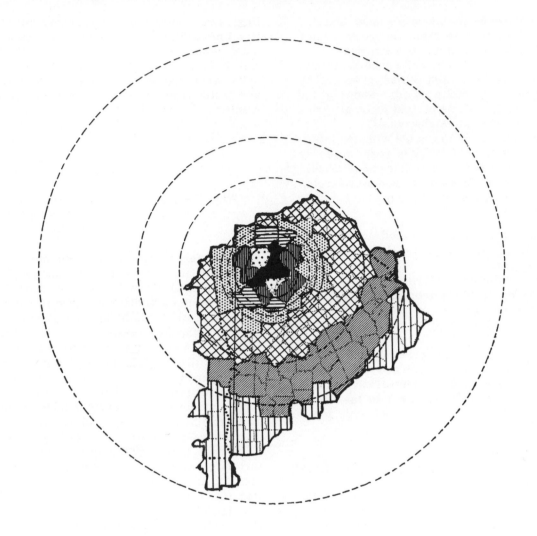

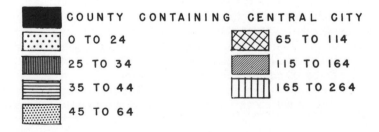

DISTANCE ZONES (MILES)

COUNTY CONTAINING CENTRAL CITY

0 TO 24   65 TO 114

25 TO 34   115 TO 164

35 TO 44   165 TO 264

45 TO 64

MAP 2-1   ZONAL CLASSIFICATION OF COUNTY UNITS IN
          THE ATLANTA, GEORGIA METROPOLITAN
          COMMUNITY

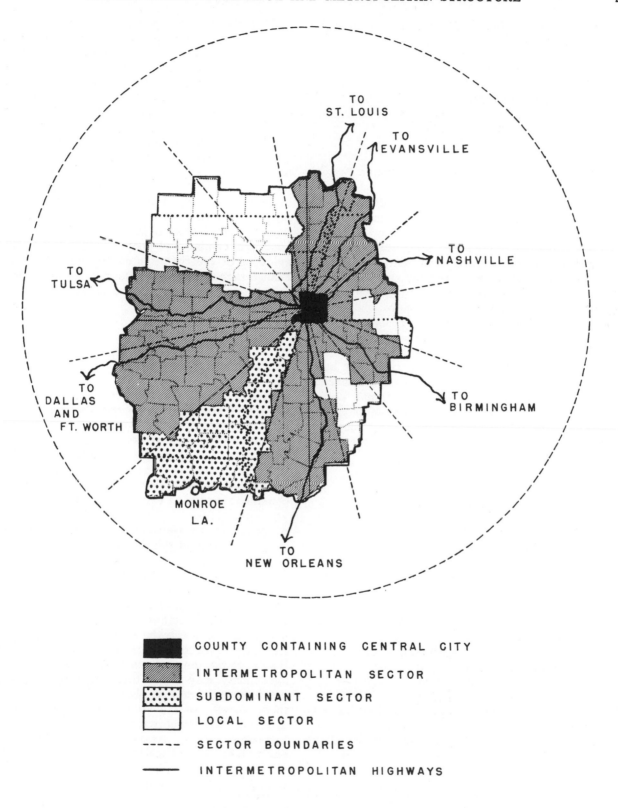

MAP 2-2   CLASSIFICATION OF COUNTY UNITS BY TYPE OF
SECTOR IN THE MEMPHIS, TENNESSEE
METROPOLITAN COMMUNITY

Number of Cities, United States, 1940, by size.[25]
Population, United States, 1940.[26]
    Urban
    Rural-nonfarm
    Rural-farm
Manufacturing, United States, 1939.[27]
Wholesale Trade, United States, 1939.[28]
Retail Trade, United States, 1939.[29]
Services, United States, 1939.[30]

All data were taken from the United States Census for the years indicated.

Although it would have been very desirable to study each one of these types of sustenance functions by major subtypes (e.g., the iron and steel industry, services to business, food stores, wholesale grocery activities, etc.) the many tabulations which would have been required for such an operation appeared not to be justified until the fact of dominance of any kind, and its general pattern, if any, had been described. For this reason, only the total amount of manufacturing, of wholesale trade, of retail trade, and of service activities have been analyzed. Each one of these functions has been measured in terms of three indexes. Number of establishments, number of employees, and "dollar value" of the activity. Singly, no one of these indexes can tell the "whole story" of that function. Together they characterize it much more adequately.

IX

How Shall the Metropolitan Pattern of Each Variable Be Studied?

In this chapter hypotheses have been advanced to the effect that metropolitan dominance varies with four variables:

    Size of metropolis
    Size of subdominant hinterland city
    Distance from metropolis
    Type of sector (direction)

The analysis will consist of a simultaneous examination of each type of population and each function (manufacturing, retail trade, etc.) by the above four variables.

A. <u>The Pattern of Aggregation of Function</u> — What percent of the total function is concentrated in any specific accessibility area under given conditions? How does this concentration compare with concentration in other accessibility areas? How does it compare with concentration of other functions in the same area?

B. <u>The Pattern of Intensity of Performance of Functions</u> — What amount of the function is performed by each 100 inhabitants in each accessibility area? How does the amount vary with changes in degree of accessibility? Size of community being held constant, a consistent change in the intensity of distribution with distance, size of metropolitan center, and sector type will be taken as evidence of metropolitan dominance. A consistent change in the intensity of distribution with increasing size of local city will be accepted as evidence of subdominance.

X

Limitations of the System of Zones and Sectors.

There are several characteristics of the system of sectors and zones described above which, though not readily apparent, do set limits to the degree of precision which can be obtained in this study. It is necessary, therefore, to examine each of these characteristics, to discuss the limits of trustworthiness imposed by each, and to foresee the possible bias which each can introduce.

A. <u>Adopting the Geographic Center of the County as the Location of the County.</u>
The median area of counties in the United States is about 623 square miles. If all counties were perfectly square in shape, each side of an average county would be almost exactly 25 miles long. Yet at the inner distance zones there are distance categories in which the interval between the upper and lower limits are much smaller than this. Hence, at the inner zones, though parts of an average county may lie in three different zones, the entire county must be classified as lying in one of these zones. In the vicinity of large cities very different conditions may exist on opposite sides of the same county. Assigning to the entire county one distance classification, according to the position

25. Sixteenth Census of the United States. Census of Population, Vols. I and II.
26. Ibid.
27. Sixteenth Census of the United States, Manufactures, Vol. III.
28. Sixteenth Census of the United States, Census of Business, Wholesale Trade, Vol. II.
29. Sixteenth Census of the United States, Census of Business, Retail Trade, Vol. I.
30. Sixteenth Census of the United States, Census of Business, Service Establishments.

of its geographic center, means that no allowances can be made for such differences. Those differences which exist with distance will tend to be revealed, but only roughly. The error will consist of underestimating the amount of difference which exists, for in each case the value is only on average value for a range of distance.

The size of the average county also impairs the ability of the individual sectors to classify areas correctly as to location in an intermetropolitan, or subdominant, or a local direction from the metropolis. The central city will be contained in a county roughly 25 miles square. Inasmuch as the county data cannot be divided, no sector units can be postulated for the county in which the central city lies. Hence almost nothing can be said about sector type in regard to the open country area immediately surrounding the metropolis. Because the arc of a 30° sector is shorter than the width of an average county at near distances, the sector classification at near distances will be frequently in error. To offset this apparent lack of ability of the sectors to classify county units properly at the near distances is the fact that, to be coded as "intermetropolitan," a route must traverse the county between its geographic center and one side. Since the sector is centered with respect to the route, the probability that the centers of counties so traversed by the route will be classed as intermetropolitan is considerably greater than the statement above would indicate.

Chart 2-3 illustrates the ability of the sectors under varying types of conditions to include intermetropolitan counties. As shown in the "A" section of this chart, when the highway runs down the center of the sector there is very little error in the classification of areas, even at short distances. Section "B" shows that the greatest possible error is likely to occur when the highway runs along one extreme side of a sector. Since the procedure for "fitting" the sectors calls for centering all major intermetropolitan routes as closely as possible, this extreme type of error should be very infrequent. This entire limitation is upon the rural, or county, units only. Cities can be classified properly by sector type in all of the distance zones.

B. Measuring Intermetropolitan Dominance with Respect Only to Adjacent Metropolitan Areas.

This system of distance zones and sectors permits the study of the change in population distribution from one central city to the next. Implicit in the above mentioned system is the assumption that each metropolis provides all of the dominance which may exist in its surrounding hinterland. This, of course, is not strictly true. The size of Detroit, Pittsburgh, Chicago, and New York City

cannot be understood merely in terms of their domination of the territory immediately surrounding them and their carrying on of trade with adjacent centers. Metropolitan influence, apparently, can extend completely across several intervening metropolitan areas. In other words, beyond the metropolitan economy there is the intermetropolitan or national economy, in which each of the various metropolitan centers diffuses its dominance over the entire nation and in which each center is itself but a unit joined with other metropolises in a division of labor. This study cannot explain "why" population density or the intensity of a given activity is greater in one metropolitan community than in another, nor can it claim that the actual population density at one point is due entirely to the combined activities of the population of the hinterland and of the metropolis. If the various indexes quickly level off with distance, revealing a stable, almost unchanging relationship with further distance, metropolitan dominance cannot be said to be present, for apparently the activity involved would be conducted on this plateau in the absence of any one metropolitan center, or only in the presence of all existing metropolitan centers.

C. Vagaries of the Transportation System.

Our modern transportation system is relatively new, and is still in the process of expansion and change. The channels of mobility of which it is composed, therefore, are not necessarily like rivers, flowing in a path of least resistance to time and space.

1. Some central cities have no direct routes to neighboring central cities (e.g., Peoria to Chicago, Wichita to Kansas City, Rochester to Albany). In such instances a considerable volume of goods may move via an extended branch to another major route, following two sides of a triangle rather than the one direct side. This may be altered in time, but if transportation routes are effective differentiators of accessibility, the sectors must represent what actually exists. Therefore, some of the intermetropolitan highways do not go in a direct line between adjacent metropolitan centers, or in some cases there may not be a direct intermetropolitan highway at all, a branch route from another metropolis being used to reach the center.

2. The skirting of lakes and other barriers may make it necessary to use two intermetropolitan sectors to include all of the route from one metropolitan center to a neighboring one. In this case, the route must curve from one sector into another one, the remainder of the original sector passing over water or some other barrier. The second sector is really a continuation of the first sector

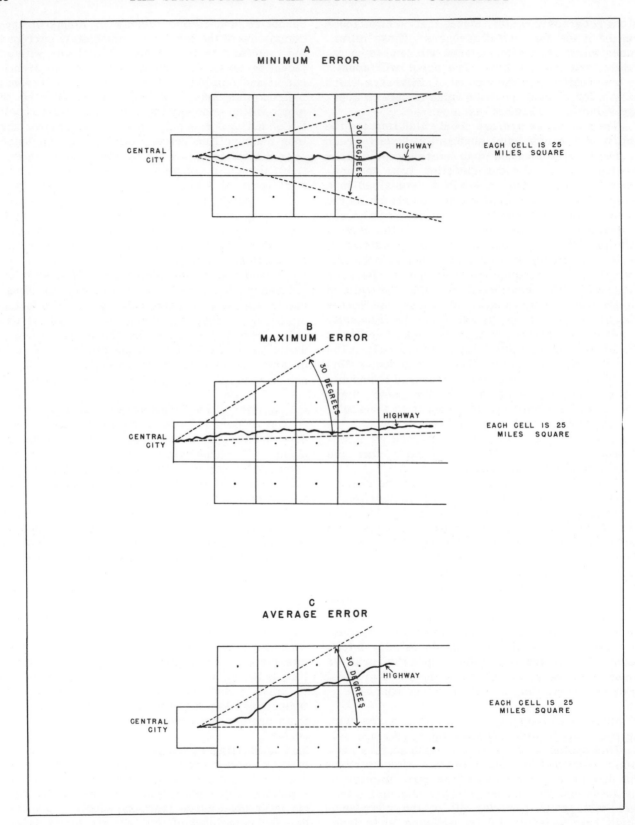

CHART 2-2   SCHEMATIC   REPRESENTATION OF   THE   ABILITY   OF   SECTORS
TO PROPERLY   CLASSIFY   INTERMETROPOLITAN   AREAS
USING   COUNTY   UNITS   OF   AREA

at the point where the first sector "loses" the route due to the intervening barrier. Here, both sectors must be coded as intermetropolitan, even if considerable wasteland is thereby added to the intermetropolitan classification.

3. A third vagary is the presence between two centers of two equally long and equally traveled routes, instead of a single route. In such cases, both routes have been termed intermetropolitan.

The net effect of these transportation peculiarities has been to introduce an element of inexactness into the classification of sectors. This study accepts these approximations as a part of the hinterland, and attempts to discover whether, on the average, certain patterns manifest themselves in spite of the accidents of topography and history.

D. The Locational Pattern of Metropolitan Centers Themselves.

Another circumstance which this study does not control is the tendency for certain of the metropolitan centers themselves to be strung out along main transportation routes. For example, a line of heavy mobility connects New York–Albany–Schenectady–Rochester–Buffalo–Erie–Cleveland–Toledo–Fort Wayne–Chicago. A similar one connects Boston–Hartford–New York–Philadelphia–Baltimore—Washington—Richmond—Jacksonville. The influence of nonadjacent metropolitan areas can easily become cumulative under these circumstances, since certain intermetropolitan sectors of small metropolises in these chains may exhibit an unusually intense concentration of population or sustenance activities. As in the case of most previous limitations, the effect is to destroy differences which would otherwise be marked. In this case, the differences between the dominance of various sizes of metropolises will be understated.

E. Lack of Sufficient Cases for Making Full Use of the Classifications Established.

Where communities are simultaneously cross-classified by the four classifications — size of metropolis, sector type, distance, and size of local community — the number of cases which fall into some cells of the table is too small to permit statistical inference. In all such cases the procedure has been to combine the classifications into broader groupings. Thus, in the tabulations which follow, the reader will find that wherever each of these variables is treated singly, a detailed classification of distance zones or sizes of communities has been used, but that in the multiple cross-classifications fewer and broader groupings have been made in order to obtain sufficient cases for statistical treatment.

XI

Mechanics of Tabulation for Statistical Analysis

Two alternatives for the tabulation of the data presented themselves within the framework which had been established. The data for each individual metropolitan community could have been classified and tabulated separately, or the data for all metropolitan communities could have been tabulated together by dividing them into the four size classes and allowing the data for all those of one size to fall into one set of categories. While the former experimental design is the more efficient, it entails many times more labor than does the second. Its chief virtue lies in the opportunity it provides for a study of the deviations of individual metropolitan communities from the general pattern. Because of the exploratory nature of the study, the entire theoretical framework upon which the procedure rests was relatively untried and thus could give no guarantee that the mass of detailed computations for individual metropolitan communities would be justified. It appeared wiser to determine first, using the simplest and most direct means, whether there was a general pattern, than to include a study of variations. The method followed, therefore, was that of using groupings of metropolitan communities.

XII

What Differences Should Be Considered Significant for this Study?

All judgments concerning the existence and pattern of dominance must be based upon a series of statistical tables in which the data listed in Section IX have been classified by the categories of the variables listed in Section X. Because the total number of people, establishments, wage earners, or dollars which will fall into each cell of such tables is large, even very small differences between the various categories will be "statistically significant" when measured by conventional standards. This does not mean, however, that all such differences are meaningful for the problem at hand. Since this is a study of patterns, and since each variable consists of three or more categories, the meaningful differences will be those patterns of differences which persist when the data are further cross-classified by other variables. If no such regular patterns of differences appear the hypothesis must be abandoned, even though each of the differences is statistically significant. In such a case it must be presumed that the differences result from the action of other variables not included in the study. Because formal tests of significance can be of little aid in determining the meaningfulness of differences, no such measures will accompany the tables. The reader may assume, for practical purposes, that every distribution is non-random with respect to the parent group from which it has been drawn. Only those differences which become a part of a general pattern will be considered significant. Failure to fit into such a pattern will be regarded as evidence against the hypothesis, even though such differences may differ greatly from their parent group. The significance of differences will be determined not by their magnitude alone, therefore, but also by their direction and their consistency with other differences.

XIII

Summary

1. Metropolitan dominance may be inferred from a demonstration that nonrandom and patterned sets of differences exist between the distribution over the land of population and sustenance activities on the one hand, and conditions which may be attributed only to the metropolis on the other hand.

2. Dominance is not regarded as a fixed attribute, but as a status which can vary in degree from unit to unit. All local communities in the metropolitan community are considered to possess some degree of dominance over some portion of the hinterland. They may be classified into four broad classes according to the range and variety of the controls which they exercise as dominants (metropolitan centers), as subdominants (hinterland cities), as influents (rural-nonfarm populations), and as sub-influents (rural-farm populations).

3. Each of these major dominance types may be subdivided and considered to represent a continuum. Metropolitan centers and, hence, all metropolitan communities, are classified into four major classes on the basis of the size of each metropolis. Hinterland cities are classified on the basis of their size in 1940, and rural-nonfarm and rural-farm populations are classified according to the size in 1940 of the largest city contained in the county in which they reside.

4. The degree of dominance which the metropolis exercises over the hinterland is limited by the relative opportunity which each metropolis has to enter into some functional division of labor with the hinterland communities. This opportunity varies with the degree of accessibility of the hinterland to the metropolis.

5. Accessibility, and consequently degree of dominance, may be expressed as a function of:

a. Distance over standard highway routes, measured in miles and grouped by class intervals, or distance zones.

b. Direction from metropolis, denoted by the type of sector in which the community is located. Three types of sectors are recognized: those containing intermetropolitan highways, those not containing such a route but containing a hinterland city of 25,000 or more inhabitants, and those containing neither a route nor a major city.

Through cross-classification of all hinterland units by these two variables, the hinterland may be subdivided into areas of hypothetically like degree of dominance.

6. Metropolitan dominance may be expected to vary with two additional variables:

c. Size of metropolitan community.

d. Size of hinterland city (or size of largest city contained in county of residence for the rural populations).

7. Functions involving sustenance, or the earning of a livelihood, may be expected to reveal most clearly the existence of a pattern of metropolitan dominance. The raw data of this study consist of data for population, manufacturing, wholesale trade, retail trade, and services, and are taken from the Sixteenth Census of the United States for the years 1939-40.

8. In order to test the above postulates, 67 metropolitan centers were established. The entire area of the United States was divided as the hinterlands of these centers. Classifications of distance, direction, size of metropolitan community, and size of local community were given to each city and county hinterland unit.

9. The full pattern of dominance may be studied by seeking consistent, nonrandom differences in fourfold cross-classifications of variables a, b, c, and d ("5" and "6" above, this summary).

10. The procedure which has been outlined above has certain limitations. In most cases the limitations consist in an underestimation of the amount of difference which exists, or in the fact that broad categories are necessarily employed in instances where narrower ones would be desirable.

CHAPTER THREE

THE STRUCTURE OF THE METROPOLITAN COMMUNITY: A SUMMARY OF FINDINGS

I

Introduction

Each of the analytical chapters of this study deals with only one aspect of population distribution or of the distribution of sustenance activities, as the case may be. It is necessary, therefore, that at some point the findings be assembled and related to each other and to the hypothesis of metropolitan dominance. Such a synthesis is made in this chapter, rather than at the end of the analysis, for two reasons. First, the analysis is a rather lengthy one. A preliminary summary of the materials which are to be examined in detail later will enable the reader more readily to place each of the remaining chapters in its proper relation to those which precede it and those which follow it. A second reason for placing the summary here is that it makes Part I a complete and abbreviated unit of the entire study. The reader who desires only to review the study in its broadest outlines will find all of the information necessary for accomplishing his objective in Part I.

In order to establish the major conclusions upon concrete and illustrated facts, a few tables and charts have been prepared in condensed form for use in this summary. This has been accomplished by combining the data into broad classifications. If the reader does not intend to read beyond this summary, he should be warned that the full picture is not as neat and orderly as these condensed tabulations might lead him to believe. In the area of 2,977,000 square miles comprising the United States, the range of diversity is so great, particularly since that area has been occupied by a population of city-builders for more than three centuries, that any general tendency, upon closer examination, reveals sufficient complexity to make unqualified conclusions difficult to reach with the use of only a few variables.

II

Distance from the Nearest Metropolis and Size Class of Metropolitan Community

A. Population and Sustenance Activities per Unit of Land Area. (Table 3-1 and Chart 3-1)

On the average, as the distance from the metropolis increases, the number of persons per square mile of land area decreases. With increasing distance, each square mile of land area supports steadily decreasing average amounts of retail trade, services, wholesale trade, and manufacturing activities. This finding is noteworthy for the following reasons: first, it is a statement of a set of conditions which applies to the entire land area of the United States. The data shown in Chart 3-1 are statistical averages of the data for all urban places and for the rural portions of all counties in the United States, classified by the distance which they lie from one of the central cities. Undoubtedly there are many areas which deviate from this average pattern. Nevertheless, marked changes in the intensity of land settlement and in the degree of specialization in sustenance activities must be the usual, rather than the unusual, correlates of increased or decreased distance from the metropolis.

Second, the distance pattern encompasses the entire area which has been called the "hinterland." The effect of distance from the metropolis does not cease to exist at the suburbs, but continues throughout all distances. Distance from the metropolis appears to be a factor in determining the level of land occupancy and the intensity with which sustenance activities are performed in zones which are a full day's journey from the central city via automobile or rail. Such areas cannot possibly be related to each other on the basis of intimate daily contact between their populations.

Third, the distance pattern for the suburban and for the most distant zones are shown here to be only different aspects of the same phenomenon. There is a fairly constant rate of change between relative decreases in land occupancy and relative increases in distance.[1] Thus, the suburb, the industrial satellite, or the metropolitan district represent only one aspect of an apparent tendency for population and the sustenance activities to resist decreasing accessibility to the metropolitan center. This reaction to distance is not directly proportional to the change in the number of miles, but is related to proportional changes in distance.

Fourth, although the four sustenance activities have approximately the same general distance

---

1. Note that Chart 3-1 is plotted on logarithmic scales.

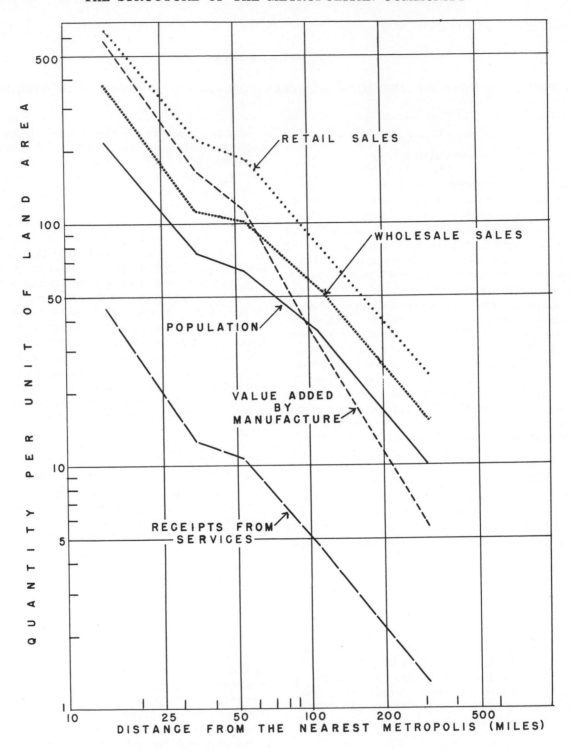

CHART 3-1   POPULATION PER SQUARE MILE AND DOLLAR
VALUE OF SELECTED SUSTENANCE ACTIVITIES
PER 1/100 SQUARE MILE OF HINTERLAND
AREA, BY DISTANCE OUTWARD FROM THE
NEAREST METROPOLIS. 67 METROPOLITAN
COMMUNITIES, UNITED STATES, 1939-40.

SOURCE: COMPILED FROM SIXTEENTH CENSUS OF THE
UNITED STATES

pattern as does population, the rates of their change with distance are not identical to those for population, nor are they like each other. Because this is true, it is apparent that the population of some zones must be more specialized in some types of activity than the populations of other zones. This immediately raises the question:

Is the pattern for population distribution accompanied by a pattern of territorial and local community specialization, division of labor, interdependency, and exchange?

This question may be answered by expressing the data for the sustenance activities in terms of "amount per unit of population" rather than in terms of "amount per unit of land area." A community with a higher than average per capita wholesale sales, for example, is more specialized in wholesale trade than a community with a lower than average per capita wholesale sales. Since specialization in any activity is indicative of a division of labor and of interdependence with other portions of the population, the indexes of specialization can be used to study the pattern of interdependency among the parts of the metropolitan community. Throughout this study the distribution of population has been studied in terms of the population per unit of land area, while the distributions of the sustenance activities have been analyzed in terms of amount per unit of population.[2]

B. Size Class of Metropolitan Community and Intensity of Land Settlement. (Table 3-1 and Chart 3-2).

The size of the central city also is related to the intensity with which the entire hinterland is occupied. Metropolitan communities with large central cities (here considered to be central cities of 500,000 or more inhabitants) have a considerably higher population per square mile than metropolitan communities with small central cities (central cities of less than 500,000 inhabitants). Moreover, the rate of change in land occupancy with relative change in distance is much greater for the hinterlands of large than of small central cities. The suburban zone of the large metropolitan communities fades into the intermediate and distant zones

with only a slight deceleration in rate of change, whereas in the small metropolitan communities populations have a more pronounced tendency to attain an equilibrium with respect to distance at the intermediate zone between 45 and 64 miles.[3] This more rapid decline of settlement with distance, in the case of the larger units, results from a much higher level of land occupancy at the inner zones and an only moderately higher level of land occupancy in the outer zones.

C. Types of Hinterland Population and Intensity of Land Settlement. (Table 3-1 and Chart 3-2)

The urban, the rural-nonfarm and the rural-farm population each occupies the hinterland with its own characteristic distance pattern. The differences between them arise primarily from differences in the level of their land occupancy, their average rate of change with relative change in distance, and differences in their characteristic alterations in this rate of change with change in distance. All three types, however, tend to cluster toward the metropolis.

This clustering tendency is most marked in the case of hinterland urban populations. With increasing distance from the central city the number of urban residents per unit of hinterland area falls off very rapidly. With each increase in distance the rural-nonfarm population also decreases, but at a much less rapid pace than does the urban population. Although there is a very high concentration of rural-farm population within the suburban zone (out to 25 miles), this concentration is almost equally high in the intermediate zone of daily railway and trucking service (35 to 64 miles). In all of the above comparisons of the distance patterns for the three types of population, the differential effect of the large and of the small metropolis is very much in evidence. Thus, there are more urban, more rural-nonfarm, and more rural-farm residents per square mile at all distances in the hinterlands of large metropolitan communities than in those of small metropolitan communities.

D. Urban-Rural Composition of the Hinterland Populations. (Chart 3-3).

The differential change in the intensities with which the urban, the rural-nonfarm, and the

2. In most cases only one of the three indexes of sustenance activities, the "per capita dollar value," is used in this summary. For similar information concerning the "number of establishments per 1,000 inhabitants" and "number of wage earners per 1,000 inhabitants" see Chapters 10-14. I am indebted to the United States Bureau of the Census for preparing special tabulations in which the manufacturing and wholesale information for areas for which information had been withheld to avoid disclosure of the operations of individual establishments was provided in the form of group totals which matched the categories of this study.

3. "Large" and "small" metropolitan communities are used throughout this chapter to refer to the size of the central city, as defined above.

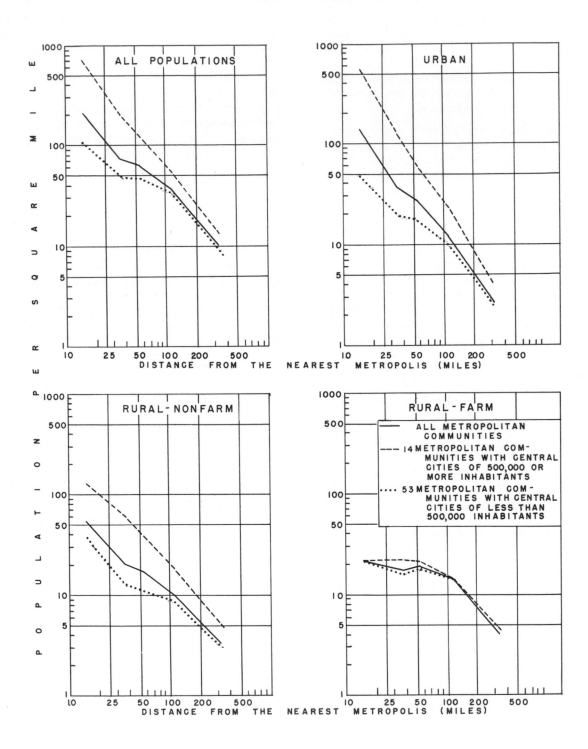

CHART 3-2   URBAN AND RURAL POPULATION PER SQUARE MILE
OF HINTERLAND BY DISTANCE FROM THE NEAREST
METROPOLIS AND SIZE CLASS OF THE METROPOLIS.
UNITED STATES, 1940

SOURCE: COMPILED FROM SIXTEENTH CENSUS OF THE UNITED STATES

Table 3-1

Indexes of land occupancy and territorial specialization - distance and city size. Urban and rural population per square mile of land area, and per capita dollar value of retail, service, wholesale, and manufacturing activities of central cities and all hinterland areas classified by distance from the nearest metropolis. United States, 1939-40.

Distance from nearest metropolis (miles)	Population per square mile [a]				Sustenance activities (per capita dollar value)			
	Total	Urban	Rural-nonfarm	Rural-farm	Retail sales	Receipts from services	Wholesale sales	Value added by manufacture
All classes of metropolitan communities								
Central cities	9,046.7	9,046.7	-	-	471	55.4	1172	284
0-24 [b]	214.6	138.8	54.5	21.3	303	21.2	175	273
25-44	74.7	35.9	21.2	17.6	301	17.0	146	224
45-64	63.3	27.0	17.5	18.8	293	16.7	161	178
65-164	36.0	11.6	9.8	14.6	236	13.4	157	95
165-over	10.0	2.6	3.1	4.3	240	12.7	156	56
All hinterland [c]	32.9	13.7	9.1	10.2	267	15.8	160	154
All metropolitan communities [d]	44.2	25.0	9.1	10.2	319	26.0	420	187
Classes A and B: Metropolitan communities with large central cities (500,000 or more inhabitants)								
Central cities	13,012.0	13,012.0	-	-	457	60.2	1295	302
0-24	711.8	561.6	128.4	21.7	346	26.8	192	317
25-44	216.1	130.3	63.2	22.7	351	20.6	166	313
45-64	122.8	61.4	39.8	21.6	347	19.1	175	249
65-164	57.1	24.1	18.5	14.5	306	16.5	162	157
165-over	13.4	4.0	4.9	4.6	290	15.0	169	111
All hinterland [c]	96.3	57.8	25.6	12.9	335	21.4	176	259
All metropolitan communities [d]	164.4	126.1	25.5	12.8	386	37.6	643	277
Classes C and D: Metropolitan communities with small central cities (100,000 - 499,999 inhabitants)								
Central cities	5,672.3	5,672.3	-	-	499	46.0	933	250
0-24	107.0	47.4	38.5	21.2	243	13.4	150	209
25-44	50.2	19.6	13.9	16.7	264	14.3	132	160
45-64	48.0	18.1	11.7	18.1	256	15.0	152	129
65-164	33.1	9.9	8.6	14.6	219	12.7	156	80
165-over	9.7	2.5	3.0	4.3	234	12.4	154	49
All hinterland [c]	25.1	8.2	7.1	9.8	235	13.2	152	105
All metropolitan communities [d]	29.4	12.6	7.1	9.8	273	18.0	266	126

a) All populations divided by total land area of each zone.

b) Includes counties containing central cities.

c) Excludes central cities.

d) Includes central cities.

Source: Compiled from Sixteenth Census of the United States.

rural-farm populations inhabit the hinterland, as distance from the metropolis increases, produces a change in the urban-rural composition of the hinterland from the center to the periphery. With increasing distance the proportion of the total population which is urban decreases, and the proportion of the population which is rural-farm increases. The proportion of the population which is rural-nonfarm does not follow the same pattern in the metropolitan communities with large central cities as it does in those with small central cities. In the former, the proportion of the population which is rural-nonfarm steadily increases with distance. In the latter, the proportion of the population which is rural-nonfarm tends to decrease from the central city out to about 65 miles from the metropolis, and then to increase with further increases in distance. At all distances, the hinterlands of large metropolitan communities are more urban in composition than are the hinterlands of small metropolitan communities. The activities of small metropolitan communities include a much larger agricultural element than do those of large metropolitan communities.

E. Relative Population Concentration (Chart 3-4)

The tendency for all hinterland populations to settle the land more sparsely with increasing distance produces broad patterns of positive and negative population concentration about the metropolis. Populations are usually thought of as being concentrated only in central cities and their immediate environs. Relative to the average intensity with which the entire land area of the United States is occupied by each population, all zones within 65 miles of the metropolis are areas of positive

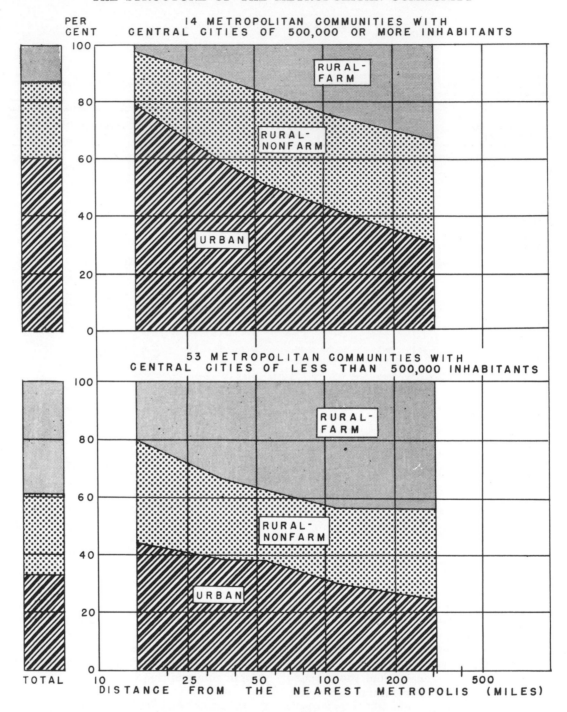

CHART 3-3 URBAN-RURAL COMPOSITION OF THE
          HINTERLAND POPULATION BY DISTANCE
          FROM THE NEAREST METROPOLIS AND
          SIZE CLASS OF THE METROPOLIS.
          UNITED STATES, 1940

SOURCE: COMPILED FROM SIXTEENTH CENSUS OF THE
        UNITED STATES

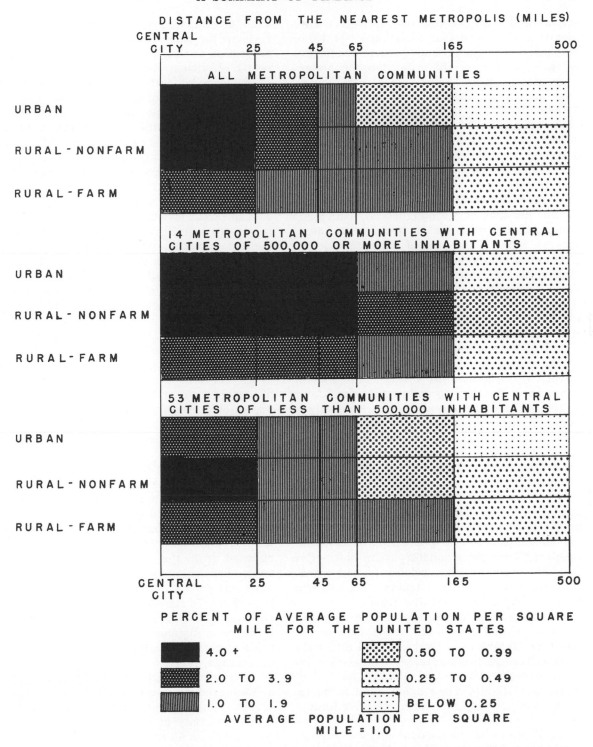

DISTANCE FROM THE NEAREST METROPOLIS (MILES)

CHART 3-4   RELATIVE POPULATION CONCENTRATION
——— RATIOS OF HINTERLAND URBAN AND
RURAL POPULATIONS PER SQUARE MILE
TO THEIR AVERAGE POPULATION PER
SQUARE MILE IN THE NATION, BY DISTANCE
FROM THE NEAREST METROPOLIS AND SIZE
CLASS OF THE METROPOLIS. UNITED STATES, 1940

SOURCE: COMPILED FROM SIXTEENTH CENSUS OF THE UNITED STATES

concentration for all populations. In metropolitan communities whose central cities are 500,000 or more inhabitants this zone of positive concentration extends as far as 165 miles into the hinterland. In metropolitan communities with central cities of less than 500,000 inhabitants, only the rural-farm population is concentrated to this distance Beyond 165 miles from central cities of all sizes there are, on the average, fewer urban and rural people per square mile than in the nation as a whole. Thus, the ability of the metropolis to concentrate people about itself extends over an area which is much larger than the metropolitan district or the suburbs of the metropolis. This positive concentration over such a broad area has as its obverse side a huge ring of population deficit lying 165 miles or more from the metropolis.

Relative to their own levels of land occupancy, the rural-nonfarm and the urban populations are much more concentrated toward the center than are the rural-farm populations. The urban population in particular tends to be very concentrated in the zones within 45 miles of the metropolis. Although the rural-nonfarm population also is very intensively concentrated in these same shorter distance zones, it tends to follow the rural-farm population out into the outer zones, presumably to act as a local service population in place of the urban population which becomes increasingly sparse. The concentration of rural-nonfarm population near the center reflects the great suburban aggregation.

F. Specialization of Function in the Hinterland. (Table 3-1 and Chart 3-5).

The above patterns of population distribution with distance have their counterpart in distinctive patterns of retail, service, wholesale, and manufacture specialization with distances. The patterns for no two of these functions are alike.

1. Central cities are more specialized in retail trade, service, and wholesale trade than is any zone of their hinterlands. Large central cities are less specialized in manufacturing than are the inner zones of their hinterlands, although small central cities are slightly more specialized in manufacturing than are the inner zones of their hinterlands.

2. Within 35 miles of the central city the population tends to have a low retail specialization index. This reflects a dependence of suburban and other areas upon the central city for the purchase of many items, presumably the more specialized ones. Beyond the 35 mile zone there is little evidence that the metropolis functions to any great extent as a retail center for the hinterland population. The gradual decrease in per capita retail

sales at distances greater than 65 miles probably reflects the increasing rural composition of the population and hence a smaller need per capita for retail activities. In other words, the function of retailing is so intimately related to the current needs of the population that it tends to be distributed much as the population is distributed. Metropolitan communities with large central cities tend to have a higher per capita retail index at all distances than those with smaller central cities. This fact is also interpreted as being due primarily to the more urban composition of the hinterlands of the larger central cities.

3. The extent to which hinterland areas specialize in service activities is influenced considerably by their metropolitan position. In metropolitan communities with large central cities such specialization declines steadily with increasing distance. In metropolitan communities with small central cities, the hinterland areas within 45 miles of the metropolis appear to be dependent upon the metropolis for many services, as they are for retail trade. At distances greater than this the hinterland appears to provide a somewhat larger share of the services which it requires. The full extent of dependency upon the metropolis can be estimated only roughly, for the rural populations can forego many services or produce them in their own households. (See Section H, "Dependence upon the Metropolis").

4. Wholesale trade is a function which is extremely concentrated in the metropolis, and one in which the metropolis is highly specialized. No distance zones seem able to provide all of the wholesale trade activities that their populations require. This type of activity is also somewhat dispersed outward from the metropolis into the 0-24 mile zone. The 25-44 mile zone appears to be in considerable deficit compared to the remainder of the hinterland. In the 45-64 mile zone there is a small revival in wholesale specialization; with further increase in distance, specialization in this function tends to remain on a plateau far below the national, or average, level.

5. Although specialization in manufacturing is not a distinguishing characteristic of central cities, certainly manufacturing is a function which has flourished only in the metropolis and the inner zones. Within 45 miles of the central city the population tends to be highly specialized in manufacturing. Beyond this distance each zone is considerably less specialized than the zone which it surrounds.

G. Dominance and Relative Functional Specialization of the Distance Zones. (Chart 3-6).

After having observed the general pattern of specialization of each of the major functions

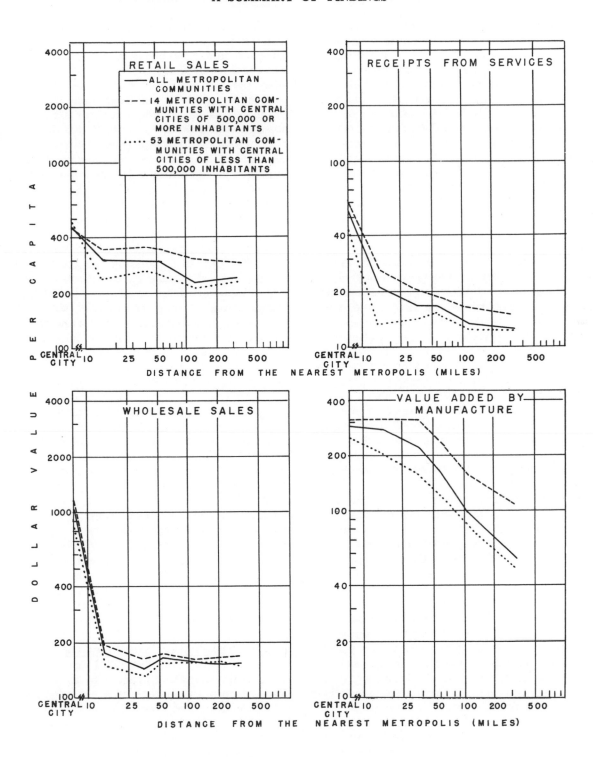

CHART 3-5 INDEXES OF SPECIALIZATION IN RETAIL TRADE,
           SERVICES, WHOLESALE TRADE AND MANUFACTUR-
           ING BY DISTANCE FROM THE NEAREST METROP-
           OLIS AND SIZE CLASS OF THE METROPOLIS.
           UNITED STATES, 1939-40

SOURCE: COMPILED FROM SIXTEENTH CENSUS OF THE UNITED STATES

individually, it is important for the development of a test of the dominance hypothesis that all four of these patterns be compared with each other directly. A comparison may be accomplished by expressing each of the per capita indexes for each function as a ratio of its average per capita value for the nation as a whole. A ratio of 1.0, then, means "as specialized as the nation as a whole." Values above and below 1.0 indicate greater or lesser specialization than the national average. Thus, the functions, within each distance zone as well as in the central cities, of larger and smaller metropolitan communities may be compared directly. A lower than average value for any distance zone is indicative of some degree of dependence upon another area.

If the index for degree of specialization is used to measure the extent of the dependency of any zone upon another part of the metropolitan community for services, wholesale trade, and manufactures, then it can be stated categorically that every zone in the hinterland is dependent upon the metropolis for wholesale trade and services, and that the outer zones are dependent upon the metropolis and the inner zones for manufacturing. In short, from the point of view of this study, a large part of the dominance of the metropolis rests upon the inability of the hinterland populations to provide most economically or most expeditiously all of the wholesale, service, and manufacturing activities which they require to sustain themselves at present levels of living.

The fact that the metropolis and those zones which are in daily contact with the metropolis (in the case of manufacturing) are the principal source of such needed activities constitutes one of the "conditions of life" for the individual community lying in the hinterland, and a very real condition to which an adaptation must be made. Because these necessary goods and services must perforce be transported from the center to the dependent community, one very obvious adaptation, other things being equal, is for individual units of the population to locate near the source of supply. Because a dependent community must obtain needed wholesale, service, and manufacturing services from the center, it must specialize in some other activity and then exchange the product of that specialization in order to supply its needs. Since the metropolitan market center is the principal mechanism by which these exchanges are effected, there is additional reason in the modern industrial-commercial society for population to concentrate in the vicinity of the metropolis. Hence it is not surprising to find the pattern of decreasing land occupancy with increasing distance from the source of needed goods and services and the principal market center.

From this point of view, metropolitan dominance is akin to the dominance which exists in nature, — it is a controlling of the conditions of life. The local community must accept its dependence upon the nearest metropolis for those needed wholesale services and manufacturing activities which it cannot provide itself, or else sustain its population at a level lower than that of other communities which do accept those conditions. But acceptance of those conditions entails specialization in some activity which will cause the needed goods and services to flow into the community from the central city or other specialized areas. The valuation placed upon each of various potential specialties by the metropolitan market will ultimately influence the activity which is chosen as a specialty.

If this view is a plausible one, then the consistent patterns of population distribution and of territorial specialization constitute a broad territorial organization, a true community with form and structure. It is because of this view that the existence of a metropolitan community is accepted as one conclusion of this study. This conclusion, however, has as a corollary the fact that this pattern of organization, this structure, embraces and characterizes the way in which almost all, if not all, areas in the entire nation support themselves. The area of close interdependence, over which the metropolitan pattern extends, is much larger than the metropolitan district, and embraces many more people and their sustenance activities than does the metropolitan district. The data which have been marshalled to develop these patterns account for all land area, all populations, all retail trade, all services, all wholesale trade, and all manufacture in the United States. Although individual areas may conform less closely than other areas, or may even appear to constitute major exceptions for one reason or another, the average remains as the typical structure of land occupancy and sustenance activities.

H. The Dependence of the Hinterland Upon the Metropolis. (Table 3-2, Chart 3-7 and Chart 3-8).

In order to make a precise measurement of the dependence of the hinterland areas upon the metropolitan center, and hence to be able to know fully the extent of the division of labor and exchange between them, it would be necessary to know the actual requirements of the hinterland population in regard to retail trade, services, wholesale trade, and manufacturing. If the requirements of each part of the hinterland population were known for each type of activity they could be compared with the actual quantity of those activities performed in each zone. A very crude estimate of the requirements of the population of central cities and of the

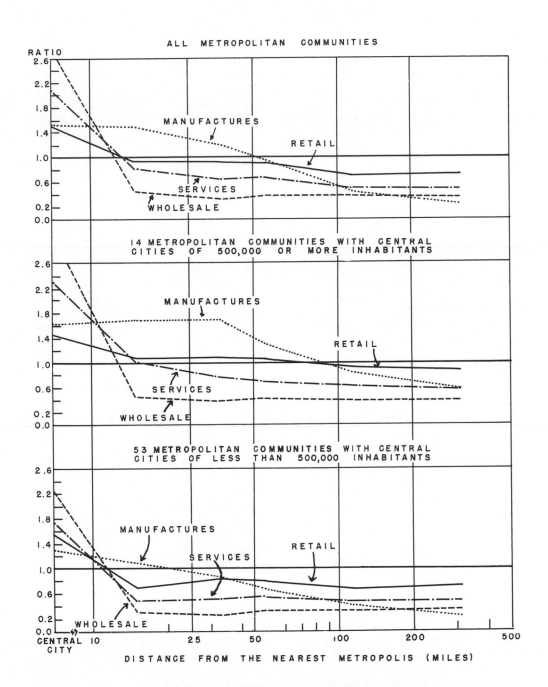

ALL METROPOLITAN COMMUNITIES

14 METROPOLITAN COMMUNITIES WITH CENTRAL
CITIES OF 500,000 OR MORE INHABITANTS

53 METROPOLITAN COMMUNITIES WITH CENTRAL
CITIES OF LESS THAN 500,000 INHABITANTS

DISTANCE FROM THE NEAREST METROPOLIS (MILES)

PER CAPITA VALUE FOR NATION = 1.0

CHART 3-6 RELATIVE CONCENTRATION OF SELECTED
SUSTENANCE ACTIVITIES. RATIO OF PER
CAPITA DOLLAR VALUES TO AVERAGE PER
CAPITA VALUE FOR THE NATION, BY DISTANCE
FROM THE NEAREST METROPOLIS AND SIZE
CLASS OF THE METROPOLIS. UNITED STATES,
1940.

SOURCE: COMPILED FROM SIXTEENTH CENSUS OF THE UNITED STATES

residents of each distance zone has been made and expressed as a ratio of the actual quantities of retail trade, services, wholesale trade, and manufacturing performed by the population of each distance zone.[4] Chart 3-7 presents graphically the pattern which these ratios take for each of the functions. A ratio of 1.0 indicates self-sufficiency in that activity. A ratio of less than 1.0 indicates dependence upon other areas, whereas a ratio larger than 1.0 is indicative of production in excess of local requirements.

It is obviously impossible to make an accurate estimate, on any simple basis, of the requirements of a population for such activities as wholesale trade or manufacturing. The procedure adopted here has been to establish a per capita requirement figure for the urban, the rural-nonfarm, and the rural-farm population which, when multiplied by the population of each, would yield the total "dollar value" of the activities as reported by the Census for the year 1939. Differences between the requirements of the urban, the rural-nonfarm, and the rural-farm populations were established by the use of consumer expenditure data prepared by the National Resources Planning Board.[5] If it is assumed that those general levels roughly measure the per capita requirements for retail trade, services, wholesale trade, and manufacture, then the total dollar value of these activities as reported by the Census may be assigned to the various populations on the basis of requirements. Using the National Resources Planning Board levels of expenditure as a basis, the following per capita requirements were estimated for each population:

tral cities, the total estimated requirements of each of these populations are determined. Table 3-2 and Chart 3-7 present, by distance zones, the ratio of actual dollar values of the activity performed to the estimated total requirements. To the extent that the requirements of the rural-farm population have been underestimated (requirements of the urban population overestimated), the extent of the dependence of each part of the hinterland has been understated.

1. If the estimated requirements of the population are even approximately correct, the hinterland population is dependent upon the metropolis for retail trade for a distance of only about 45 miles into the hinterland. According to the estimates, in the zone 25-44 miles the population obtains 98 percent or more of its retail requirements locally. Even if allowance is made for a considerable error in the factors used, the fact remains that at about 45 miles the hinterland appears to become completely self-sufficient in retail trade. The excesses of retail activity at the greater distances, and the deficit of retail trade at distances between 65 and 265 miles from the metropolis, may reflect: (a) changing consumption patterns of the three populations with distance, (b) the use of mail orders, and (c) regional differences in consumption (a larger than average proportion of the population of the South falls in the 65-264 mile interval. See Chapter 9). Only a very small proportion of the hinterland may be said to be dependent upon the metropolis as a shopping center, and in no case is the extent of this dependence large. On the average, the retailing activities of central cities are

| Function | Type of Population | | | |
	All populations	Urban	Rural-nonfarm	Rural-farm
Retail sales	$319.0	$402.0	$283.0	$149.0
Receipts from services	26.0	32.7	23.0	12.1
Wholesale sales	420.0	529.0	372.0	196.0
Value added by manufacture	187.0	235.0	165.0	87.0

Since these values "account for" the total quantity of each of the functions, any errors made in establishing these per capita estimates must necessarily consist of an overestimation of the requirements of one type of population and, thereby, an underestimation of the requirements of another population type.

When the above estimated per capita requirements are multiplied by the urban, the rural-nonfarm, and rural-farm population residents in each zone of the hinterland and by the residents of cen-

only 17 percent greater than the estimated volume of requirements of their own populations. The residents of the suburbs (0-24 miles) consume almost all of this excess, leaving very little apparent dependency at distances between 25-45 miles and beyond 45 miles, none save that which might arise from purchases via mail or infrequent shopping trips on the part of a small segment of the population.

2. All parts of the hinterland are dependent upon the central city for services and wholesale trade.

4. These estimates are not reported in the detailed analysis for each sustenance activity in Chapters 11-14, but are reported here for use in testing the hypothesis of the study.

5. National Resources Planning Board, Family Expenditures in the United States, 1941. Table 40, p. 13.

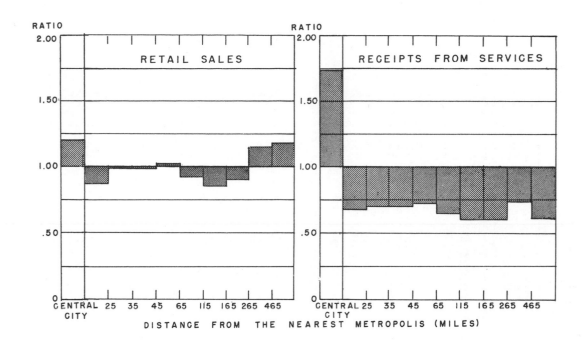

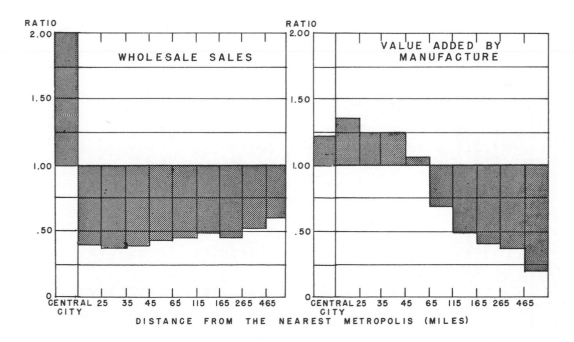

CHART 3-7 RATIO OF ACTUAL RETAIL SALES, RECEIPTS
FROM SERVICES, WHOLESALE SALES, AND VALUE
ADDED BY MANUFACTURE TO ESTIMATED
REQUIREMENTS FOR THESE FUNCTIONS, BY DIS-
TANCE FROM THE NEAREST METROPOLIS.
UNITED STATES, 1939-40

SOURCE: COMPILED FROM SIXTEENTH CENSUS OF THE UNITED STATES

Table 3-2

Ratios and cumulative ratios of actual dollar value of retail sales, receipts from services, wholesale sales, and value added by manufacture to the estimated requirements of the population for these activities, by distance from the nearest metropolis and size class of metropolis. United States, 1939-40.[a]

Distance	ALL METROPOLITAN COMMUNITIES				METROPOLITAN COMMUNITIES WITH CENTRAL CITIES OF 500,000 OR MORE INHABITANTS				METROPOLITAN COMMUNITIES WITH CENTRAL CITIES OF LESS THAN 500,000 INHABITANTS			
	Retail sales	Receipts from services	Wholesale sales	Value added by manufacture	Retail sales	Receipts from services	Wholesale sales	Value added by manufacture	Retail sales	Receipts from services	Wholesale sales	Value added by manufacture
Ratio of actual dollar value to estimated requirements												
Central city	1.17	1.74	2.22	1.21	1.14	1.87	2.45	1.29	1.24	1.47	1.76	1.06
0-24[b]	.86	.66	.38	1.34	.91	.81	.39	1.45	.78	.41	.37	1.14
25-34	.98	.68	.36	1.25	1.04	.76	.41	1.46	.90	.60	.31	1.03
35-44	.99	.68	.37	1.25	1.04	.74	.32	1.72	.96	.64	.40	.92
45-64	1.01	.71	.42	1.05	1.13	.76	.43	1.38	.92	.66	.41	.79
65-114	.91	.63	.43	.67	1.02	.68	.41	.92	.87	.61	.44	.59
115-164	.83	.59	.48	.49	.98	.62	.40	.79	.81	.59	.49	.44
165-264	.87	.58	.44	.39	1.07	.71	.49	.72	.84	.56	.44	.34
265-464	1.13	.73	.52	.36	1.09	.55	.42	.60	1.13	.75	.53	.35
465-over	1.16	.60	.59	.21	-	-	-	-	1.16	.60	.59	.21
Total	1.00	1.00	1.00	1.00	1.06	1.27	1.34	1.30	.95	.77	.70	.75
Cumulative ratio of actual dollar value to estimated requirements (center to periphery)[c]												
Central city	1.17	1.74	2.22	1.21	1.14	1.87	2.45	1.29	1.24	1.47	1.76	1.06
0-24[b]	1.07	1.37	1.59	1.25	1.06	1.52	1.77	1.34	1.08	1.09	1.27	1.09
25-34	1.06	1.30	1.47	1.25	1.06	1.46	1.66	1.35	1.05	1.03	1.14	1.08
35-44	1.05	1.26	1.39	1.25	1.06	1.43	1.59	1.37	1.04	.98	1.06	1.06
45-64	1.05	1.18	1.26	1.22	1.07	1.36	1.48	1.37	1.02	.92	.93	1.01
65-114	1.02	1.08	1.11	1.12	1.06	1.30	1.39	1.33	.98	.83	.79	.89
115-164	1.01	1.04	1.05	1.07	1.06	1.28	1.36	1.32	.95	.79	.74	.82
165-264	1.00	1.01	1.01	1.02	1.06	1.27	1.35	1.30	.94	.77	.71	.76
265-464	1.00	1.00	1.00	1.01	1.06	1.27	1.34	1.30	.94	.77	.70	.75
465-over	1.00	1.00	1.00	1.00	-	-	-	-	.95	.77	.70	.75
Cumulative ratio of actual dollar value to estimated requirements (periphery to center)[d]												
Central city	1.00	1.00	1.00	1.00	1.06	1.27	1.34	1.30	.95	.77	.70	.75
0-24[b]	.92	.65	.42	.91	1.00	.76	.40	1.32	.87	.58	.43	.67
25-34	.93	.64	.43	.77	1.06	.72	.41	1.22	.89	.61	.44	.59
35-44	.93	.64	.44	.71	1.06	.71	.41	1.16	.88	.61	.45	.55
45-64	.92	.63	.44	.65	1.06	.71	.42	1.07	.87	.60	.45	.52
65-114	.90	.61	.45	.54	1.02	.67	.42	.86	.87	.60	.46	.47
115-164	.89	.60	.47	.43	1.02	.65	.44	.75	.92	.60	.48	.38
165-264	.94	.61	.47	.38	1.07	.69	.48	.70	1.14	.73	.53	.33
265-464	1.13	.72	.53	.35	1.09	.55	.42	.60	1.16	.60	.73	.35
465-over	1.16	.60	.59	.21	-	-	-	-	1.16	.60	.59	.21

a) Adjusted for differences in levels of consumption between the urban, the rural-nonfarm, and the rural-farm populations.
b) Includes county containing the central city.
c) Ratios computed from cumulative distributions of actual and estimated dollar values from central city to outer zone.
d) Ratios computed from cumulative distributions of actual and estimated dollar values from the outer zones to the center.

Source: Based upon average per capita requirements estimated from expenditure data reported in National Resources Planning Board, Family Expenditures in the United States, 1941, Table 40, p. 13. Population data compiled from Sixteenth Census of the United States.

The dependence upon wholesaling is of particularly great magnitude It is assumed that the dependence of the hinterland population in regard to services is primarily of the "service to business" type or some other specialized form. Barber shops, laundries, and the other personal service establishments are thought to be distributed in much the same way as is retail trade. If data were available concerning the distribution of capital for new enterprises, banking, and other financial activities they would probably show a per capita distance pattern similar to that for wholesale and services. One condition of life to which hinterland populations must adjust, therefore, is a sizeable dependence upon the wholesale and business service activities of central cities, and a similarly large dependence in financial matters.

3. In the case of manufacturing the dependency pattern differs from both of the other two types of patterns. The entire area beyond 65 miles is dependent upon the entire area within 65 miles. The central city, and a broad zone surrounding it, produce quantities of manufactured products which are in excess of their requirements.

Thus, within the hinterland, there does exist a broad territorial division of labor which makes for interdependence of the various parts and for exchange. The fact that, in regard to certain basic activities, this interdependence takes the form of a dependence of the entire hinterland upon the center gives rise to the apparent dominance of the metropolis.

Another way of viewing the structure of dependency in the hinterland is to show how the excesses of each activity balance the deficits. The surplus of wholesale trade activity in the central city, for example, is gradually consumed by the hinterland, which is deficient in this activity, until at the outermost zone the surplus is zero because it has all been distributed. Table 3-2 presents the cumulative excesses and deficits out through distance zones for each of the four sustenance activities in large and small metropolitan communities.[6] Chart 3-8, illustrating this tabulation, shows that at 45 miles, for example, the cumulative retail excess of the central city has been reduced to a relative value of 105 percent of estimated requirements, while the index for services is 118, for wholesale trade 126, and for manufacturing 122 percent. The deficits, calculated from the outer zone toward the center, represent the load of hinterland dependency carried by the metropolis, or

the metropolis and the inner zones (in the case of manufacturing).

III

Type of Sector and the Metropolitan Pattern

In spite of the fact that all hinterland zones appear to be dependent upon the metropolis for some of their sustenance needs, this dependence is far from being complete dependence for any single type of activity. In every zone there is some retail trade, some wholesale trade, some service, and some manufacturing activities. Within the hinterland there are 3464 cities and urban places ranging in size from 2500 to more than 100,000 inhabitants. In addition there are many thousands of incorporated and unincorporated villages and hamlets which serve as local community centers. Through these centers must flow the goods which the local population must obtain from the metropolis or from other areas. To them falls the task of producing or collecting a large share of the surplus commodities which are needed for exchange. Because of them, the hinterland is not directly dependent upon the metropolis for all of its retail, wholesale, service, and manufacturing needs. Conceivably the broad distance structure may be accompanied by many other basic patterns of population distribution and functional dependency which arise from the functioning of these hinterland centers. It was hypothesized in Chapter Two that one such pattern is "direction from the metropolis," or "type of sector."

A. Population Distribution (Table 3-3 and Chart 3-9).

1. Those sectors which contain a major transportation route between two neighboring central cities (intermetropolitan sectors) have a high average level of land occupancy of urban, rural-non-farm, and rural-farm populations. Such sectors comprise 57 percent of the total land area of the hinterland.

2. Those sectors which do not contain a major intermetropolitan thoroughfare, but do contain a major hinterland city of 25,000 or more inhabitants ("subdominant" sectors) have an even larger population per square mile than do the intermetropolitan sectors. This greater intensity of land occupancy includes not only the urban population (something to be expected because of the large hinterland

---

6. Note that the estimates of Table 3-2 indicate that small metropolitan communities are dependent upon large metropolitan communities for a part of their needs in the case of each of the four sustenance activities. It is interdependences of this type, presumably, which give rise to extensive intermetropolitan exchange.

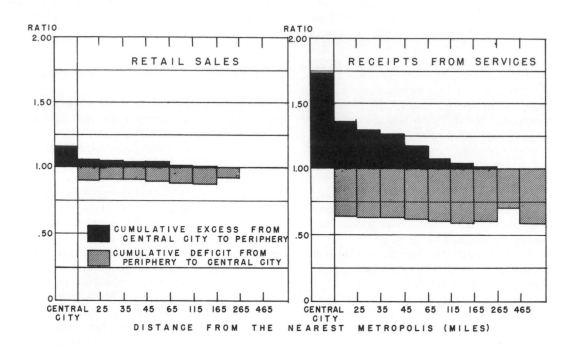

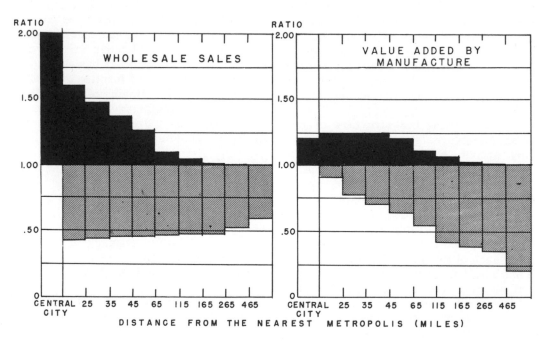

CHART 3-8 RATIO OF CUMULATIVE RETAIL SALES, RECEIPTS FROM
SERVICES, WHOLESALE SALES, AND VALUE ADDED BY
MANUFACTURE TO ESTIMATED REQUIREMENTS FOR
THESE FUNCTIONS, BY DISTANCE FROM THE NEAREST
METROPOLIS. UNITED STATES, 1939-40

SOURCE: COMPILED FROM SIXTEENTH CENSUS OF THE UNITED STATES

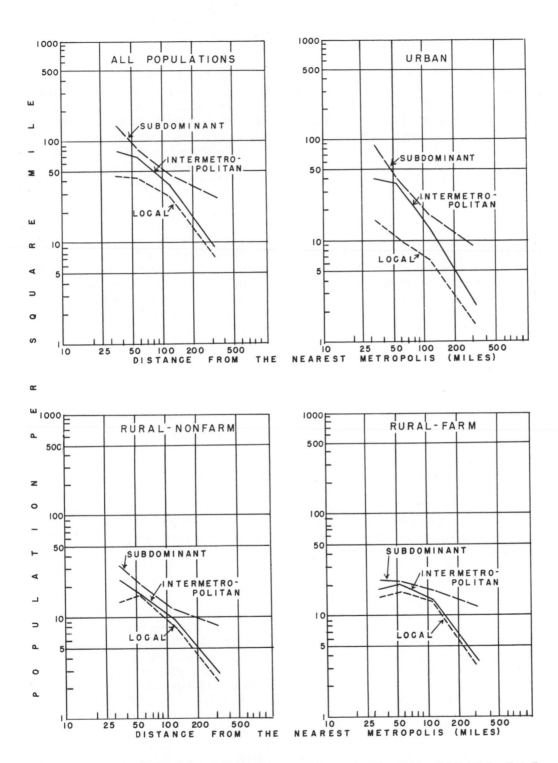

CHART 3-9 URBAN AND RURAL POPULATION PER SQUARE MILE
OF HINTERLAND BY DISTANCE FROM THE
NEAREST METROPOLIS AND TYPE OF SECTOR.
UNITED STATES, 1940

SOURCE: COMPILED FROM SIXTEENTH CENSUS OF THE UNITED STATES

city contained by definition), but also both the rural-nonfarm and the rural-farm populations as well. Such sectors comprise 10 percent of the total hinterland area.

3. Those "local" sectors which contain neither an intermetropolitan thoroughfare nor a major hinterland city have considerably lower than average levels of land occupancy of all three types of population. Such sectors constitute 33 percent of the land area.

4. Thus, intermetropolitan and subdominant sectors tend to disperse the population farther into the hinterland and to support concentrations of population at much greater distances from the metropolis than would otherwise seem possible.

B. Functional Specialization (Table 3-3 and Chart 3-10).

1. These intersector differences are accompanied by definite differences in the degree of specialization in sustenance activities among the sectors. Intermetropolitan sectors are slightly more specialized in three of the four types of functions than are the other two types of sectors, i.e., in retail trade, in services, and in wholesale trade. This relative advantage of the intermetropolitan over the subdominant sectors is of very minor importance compared to the much higher specialization of both of these types of sectors compared with local sectors. Wholesale establishments which are located in the hinterland appear to prefer a location along an intermetropolitan route which will enable them to draw upon the elaborate wholesale mechanism of two or more metropolitan centers, or a location in a sector containing a hinterland city of 25,000 or more inhabitants.

2. The existence of a set of local conditions favorable to manufacturing (such as a fortuitous combination of natural resources) appears to be one major cause for the rise of large hinterland cities away from the intermetropolitan transportation routes. This is indicated by a smaller index of manufacturing specialization in intermetropolitan than in subdominant sectors, at all distances. Yet manufacturing is not the sole specialization of the sectors containing such cities, as is indicated by their greater than average specialization in the other three types of functions.

3. The local sectors, having a much lower degree of accessibility to the metropolis and to major hinterland cities than have the other two sector types, are much less specialized than the other sectors. This deficit is greatest for wholesale trade and manufacturing, which average only 69 percent of the average hinterland specialization in these two activities. It is least, as would be expected, for retail trade. The extent of the deficit

for services is about midway between that for retail trade and that for manufacturing and wholesale.

4. When the metropolis-centered activities of wholesale trade and manufacturing do "go to the hinterland," they tend to cling to their metropolitan moorings and choose a location which will permit them ready access to the metropolis. It would appear that these outlying units, for the most part, are not independent enterprises operating in direct competition with the wholesale and manufacturing units of the central city. Rather, the evidence indicates that they are appendages of an extended metropolis-centered system of production, marketing, and distribution. If the hinterland wholesale and manufacturing units were competitive rather than supplemental units, then the relative indexes for the local sectors would be higher than those for the intermetropolitan sectors. For it would appear that hinterland populations would develop their own service, wholesale, and manufacturing units in competition with the central city most successfully in those local sectors which are most remote and inaccessible to the metropolis, and least subject to competition from the metropolis. In such a case the more accessible intermetropolitan and subdominant sectors would remain relatively unspecialized and more dependent upon the wholesale and manufacturing institutions of the central city. Since the actual situation is the opposite of this, it can only be surmised that wholesale trade and manufacturing in the hinterland are highly integrated with an extensive system, the center of which is located in the central city. In that case, such establishments located in the hinterland must adapt also to the activities of the metropolis. The individual wholesale establishment undoubtedly finds its sources of supply, or its market (if it is an assembler of products), located in the central city. The individual manufacturer undoubtedly finds that his only source of some raw materials and component parts which are necessary for the fabrication of his product, as well as the distribution outlet for his product, is located in the metropolis. It may be presumed that it is for these reasons that the shorter distance zones and the more accessible sectors have a pattern of sustenance activities more nearly like that of the metropolis than have local sectors. Beyond certain distance limits the cost of serving the entire hinterland area from the central city appears to become prohibitive and the task to become a physical impossibility. Under such conditions local establishments tend to arise at those points which most nearly approximate the conditions of the metropolis and which provide easy access to the metropolis.

Table 3-3

Indexes of land occupancy and territorial specialization — type of sector. Urban and rural populations per square mile of land area, and per capita dollar value of retail, service, wholesale and manufacturing activities of all hinterland areas classified by type of sector and distance from the nearest metropolis. United States, 1939-40,a)b)

Distance from the nearest metropolis (miles)	ALL METROPOLITAN COMMUNITIES								METROPOLITAN COMMUNITIES WITH CITIES 500,000 AND OVER - CLASS A AND B								METROPOLITAN COMMUNITIES WITH CITIES OF LESS THAN 500,000 - CLASS C AND D							
	Population per square mile of hinterland				Sustenance activities (per capita dollar value)				Population per square mile of hinterland				Sustenance activities (per capita dollar value)				Population per square mile of hinterland				Sustenance activities (per capita dollar value)			
	Total	Urban	Rural-nonfarm	Rural-farm	Retail trade	Services	Wholesale trade	Manufacturing	Total	Urban	Rural-nonfarm	Rural-farm	Retail trade	Services	Wholesale trade	Manufacturing	Total	Urban	Rural-nonfarm	Rural-farm	Retail trade	Services	Wholesale trade	Manufacturing
Intermetropolitan sectors																								
0-24a)	244.6	138.8	54.5	21.3	303	21.2	175	273	711.8	561.6	128.4	21.7	346	26.8	192	317	107.0	47.4	38.5	21.2	243	13.4	150	209
25-44	81.2	39.6	23.4	18.3	305	17.7	158	226	235.2	139.5	71.9	23.8	361	21.7	177	301	54.8	22.4	15.1	17.3	264	14.8	143	171
45-64	71.6	34.8	17.1	19.7	305	17.8	179	191	133.9	74.3	38.5	21.1	348	19.7	183	257	55.6	24.7	11.6	19.4	277	16.6	176	149
65-164	37.3	13.3	9.9	14.1	245	14.5	173	100	62.2	29.2	19.1	14.0	322	18.3	170	175	34.0	11.2	8.7	14.2	228	13.7	173	82
165-over	9.1	2.4	2.9	3.8	248	13.2	169	46	8.0	2.3	2.9	2.8	304	15.2	170	76	9.2	2.4	2.9	3.9	244	13.0	168	45
All distances	33.0	15.5	8.1	9.5	283	17.7	183	164	112.2	74.8	25.0	12.4	354	24.2	198	277	24.5	9.1	6.2	9.2	249	14.5	176	108
Subdominant sectors																								
0-24a)	244.6	138.8	54.5	21.3	303	21.2	175	273	711.8	561.6	128.4	21.7	346	26.8	192	317	107.0	47.4	38.5	21.2	243	13.4	150	209
25-44	141.0	86.8	31.8	22.4	330	19.2	151	271	280.6	189.8	67.3	23.6	347	21.0	175	338	76.4	39.2	15.4	21.8	300	16.3	110	168
45-64	84.9	41.4	21.7	21.8	311	18.8	188	246	143.9	81.3	38.6	23.9	348	20.1	210	309	53.9	20.4	12.8	20.7	258	17.0	158	154
65-164	47.6	17.6	12.0	18.0	244	14.1	173	114	58.2	27.3	16.9	13.9	312	16.4	180	170	44.6	10.6	10.6	19.1	220	13.3	171	94
165-over	29.4	8.9	8.3	12.1	227	13.5	168	81	22.6	7.2	8.1	7.3	293	15.7	177	131	33.9	10.1	8.5	15.3	197	12.5	164	58
All distances	57.0	27.6	13.0	16.4	276	16.5	166	171	80.7	50.5	18.1	12.1	335	19.9	173	262	46.8	17.7	10.8	18.3	232	14.0	160	106
Local sectors																								
0-24a)	244.6	138.8	54.5	21.3	303	21.2	175	273	711.8	561.6	128.4	21.7	346	26.8	192	317	107.0	47.4	38.5	21.2	243	13.4	150	209
25-44	45.1	15.7	14.3	15.1	264	12.4	105	180	114.6	57.8	37.8	19.2	308	13.6	82	336	37.1	10.8	11.6	14.7	248	11.9	113	126
45-64	43.6	10.6	16.5	16.5	255	12.6	102	102	85.1	21.4	43.0	20.8	344	16.0	105	150	35.9	8.6	11.6	15.7	214	11.0	100	79
65-164	28.8	6.3	8.6	13.9	209	10.4	111	70	44.8	9.5	18.9	16.3	251	11.4	113	87	27.2	6.0	10.6	13.7	202	10.3	111	68
165-over	7.2	1.5	2.4	3.4	233	10.9	117	54	6.3	0.8	2.5	3.1	188	7.4	76	55	7.2	1.5	2.3	3.4	235	11.0	118	54
All distances	22.7	6.9	6.9	8.9	239	12.1	111	107	72.7	32.2	26.0	14.5	305	16.0	108	192	19.1	5.1	5.5	8.5	221	11.0	111	84

a) Includes counties containing the central cities. Because intersector comparisons of population are unreliable in the 0-24 mile zone, all sectors have been combined and a single figure reported for comparison with other zones. The"all distances,"however, exclude the counties containing the central cities and include the remaining counties in the 0-24 mile zone.

b) Per capita values are for retail sales, receipts from services, wholesale sales, and value added by manufacture.

Source: Compiled from Sixteenth Census of the United States.

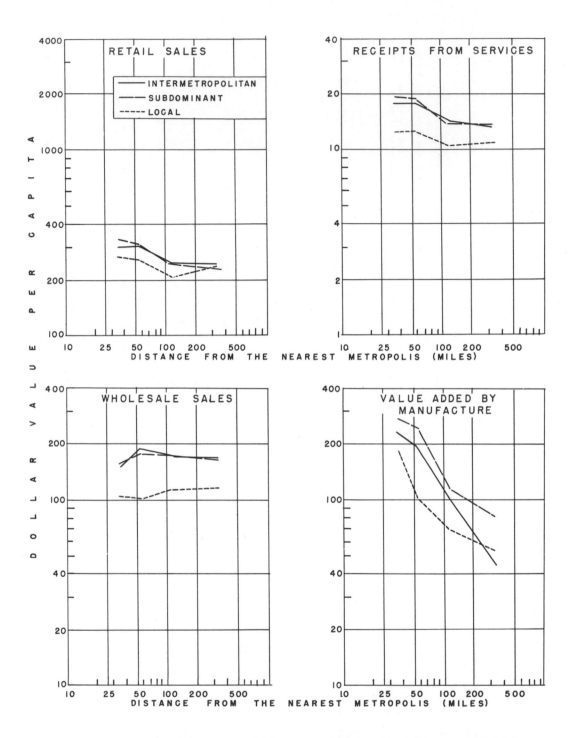

CHART 3-10 INDEXES OF SPECIALIZATION IN RETAIL TRADE, SERVICES, WHOLESALE TRADE AND MANUFACTURING BY DISTANCE FROM THE NEAREST METROPOLIS AND TYPE OF SECTOR. UNITED STATES, 1940

SOURCE: COMPILED FROM SIXTEENTH CENSUS OF THE UNITED STATES

Thus, an additional element in the metropolitan structure is the transportation system between central cities, and the close interfunctioning of central cities and large hinterland cities of 25,000 or more inhabitants. Each such route appears to have become an axis along which the urban, the rural-nonfarm and the rural-farm populations cluster more intensively than is the case in local sectors which contain no such thoroughfare. This clustering does not appear to produce competition with the metropolis as much as it does further integration into the metropolitan system. It appears to be opportunity to enter into a division of labor with the metropolis, rather than opportunity to compete with the metropolis, which leads to specialization in wholesale trade, manufacturing and, to a lesser extent, services.

IV

The Place of Principal Hinterland Cities and Other Areas in the Metropolitan Structure (Table 3-4 and Chart 3-11)

In the study of sector types it was noted that those sectors which contain large hinterland cities promote greater population concentration and higher indexes of specialization than do local sectors containing no such cities. This would indicate that the larger cities of the hinterland are focal points of concentration and specialization. This question is further explored in Table 3-4 and Chart 3-11, where the per capita value of each function for cities of 10,000 inhabitants or more is compared, by distance, with the same value for other hinterland areas. The question here is: what part do the principal hinterland cities play in the pattern of interdependency and exchange between the metropolis and the hinterland?

1. The central city is more specialized in services and wholesale trade than are the principal hinterland cities lying in any zone. This is not true, however, in regard to retail trade and manufacturing activities. The principal hinterland cities lying more than 45 miles from the metropolis are all more specialized in retail trade than is the metropolis. As a whole, the principal hinterland cities lying less than 65 miles from the metropolis are more specialized in manufacturing than is the central city.

2. With increasing distance from the central city the specialization of the principal hinterland cities in retail, services, and wholesale tends to increase. The specialization of the other areas tends either to decrease somewaht with increasing distance or to remain relatively unchanged. Thus, as one progresses from the metropolis into the hinterland,

the hinterland cities of 10,000 or more inhabitants tend to be a great deal more specialized in retail and wholesale trade, and slightly more specialized in services. Beyond about 45 miles these same cities become steadily less specialized in manufacturing with increasing distance.

3. The fact that the "other" hinterland areas, comprised of rural areas and cities of less than 10,000 inhabitants, make no change of such magnitude with increasing distance indicates that the type of retail, service, and wholesale activities found in these areas is of such a nature that such activities must follow the distributional pattern of population closely. Presumably a great proportion of these enterprises is concerned with the distribution of those nonspecialized items for which there is a general and frequently recurring need. Grocery stores, filling stations, and barber shops, as well as wholesale grocers and assemblers of farm products would fall in this class.

4. One should avoid the temptation to infer from Chart 3-11 that, because the degree of specialization of the hinterland cities increases with increasing distance from the metropolis, the hinterland areas as a whole tend to become more independent of the metropolis in regard to these functions. While it is true that the rising indexes for commercial activities with greater distance do reflect an increasing tendency for cities to perform as shopping and distributing centers for a broad "trade territory," it does not follow that the dominance of the metropolis decreases in proportion to the rise in the indexes of specialization of the hinterland cities. In Chapter 7, Section IV it is demonstrated that as the distance from the metropolis increases the average size of the trade territory of each hinterland city also increases. This enlarged territory occurs because cities are more sparsely distributed at these distances, leaving a larger number of square miles as well as a larger total population to be included in the average trade territory of each hinterland city. As the distance from the metropolis increases, populations must travel greater average distances to patronize the retail, service, and wholesale establishments of a city of 10,000 or more inhabitants. The average number of people who are dependent upon each such center is also greater at the greater distances. Hence, the total volume of business, relative to the size of the city, is also larger. For example, the rise in the index of retail specialization with increasing distances beyond 45 miles from the metropolis may be attributed almost entirely to the enlarging trade territories of cities of 10,000 inhabitants or more. The fact that there is no comparable rise for services indicates that the population and business units of outlying areas

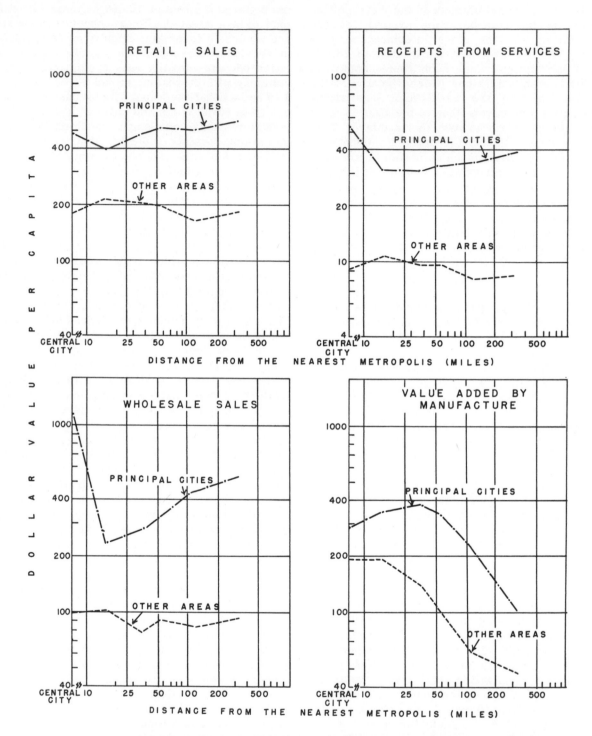

CHART 3-11 INDEXES OF SPECIALIZATION IN RETAIL TRADE,
           SERVICES, WHOLESALE TRADE, AND MANUFACTURING
           FOR CENTRAL CITIES AND HINTERLAND CITIES
           OF 10,000 OR MORE INHABITANTS AND "OTHER
           AREAS", BY DISTANCE FROM THE NEAREST METROP-
           OLIS   UNITED STATES, 1939-40

SOURCE: COMPILED FROM SIXTEENTH CENSUS OF THE UNITED STATES

Table 3-4

Indexes of territorial specialization - Principal hinterland cities and "other areas."
Per capita dollar value of retail, service, wholesale, and manufacturing activities of
hinterland cities of 10,000 or more inhabitants and of other hinterland areas classified by distance from the nearest metropolis and size class of the metropolitan community. United States, 1939-40.[a]

Distance from the nearest metropolis (miles)	PER CAPITA DOLLAR VALUE							
	Retail sales		Receipts from services		Wholesale sales		Value added by manufacture	
	Principal cities	Other areas	Principal cities	Other areas	Principal cities	Other areas	Principal cities	Other areas
All classes of metropolitan communities								
Center[b]	471	181	55.4	9.2	1,172	99	284	191
0-24	397	213	31.3	10.7	239	102	351	195
25-44	483	204	30.6	9.7	273	79	380	141
45-64	511	199	32.8	9.7	325	90	347	105
65-164	502	167	33.7	8.1	443	83	225	61
165-over	563	186	38.6	8.4	534	93	103	48
All distances	466	183	32.5	8.8	331	87	303	85
Classes A and B: Metropolitan communities with large central cities (500,000 or more inhabitants)								
Center[b]	457	222	60.2	13.8	1,295	155	302	241
0-24	400	236	33.3	12.8	216	130	370	216
25-44	492	237	31.0	12.1	276	76	407	235
45-64	517	241	32.4	10.8	318	85	395	160
65-164	526	215	33.1	9.6	353	83	320	90
165-over	596	234	36.3	11.1	484	111	196	95
All distances	453	230	32.8	11.0	264	91	370	156
Classes C and D: Metropolitan communities with small central cities (100,000-499,999 inhabitants)								
Center[b]	499	162	46.0	7.0	933	73	250	165
0-24	389	189	25.3	8.4	306	72	299	168
25-44	473	186	30.0	8.4	271	81	347	91
45-64	504	175	33.2	9.0	333	92	297	74
65-164	494	157	33.9	7.8	476	83	191	55
165-over	559	180	38.9	8.0	540	91	91	43
All distances	481	169	32.3	8.1	402	85	235	63

a) Hinterland cities of 10,000 or more inhabitants are termed "principal cities". County
units of rural areas and cities of less than 10,000 inhabitants are classified as "other
areas".

b) Values shown under "principal cities" are those for central cities; values shown under
"other areas" are those for counties containing central cities.

Source: Compiled from Sixteenth Census of the United States.

either forego many services or obtain a considerable share of them directly from the central city. The sharp increase, even above the rate for retail, in wholesale specialization of the hinterland cities, indicates that in those cases in which it is more economical for a wholesale establishment to be located in the hinterland than in the metropolis, the larger hinterland city is preferred to the small city and open country. Meanwhile, the other areas are thereby made more heavily dependent upon the principal hinterland city for wholesale activities than for retail; yet Chart 3-7 has indicated that there is an apparent decrease in total dependency for wholesale sales with increasing distance. Therefore, the rise in the wholesale specialization indexes of large hinterland cities is a function both of increasing average size of trade territory and increasing self-sufficiency. The data for manufacturing indicates that this is one activity in which the opportunity for even a large hinterland city to specialize is restricted to a fairly narrow zone within or about the central city.

5. Although cities of 10,000 or more inhabitants occur much less frequently in the hinterland than do cities of 2,500 to 9,999, the greater relative importance of the former is indicated by the fact that the population per square mile of hinterland is much greater for the large hinterland cities than for the smaller ones. Although there are more of the smaller places, the total number of people actively engaged in serving each unit of area is greater for the cities of 10,000 or more inhabitants.

6. The pattern by which population occupies the land, and the tendency for the degree of specialization in the four sustenance activities to fit into that pattern, permit us to infer that an area in the hinterland may stand in one of two principal relations to the metropolis. It may participate directly in the activities of the metropolis or it may stand in an exchange relationship with the metropolis. It may also stand in a third relation which is, in reality, a mixture of the first two. This third relation may be called one of interchange.

a. The zone within 25 miles of the central city is obviously a zone of direct participation. The level of land occupancy is high; dormitory towns are numerous; the cities located there are more deficient in retail trade, wholesale trade, and services than are the cities lying in other parts of the hinterland. Because they provide space and yet are able to participate directly in the advantages of the metropolis, the principal hinterland cities in this zone attain a high degree of manufacturing specialization. For this same reason the "other areas" appear able to become more specialized in all phases of the sustenance activities than is the

case in any other zone. Throughout this zone it would appear that, to all intents and purposes, the populations and the functional establishments are residents of the metropolis. They are not "suburban," but "submetropolis" populations.

b. At about 65 miles from the metropolis begins the rise in the retail, service, and wholesale specialization of the principal hinterland cities, indicating the presence of a trade territory for each, and their subdominance over that trade territory. In this zone, the factors favoring manufacturing decline progressively, both for principal cities and "other areas." Beyond 65 miles, the "other areas" attain a plateau in retail, service, and wholesale specialization. They appear to provide locally the more standard commodities which are needed frequently or in large quantity, and to depend upon the metropolis and the hinterland city for the more specialized ones. Since such dependence must take the form of exchange, this zone may be termed the zone of exchange. The functions of collection and distribution characterize its principal cities; agricultural production and extraction characterize its "other areas." Here there is little manufacturing activity.

c. The zone between 25-64 miles appears to be a mixed zone. The level of land occupancy tends to vary with size of central city and type of sector. In Chapters Six, Seven and Eight it is shown that, at some point in this zone, population tends to attain a point of equilibrium with distance, and that there is a measurable concentration of large hinterland cities in the 45-64 mile portion of the zone. That these cities are outlying points of distribution and manufacture is evident from Chart 3-11. Because this zone does contain such a mixture, it may be called a zone of interchange, for it mediates between the metropolis and its direct participants and the outlying zone of exchange. From such outlying centers in this zone secondary highways radiate to the more remote portions of the hinterland, and for this reason the cities in this zone may be called "hinterland-access cities."

In the metropolitan communities with large central cities the zone of participation appears to have expanded outward from the center and to have merged into the zone of interchange, whereas in the metropolitan communities with small central cities the three broad zones of population distribution and of functional specialization are more distinct. If such is the case, then it must be assumed that the three types of relationship in which the hinterland cities may stand with respect to the metropolitan center were laid down in the era of rail transportation, and that motor transportation, electric power, and other technological developments are fostering their convergence. If one were to take the pattern of the large metropolitan communities as the ultimate end of the aggregation process, he would be forced to conclude that the process of dominance and subdominance has, as one end result, the almost complete elimination of the zone of exchange and the co-mingling of the zones of participation and interchange. This could come about, however, only through a multiplication of the number of metropolitan centers, as has obviously been the case in those geographic regions containing cities of 500,000 or more inhabitants. In those parts of the United States in which central cities of this class are primarily found, the average distance between centers is not in excess of the 65 miles marking the outer limits of the zone which is classified here as a zone of interchange. In the not too distant future, in other words, the number of metropolitan centers may increase to such an extent that 65 miles will be the maximum distance which most areas lie from a central city, and technological improvements in transportation may permit all communities within this radius to participate directly with the metropolis.

V

Size of Hinterland City and Metropolitan Structure
(Table 3-5 and Chart 3-12)

1. The previous section demonstrated the fact that large hinterland cities are the principal focal points about which the activities of the outlying areas are oriented. From Table 3-5 and Chart 3-12 may be observed the additional fact that the larger the hinterland city is the greater its degree of specialization tends to be. Hinterland cities of 25,000 or more inhabitants are more specialized, on the average, in retail, service, wholesale, and manufacturing activities (except at extreme distances) than are cities of 10,000-24,999 inhabitants. This is true at all distances, and in metropolitan communities containing either large or small central cities. Too much emphasis, however, must not be placed upon the fact of size of city. In the detailed tabulations of Chapters Eleven to Fourteen it is found that sector type, size of metropolis, and a more detailed distance classification modify this general conclusion considerably.

2. An explanation is developed in Chapter Seven for this phenomenon of increased average specialization of the larger cities, where it is demonstrated that the average trade territory of a large hinterland city is inevitably larger than that of a small hinterland city, that it contains a larger population, and that this disparity tends to increase with greater distance from the metropolis. This

alone would account for the greater degree of specialization which the cities of 25,000 or more inhabitants have compared with those of only 10,000-24,999 inhabitants. Again reference must be made to Chart 3-7 and to the fact that, except for wholesale trade, the total degree of dependency upon the metropolis does not change materially outside the 45 mile zone.

3. Because data concerning all four of the sustenance activities are not available for small cities, this analysis of the specialization of the various sizes of cities cannot be carried out for urban places of less than 10,000 inhabitants. Chapter Seven demonstrates, however, that the size of the average trade territories of these smaller cities also decreases with decreasing size of hinterland city, and that the trade territory of small cities increases in area and population with distance in the same manner as cities of 10,000 or more inhabitants. It is almost certain to be true, therefore, that these smaller sized cities tend to be progressively less specialized than the larger cities in all functions, with the possible exception of retailing, and that with increasing distance the degree of their specialization in all activities also increases. Whatever the size of a city, it must be specialized in some function at a level above the hinterland average; otherwise it has no reason for existence, no function to perform in the hinterland, and no visible means of supporting its population. The great concentration of wholesale, service, and manufacturing activities in the large hinterland cities and/or in the inner zones indicates that the hinterland city of less than 10,000 inhabitants which is located 65 miles from the metropolis must support itself primarily by retail specialization, with a much lower level of specialization in services and wholesale trade.

4. Specialization in manufacturing, because it involves many unique "production factors" of which access to markets is only one aspect, (and a secondary one when compared to all of the other factors combined) does not show this total response to changes in the average size of trade territory. The fact seems to exist that within about 65 miles of the metropolis these production factors appear to be present in a favorable combination, that outside the 65 mile zone they become increasingly unfavorable, and that no other consideration will suffice to promote manufacturing. Opportunity to escape competition from the metropolis appears to be less important to the manufacturer than does access to the factors of production. Increasing size of trade territory seems to provide him with no incentive whatsoever to move into the hinterland if it means the sacrifice of a location which provides these factors economically.

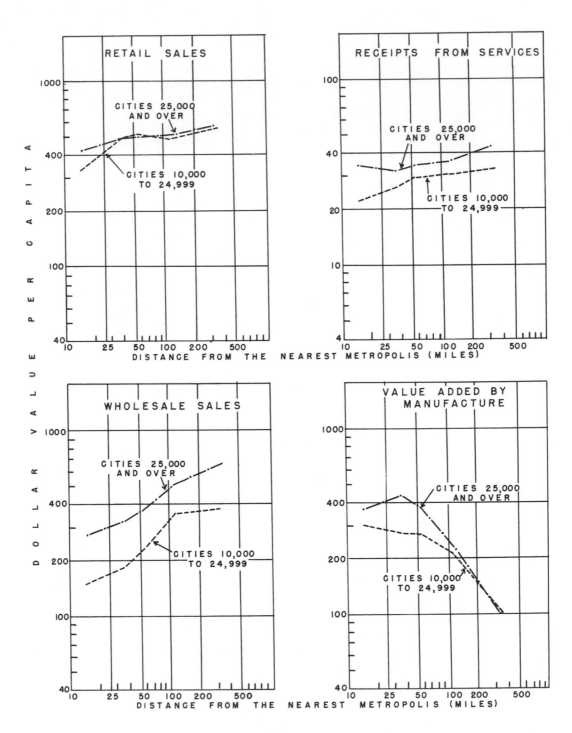

CHART 3-12   INDEXES OF SPECIALIZATION IN RETAIL TRADE, SERVICES, WHOLESALE TRADE, AND MANUFACTURING FOR HINTERLAND CITIES OF 10,000 OR MORE INHABITANTS, BY SIZE AND DISTANCE FROM THE NEAREST METROPOLIS. UNITED STATES, 1939-40

SOURCE: COMPILED FROM SIXTEENTH CENSUS OF THE UNITED STATES

Table 3-5

Indexes of land occupancy and specialization - Principal hinterland cities, by size. Population per square mile of hinterland and per capita dollar value of retail, service, wholesale and manufacturing activities of hinterland cities of 10,000 or more inhabitants, classified by size, distance from the nearest metropolis, and size class of metropolitan community. United States, 1939-40.

Distance from the nearest metropolis (miles)	Population per square mile		PER CAPITA DOLLAR VALUE							
			Retail sales		Receipts from services		Wholesale sales		Value added by manufacture	
	10,000-24,999	25,000-over	10,000-24,999	25,000-over	10,000-24,999	25,000-over	10,000-24,999	25,000-over	10,000-24,999	25,000-over
All classes of metropolitan communities										
0-24 a)	31.8	81.7	333	422	22.5	34.6	149	274	303	369
25-44	9.1	17.0	480	485	26.6	32.7	182	323	278	435
45-64	6.2	13.1	517	508	29.2	34.6	230	370	272	382
65-164	3.1	4.3	499	505	30.2	36.1	353	506	212	235
165-over	0.7	0.8	558	567	32.9	43.5	383	661	106	101
All distances	3.4	6.4	455	473	27.5	35.2	252	373	245	333
Class A and B: Metropolitan communities with large central cities (500,000 or more inhabitants)										
0-24 a)	129.1	346.9	336	425	22.8	37.1	92	262	312	390
25-44	29.0	68.9	480	497	27.3	32.6	161	324	300	452
45-64	12.7	36.0	530	513	29.9	33.3	226	350	306	425
65-164	6.5	9.9	497	545	29.6	35.4	268	408	358	296
165-over	1.1	1.0	455	748	22.0	51.7	237	750	208	183
All distances	13.5	32.1	418	468	25.7	35.7	157	309	315	392
Classes C and D: Metropolitan communities with small central cities (100,000-499,999 inhabitants)										
0-24 a)	10.7	24.3	326	416	21.7	26.9	299	310	280	307
25-44	5.7	8.0	480	468	25.9	32.9	200	321	259	410
45-64	4.5	7.3	507	502	28.6	36.1	233	395	248	327
65-164	2.6	3.6	499	490	30.5	36.4	383	544	162	212
165-over	0.6	0.8	574	547	34.5	42.6	405	651	91	91
All distances	2.1	3.2	484	479	28.8	34.5	326	452	194	263

a) Land area of counties containing central cities included in 0-24 mile zone for computation of population per square mile.

Source: Compiled from Sixteenth Census of the United States.

5. The inevitable conclusion from the analysis of the specialization of hinterland cities of each size is that <u>within the hinterland there is a very definite pattern of functional specialization corresponding to the distribution of population in cities of various sizes.</u> Some set of conditions, associated with distance from the metropolis and type of sector, seems to have operated to produce a characteristic distribution of cities in the hinterland and to regulate the size which they have been able to obtain. Individual cities appear to have adapted to this frame of reference and to have achieved degrees of specialization in retail trade, services, and wholesale trade commensurate with the degree of dependence of the hinterland population upon the central city, the size and population of the local trade territory available to them, and the type of relationship which they can establish with the metropolis. In those areas of the metropolitan community which possess conditions favorable to manufacturing, the hinterland cities have specialized in this activity.

VI

The Place of Rural Areas and Minor Cities in the Metropolitan Structure
(Table 3-6 and Chart 3-13)

The problem of subdominance may be explored through a comparison of the intensity of land occupancy and functional specialization to be found in the immediate vicinity of hinterland cities of various sizes. The classification of the rural areas of counties which remained after all cities had been subtracted (population analysis), and of the "other areas" which remained after all principal cities had been subtracted (analysis of specialization), provides a most useful framework

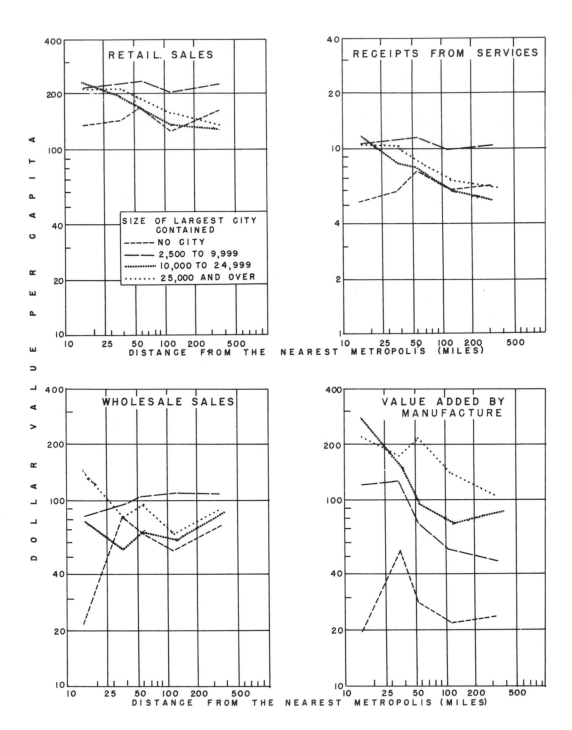

CHART 3-13   INDEXES OF SPECIALIZATION IN RETAIL TRADE, SERVICES, WHOLESALE TRADE, AND MANUFACTURING FOR RURAL HINTERLAND AREAS AND CITIES OF LESS THAN 10,000 INHABITANTS. COUNTY UNITS CLASSIFIED BY SIZE OF LARGEST CITY CONTAINED AND DISTANCE FROM THE NEAREST METROPOLIS. UNITED STATES, 1939-40

SOURCE: COMPILED FROM SIXTEENTH CENSUS OF THE UNITED STATES

for this exploration. In this study these county units of the "rural areas" and the "other areas" have been classified on the basis of the "size of the largest city contained."[7]

1. The presence of a city in a county area, and the size of that city are very closely related to the average number of people per square mile in the rural portion of the county. Each increase in the size of the largest city contained by the county area is accompanied by an increase in the average intensity of land settlement. This phenomenon extends to both the farm and the nonfarm population, to the hinterlands of large and of small central cities, and is present at all distance zones and in all sector types. Just as there is an intense aggregation of population in the immediate vicinity of central cities, so there is a similar aggregation of rural populations about hinterland cities. The intensity of the aggregation, also as in the case of central cities, increases with city size.

2. This tendency to cluster about hinterland cities has its functional aspect. The "other area" portions of the county units are extremely deficient in all three of the commercial sustenance activities, but the deficiency is particularly marked in regard to wholesale trade and services. The small hinterland cities of less than 10,000 inhabitants, and the rural shopping centers, appear to be able to satisfy a considerable proportion, though not all, of the retail requirements in each county unit, but are themselves heavily dependent upon larger hinterland cities, as well as upon the metropolis, for a great deal of their wholesale and service requirements. County units containing no city have low indexes of specialization in all four functions. The presence of a city of less than 10,000 inhabitants is associated with an increase of several points in the commercial activities, indicating that such counties as a whole are more specialized, Yet the "other area" of counties containing a city of 10,000-24,999 is very little more specialized than are the rural areas of counties containing no city, indicating that the small cities which are present in counties with larger cities, as well as the rural populations, are heavily dependent upon the principal hinterland city.

3. Manufacturing, as in all previous cases, occurs in those rural areas in which there is a high level of urban land occupancy. The presence in a county unit of a city of 10,000 or more inhabitants is con-

ducive to manufacturing in the small cities and rural areas. With each increase in size of largest city contained in a county unit there is a marked increase in the degree of manufacturing specialization, particularly in the inner zones. This does not indicate that the manufacturing institutions of the larger hinterland city are a substitute for establishments which would otherwise be located in small cities and rural areas. The situation is quite the reverse; the presence of manufacturing in the large hinterland city is conducive to manufacturing in the remainder of the county.

4. In perhaps no other single tabulation of this study can the simultaneous operation of the dominance of the metropolis and the subdominance of the hinterland city be more clearly envisaged than in Table 3-6. Even as the hinterland cities aggregate rural populations in accordance with their size, and as the populations of the "other areas" attain a given degree of specialization commensurate with the size of the largest city contained in their county, the factors of distance from the metropolis and size of the metropolis are seen to be in operation at all points. This fact should make it obvious that dominance and subdominance are two coacting sets of forces in the hinterland. The rural populations adapt to conditions associated with both hinterland cities and metropolitan centers. Hinterland cities adapt to conditions associated with the presence of other hinterland cities larger than themselves and to the presence of the metropolis. The evidence presented here indicates most clearly that the distribution of population and of sustenance activities in the metropolitan community cannot be understood without reference to the influence of the individual hinterland city, just as the influence of the individual hinterland city cannot be understood without reference to the influence of the nearest metropolis. The metropolitan community thus appears to be an organization of many mutually interdependent and inter-functioning subcommunities oriented about the hinterland cities, which, in turn, are subdominant to and interdependent with the dominant metropolis, and inter-function with it. The entire community organization appears to be held together by a system of community specialization in, and exchange of, locally produced surpluses to fill those needs which cannot be most efficiently satisfied by local institutions.

7. The analysis of the four functions was made for cities of 10,000 inhabitants or more only. The "other areas" remaining after these city totals were subtracted from county totals therefore included the small cities of less than 10,000 inhabitants. The analysis of population, on the other hand, included all urban places. The residual areas after all urban places were subtracted were therefore the completely rural areas. In Table 3-5 the population section refers to rural areas, while the sections for the sustenance activities refer to the "other areas," or the rural area plus the cities of 2,500 to 9,999 inhabitants.

Table 3-6

Indexes of land occupancy and specialisation. Rural population per square mile of hinterland and per capita retail sales, receipts from services, wholesale sales and value added by manufacturing for county units classified by size of largest city contained, distance from the nearest metropolis, and size class of metropolitan community. United States, 1939-40.

Distance from the nearest metropolis (miles)	ALL METROPOLITAN COMMUNITIES				METROPOLITAN COMMUNITIES WITH CENTRAL CITIES OF 500,000 OR MORE INHABITANTS. CLASSES A and B.				METROPOLITAN COMMUNITIES WITH CENTRAL CITIES OF LESS THAN 500,000 INHABITANTS. CLASSES C and D.			
	No city	2,500-9,999	10,000-24,999	25,000-over	No city	2,500-9,999	10,000-24,999	25,000-over	No city	2,500-9,999	10,000-24,999	25,000-over
Population per square mile of hinterland												
0-24	44.6	54.2	98.0	145.0	68.5	135.0	239.2	180.5	43.5	45.0	59.8	95.7
25-44	29.8	28.7	47.5	71.5	40.9	65.5	102.3	110.0	28.9	25.9	34.3	49.7
45-64	26.8	33.4	38.0	59.2	36.4	54.4	56.5	85.7	25.7	30.0	30.9	38.8
65-164	19.8	23.5	30.0	39.3	27.9	29.7	39.5	37.4	19.3	22.8	28.0	40.3
165-over	5.7	8.5	10.1	14.5	6.0	11.9	17.5	8.7	5.7	8.2	9.6	19.2
All distances	11.5	18.1	28.2	41.3	16.9	29.2	56.0	48.6	11.2	17.0	23.0	36.3
Per capita retail sales (dollars)												
0-24	135	215	228	214	252	232	268	224	126	209	187	179
25-44	142	225	193	215	188	277	229	232	137	214	162	190
45-64	166	232	170	183	277	313	221	204	148	208	131	140
65-164	128	202	137	153	158	253	192	214	125	195	119	118
165-over	161	226	129	135	162	289	175	202	161	219	122	107
All distances	143	215	161	179	181	273	219	218	139	205	133	137
Per capita receipts from services (dollars)												
0-24	5.3	10.8	11.9	10.7	6.6	12.1	16.1	11.7	5.2	10.4	7.4	6.9
25-44	6.0	11.4	8.5	10.4	7.1	17.2	9.7	12.5	5.9	10.3	7.5	7.4
45-64	7.6	11.6	8.1	8.7	10.4	14.0	10.2	9.1	7.1	10.9	6.5	7.8
65-164	6.2	10.1	6.3	6.9	7.6	11.4	8.3	9.4	6.1	9.9	5.7	5.6
165-over	6.5	10.7	5.4	6.4	6.4	13.8	6.1	11.7	6.6	10.4	5.2	4.3
All distances	6.4	10.7	7.5	8.5	7.7	13.1	10.1	10.7	6.3	10.2	6.2	6.1
Per capita wholesale sales (dollars)												
0-24	22	84	77	141	13	64	102	157	22	90	51	85
25-44	82	95	56	81	51	69	52	99	85	101	59	55
45-64	69	104	68	94	69	110	73	79	69	103	64	124
65-164	55	110	62	67	64	109	71	70	54	110	59	65
165-over	73	110	84	91	41	146	50	120	75	106	89	80
All distances	63	107	65	89	58	107	69	101	64	107	64	75
Per capita value added by manufacture (dollars)												
0-24	20	122	272	219	74	98	197	244	16	130	352	105
25-44	55	127	159	177	22	345	219	221	59	82	108	117
45-64	28	75	96	213	23	100	94	253	29	68	97	134
65-164	22	54	77	139	32	62	96	145	21	52	70	136
165-over	24	48	85	105	54	77	171	123	22	44	73	98
All distances	25	66	116	171	35	111	149	212	24	59	100	125

Source: Compiled from Sixteenth Census of the United States.

VII

The Metropolitan Community and the Physical Environment

In Chapter Two it was acknowledged that the patterns which have been described here would have meaning only if it could be demonstrated that these patterns are not completely required by conditions of the environment. The simplest and most direct way of making this demonstration is to show, as has been done in Chart 3-14, that within each broad geographic region (generally regarded as a fairly homogeneous part of the total physical environment) the metropolitan pattern still exists. This does not deny the existence of regional differences. Throughout this study emphasis has been placed upon the fact that the metropolitan community must be regarded as a means of adapting to the environment; therefore, differences in that environment must necessarily become an element in the adjustment. The general elements of the metropolitan pattern are present, nevertheless, in each geographic region. With the exception of the farm populations, differences associated with dominance and subdominance within each region are greater than the average differences between regions.

VIII

Conclusion

1. A dominant city is a city which controls many of the conditions of life of all the communities lying within a broad area surrounding it. This control arises from a higher than average degree of specialization in such functions as services and wholesaling, and from an ability to foster industrial development in its immediate vicinity by provision of favorable combinations of the factors of production. Other communities must accept these conditions of life by specializing in other activities and by becoming dependent upon the central city for those goods and services which their residents require but which they cannot provide locally. The metropolitan market center mediates a complex intercommunity exchange, and thereby integrates the activities of outlying communities with each other and with the activities of the metropolis. The single hinterland community must rely upon the central city to preserve the balance which is thus attained among the parts. Not a small part of this balance depends upon the interfunctioning of the dominant units with each other. Organizational patterns based upon these principles are common in plant and animal communities.

2. A subdominant city is a city which adapts to the condition of general dependence upon the center and which functions, through specialization in one or more of the sustenance activities, as an intermediary between the metropolis and the outlying areas. The subdominant city, therefore, has a trade territory comparable to the hinterland of the metropolis, but smaller in size. The subdominant city cannot specialize in all sustenance activities. To the extent that a large hinterland city is able to provide its trade territory with all of the principal sustenance activities required, and to promote a higher than average level of manufacturing in its immediate environs, it is passing from a subdominant to a dominant status. Dominance and subdominance, hence, are only two parts of one continuum of degree of control.

3. A metropolitan community is an organization of many subdominant, influent, and subinfluent communities, distributed in a definite pattern about a dominant city, and bound together in a territorial division of labor through a dependence upon the activities of the dominant city. Subdominant communities produce surpluses for exchange throughout the area. They aid in the interchanging which takes place between the central city and the rural populations. The metropolitan community is not independent of the physical environment, but is, rather, an adaptation to the environment. It utilizes the techniques of production and exchange which are common to populations with industrial-commercial cultures in order to exploit environmental resources and maintain maximum security against catastrophe. Many other conditions of life undoubtedly are subject to control or modification by the central city. The complete structure of the metropolitan community may include the functions of finance, government, education, religion, and innumerable other aspects of the institutional composition of the individual hinterland community. The four broad types of functions which have been considered here can only hint at the detailed patterns which will emerge as a consequence of the application of further research employing new varieties of data, finer subdivisions of the functions than the broad categories used here, and additional variables measuring position in the metropolitan community.

4. The metropolitan community has come to be a characteristic pattern by which at least one urbanized commercial-industrial society, the United States, is organized. This pattern reflects an underlying set of interrelationships which are based on interdependency and on a division of labor. In making use of new techniques of production, transportation, distribution, and exchange the population of the nation appears to have arranged itself by

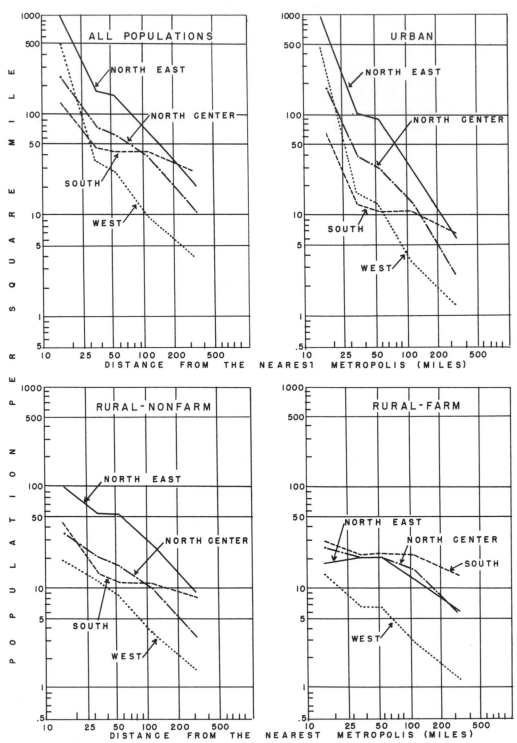

CHART 3-14 POPULATION PER SQUARE MILE OF HINTERLAND,
BY GEOGRAPHIC REGION AND DISTANCE FROM
THE NEAREST METROPOLIS. UNITED STATES, 1940

SOURCE: COMPILED FROM SIXTEENTH CENSUS OF THE UNITED STATES

a pattern which is repeated, with individual variations, many times.

5. Even newer techniques in all of these activities are being introduced daily, and improvements are being made upon the old ones; added to the fact that more extensive use is also being made of the old techniques, this means that the patterns which have been presented here for the years 1939-40 can at best be regarded as representing a moving equilibrium. Observations for other points in time can establish the extent to which these patterns are changing.

6. The statistical evidence which has been assembled here supports and adds detail to the work of Gras and McKenzie, and to their hypothesis. The introduction of the principle of subdominance places considerable emphasis upon the unity and integrity of the individual hinterland community as one aspect of metropolitan structure. In the past there has been a temptation to view such communities as vestiges of a former era. The fact that the local hinterland community functions as a subdominant is here regarded as basic to dominance itself, and implies that the communities which have survived from a pre-metropolitan era have done so by undergoing an internal reorganization and reorientation of their activities. Dominance on a broad scale appears to be possible only when it is accompanied by the phenomena of subdominance, influence, and subinfluence. If this be a valid inference from the data which have been presented here, the importance of the local hinterland community as a unit in social organization will not diminish with time. Such communities may increase or decrease in number. They may gain additional functions from other hinterland communities or from the central city, or lose them, as the case may be. But in the foreseeable future the element of intercommunity exchange remains the basis for the metropolitan pattern of population distribution. Many more metropolitan centers may arise, and some of the present ones may decline in importance. Yet the probability remains high that there will be a definite pattern of population distribution about points which supply a variety of needs to a dependent population, and that this pattern will reflect the manner in which the entire population supports itself. As Gras has stated, "Interdependence of parts is really the key to the whole thing."

PART II

THE POPULATION STRUCTURE OF METROPOLITAN COMMUNITIES

INTRODUCTION TO PART II

The study of the distribution of population with respect to metropolitan centers will be treated in the four succeeding chapters, each chapter dealing with one of the four major variables — distance, sector type, size of metropolis, and size of local community.

Although the analysis which follows is statistical, the methods employed are very simple and will give the nonstatistical reader no trouble. The major points are clarified by charts and diagrams. Perhaps an understanding of the analysis will be facilitated if the reader selects the metropolitan community with which he is most familiar and keeps it in mind as he reads, informally verifying the findings of this study from his own experience, or noting exceptions, as the case may be.

CHAPTER FOUR

DISTANCE FROM THE METROPOLIS

I

Description of the Distribution
of Land Area and Population

A. What is the Shape of the Average Metropolitan Community?

At first thought, one might expect the typical shape of the metropolitan community to be circular, with the metropolis at the center. For several reasons, however, a circle is not the usual shape of a hinterland, and the central city does not actually lie at the geographic center:

a. Many of the metropolitan centers have less than the full twelve sectors (one complete circle) because they are seaboard and lake front cities, and have no land area in certain sectors.
b. Metropolitan centers lying near a seacoast or lake have abnormally short sectors on the side toward water.
c. The sectors are of varying lengths, depending on the distance which it lies from the nearest neighboring metropolis.
d. The sparsity of metropolitan centers in the Southwest and Mountain divisions permits some of the metropolitan centers to have hinterlands which are extremely large and quite irregular in shape.

To obtain a picture of the accessibility pattern of the hinterland, one can compare the land area actually lying in each distance zone of all metropolitan communities with the land area which would be expected to be within that zone if every hinterland contained all twelve sectors and if each metropolis lay in the exact geographical center of its hinterland. Chart 4-1, by expressing the actual area in each zone as a percentage of the expected area, illustrates the total departure from the circular pattern. At the very shortest distance zone the actual land area is approximately three-quarters of the expected area, indicating that water fronts, shore lines, and extremely short sectors cut away approximately one-fourth (three sectors) of the average hinterland.[1] In the second and succeeding zones outward, as the shorter sectors encounter the boundaries of neighboring metropolitan centers, there is a steady decrease in the percentage which the actual area comprises of the expected area. At 365 miles, the actual land area is only about 2 percent of the amount which would be expected at this distance if all sectors were present and extended through the 265-464 mile zone.

B. What Percentage of Land Area and Population Lies in Central Cities and in Each Distance Zone?
1. It should not be inferred from the foregoing that the great bulk of the land area of the United States lies within a very few miles of the metropolis. Fully half of the hinterland lies 165 miles, or more, from its central city. The maximum extension of a hinterland seems to be about 465 miles, since less than 5 percent of the total land area lies at a distance greater than this.
2. The population of the United States, and particularly the urban population, is distributed about the metropolis in a very different fashion than is the land area. One out of four people lives in the 0.126 percent of the total area of the United States which is occupied by the 67 central cities. One additional person in seven lives within easy commuting distance (0-24 miles) of the metropolis,[2] and three out of five people live either in a metropolis or within 65 miles (about two hours

1. Of the sectors which make up the 67 metropolitan communities, a combined total of 628 sectors contain at least some land area. This is an average of 9.4 sectors per metropolitan community, or a loss of 2.6 sectors per metropolitan community because of the factors named.
2. The inner zone is always of indeterminate size because the metropolis is also located in that zone, and because the county containing the central city can be given no distance value. Although "O" is used to indicate the inner distance value of this zone, in every case the central zone consists of the land area from the city limits of the metropolitan centers out to some specified distance in the hinterland. Thus "0-24 miles" means "from the city limits of the metropolis out to 25 miles from the center of the metropolis, including all of the counties containing the central cities." In plotting the data for the inner zone on the charts which follow, a radius of five miles has arbitrarily been assigned to the central city. The midpoint used for plotting purposes, therefore, falls midway between five miles from the metropolis and the outer limit of the zone.

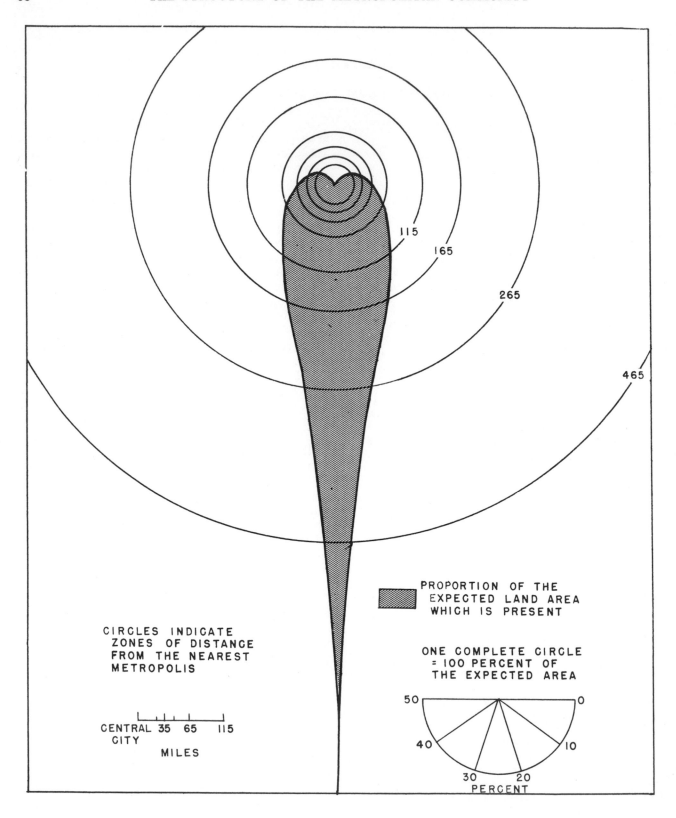

CHART 4-1 PERCENT WHICH ACTUAL LAND AREA IS OF THE LAND AREA
EXPECTED IF THE METROPOLITAN COMMUNITIES WERE
CIRCULAR, BY DISTANCE FROM THE NEAREST METROPOLIS

Table 4-1

Percentage distributions of land area, total population, and urban population, by distance from the nearest metropolis. United States, 1940.

Distance zone (miles)	Percentage distribution			Difference, in percentage points, between land area and--	
	Land area	Total population	Urban population	Total population	Urban population
Central cities	0.126	25.7	45.4	25.6	45.3
Hinterland:					
0-24a	3.1	15.2	17.5	12.2	14.4
25-34	2.6	5.4	5.0	2.8	2.4
35-44	3.3	4.6	3.6	1.3	0.3
45-64	7.0	10.0	7.5	3.0	0.5
65-114	18.3	17.3	10.8	-1.0	-7.5
115-164	15.9	10.5	5.1	-5.4	-10.8
165-264	24.3	8.4	3.7	-15.9	-20.6
265-464	20.8	2.5	1.3	-18.3	-19.5
465-over	4.6	0.4	0.1	-4.2	-4.5
All zones	100.0	100.0	100.0	44.8b	62.9b

aIncludes counties containing central cities.

bCoefficient of dissimilarity between distribution of land area and population.

Source: Sixteenth Census of the United States. Compiled from Population, Vol. I, State Tables 3 and 5; Areas of the United States, 1940, Tables 2, 3, and 4.

journey) by automobile of the metropolis. Only one person in 34 lives 265 or more miles (more than six and one-half hours via automobile) from the metropolis. This tendency for population to concentrate toward the shorter distances is even more marked in the case of the urban population. Almost two out of three urbanites live either in or within easy commuting distance of the metropolis. Almost four out of five urbanites live within two hours journey, and only seven in 500 urban people live more than six and one-half hours via auto from a metropolis.

This apparent concentration of population at the shorter distances is the first evidence of metropolitan control. Through further analysis it can be measured, and its pattern described.

II

Concentration of the Population About the Metropolis

A. Differences Between the Distributions of Land Area and Population.

It might appear that there is little new in this discovery of a concentration of people in and about the metropolis. The inclusion of the population of central cities in the above percentage comparisons will necessarily denote an unusual concentration of people relative to land area. Also, the fact is well known that a concentration of population in suburban cities and rural areas immediately surrounds each of the major cities. This peripheral concentration is commonly regarded as a circumstance arising from the relative inflexibility of city boundaries despite persistent urban growth. The Census Metropolitan District, delimited on the basis of continuous density outward from the city, has been established in order to delimit the large urban community more realistically. A closer examination, however, reveals that the patterning of population does not stop at the boundaries of the metropolitan district.

More exact measurements of concentration can be made by a comparison of the percent of population with the percent of land area present in each zone after the central cities have been removed from the distributions. Judgments concerning the amount of concentration are further facilitated if, in place of laborious comparisons of pairs of percentages, percentage-point differences are computed between the distributions of land area and population. Such percentage-point differences, for each type of population for each distance zone, are presented in Table 4-2. As an aid to the understanding of the full-extent of population concentration about the metropolis, the 0-44 mile zone has been divided into two parts: the metropolitan districts of the 67 central cities and the remainder of the area of the 45 mile zone. Such a division permits a comparison of population concentration in the metropolitan districts with concentration in the areas immediately outside the metropolitan districts.

If people were distributed in all zones in exactly the same proportions as is land area, there would be no concentration with respect to the metropolis. But since a larger proportion of the total population actually resides in some zones than zero concentration (equal percentages of people and land area) would indicate, one is justified in terming all percentages of population in excess of the percentage of land area "population concentration." When used in this sense, concentration is a relative term, and means that the intensity with which a given type of population occupies one area is greater than the average intensity with which that population occupies all areas. These same assumptions mean that an area may have a deficiency, or disproportionately small share, of population in relation to its area. The percentage-point differences, therefore, show proportions of the total which are concentrated or deficient in each category.[3]

The percentage-point differences between the distance distribution of land area and the three types of hinterland population (reported in Table 4-2) are most revealing. Note particularly that:

a. All three hinterland populations show a distinctive pattern of concentration with respect to the metropolis.

b. This concentration is not merely a "suburban" phenomenon: population is consistently concentrated at great distance into the hinterland — as far as 115 miles.

c. The pattern of concentration does not fade merely to zero difference, but passes over into a negative value at the greater distances and continues out through the last zone of the hinterland as a relative lack of concentration.

d. The metropolitan district accounts for about 90 percent of the concentration of the hinterland urban population, as well as for about 60 percent of the rural concentration in the 0-44 mile zone; the concentration of population, however, extends far beyond metropolitan district boundaries.[4]

e. Each of the major types of hinterland population has a definite pattern of distribution with distance from the metropolitan center.

Imagine for a moment what the above distribution would have been without a pattern of concentration with distance. Either the differences all would have been small (near zero) or they all would have been randomly positive or negative, with little regard for distance. The fact that this definite pattern of differences is obtained by arranging the urban, the rural-farm, and the rural-nonfarm populations of the United States by distance from the nearest metropolis indicates that distance from large cities measures a set of elements which are a deep and universal part of our organization as a nation.

---

3. The sign before a percentage-point difference is a matter of arbitrary choice as to which distribution is to be subtracted from the other. The choice made here has been such that relative concentration will always appear as a positive quantity and relative scarcity as a negative one.

4. The subtraction of the metropolitan district area and population from its 0-44 mile zone understates slightly the amount of concentration outside the metropolitan district in that zone, since in a few instances metropolitan districts include distances greater than 45 miles from the central city (e.g. Pittsburgh and San Francisco Metropolitan Districts). This has the effect of subtracting some land and population which actually is not there from the 0-44 mile zone.

Table 4-2

Differences, in percentage points, between the percentage distributions of land area and population, by distance from the nearest metropolis. United States, 1940.

Distance zone (miles)	Hinterland population[a]				
	Total	Urban	Rural	Rural-nonfarm	Rural-farm
Central county	b	b	5.4	9.6	1.6
0-24[c]	17.4	29.0	3.9	6.1	1.9
25-34	4.7	6.5	3.4	4.4	2.5
35-44	2.9	3.2	2.6	3.5	1.9
45-64	6.5	6.8	6.2	6.4	6.0
65-114	5.0	1.5	7.4	5.0	9.5
115-164	-1.8	-6.6	1.6	-2.6	5.4
165-264	-13.0	-17.5	-9.7	-11.7	-7.9
265-464	-17.5	-18.4	-16.8	-16.7	-16.9
465-over	-4.1	-4.4	-3.9	-4.0	-3.8
0-44 mile zone	25.0	38.7	15.3	23.6	7.9
Metropolitan districts	18.8	32.5	9.0	d	d
Remainder of zone	6.2	6.2	6.3	--	--
Coefficient of dissimilarity	36.4	46.9	30.4	35.0	28.7
Coefficient of similarity	63.6	53.1	69.6	65.0	71.3

[a]Positive values indicate concentration of population; minus signs indicate a deficit of population relative to land area.

[b]Urban population distributed by actual distance of city rather than location inside or outside central county.

[c]Grouping of inner zones necessary to make urban population coincide with land area.

[d]Data for rural-farm and rural-nonfarm populations by metropolitan districts not reported.

Source: Sixteenth Census of the United States. Compiled from Population, Vol. I, State Tables 3 and 5; Population, Vol. II, State Tables 26 and 27; Areas of the United States, 1940, Tables 2, 3, and 4.

B. The Amount of Population Concentration in the Metropolitan Community.

Adding together all of the positive (or negative) percentage-point differences makes it possible to obtain a measure of the proportion of the total population which is concentrated.[5] Had there been absolutely no difference between the percentage distributions of land area and of population, all percentage-point differences would have been zero, and their sum also would have been zero. The greater the differences between two distributions,

the metropolis and forms a definite pattern. The sum of the differences of one sign is a summary measure of total concentration produced by this pattern. This measure may be called a "coefficient of dissimilarity" and, theoretically, it can vary in value between 0 and 100 percent (or 1.0).[6] In Tables 4-1 and 4-2, where the coefficients of dissimilarity and of similarity are reported for the zonal distributions of the various populations with respect to the comparable distributions of land area, it is found that the values of these measures are as follows:

Population type	Coefficient of dissimilarity	Coefficient of similarity
United States total	44.8	55.2
United States urban (including central cities)	62.9	37.1
Hinterland urban	46.9	53.1
Hinterland rural	30.4	69.6
Rural-nonfarm	35.0	65.0
Rural-farm	28.7	71.3

the larger must be some of the percentage-point differences between them. The sum of either their positive or their negative values is an index of over-all difference between any two percentage distributions. If the positive differences are all in the inner zones, and the negative ones all in the outer zones, it is evident that the concentration of population with respect to land is oriented toward

All the hinterland populations, when considered separately, are found to have an impressively high degree of concentration. Thus 46.9 percent of the hinterland urban population is concentrated relative to distance from the central city, while 28.7 percent of the rural-farm population is so concentrated. The rural-nonfarm population has a concentration value about midway between these two (35.0 percent).

5. Since each of two percentage distributions adds to 100, the sum of the individual differences between them must add to zero. In other words, the sum of the positive quantities will equal the sum of the negative ones.

6. This device can be employed to summarize the total amount of dissimilarity between any two percentage distributions in which the two sets of percentages are distributed by the same classes and refer to the same units. If it is subtracted from 100 per cent, the total proportion of similarity between two distributions can be found. Such a measure will be referred to hereafter as a "coefficient of similarity." It measures the amount of correspondence between the pairs of percentages in two comparable percentage distributions.

Because of their extreme simplicity, ease of calculation, and ready interpretability, several measures of this general type will be used throughout this study. The values obtained indicate the proportion of the total of one distribution which must be redistributed among the categories of opposite sign in order to render the two distributions alike. The value obtained varies with the number of units into which the percentage distribution is divided; increasing the number of categories tends to give higher values. The manner in which the whole has been subdivided also affects the value. Coefficients of this type, therefore, can be compared only with similar coefficients, computed from data which refer to the same units and which are divided into the same classes. In some applications a coefficient of complete dissimilarity (coefficient of 100 per cent) is impossible, as in the case of a comparison of the distribution of people and land, which would require all of the people to live on zero land area.

For a full description of this device, and some applications, see: PEP (Political and Economic Planning), Report on the Location of Industry (London: PEP, 1939) pp. 291-293.

E. M. Hoover, "Interstate Redistribution of Population, 1850-1940," Journal of Economic History, l (May 1941) pp. 199-205.

P. S. Florence, W. G. Fritz, and R. E. Gilles, "Measures of Industrial Distribution," Chapter 5, National Resources Planning Board, Industrial Location and National Resources, (Washington, D.C.: Government Printing Office, 1943).

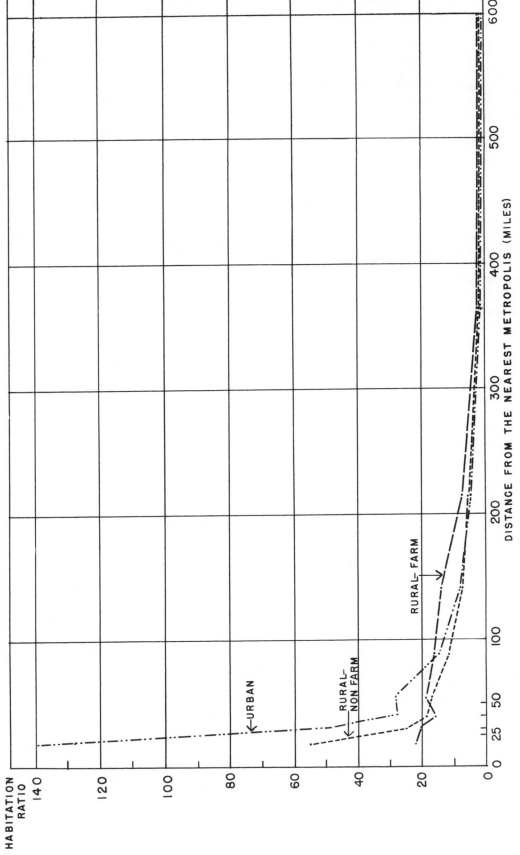

CHART 4-2 HABITATION RATIOS: POPULATION PER SQUARE MILE OF HINTERLAND, BY DISTANCE
FROM THE NEAREST METROPOLIS. UNITED STATES, 1940

It would be necessary to move 44.8 percent of the total population of the United States (including population of the central cities) from the central zones out into the periphery before a complete "decentralization" of the metropolitan community, as delimited here, could be obtained. If one desired to decentralize the urban population completely, including the residents of central cities as well as the hinterland urban population, it would be necessary to move 62.9 percent of the total city dwellers from the inner zones out beyond the 115 mile zone. Such is the magnitude of the concentration of urban population in the inner portions of the metropolitan community.

The remarkable position of the rural-nonfarm population, half way between the values for the hinterland urban and the rural-farm populations, leads to an inference that the rural-nonfarm population is influenced in its distribution both by those factors which give the urban population its characteristically high degree of independence from the land, and by those which give the rural-farm population its relative dependence on the land.

III

The Pattern of Population Settlement with Distance from the Metropolis

Having demonstrated the existence of concentration and measured its amount, the next step is to find whether or not there is a definite pattern of distribution of population with distance from the metropolis. Only in this way will it be possible to generalize a population structure for metropolitan communities. Evidence that such a pattern exists has been indicated by the large percentage-point differences in the inner zones, and by the neat division of all the plus differences in the inner zones from all the minus differences in the outer zones.

The preceding observations make it apparent that the distinctive pattern of population distribution with respect to the metropolis will be one of varying intensity of land settlement. Although the method of percentage-point differences is very useful in demonstrating that concentration exists, and in measuring its amount, it cannot state the intensity with which the populations settle different

areas. This inability results from the fact that the method cannot eliminate differences which are due solely to the existence of more land area in some zones than in others.

The "number of persons per square mile" (or per 100 square miles), a familiar measure of the intensity of land occupancy, will be used to eliminate such differences in area. The computation is made by dividing the population of each zone (urban, rural-nonfarm, or rural-farm) by the land area of the zone.[7] With differences in land area eliminated, all parts of the hinterland become directly comparable to each other. In order to avoid confusion with density figures as they are usually interpreted, the measures used in this study of the number of people per unit of hinterland area are called "habitation ratios." The habitation ratios are not intended as measures of the number of persons which each square mile of the hinterland "supports" or is capable of supporting. They are interpreted, rather, as rates of occupancy, measures of the intensity of land settlement, or indications of the degree to which the hinterland is utilized and manipulated by the population of a given type.

A. The Intensity of Land Settlement — Habitation Ratios by Distance Zones.

That there is a distinctive pattern of intensity of land occupancy with distance from the metropolis is obvious from Table 4-3 and Chart 4-2, which report the urban, the rural-nonfarm, and the rural-farm population per square mile of hinterland for each distance zone. In the inner zone the habitation ratio for each population type is at a maximum. With increasing distance the number of residents per square mile decreases until, at the greatest distances, the population per square mile is only a small fraction of its original value. The habitation ratio of all hinterland population for the areas beyond 465 miles from the metropolis, for example, is only 3.9 percent of the habitation ratio in the 25-34 mile zone.

The over-all pattern of land settlement in metropolitan communities appears to take the form of a precipitous decline from the central city out through the 35-44 mile zone, a leveling off or even a slight rise in the 45-64 mile zone, and a very

---

7. Although the arithmetic procedure used in computing this measure is the same as that used in computing "densities," e.g., the number of persons per square mile in cities, the interpretation made here is not that which is usually associated with density figures. The term "density," when applied to population, frequently connotes crowding or the average proximity of residence. In this sense, the number of urban persons per square mile of hinterland can scarcely be spoken of as the "density" of the urban population in the hinterland, for in no way does it measure the crowding of urban residents or their proximity to each other. It does measure, however, the extent to which the urban population is present in any one part of the hinterland.

Table 4-3

Habitation ratios: Urban and rural population per square mile of hinterland, by distance from the nearest metropolis. United States, 1940.[a]

Distance zone (miles)	All hinterland population	Type of hinterland population			
		Urban	Rural	Rural-nonfarm	Rural-farm
Mean habitation ratio	32.9	13.7	19.3	9.1	10.2
0-24	214.6	138.8	75.8	54.5	21.3
25-34	92.6	47.9	44.8	24.7	20.1
35-44	60.8	26.6	34.1	18.4	15.7
45-64	63.3	27.0	36.3	17.5	18.8
65-114	41.9	14.8	27.1	11.6	15.5
115-164	29.2	8.0	21.2	7.6	13.6
165-264	15.4	3.8	11.6	4.7	6.9
265-464	5.2	1.6	3.6	1.8	1.9
465-over	3.6	0.7	2.8	1.1	1.7

[a]Total land area of the United States, excluding area of central cities, used in computing all habitation ratios.

Source: Sixteenth Census of the United States. Compiled from Population, Vol. I, State Tables 3 and 5; Population, Vol. II, State Tables 26 and 27. Areas of the United States, 1940, Tables 2, 3, and 4.

steady decline to the outer limits of the hinterland. Within 65 miles of the metropolis the land is more intensively occupied by urban than by rural populations. Within 35 miles of the metropolis the land is more intensively occupied by the rural-nonfarm than by the rural-farm populations. At distances greater than 115 miles the rural-farm population occupies the hinterland more intensively than does either the urban or the rural-nonfarm. At about this same point the rural-nonfarm surpasses the urban population in the rate of land occupancy. Thus, at the very periphery of the hinterlands, all populations occupy the land with a very low intensity and in a combination which is the complete reverse of the one found in the inner zones. As will be seen in later chapters, the introduction of other variables modifies this general pattern somewhat.

Chart 4-3 presents the same information which is plotted on Chart 4-2. In Chart 4-3, however, the distance scale and the scale for the habitation ratios are logarithmic instead of arithmetic. The "reverse J" shape of the curves in Chart 4-2 reveals the fact that a given mileage change in distance is not accompanied by a constant amount of change in the habitation ratios; with a given change in mileage distance, the amount by which the habitation ratios change tends to decrease as the distance increases. There tends to be a fairly constant rate of change, however, in the habitation ratios with proportional change in distance. This fact is demonstrated graphically by the logarithmic plotting of Chart 4-3. The urban and the rural-nonfarm populations approximate a linear pattern with distance when plotted on scales of this type. Change in relative distance, rather than in linear

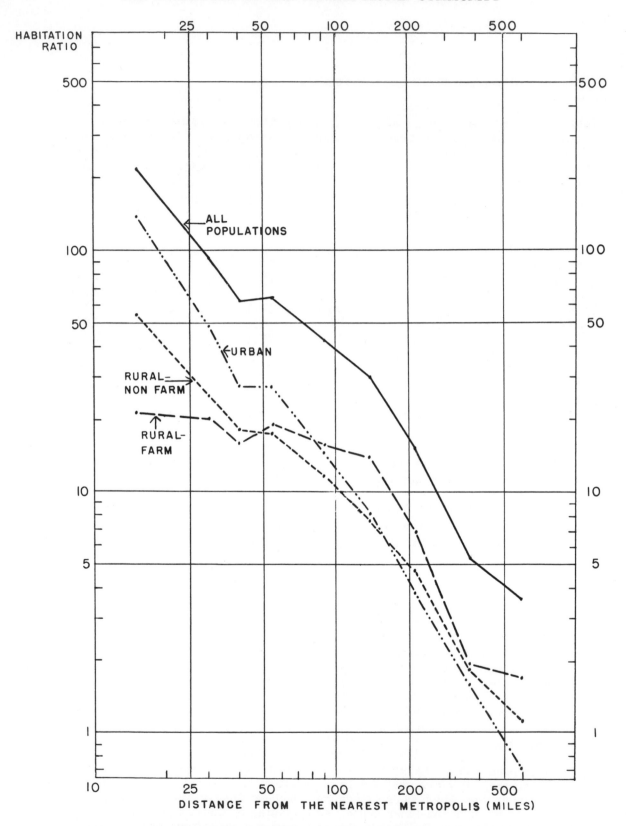

CHART 4-3 HABITATION RATIOS: POPULATION PER SQUARE
MILE OF HINTERLAND, BY DISTANCE FROM THE
NEAREST METROPOLIS. UNITED STATES, 1940

distance, has a tendency to be accompanied by a fairly constant rate of change in the intensity of land occupancy. Proportional changes in distance from the metropolis tend to be more directly associated with a constant rate of change in the intensity with which the land is occupied than is the addition or subtraction of a given number of miles. Because logarithmic charts illustrate more clearly the nature of the relationships between land occupancy and distance, they will be used in preference to arithmetic charts throughout this study.

A comparison of the slopes of the lines representing the different populations at different distances makes it possible to observe patterns in the rates of change. Thus, the existence of a more gentle slope for the rural-nonfarm than for the urban population indicates that the rate of change in the intensity of land occupancy with relative change in distance is smaller for the rural-nonfarm than for the urban population. The pattern for the rural-farm population appears to consist of two separate rates of change, one extending from the metropolis out to about 165 miles, and the other continuing from that point out to the edge of the hinterland. At distances of less than 115 miles, the rural-farm population exhibits a small increase in the rate of land occupancy with relative increase in proximity to the central city. In this respect it is very different from both the urban and the rural-nonfarm populations, which tend to show a rapid decrease in habitation ratio with each increase in distance from the metropolis. At the far distances (beyond 165 miles) the rural-farm population seems to undergo a marked alteration in its pattern of distribution, and to approach the rate of change which is characteristic of the other two populations at these distances.

There is a tendency for all three populations to attain a habitation ratio in the 35-44 mile zone which is the same as or even smaller than that which they attain in the 45-64 zone before plunging further into the dispersion side of the chart. This is a phenomenon worthy of more than passing note. It appears that whatever effect the metropolis exerts upon population at this distance is in the direction of stabilizing or even discouraging settlement of the land. Beyond the 35-44 mile zone the metropolis tends to be ringed with a greater concentration of urban and rural-farm population. This tendency persists in some degree, as will be

seen, for all sizes of metropolitan communities and for all sector types in one or another of the intermediate zones between 25 and 65 miles. Several hypotheses can be formulated to explain this tendency:

a. Thirty-five miles marks the outer limit of the influence of the metropolis, and the remainder of the pattern of land settlement is due entirely to other factors not controlled by this study.
b. The metropolis may impose one set of limiting conditions upon the area immediately surrounding it and another set upon more distant areas. The 35-64 mile zone may represent either a shift from one type of metropolitan control to another, or a point of equilibrium between the two types of control.
c. The 25-34 and the 35-44 mile zones are the only two distance zones which are as small as ten miles in width. The other zones are two or more times as wide. The low value for the 25-34 mile zone represents only a random fluctuation which would not appear at all if the distance limits of the zones were larger.[8]

Examining this detail of the population patterns and choosing among the above hypotheses would require the introduction of the remaining three variables by which the distribution of population is to be examined. For the present it is sufficient to call attention to this unique trait of population distribution with distance from the metropolis. As the other variables are introduced these variations will be traced to their source.

The evidence presented thus far indicates that the general pattern of land occupancy in the hinterland is one of:

a. Sharply decreasing intensity of settlement out to about 45 miles from the metropolis.
b. A zone of little change or slight increase over the 35-44 mile zone in the intensity of settlement between 45-64 miles from the metropolis.
c. Continuation of the decrease in intensity of settlement with increasing distance beyond 65 miles from the metropolis.

* * *

8. The 25-34 mile zone contains 142 counties, and the 35-44 mile zone contains 158 counties. Evidence that ratios computed on the basis of such a large area are stable ones is given by the fact that this tendency persists at some intermediate point in each size class of metropolitan community, and hence is not caused by one extreme case. It is true, nevertheless, that if the 25-44 mile zones are combined into one zone, the leveling off in the rate of change with relative distance disappears completely and is replaced in this zone by a more gentle slope of the curve than is the case in the other zones.

B. <u>The Amount of Dissimilarity Between the Distributions of Urban and Rural Populations.</u>

How independently are the urban and rural populations distributed with respect to each other at each distance? The method of computing percentage-point differences, and of computing coefficients of dissimilarity and of similarity, which was employed for comparing the distribution of population and land area, may be used to answer this question. The differences are much smaller in this case than for land area, since the common tendency for all populations to be distributed with respect to land area reduces the amount of difference between them. The measures of dissimilarity and similarity between the distributions are:

Comparison of Hinterland Populations	Coefficient of Dissimilarity	Coefficient of Similarity
Urban with rural-farm	31.6	68.4
Rural-nonfarm with rural-farm	16.3	83.7
Urban with rural-nonfarm	15.8	84.2

A total of 31.6 percent of the hinterland urban population fails to correspond to the distribution of the rural-farm population, and all of this difference is in the direction of concentration in the near zones. Compared to the urban population, the rural-nonfarm population shows a deficit in the inner zones and a relative concentration in the outer zones, but compared to the rural-farm population the rural-nonfarm group is concentrated in the inner zones and is deficient in the 65-264 mile zones, with an extremely small concentration in the outer two zones. In general:

a. These populations which have been considered the farthest apart in the dominance scale show the least degree of similarity of distribution.

b. The rural-nonfarm population, occupying the middle position in the dominance scale, shows an almost identical degree of association both with the rural-farm and with the urban population.

c. The rural-farm population is only slightly more independent of the distribution of hinterland urban population (31.6) than it is of the land itself (28.7 with respect to land).

IV

Summary

1. In metropolitan communities there is a tendency for the land to be occupied with decreasing intensity as the distance from the central city increases.
2. The urban, the rural-nonfarm, and the rural-farm populations all exhibit this tendency, although each has its own characteristic pattern.
3. The suburbanization of the population in the immediate environs of the central city is, therefore, only one aspect of a general pattern of land occupancy which extends to the very periphery of the area which has been defined as the metropolitan community.
4. The pattern of change in land occupancy with distance tends to be exponential in nature. Proportional increase in distance, rather than mileage change, appears to have a roughly linear relationship to proportional decline in the intensity of land occupancy.

*   *   *

CHAPTER FIVE

DIRECTION FROM THE METROPOLIS: SECTOR TYPE

I

Introduction

Evidence was presented in the procedural notes of Chapter Two in support of a thesis that, since population is not uniformly distributed within each distance zone, direction from the metropolis is an important element to be considered in studying distributional patterns of hinterland populations. The evidence there cited suggested the hypothesis that a seeming tendency for population to concentrate in one direction rather than another from the metropolis is associated with the presence of major routes of transportation and with movement to and from the metropolitan centers. In order to provide for the testing of this hypothesis, the hinterlands of the 67 metropolitan communities were subdivided into sectors. Each sector was then classified as one of three types — intermetropolitan, subdominant, or local — depending upon whether it contained a major intermetropolitan route, a major hinterland city, or neither of the two.

This chapter is devoted to a comparison of the distributions of population within these three types of sectors. An attempt will be made to demonstrate the fact that some types of sectors are more intensively occupied than are other types of sectors, and that a pattern of intersector differences is superimposed upon the distance pattern. This demonstration is made possible through a cross-classification, by both their distance and their sector type classifications, of the population and land area data for the hinterland units. Differences in the intensity with which the types of sectors are occupied can then be observed for each distance zone.

It will be remembered that certain limitations which are inherent in the use of county units make intersector comparisons untrustworthy at distances of less than 25 miles. Moreover, the counties which contain the central cities necessarily lie in all sectors and, therefore, cannot be assigned to any one type of sector. In the tables which follow, the entire 0-24 mile zone has not been subdivided into sector types, but is presented as a unit at the head of each column for comparison with the sector-type data for the remaining distances.

II

Description of the Location and Distribution of Land and Population in the Three Types of Sectors

A. Land Area.
1. More than one-half (56.4 percent) of the land area of the United States, due to the direction of its location from the nearest metropolis, is placed in a sector which contains a major intermetropolitan thoroughfare connecting pairs of metropolitan centers. Such a large proportion of the hinterland must be classified as intermetropolitan because each metropolis has an average of six or seven metropolitan communities bounding it and, in most cases, a highway route to each of these communities. This multiplicity of neighboring metropolitan centers results in the exposure of a very large share of the hinterland to any influence which is associated with an intermetropolitan location.
2. Only about one-tenth (10.4 percent) of the hinterland is located in a sector containing a hinterland city of 25,000 inhabitants or more.
3. One-third (33.2 percent) of the hinterland does not have ready access either to the intermetropolitan or to the metropolis-hinterland city streams.

B. Population.
1. An even higher proportion of population than of land area is located in intermetropolitan and subdominant sectors. More than three-fourths of the hinterland population has a locational position permitting either participation in the stream of movement between metropolitan centers or the enjoyment of easy access to a major hinterland city. Less than one-fourth of the population has a location in a local sector. There is a measurable concentration of population, therefore, in intermetropolitan and subdominant sectors, and a deficit of population in the local sectors.
2. The three types of population are not distributed in the same way among the types of sectors. Unduly large proportions of the urban population are found, relative to land, in the intermetropolitan and subdominant sectors. The rural-nonfarm and the rural-farm populations are concentrated, relative to land, in the subdominant sectors, and show a slight deficit both in the

Table 5-1

Distribution of land area and hinterland population, by sector type, United States, 1940.

Area and population	Type of sector			
	All sectors	Inter-metropolitan	Subdominant	Local
Land area[a] (thousand square miles)	2920.9	1648.5	303.9	968.5
Population (thousands)				
Total hinterland	93793	54453	17324	22015
Urban[b]	40602	25524	8380	6697
Rural[a]	53191	28929	8944	15318
Nonfarm	23981	13317	3958	6706
Farm	29210	15612	4986	8612
	Percentage distribution			
Land area	100.0	56.4	10.4	33.2
Population				
Total hinterland	100.0	58.1	18.5	23.5
Urban	100.0	62.9	20.6	16.5
Rural	100.0	54.4	16.8	28.8
Nonfarm	100.0	55.5	16.5	28.0
Farm	100.0	53.4	17.1	29.5

a) Excludes counties containing the central cities.

b) Includes urban population outside central cities but located in county containing the central cities.

Source: Sixteenth Census of the United States. Compiled from Population, Vol.I, State tables 3 and 5; Population, Vol.II, State tables 26 and 27; Areas of the United States, 1940, Tables 2, 3, and 4.

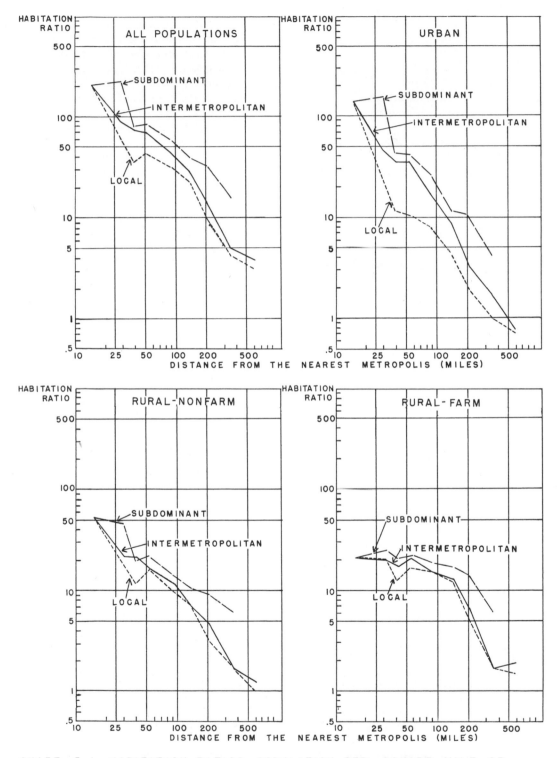

CHART 5-I HABITATION RATIOS: POPULATION PER SQUARE MILE OF
HINTERLAND, BY TYPE OF SECTOR AND DISTANCE FROM THE
NEAREST METROPOLIS. UNITED STATES, 1940

intermetropolitan and the local sectors. This deficit is greatest for rural-farm population in the intermetropolitan sectors, and for rural-nonfarm population in the local sectors.

III

The Pattern of Population Settlement in the Three Types of Sectors

A. The intensity of land occupancy: habitation ratios. (Chart 5-1)

1. The overall distance pattern for each sector type for all populations is one of fairly steady and very marked decrease in the intensity of occupancy with increasing distance from the metropolis. Hence, no one sector deviates from the general distance pattern for the hinterland as a whole.

2. The subdominant sectors are much more intensively settled than are the other two types of sectors. With only minor exceptions, this is true for all distances and for all types of hinterland population.[1]

3. The intermetropolitan sectors are more intensively occupied than are the local sectors. This, too, is a difference which exists, with only very minor exceptions, for each of the three population types through all distances.

4. The subdominant sectors have a considerably higher habitation ratio than do the intermetropolitan sectors. With only one exception, a minor one involving the rural-nonfarm population in one distance zone, this difference persists through all distances for all populations.[2]

5. The intermetropolitan sectors seem to be more effective in facilitating intense settlement at distances of 115 miles or less from the metropolis. At distances greater than this the advantage which the intermetropolitan sectors possess over the local sectors in regard to promoting settlement decreases, even though evidences of this advantage remain at even the greatest distances. At these greater distances the sectors have "spread" to such an extent that those counties through which the intermetropolitan route does not actually pass are also classified as "intermetropolitan." It may be, of course, that this slight leveling off of actual concentration at the greater distances represents a fairly heavy concentration of population in the immediate area through which the intermetropolitan route passes, and that this concentration is hidden by the inclusion of the broad sector area. In such a case, the concentrative effect of main thoroughfares would be confined to a small strip of area along each side. The validity of this possibility cannot be tested here, however, since the interest of this study is in measuring the effect upon broader segments of the hinterland, and no provision has been made for holding "distance from intermetropolitan route" constant.

6. Each of the three types of sectors participates in the previously noted tendency of population to level off or decline in the 35-44 mile zone and to rise in the 45-64 mile zone.[3] The population of intermetropolitan sectors exhibits this tendency to the least extent and the local sectors exhibit it in the strongest degree. It is least evident for the urban population in each type of sector. It is most evident for the rural-nonfarm population in the local and subdominant sectors, and for the rural-farm population it is quite marked in all sectors. Since this "leveling off" tendency remains after further subdivision of the data, it would appear that the hypothesis which considers it a completely random combination of events must be discarded. The fact that all types of sectors including those

---

1. A portion of the more intense settlement of urban population in the subdominant sectors, and of the lack of urban population in the local sectors, is to be expected because of the definition used in classifying these sectors. The requirement that a sector must contain a hinterland city of 25,000 or more inhabitants before it can be classified as a subdominant sector would necessarily raise the average number of urban persons per square mile in this type of sector. Similarly, classifying as local all sectors which do not contain such a large hinterland city necessarily lowers the habitation ratio for sectors of this type. In Chapter Seven, however, it will be shown that all of this difference in occupancy is not due solely to the population of a large hinterland city in the sector. The large habitation ratios in subdominant sectors of the rural-nonfarm and rural-farm populations cannot possibly be considered products of the manner of definition.

2. Some of the difference, at least, in habitation ratios between the subdominant and the intermetropolitan sectors is due to the definitions used in classifying the sectors by type. The requirement that each subdominant sector contain a large hinterland city, whereas the intermetropolitan sectors were required only to contain an intermetropolitan route, with or without hinterland cities, would tend to account for some of the greater concentration of urban population in the subdominant sectors. Chapter Seven, which studies concentration by size of community, will eliminate this element of necessary difference and will measure the absolute concentration in the two types of sectors in a manner which will permit more precise comparisons between the two.

3. See Chapter Four, Section III.

Table 5-2

Habitation ratios: Urban and rural population per square mile of hinterland, by sector type and distance from the nearest metropolis. United States, 1940.

Distance zone (miles)	Type of hinterland population and type of sector											
	All populations			Urban a)			Rural-nonfarm			Rural-farm		
	Intermetropolitan	Subdominant	Local	Intermetropolitan	Subdominant	Local	Intermetropolitan	Subdominant	Local	Intermetropolitan	Subdominant	Local
Mean habitation ratio	33.0	57.0	22.7	15.4	27.6	6.9	8.1	13.0	6.9	9.5	16.4	8.9
0-24 b)	214.6	214.6	214.6	138.8	138.8	138.8	54.5	54.5	54.5	21.3	21.3	21.3
25-34	88.8	222.2	61.0	45.1	149.2	22.5	24.2	48.3	18.5	19.5	24.6	20.0
35-44	74.2	82.7	36.2	34.4	42.0	11.8	22.7	19.9	12.0	17.2	20.8	12.4
45-64	71.6	84.9	43.6	34.8	41.4	10.6	17.1	21.7	16.5	19.7	21.8	16.5
65-114	44.0	59.6	32.5	16.8	26.1	7.8	12.1	14.4	9.8	15.1	19.1	14.9
115-164	28.9	39.1	23.9	8.9	11.6	4.3	7.1	10.3	7.0	12.9	17.2	12.6
165-264	14.6	33.1	10.3	3.5	10.3	2.0	4.7	9.0	3.2	6.5	13.9	5.0
265-464	5.0	16.1	4.3	1.7	4.0	1.0	1.6	6.2	1.6	1.7	5.9	1.7
465-over	3.8	c)	3.1	0.8	c)	0.7	1.2	c)	1.0	1.9	c)	1.5

a) Excludes area and population of central cities.

b) Includes land area and population outside central cities but in counties containing central cities. All sectors are combined in this zone. The combined figure is reported as the value for each sector type for comparison with values for other distances.

c) No land area at this distance and sector type.

Source: Sixteenth Census of the United States. Compiled from Population, Vol.I, State tables 3 and 5; Population, Vol.II, State tables 26 and 27; Areas of the United States, 1940, Tables 2, 3, and 4.

containing large hinterland cities, still exhibit the typical pattern of distribution as the distance increases beyond 65 miles, makes less plausible the hypothesis that 35 miles is the outer limit of metropolitan dominance. This characteristic of the pattern of land settlement will be explored further in the succeeding chapters.

7. The fact that the intensity of settlement, even in those sectors which contain large hinterland cities, declines in all directions with increasing distance from the metropolis, lends additional support to the inference that the metropolitan community is a functional organization of a broad expanse of territory. The steady decrease in intensity of land occupancy with distance, under the three very different sets of conditions represented by the three sector types, can be rationalized only by some such hypothesis.

B. Population concentration relative to average settlement of the hinterland. (Chart 5-2)

In the construction of Chart 5-2, the average population per square mile for all hinterland areas has been subtracted from the average population per square mile in each sector type and each distance zone. These excesses and deficits have been expressed as ratios of the national average for the population of each type. This measure may be called an "index of concentration." An index of concentration of 2.0, for example, is obtained for the urban population settlement in subdominant sectors of the 45-64 mile zone. Such an index in-

dicates the presence in this zone of an average excess of urban population which is twice the national average intensity of urban settlement in the hinterland. Stated another way, the urban habitation ratio of this type of location in the hinterland is 200 percent greater than the urban habitation ratio for the hinterland as a whole.

1. There is a marked and uniform pattern of population concentration in all of the sector types. This pattern is one of decreasing concentration with increasing distance.

2. The subdominant sectors are relatively more concentrated, throughout their entire length, than are the intermetropolitan and local sectors.

3. The intermetropolitan sectors, throughout their entire length, are equally as concentrated as the local sectors, and sometimes more concentrated. The one exception is the greater concentration of the rural-farm population in the 25-34 mile zone of local sectors.

4. Aside from the deficit of urban population in the local sectors, there is positive concentration of all populations in all zones out to 115 miles from the metropolis. Except for a near-zero concentration of rural-farm population in the subdominant zone, there is a deficit of concentration in all sectors at distances beyond 165 miles.

5. Population concentrations in excess of the national average, therefore, appear to be associated with proximity to the metropolis, with a location along a major intermetropolitan thoroughfare, or with a location in a sector of the hinterland

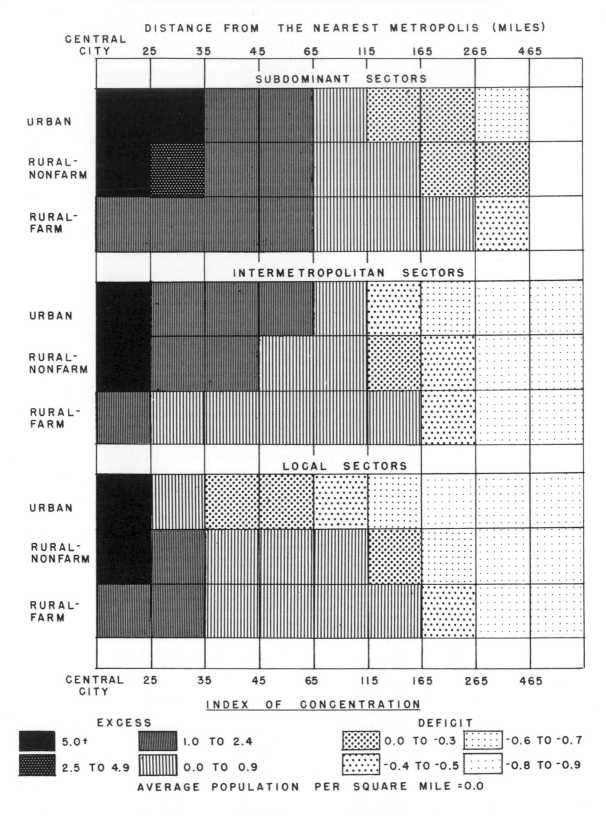

CHART 5-2 RELATIVE EXCESS OR DEFICIT OF POPULATION
          PER SQUARE MILE, BY TYPE OF SECTOR AND
          DISTANCE FROM THE NEAREST METROPOLIS.
          UNITED STATES, 1940

containing a major subdominant city. The greatest deficits of settlement occur in local sectors and at distances of more than 165 miles from the metropolis along intermetropolitan routes. This generalization holds for the urban as well as for both the rural-farm and rural-nonfarm populations.

IV

Summary

1. Differences in the intensity of population settlement are associated unmistakably with direction from the metropolis as expressed by the type of sector. Sectors containing a major hinterland city have higher habitation ratios than do the intermetropolitan and the local sectors. The intermetropolitan sectors, in turn, have higher habitation ratios than do the local sectors.

2. The pattern of concentration (population in excess of the average population per square mile in the hinterland as a whole) is also different between sector types. In the local sectors such a concentration exists only in the inner zones. The subdominant sectors have a concentration of population throughout almost their entire length. The intermetropolitan sectors show a concentration of population only slightly less intense than that of the subdominant sectors out to about 115 miles, but at greater distances this type of sector tends to show a deficit of population concentration almost as great as that of the local sectors at these distances.

CHAPTER SIX

THE EFFECT OF THE SIZE OF THE METROPOLIS
UPON THE DISTRIBUTION OF POPULATION

I

Introduction

Up to this point the data for the hinterland areas of all 67 of the metropolitan communities have been combined in order to develop one "average" metropolitan pattern. Because the population in the environs of the very largest cities is many times larger than the population in the vicinity of the smaller places selected as metropolitan centers, one might well be doubtful that the patterns of population distri-

Identification letter	Number of inhabitants in central city	Number of metropolitan communities
A	1,000,000 or more	5
B	500,000 to 999,999	9
C	250,000 to 499,999	19
D	100,000 to 249,999	34

bution which have been described exist at all in the areas about the smaller central cities. It is possible that such patterns may be very pronounced in the hinterlands of the largest cities, and that the combining of all hinterlands has made them only appear to extend to the hinterlands of the smaller places. If such were the case, nothing in the preceding analysis would have revealed the fact, since all of the data have been added together to obtain a single average value for each sector type and each distance.

In order to make it unmistakably clear that the principles which have been developed hold true for the smaller as well as for the larger metropolitan communities, the 67 metropolitan communities are now divided into four size groups, or classes, and a separate examination of the distance-sector type pattern is made for each group. This chapter has a second objective. In the statement of procedure (Chapter Two) it was hypothesized that the intensity of metropolitan dominance is related to the size of the metropolis — In general, the larger the metropolis the greater its dominance. To submit this hy-

pothesis to partial test is the second objective. The division of the metropolitan communities into four size classes will permit not only a separate test of the distance and type of sector patterning in metropolitan communities with small and large central cities, but will also permit a determination of whether there is a consistent change in those patterns as one progresses from the metropolitan communities with the largest to those with the smallest central cities.

The size grouping of the 67 metropolitan communities is as follows:

In order to save space in the headings of the tables which follow, the identification letter (A, B, C, D) will be used, rather than the class limits.[1]

II

Description of the Distribution of Land Area and Population Among the Various Size Classes of Metropolitan Communities.

A. The Proportion of the Total Land Area and of Population in Each Size Class of Metropolitan Community. (Table 6-1)

1. The five largest metropolises claim as hinterland only about one twenty-fourth (4.2 percent) of the land area of the United States, yet they contain 22.4 percent of the total population. Disproportions between land area and population are the rule rather than the exception in each of the four size classes. The two largest sizes have a sizeable concentration, relative to the proportion of land, of all populations except rural-farm. In class C there is a deficit of

---

1. This grouping of metropolitan communities according to the size of their central cities is the only size classification for metropolitan communities, as units, made in this study. The term "size of metropolitan community" is used frequently in examining the differences between the metropolitan communities when they are grouped according to the size of their respective metropolises, and refers to the size of the metropolis in 1940, not to the amount of land area or population contained in the metropolitan community as a whole or in its hinterland.

Table 6-1

Population and land area distributed by size class of metropolitan community.
United States, 1940.

Population and land area	All metropolitan communities[b]	Size class of metropolitan community[a]			
		A	B	C	D
Population (000)[c]					
Total	131,673	29,456	24,184	35,317	42,716
Urban	74,428	25,057	16,079	15,572	17,719
Metropolis	33,826	15,911	6,457	6,507	4,951
Hinterland	40,602	9,146	9,622	9,065	12,768
Rural	57,246	4,399	8,104	19,745	24,997
Nonfarm	27,029	3,320	4,991	7,620	11,098
Farm	30,216	1,079	3,113	12,125	13,899
Land area (sq.mi.)[c]					
Total	2,976,325	124,363	201,957	992,106	1,657,899
Urban	19,213	3,697	4,947	4,326	6,243
Metropolis	3,739	1,219	500	1,014	1,006
Hinterland	15,474	2,478	4,447	3,312	5,237
Rural	2,957,109	120,665	197,010	987,779	1,651,655
		Percentage distribution			
Population					
Total	100.0	22.4	18.4	26.8	32.4
Urban	100.0	33.7	21.6	20.9	23.8
Metropolis	100.0	47.0	19.1	19.2	14.6
Hinterland	100.0	22.5	23.7	22.3	31.4
Rural	100.0	7.7	14.2	34.5	43.7
Nonfarm	100.0	12.3	18.5	28.2	41.1
Farm	100.0	3.6	10.3	40.1	46.0
Land area					
Total	100.0	4.2	6.8	33.3	55.7
Urban	100.0	19.2	25.7	22.5	32.5
Metropolis	100.0	32.6	13.4	27.1	26.9
Hinterland	100.0	16.0	28.7	21.4	33.8
Rural	100.0	4.1	6.7	33.4	55.9

a) Size class of each metropolitan community determined by population of
   metropolitan center in 1940.
b) Equivalent to U.S. total.
c) Individual cells rounded to nearest thousand, hence, some totals do not
   equal sum of parts. The population of cities with 10,000 or more inhabitants
   was tabulated with numbers rounded to the nearest hundred persons. The land
   area of cities was tabulated to the nearest tenth of a square mile; in subtracting city from county totals to obtain rural area by machine tabulation
   it was not possible to round exactly the resulting rural areas to the nearest square mile. For these reasons, the totals for urban population and for
   land area do not exactly match the U.S. totals of the original data.

Source: Sixteenth Census of the United States. Compiled from Population, Vol.
         I, State tables 3 and 5; Population, Vol. II, State tables 26 and 27;
         Areas of the United States, 1940, Tables 2, 3, and 4.

all except rural-farm population, and in class D a deficit of all populations, relative, in both cases, to the proportion of land.

2. In general, the larger metropolitan communities contain the greatest excesses of the urbanized populations — metropolis, hinterland urban, and rural-nonfarm — while the smaller ones contain the largest shares of the rural population.

3. It should be noted in passing that of the almost 3,000,000 square miles of land area in the United States, only 19,213 square miles are devoted to urban land uses. If all of the cities of the United States were fitted into a square, with no vacant space between the cities, each side of that square would be only 139 miles long. The 67 metropolitan centers, if similarly placed, would make a square only 61 miles long on each side. San Bernardino County, California, is larger by more than 900 square miles than the total area of the 3,464 urban places in the United States. Almost one-fourth of this urban land area is occupied by the metropolises, and three-fourths by the hinterland cities. Compared to the proportion of the total land area which they comprise, and to the number of central cities of their class, the larger metropolitan centers and their hinterlands contain a very high proportion of this urban land area.

B. The Average Metropolitan Community of Each Size. (Table 6-2)

While there is a great deal of variation in size among metropolitan communities, even within each size class, an average land area and an average number of each type of inhabitants are presented for each size class of metropolis, in order that the general magnitude of the populations under consideration may be known.

1. The class A and B metropolitan communities have hinterlands which are, on the average, less than half as large as those of the class C and D groups.

2. In spite of this difference in land area, there is a consistent increase in average population from class D to class A. The average class D metropolitan community contains a million and one-quarter inhabitants, while the class A group contains an average of 6 million inhabitants.

3. Each size class has a larger average metropolis, urban, and rural-nonfarm population than has the next smaller one.

4. The rural-farm population shows no such uniform increase or decrease in numbers with change in the size of the metropolis. There tend to be fewer rural-farm people in the large metropolitan communities than in the smaller ones.

C. The Population Composition of Metropolitan Communities of Each Size. (Table 6-3)

1. With increasing size of metropolis, an increasing proportion of the total population of the metropolitan community tends to live in the metropolis itself.

2. With increasing size of metropolis, a decreasing proportion of the total population tends to live in village and other rural-nonfarm locations.

3. The rural-farm population constitutes a very small share of the total population of class A and B metropolitan communities, but a very large share of the population of classes C and D.

4. The population of hinterland cities constitutes a smaller proportion of the total population in the two smallest than in the two largest size groups, but there is no consistent trend in this respect along the scale of size of metropolis. Class B has a higher proportion than class A, and class D a higher proportion than class C.

5. In class A and B metropolitan communities, the rural population is preponderantly of the nonfarm type; in class C and D metropolitan communities the rural population is preponderantly of the farm type.

III

The Comparative Intensity of Land Occupancy in Metropolitan Communities of Each Size Class. (Table 6-4, Chart 6-1)

Table 6-4 presents the habitation ratios, for each distance zone of each sector type, for each of the four classes of metropolitan communities.

A. The Total Hinterland Population. (All sector types combined)

1. In general, the same pattern of decreasing intensity of land occupancy with relative increase in distance from the metropolis, which has been observed for all metropolitan areas combined, now may be seen to exist for each size of metropolitan community. This pattern is no less definite and uniform for the smallest metropolitan communities than for the largest. Thus, the pattern of land settlement by distance which was described in the two preceding chapters is not confined to a few of the metropolitan communities.

2. The uniformity of this trend in regard to each size of metropolitan community must lead to the inference that this pattern expresses one characteristic way in which population in the United States is arranged with respect to large central cities. While similar data cannot be presented here for each of the 67 metropolitan communities, to show that this same tendency exists for each one individually, the inference can be made that a complete absence of this pattern in any one hinterland would be the exception rather than the rule. The grouping

Table 6-2

Population and land area per metropolitan community of each size class,
United States, 1940.

Population and land area	All metropolitan communities[b]	Size class of metropolitan community[a]			
		A	B	C	D
Population (000)[c]					
Total	1,965	5,891	2,687	1,859	1,256
Urban	1,111	5,011	1,787	820	521
Metropolis	505	3,182	717	342	146
Hinterland	606	1,829	1,069	477	376
Rural	854	880	900	1,039	735
Nonfarm	403	664	555	401	326
Farm	451	216	346	638	409
Land area (sq.mi.)					
Total	44,423	24,873	22,440	52,216	48,762
Urban	287	739	550	228	184
Metropolis	56	244	56	53	30
Hinterland	231	496	494	174	154
Rural	44,136	24,133	21,890	51,988	48,578

a) Size class of each metropolitan community determined by population
    of metropolitan center in 1940.

b) Equivalent to U.S. total.

c) Individual cells have been rounded to the nearest thousand; hence,
    all totals do not exactly equal sum of their parts.

Source: Sixteenth Census of the United States, compiled from Population,
         Vol.I, State Tables 3 and 5; Population, Vol.II, State Tables 26 and
         27; Areas of the United States, 1940, Tables 2, 3, and 4.

Table 6-3

Percentage distributions of population and land area by size class of metropolitan community, United States, 1940.

Population and land area	All metropolitan communities	Size class of metropolitan community			
		A	B	C	D
Population					
Total	100.0	100.0	100.0	100.0	100.0
Urban	56.5	85.1	66.5	44.1	41.5
Metropolis	25.7	54.0	26.7	18.4	11.6
Hinterland	30.8	31.0	39.8	25.7	29.9
Rural	43.5	14.9	33.5	55.9	58.5
Nonfarm	20.5	11.3	20.6	21.6	26.0
Farm	22.9	3.7	12.9	34.3	32.5
Land area					
Total	100.0	100.0	100.0	100.0	100.0
Urban	0.6	3.0	2.4	0.4	0.4
Metropolis	0.1	1.0	0.2	0.1	0.1
Hinterland	0.5	2.0	2.2	0.3	0.3
Rural	99.4	97.0	97.6	99.6	99.6

Source: Sixteenth Census of the United States. Based upon compilations for Table 6-? of this study.

of metropolitan communities by size makes it virtually impossible for the pattern of any one metropolitan community to overbalance the general pattern for the size group as a whole. While a detailed analysis of the individual metropolitan communities undoubtedly would lead to a qualification and refinement of these findings, it could not do much more than reverify the general nature of the pattern for most hinterlands, and perhaps suggest more appropriate subdivisions of the land area between individual metropolitan communities. Since this pattern of population distribution could have emerged only over a period of time, an analysis of the individual metropolitan communities for two or more decades could also reveal areas where this pattern appears to be in the process of emerging but is, as yet, incomplete.

3. In spite of the fact that the general pattern of land settlement is manifest in all sizes of metropolitan communities, there are variations in this pattern which appear to be associated with the size of the metropolis itself. When all sector types are considered together, there is a consistent tendency for the intensity of land occupancy at any given distance to increase with increasing size of the metropolis.[2] At even 65-114 miles from the

See footnote on page 91.

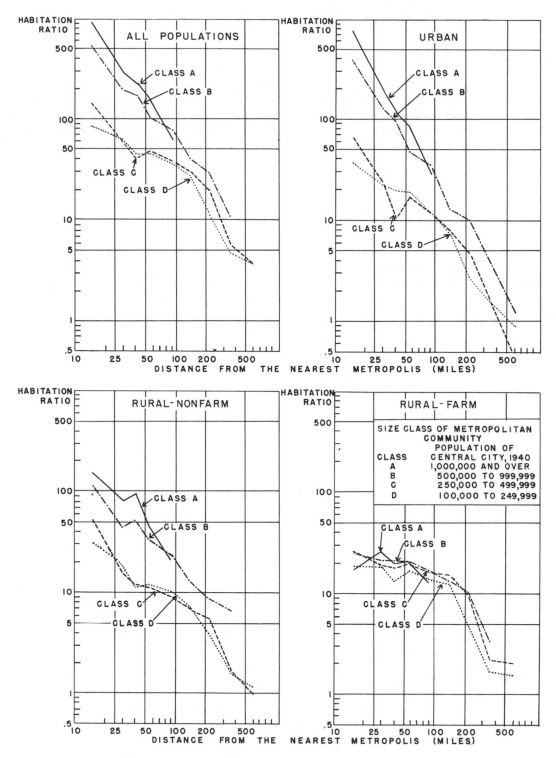

CHART 6-1 HABITATION RATIOS: POPULATION PER SQUARE MILE OF
         HINTERLAND, BY SIZE CLASS OF THE METROPOLITAN
         COMMUNITY AND DISTANCE FROM THE NEAREST
         METROPOLIS. UNITED STATES, 1940

metropolis, the number of persons per square mile in the class A and B metropolitan communities is almost twice that in the class C and D metropolitan communities. The differences between the C and D sizes of metropolitan communities are small compared to the differences between the C, B, and A metropolitan communities. Location in a metropolitan community whose central city contains 100,000 to 249,999 inhabitants appears to be associated with an average intensity of settlement only slightly smaller than in the case of location in a metropolitan community whose central city contains 250,000 to 499,999 inhabitants. On the other hand, an increase in size of metropolis beyond 500,000 inhabitants tends to be associated with a large increase in the habitation ratio. The largest single difference between class D and class C metropolitan communities is in the 0-24 mile zone, the zone in which the increased size of the central city is very definitely accompanied by an increase in the intensity of land occupancy.

4. At distances greater than 45 miles from the metropolis, the habitation ratios are patterned, in almost perfect array, according to size of metropolitan community by distance.[3] Each size of metropolis has a higher habitation ratio at a given distance in its hinterland than has the next smaller size of metropolis. Simultaneously, each zone has a higher habitation ratio than the zone lying outside it. This same uniformity is exhibited by the intermetropolitan sectors. In the local and subdominant sectors, class D metropolitan communities tend to have a habitation ratio higher than that of class C metropolitan communities. This difference may be due, in part, to the fact that proportionately more areas from the southern and central portions of the United States are included in the class C communities, whereas proportionately more areas from the northern and eastern portions of the United States are included in the class D. It must be concluded that, while class C and D centers both have the same pattern of population distribution as the larger metropolitan centers, the concentrative effect of the size of the metropolis, considered as an additional variable in the analysis, operates only weakly in hinterlands dominated by a metropolis of less than 500,000 inhabitants, and operates even then primarily in the intermetropolitan portion (about 50 percent) of the hinterland. Whatever the factors are which operate to nullify the association between intensity of land occupancy and size of

metropolis in the subdominant and local sectors of these smaller metropolitan communities, they appear to be inoperative, or counterbalanced by other forces, in the hinterlands of the larger metropolitan communities.

B. The Urban Population of the Hinterland.

1. A Comparison of the habitation ratios for the urban population with those for the total population indicates that many of the differences noted above in land occupancy between the sizes of metropolitan communities are produced by the hinterland urban population. The general pattern for the urban population, by size of metropolis, distance, and sector type, is, on the whole, an accentuated form of the pattern which exists for the total hinterland population. The rate of change in intensity of land occupancy with relative change in distance is much greater for the urban than for the total population. The differences between the metropolitan communities of class A, B, and C - D (C and D considered together) are also much greater. The tendency for population to be distributed with decreasing intensity according to distance is evident in all sectors except the subdominant sectors of the class A metropolitan communities.

2. The tendency for urban habitation ratios to level off or even to decline between 25 and 44 miles, and to rise in the 45-64 mile zone, may now be found present in all four of the size classes of metropolitan communities. This phenomenon, therefore, is not associated with absence of great metropolitan influence, but, rather, with the very situations in which the most intense metropolitan influence may be expected to exist.

The population lying more than 65 miles from the metropolis is distributed about the metropolis, by distance and sector type with considerable uniformity. It cannot easily be concluded, therefore, that these variations in the habitation ratio between 25 and 44 miles represent the outer limits of metropolitan influence, and that, beyond this point, the population is distributed by some new principle. If the population were distributed by factors which are independent of the metropolis, it is difficult to visualize how the distribution of population can be so well and so uniformly characterized by a set of variables which measure location with respect to the metropolis. If the possibility of some new variable is thus ruled out, the only possible conclusion is that the variations in the pattern of population

2. Since, in the case of class A metropolitan communities, the land area lying 115 miles or more from central cities belongs almost entirely to the Los Angeles metropolitan community, and consists of wasteland, it will be disregarded in discussing the pattern of distribution in class A metropolitan communities, for it cannot be said to represent the group.

3. Note the single exception in the class A metropolitan communities.

Table 6-4

Habitation Ratios: Urban and rural population per square mile of hinterland, by size class of metropolitan community, sector type, and distance from the nearest metropolis. United States, 1940.

Distance zone (miles)	Type of sector — All sector types A	B	C	D	Intermetropolitan A	B	C	D	Metropolitan community — Subdominant A	B	C	D	Local community A	B	C	D
A. All populations																
0-24[a]	957.0	532.9	145.4	86.9	957.0	532.9	145.4	86.9	957.0	532.9	145.4	86.9	957.0	532.9	145.4	86.9
25-34	291.6	197.0	59.5	60.2	372.8	159.6	58.8	58.0	216.3	470.0	158.8	76.7	146.1	76.4	43.2	62.6
35-44	227.1	167.8	40.2	45.0	248.6	195.1	50.3	52.3	210.9	142.8	45.6	64.5	175.5	111.4	29.7	28.7
45-64	155.9	103.0	48.6	47.6	177.7	111.7	57.9	54.1	163.2	129.3	51.7	55.2	115.5	64.7	33.5	37.3
65-114	62.8	76.3	38.0	36.5	59.0	82.3	41.5	37.0	187.7	110.9	48.8	50.0	44.7	51.2	27.6	31.7
115-164	d)	40.2	30.5	27.4	d)	39.2	32.5	25.1	d)	46.8	39.4	42.1	e)	27.4	20.2	25.6
165-264	d)	29.4	20.5	11.7	d)	39.7	21.7	10.6	c)	29.6	35.1	34.4	c)	16.0	12.4	9.6
265-464	d)	11.4	5.7	4.9	d)	c)	6.7	4.8	c)	10.9	46.3	17.9	c)	14.8	3.8	14.6
465-over	c)	c)	3.6	3.6	c)	c)	4.6	3.4	c)	c)	c)	c)	c)	c)	2.2	4.0
B. Urban population																
0-24[a]	789.3	395.5	66.5	37.4	789.3	395.5	66.5	37.4	789.3	395.5	66.5	37.4	789.3	395.5	66.5	37.4
25-34	186.0	129.7	24.4	23.6	267.8	92.7	22.5	21.9	91.6	358.1	29.3	37.0	60.5	39.5	9.4	25.5
35-44	144.8	94.4	17.0	19.7	109.8	106.8	16.2	25.5	199.3	93.2	10.5	25.2	94.3	60.6	4.9	9.2
45-64	85.7	46.9	11.9	18.8	118.9	51.8	23.1	25.8	92.8	72.6	16.4	22.7	27.4	17.3	8.1	8.9
65-114	28.1	35.2	8.0	12.0	26.3	42.4	13.8	13.2	139.5	61.1	19.1	18.2	8.1	11.6	5.8	8.4
115-164	d)	13.1	4.8	7.4	d)	13.4	9.0	8.2	a)	16.3	12.0	11.7	d)	4.7	3.5	4.7
165-264	d)	10.1	1.7	2.8	d)	12.1	5.1	2.6	c)	10.9	9.5	10.7	d)	1.1	2.3	1.9
265-464	d)	1.2	0.4	1.6	d)	c)	1.9	1.7	c)	0.9	16.9	7.9	d)	3.3	1.1	1.0
465-over	c)	c)	c)	0.9	c)	c)	0.7	0.8	c)	c)	c)	c)	c)	c)	0.1	1.2
C. Rural-nonfarm population																
0-24[a]	150.8	112.1	52.9	30.9	150.8	112.1	52.9	30.9	150.8	112.1	52.9	30.9	150.8	112.1	52.9	30.9
25-34	80.0	44.7	15.5	17.7	77.2	43.1	15.5	19.3	97.5	86.6	8.6	14.4	67.8	18.1	16.6	13.6
35-44	93.0	51.4	11.9	11.8	120.0	64.4	12.4	12.6	31.6	29.6	13.1	18.6	58.0	32.0	11.4	8.8
45-64	48.7	34.4	11.4	12.0	38.1	38.8	11.7	11.5	44.4	34.3	13.7	12.3	69.0	25.4	10.2	12.5
65-114	21.5	23.7	9.0	10.4	24.5	22.2	9.7	11.0	20.9	30.6	11.1	12.7	14.6	11.0	7.0	8.9
115-164	d)	13.3	6.9	7.4	d)	12.3	7.1	6.4	a)	15.5	8.8	10.3	d)	3.7	5.0	7.7
165-264	d)	8.7	5.6	3.9	d)	10.3	6.4	3.6	c)	9.0	8.3	9.8	d)	7.7	3.2	3.4
265-464	d)	6.7	1.7	1.6	d)	c)	1.9	1.6	c)	6.5	9.2	3.4	d)	c)	1.3	1.6
465-over	c)	c)	1.0	1.2	c)	c)	1.2	1.1	c)	c)	c)	c)	c)	c)	0.7	1.3
D. Rural-farm population																
0-24[a]	16.9	25.3	26.0	18.6	16.9	25.3	26.0	18.6	16.9	25.3	26.0	18.6	16.9	25.3	26.0	18.6
25-34	25.6	22.6	19.6	18.9	27.8	25.8	20.8	16.9	27.2	25.4	21.0	25.0	17.7	18.5	17.2	23.4
35-44	19.9	22.0	17.8	13.5	18.8	23.9	21.8	14.1	19.9	19.4	22.0	20.7	23.2	18.8	13.4	10.7
45-64	21.6	21.6	20.1	16.8	20.8	23.1	23.1	16.8	26.0	22.3	21.7	20.2	19.1	21.9	15.3	15.9
65-114	13.3	17.5	17.0	14.1	8.1	17.8	17.9	12.9	27.3	19.1	18.6	19.1	22.0	21.4	11.7	14.3
115-164	d)	13.8	15.5	12.6	d)	13.4	16.4	10.5	d)	15.1	18.6	20.1	d)	11.6	11.8	13.2
165-264	d)	10.6	10.1	5.0	d)	17.3	10.2	4.4	c)	9.6	17.3	13.9	c)	11.2	6.8	4.3
265-464	d)	3.5	2.3	1.7	d)	c)	2.8	1.4	c)	3.5	20.1	6.6	c)	3.7	1.4	2.0
465-over	c)	c)	2.1	1.5	c)	c)	2.7	1.4	c)	c)	c)	c)	c)	c)	1.4	1.5

a) Includes land area and population of counties containing central cities, but excludes central cities.

b) Excludes area and population of central cities.

c) No land area at this distance and sector type.

d) Areas consisting entirely of land and population of Los Angeles metropolitan community excluded.

Source: Sixteenth Census of the United States. Compiled from Population, Vol.I, State tables 3 and 5; Population, Vol.II, State tables 26 and 27; Areas of the United States, 1940, Tables 2, 3, and 4.

distribution represent some characteristic element of metropolitan influence, and that this element is a part of the metropolitan structure. If such is the case, it becomes necessary to develop a hypothesis concerning the nature of this element and the method by which it operates to produce this distortion of the general pattern of population distribution.

An examination of the disturbances in the 25-64 mile distances, for the purpose of discovering how they fit into the general pattern for all distances, makes it apparent that the disturbances have as much the nature of an abnormally low value in the 25-34 or the 35-44 mile zones as of an abnormally high value in the 35-44 or the 45-64 mile zones. A greater concentration of urban population appears to exist in the 35-44 mile zone of class A and B metropolitan communities, and in the 45-64 mile zone of the class C metropolitan communities, than would be expected considering the general trend of land occupancy with distance. These distances appear to be unusually favorable locations for the growth of hinterland cities. It is here hypothesized that cities in these zones are located at points where direct dominance by the metropolis changes over to indirect dominance. The area within 25 miles of the metropolis is within a distance which makes possible easy daily commuting, and direct participation in the activities of the metropolis. The metropolis organizes this inner area directly with respect to itself. Beyond 45 miles the metropolis must dominate the hinterland indirectly — that is, by working through major subdominant hinterland cities. According to this view, a location just outside the zone of easy commuting would seem to be a preferred locational point for hinterland cities. As the metropolitan community developed, these outlying centers may have sprung up quickly, leaving the process of suburbanization to "fill in" the next inner zone. The low habitation ratios in the inner zones of class B, C, and D areas may be an indication that this filling in process is still incomplete.

C. The Rural-nonfarm Population.

1. Division of the distance and type of sector distributions according to the four sizes of metropolitan communities necessitates very few modifications of the general principles which were developed earlier in regard to populations of this type. The fact that the habitation ratios, by size of metropolitan community, follow the A, B, C-D pattern makes it evident that the size of the metropolis is also associated with the intensity with which the land is occupied by rural-nonfarm population.

2. Those variations in the habitation ratios between 25 and 64 miles which have been discussed in some detail for the urban population are also present, at these same points, for the rural-nonfarm population.

The hypothesis which has been developed makes it possible to regard these unusual aggregations of rural-nonfarm populations as suburban settlements around the peripheries of the larger hinterland cities in the 45-64 mile zones.

D. The Rural-farm Population.

It seems evident that the intensity of land settlement by the rural-farm population is associated with distance and with direction from each class of metropolitan centers but the principles which govern this settlement are not readily apparent. It will be remembered that the distribution of the total rural-farm population by distance, as presented in Chapter Four, appeared to be composed of two separate trend lines. Out to approximately 115 miles from all metropolitan centers, there appeared to be only a very gradual rate of decline in the intensity of land occupancy with relative change in distance. Beyond this point the rate of decline was more rapid. When the rural-farm population is further classified by the size of the metropolis certain new facts appear:

1. The rural-farm population tends to have a lower habitation ratio in the zone surrounding the central city (0-24 miles) than in the 25-34 mile zone. Since the figures of Table 6-4 are based upon the total hinterland area, including the area of subdominant cities, it might be concluded that this low ratio is due to the "pushing out" of the farm population by urban land uses. That city areas as such do not account for all of this lower rate may be shown by the following tabulation of the rural-farm population per rural square mile of land area (area of all cities removed):

Distance zone (miles)	Class of metropolis			
	A	B	C	D
0-24	20.3	28.8	26.8	19.0

The fact remains that heavy concentrations of the rural-nonfarm population may displace the rural-farm population from the inner zone. That this appears to be the case is demonstrated by the class A metropolitan communities, in which the rural-farm population in all sectors is more concentrated in the 25-34 mile zone than in the 0-24 mile zone. This same tendency, that of the rural-farm population in the second zone to be equal to or greater than the innermost zone in land occupancy, is present in one or more sectors of every class of metropolis except the C group, in which the characteristics of the hinterlands of such places as Denver, San Antonio, Birmingham, Portland, Kansas City, and Minneapolis may produce the lower habitation ratio in the second zone.

2. In the class A metropolitan community there is a general <u>rise</u> from the central city out to a distance of 65 miles in the intermetropolitan sectors and out to 115 miles in the subdominant and local sectors. (This is the extent of the land area, in the class A metropolitan communities, which is considered representative of the class). The evidence available here indicates a slight <u>inverse</u> relationship between the intensity of land occupancy by the rural-farm population and distance from metropolitan centers of one million inhabitants or more. Whether this phenomenon can be interpreted as a lack of available space for farming, or as a lack of arable land, cannot be stated. Whatever the cause, the conclusion remains that the concentrative pattern of distribution of the rural-farm population with distance from the metropolis is inoperative in the five largest metropolitan communities.

3. The B, C, and D sizes of metropolitan community share the general tendency, in a modified form, toward a decreasing habitation ratio with relative increase in distance from the metropolis. The subdominant sectors of the C and D metropolitan communities appear able to maintain a very high ratio of population to land as far into the hinterland as 200 miles. In these classes, only the local and the intermetropolitan sectors lose population per unit of area with increasing distance. In the class B metropolitan centers the habitation ratios of all sector types decrease with distance. The deviations from this general pattern occur, as in the case of the rural-nonfarm and the urban populations, in the 25-44 mile zone. Evidence will be presented in Chapter Eight to show that these deviations are associated also with the presence of major hinterland cities in the 45-64 mile zone.

4. In addition to the fact that the rural-farm pattern of concentration with distance does not follow one single pattern for all sizes of metropolitan communities, it should also be observed that there is no great difference between the rural-nonfarm habitation ratios of the various sizes of metropolitan community. For the rural-farm population, therefor, the intensity with which land is inhabited tends to increase only slightly with increasing size of metropolis. The only way this tendency can be observed at all is through a comparison of the class A and B metropolitan communities with the class C and D, and even then this tendency fades out at 115 miles from the central city.

Chapter Four demonstrated that the rural-farm population was distributed in regard to land with a degree of association equal to its degree of association with the urban population. This finding takes on new meaning in the light of the present analysis. Great cities appear to repel in some instances, and not to encourage, at least, in other instances, an intense settlement by the rural-farm population. The size of the metropolis appears to have only a slight effect upon the intensity of agricultural activities at any given distance. It would appear that such factors as: (a) the existence of arable land, (b) a limit to the intensity with which agricultural land can be cultivated, (c) competition for space with nonagricultural land uses, and (d) the presence of major hinterland cities, condition and limit the extent to which the rural-farm population is able to follow the concentrative pattern of the other hinterland populations. Only at distances of 115 miles does distance from the metropolis become positively associated with decreased settlement. This decline may be due to the decline in the fertility of the land (if the metropolis is located toward the center of each area of arable land) or to some real change in the conditions under which agricultural activities can take place.

IV

Summary

1. The metropolitan communities of each size class conform to the general pattern of population distribution developed in the preceding two chapters. The intensity with which the land is occupied with increasing distance and with change in type of sector tends to vary according to the same general pattern as has been described in regard to all of the metropolitan communities considered as a group.

2. The size of the central city, however, appears to be a variable which is related to the intensity of land settlement under given conditions of distance and type of sector. Class A and B metropolitan communities have higher numbers of population per square mile at all distances than have class C and D metropolitan communities. The class A metropolitan communities tend to be more intensively occupied than do the class B communities. There are only minor differences between class C and D areas in this respect.

CHAPTER SEVEN

THE DISTRIBUTION OF CITIES, BY SIZE, IN THE HINTERLAND

I

Introduction

This chapter attempts to examine the distributional patterns of hinterland cities of various sizes. The very fact that hinterland cities exist at all is evidence that the dispersed rural population cannot and does not depend upon the metropolis directly for all of its urban services. Some of the functions which only a city can perform seem to be needed so universally, so frequently, and in such quantities that smaller centers spring up in the hinterland to satisfy those needs. The presence of hinterland cities appears to be an inevitable and necessary accompaniment of an intensive level of land occupancy. Under present conditions of environment, resources, markets, and technology urban units located in the hinterland appear to be more efficient locations for accomplishing some functions than does the metropolis.

The hypothesis of subdominance developed in Chapter Two provides a starting point for examining the place of the hinterland city in the metropolitan structure. The metropolis was there characterized as a unit which dominates its hinterland by controlling some of the conditions of life of other communal units, which in themselves exercise a degree of control (subdominance) over still less dominant units. If this hypothesis is true, any over-all structure, in order to be typical of the metropolitan community, must consist of some pattern of arrangement and inter-functioning of hinterland cities with each other as well as with the central city.

Perhaps the importance of this point can be further emphasized by a review of a few of some facts about hinterland cities. In this study only 67 cities have been deemed of sufficient size and complexity to be considered metropolitan centers. Scattered throughout the hinterland are 3,395 other cities and urban places ranging in size from 2,500 to more than 100,000 inhabitants. Though many of these places are mere extensions or appendages of the 67 metropolitan centers themselves, the majority of them are detached units lying outside the "built up" area of the metropolis. In addition to these numerous independent com-munities there are many times again as many villages, hamlets, and other agglomerations of urban-like populations. In 1940 the United States Census listed 13,288 incorporated places of less than 2,500 inhabitants. There are many more which have no such formal organization. The 67 metropolitan centers contain but 25.7 percent of the total population of the United States. The combined population of the hinterland cities is 30.8 percent of the national total, and an additional 20.5 percent of the population resides in the many village and rural-nonfarm areas. Thus, 77 percent of the population of the United States is agglomerated, or nucleated, and the amount of agglomerated or nucleated population outside central cities is almost exactly twice the amount concentrated inside the central cities. No realistic hypothesis of metropolitan organization could fail to take note of the fact that the hinterland everywhere contains a multiplicity of local centers and that, together, these local centers contain a large proportion of the total population.

The additional classification of "size of hinterland city in 1940" which has been superimposed upon the preceding tabulations for the urban population by distance, type of sector, and size class of central city, makes it possible to study the distribution in the hinterland of each size of subdominant center. As in the preceding chapters, the population data for each size of city have been reduced to the familiar habitation ratios — population per unit of land area. The land area which has been used as the base for these ratios is the number of square miles of land area contained in the sector type and distance zone in which are located the hinterland cities of the given size. The same land area is used as a base, in each case, in the computation of the habitation ratio for each size class of hinterland city lying in a given zone and sector type. This procedure not only eliminates differences in area between the various parts of the hinterland, but also serves to emphasize the fact that any one hinterland area is simultaneously occupied, or served, by more than one size of hinterland city, and that varying combinations of this service may be found in different parts of the hinterland.

II

Description of the Location of Cities in the Hinterland, by Size

A. The Number of Hinterland Cities of Each Size in Each Size Class of Metropolitan Community. (Table 7-1)

Of the 3,395 hinterland cities and urban places of all sizes in the United States in 1940, at least one-seventh of the members belonging to each size group are present in the hinterland of each of the four classes of metropolitan communities. No one

B. The Average Number of Hinterland Cities of Each Size Class in Each Metropolitan Community. (Table 7-2)

1. The increase in the average number of hinterland cities belonging to each size group with each increase in the size class of metropolitan communities is indicative of the increasing complexity of metropolitan communities which accompanies an increase in the size of central cities. Thus, a class D metropolitan community would consist on the average, of a metropolis and 38 hinterland cities, of which only three would be as large as 25,000 inhabitants. An average class A metropolitan communi-

Table 7-1

Number of hinterland cities, distributed by size group of city and size class of metropolitan community in which located. United States, 1940.

Size of urban place	All metropolitan communities	Size class of metropolitan community			
		A	B	C	D
All urban places	3395	556	679½ [a)]	853	1306½
2,500 - 4,999	1422	201	242	385½	593½
5,000 - 9,999	965	153	183½	247½	381
10,000 - 14,999	374	69	92	84	129
15,000 - 24,999	291	43	82	63	103
25,000 - 49,999	211	51	46	46	68
50,000- over	132	39	34	27	32
Percentage distribution					
All urban places	100.0	16.4	20.0	25.1	38.5
2,500 - 4,999	100.0	14.1	17.0	27.1	41.7
5,000 - 9,999	100.0	15.9	19.0	25.6	39.5
10,000 - 14,999	100.0	18.4	24.6	22.5	34.5
15,000 - 24,999	100.0	14.8	28.2	21.6	35.4
25,000 - 49,999	100.0	24.2	21.8	21.8	32.2
50,000 - over	100.0	29.5	25.8	20.5	24.2

a) Those cities which lie in two counties between which a metropolitan community boundary passes have been coded as one-half city in each metropolitan community.

Source: Sixteenth Census of the United States. Compiled from Population, Vol.I, State tables 3 and 5.

class of metropolitan community claims more than 41.7 percent or less than 14.1 percent of the members of any one size group of hinterland city. The larger hinterland cities tend to be more evenly distributed among the metropolitan communities of the four sizes than do the smaller ones.

ty, on the other hand, would consist of a metropolis and 111 hinterland cities, of which 18 would contain 25,000 or more inhabitants. On the whole, the larger the size-class of the central city, the larger the average number of hinterland cities of each size which it contains.

Table 7-2

Number of hinterland cities of each size group per metropolitan community of each size class, United States, 1940.

Size of urban place	All metropolitan communities	Size class of metropolitan community			
		A	B	C	D
All urban places	50.7	111.2	75.5	44.9	38.4
2,500 - 4,999	21.2	40.2	26.9	20.3	17.5
5,000 - 9,999	14.4	30.6	20.4	13.0	11.2
10,000 - 14,999	5.6	13.8	10.2	4.4	3.8
15,000 - 24,999	4.3	8.6	9.1	3.3	3.0
25,000 - 49,999	3.1	10.2	5.1	2.4	2.0
50,000 - over	2.0	7.8	3.8	1.4	0.9
Percentage distribution					
All urban places	100.0	100.0	100.0	100.0	100.0
2,500 - 4,999	41.9	36.2	35.6	45.2	45.4
5,000 - 9,999	28.4	27.5	27.0	29.0	29.2
10,000 -14,999	11.0	12.4	13.5	9.8	9.9
15,000 -24,999	8.6	7.7	12.1	7.4	7.9
25,000 -49,999	6.2	9.2	6.8	5.4	5.2
50,000 -over	3.9	7.0	5.0	3.2	2.4

Source: Sixteenth Census of the United States. Compiled from Population, Vol.I, State tables 3 and 5.

2. With increasing size of metropolis goes an important change in the size composition of the complement of hinterland cities. Not only are the larger hinterland cities more numerous in the larger metropolitan communities; they are also relatively more important, as indicated by the fact that they constitute a larger percentage of all cities in the larger than in the smaller size classes of metropolitan communities. The large metropolis not only has more cities in its hinterland than does the small metropolis; it also has, on the average, larger hinterland cities than does the small metropolis.

C. The Distribution of the Hinterland Urban Population Among the Various Sizes of Hinterland Cities, by Size of Metropolis. (Table 7-3)

The large proportion of all hinterland cities which the small hinterland cities represent should not lead to the assumption that the populations of hinterland cities are preponderantly small-city dwellers. Table 7-3, showing what proportion of the total urban population of each class of metropolitan community lives in each size group of hinterland city, indicates that large hinterland cities are a more important element of the hinterland than the number of such cities would suggest.
1. The proportion of the hinterland urban population living in cities of more than 50,000 inhabitants is more than twice as large in the class A as in the class D metropolitan communities. Between these extremes, each smaller size of metropolis has a smaller proportion of its hinterland urban inhabitants living in cities of 50,000 or more inhabitants.

Table 7-3

Percentage distribution of urban inhabitants living in central cities
and in hinterland cities, by size class of metropolitan community.
United States, 1940.

Size and type of urban place	All metropolitan communities	Size class of metropolitan community			
		A	B	C	D
2,500-4,999	12.4	7.9	8.9	15.1	16.3
5,000-9,999	16.5	11.9	13.4	18.6	20.5
10,000-14,999	11.1	9.3	11.7	11.1	11.9
15,000-24,999	13.5	8.9	16.4	13.0	14.8
25,000-49,999	18.1	19.7	16.7	17.4	18.4
50,000-99,999	17.4	18.5	19.1	16.6	16.1
100,000-over	11.1	23.6	13.8	8.2	2.0
All hinterland cities	100.0	100.0	100.0	100.0	100.0

Source: Sixteenth Census of the United States, compiled from Population,
Vol. 1, State tables 3 and 5.

2. To compensate for this high proportion of the urban population living in the very large hinterland cities, the largest metropolitan communities have a relatively small proportion of their urban inhabitants living in smaller hinterland cities. Only in class D metropolitan communities is there a relatively uniform distribution of the urban population among the city size classes, since no tendency exists in such communities for any one size of hinterland city to claim an unusually large or small share of the total hinterland urban population.
3. In the class A metropolitan communities the population of the central cities outnumbers the combined populations of all hinterland cities. In the class B, C, and D metropolitan communities, this situation is reversed; the population of the subdominant cities outnumbers that of the central cities, and does so by a ratio which becomes quite large in the smallest class. The population of all class D central cities in only 39 percent as large as the combined population of their hinterland cities.

III

The Intensity with which the Hinterland is
Occupied by Residents of Various Sizes of Cities

A. The Distribution of the Urban Population in the Hinterland, by Size of Urban Place, Size of Metropolitan Community, and Sector Type. (Table 7-4, Chart 7-1)

Chart 7-1 and Table 7-4 report the population of each size group of hinterland city per unit of area by distance, sector type, and size of metropolis. The data for the 25-34 and the 35-44 mile zones have been presented separately and have also been grouped into one zone. This procedure enables the reader to observe the deviations from the over-all pattern which occur at this distance as well as the conformity to the general pattern which results when the variations are removed by the combining of these two adjacent distance categories.

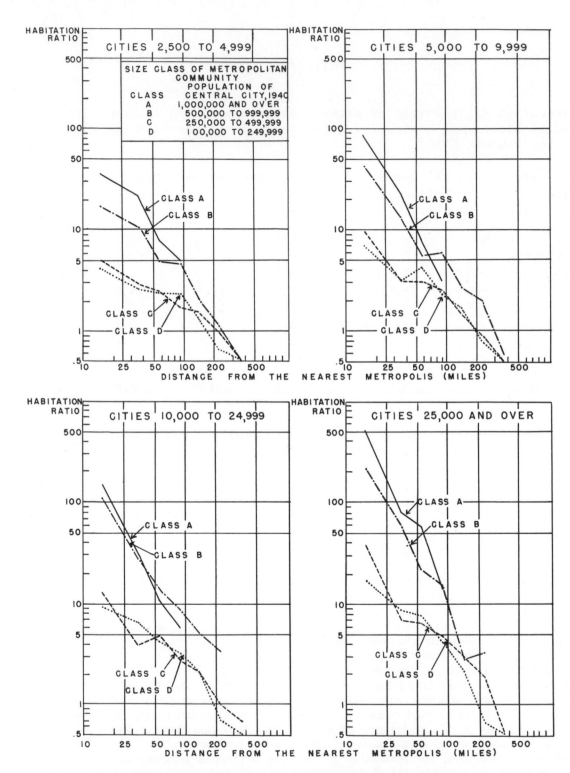

CHART 7-I HABITATION RATIOS: POPULATION PER SQUARE MILE OF
HINTERLAND, BY SIZE OF HINTERLAND CITY, SIZE CLASS
OF THE METROPOLITAN COMMUNITY, AND DISTANCE FROM
THE NEAREST METROPOLIS. UNITED STATES, 1940

1. The populations of all four sizes of hinterland cities occupy the hinterland with a pattern of decreasing intensity with increasing distance.

2. At any given distance, the larger the metropolis the higher the habitation ratio tends to be for any one size-class of hinterland city. This comparison follows the "A is greater than B is greater than either C or D" pattern noted for all hinterland urban population in Chapter Six.

3. The smaller cities are more evenly spread throughout the hinterlands of all classes of metropolitan communities than are the larger cities, as is shown by the more gentle slope of their graph.

4. The class A and B metropolitan communities tend to have similar patterns, as shown by the height and slope of their lines. The C and D classes are also in general alike.

5. The larger the size of the hinterland city, the higher its average habitation ratio tends to be. Thus, even though the small hinterland cities are much more numerous than the larger ones, a larger number of urban people per unit of area reside in larger centers of subdominance than in smaller ones. This situation exists, at all distances, in all sizes of metropolitan communities. The widespread distribution of the major hinterland cities throughout the hinterlands of all sizes of metropolitan communities, and the preponderance of their population numbers over those of the smaller centers of subdominance at each distance, is further evidence that the major subdominant center plays a very significant role in the distribution of population.

6. When the various distance zones are broken into sector types, the general pattern of decline with distance remains, although with several deviations from the trend.[1] The following conclusions seem to be warranted:

    a. Those differences in accessibility which are associated with the growth of hinterland cities to a specific size seem to differentiate the hinterlands of the class C and D metropolitan communities more clearly than they do the hinterlands of the class A and B metropolitan communities. In class C and D metropolitan communities there are fairly consistent differences between the sectors in regard to the intensities with which the inhabitants of a city in a given size group inhabit the hinterland. In general, the subdominant sectors are more intensively occupied by all sizes of cities than are the intermetropolitan or local sectors. Thus, the higher degree of urbanization of subdominant sectors is due, not to the presence of large cities alone (the basis for their classification as subdominant), but to high habitation ratios for urban populations of all sizes of cities as well. Therefore, the subdominant sector appears to have fostered the growth of smaller hinterland cities of all sizes. In sectors of this type, moreover, the populations of all sizes of cities are distributed more evenly throughout the distance zones than are the populations of the other sector types, since the habitation ratios of all sizes of cities tend to be higher in the distant zones of subdominant sectors than in the distant zones of sectors of other types.

    b. In the 45-65 mile zone the intermetropolitan sectors of class B and C metropolitan communities are more intensively occupied by all sizes of cities than are the local sectors. At distances smaller or greater than this there appear to be no consistent differences in favor of either sector type. In the near areas, where accessibility is high, the intensity with which the inhabitants of a given size of city inhabit the land is also high in all sectors, and variations in the intensity of this land occupancy are not associated in any simple way with the types of accessibility measured by the classification of sectors according to type. One can only generalize, and say that when accessibility is very high there is an intense settlement of all city-size populations in all types of sectors, but that as the distance increases the greater accessibility of the intermetropolitan sectors fosters an urban development greater than that attained by the local sectors. Beyond 165 miles, access to the central city does not seem either to encourage or discourage the intensity with which the hinterland is inhabited by the populations of cities of less than 10,000 inhabitants of given size class.

    c. In the class A and B metropolitan communities the individual sizes of cities present habitation ratios which resemble those of the near zones for all metropolitan communities. Although the intersector differences noted above for class C and D metropolitan communities have a tendency to be present also in class A and B metropolitan communities, the patterns in the latter case, are less clean-cut and are not without exceptions. To the extent that all areas in the hinterlands of the larger metropolitan communities are more accessible

---

1. Some of these deviations appear to arise from the small numbers of counties used to determine the area base. Except for unavoidable "tapering off" of the land area with distance, the areas used in these tables are quite stable. Aside from the end values, the ratios for class D are based upon 35 or more counties, those for class C upon 47 or more, class B upon 11 or more, and class A upon 6 or more counties. Distances greater than 115 miles have been excluded for the class A metropolitan communities as being unrepresentative of the class as a whole.

Table 7-4

Population of hinterland cities of each size group per 100 square miles, classified by size class of metropolitan community, sector type and distance from the nearest metropolis. United States, 1940.

Distance zone (miles)	Size group of hinterland city by size class of metropolitan community															
	2,500 - 4,999				5,000 - 9,999				10,000 - 24,999				25,000 - over			
	A	B	C	D	A	B	C	D	A	B	C	D	A	B	C	D
	All sectors				**All sectors**				**All sectors**				**All sectors**			
All distances	590	424	138	125	888	640	170	158	1353	1342	221	206	4597	2370	386	281
0-24 a)	3456	1689	498	412	8647	4280	979	698	15173	11256	1300	949	51651	22323	3871	1677
25-44	2166	1012	292	266	2339	1360	310	313	3025	2814	392	676	7950	6164	692	868
25-34	2137	1063	254	295	2439	1185	445	436	3869	3630	520	814	10099	7089	1224	813
35-44	2203	951	323	246	2146	1567	196	234	1941	1851	283	587	5188	5073	242	903
45-64	818	501	254	251	785	566	310	425	1103	1377	494	430	5860	2249	646	776
65-114	500	477	172	232	307	598	247	234	577	887	276	323	1423	1557	498	412
115-164	b)	223	155	138	b)	269	149	167	-	528	210	210	-	288	292	223
165-264	b)	124	98	67	b)	203	92	82	-	353	98	67	-	327	190	67
265-over	b)	53	25	25	b)	67	34	33	-	-	67	38	-	-	13	53
	Intermetropolitan				**Intermetropolitan**				**Intermetropolitan**				**Intermetropolitan**			
0-24 a)	3456	1689	498	412	8647	4280	979	698	15173	11256	1300	949	51651	22323	3871	1677
25-44	2564	1047	254	257	2956	1426	381	276	2780	2717	587	640	11150	4776	729	1216
25-34	3037	1055	166	193	3548	1057	542	256	4463	4046	631	690	15732	3108	909	1048
35-44	2019	1079	352	309	2271	1800	200	292	836	1822	537	598	5856	6467	1016	1353
45-64	1105	533	253	303	873	623	357	480	1023	1822	685	515	8885	2198	1016	1278
65-114	337	571	169	235	314	664	254	218	884	737	274	302	1094	2267	685	561
115-164	b)	241	179	117	-	297	138	138	-	800	297	234	-	-	289	331
165-264	b)	263	94	69	b)	398	98	52	-	546	80	94	-	-	234	43
265-over	b)	-	23	23	b)	-	44	36	-	-	91	32	-	-	-	64
	Subdominant				**Subdominant**				**Subdominant**				**Subdominant**			
0-24 a)	3456	1689	498	412	8647	4280	979	698	15173	11256	1300	949	51651	22323	3871	1677
25-44	1033	566	408	257	886	2094	562	204	3300	3056	305	817	6351	18755	4779	1584
25-34	732	623	259	308	944	2775	597	323	2606	4493	723	1769	4876	27975	11347	1301
35-44	1576	490	517	237	781	1185	536	156	4556	1136	-	432	9020	6511	-	1699
45-64	845	506	442	307	856	480	226	60	640	919	-	638	8130	5359	969	1266
65-114	c)	381	305	324	c)	746	334	256	-	2674	370	192	c)	2307	899	1053
115-164	-	180	158	197	-	350	163	196	-	342	150	401	-	756	729	425
165-264	-	106	160	104	-	202	89	203	-	371	265	65	-	414	517	693
265-over	-	42	-	54	-	46	c)	120	-	-	-	-	-	-	c)	615
	Local				**Local**				**Local**				**Local** d)			
0-24 a)	3456	1689	498	412	8647	4280	979	698	15173	11256	1300	949	51651	22323	3871	1677
25-44	2110	1261	322	286	1955	670	179	414	3480	2851	154	714	-	-	-	-
25-34	1183	1384	416	599	1243	312	240	997	3626	2247	281	957	-	-	-	-
35-44	3283	1073	266	150	2856	1216	142	162	3294	3771	79	608	-	-	-	-
45-64	565	430	204	171	550	511	261	457	1620	790	342	264	-	-	-	-
65-114	603	353	129	199	203	420	203	250	-	383	247	393	-	-	-	-
115-164	-	272	107	148	-	-	162	199	-	201	77	112	-	-	-	-
165-264	-	117	78	59	-	-	99	103	-	-	58	29	-	-	-	-
265-over	-	c)	28	29	-	204	12	20	-	-	46	55	-	-	-	-

a) No sector types shown separately for distances less than 25 miles. A combined value for all sectors is reported for each sector type at this distance zone for purposes of comparison with other zones. Zone includes land area and population of counties containing central cities.

b) Area in eastern California and western Nevada and Arizona arbitrarily excluded as being unrepresentative of average hinterland area.

c) Combined with category immediately above because of small amount of land area at these distances.

d) By definition there are no cities of 25,000 or more inhabitants at distances greater than 10 miles from the metropolis in local sectors.

Source: Sixteenth Census of the United States, Population, Vol.I, State tables 3 and 5; Areas of the United States, 1940, tables 2, 3, and 4.

than are the hinterlands of the smaller metropolitan communities, by virtue of having more highly developed systems of highways and railroads, intermetropolitan routes and large hinterland cities may be less essential to a high occupancy of the hinterland than they are in smaller metropolitan communities. The subdominant sectors, in particular, do not exhibit their customary trait of fostering greater urbanism of all sizes of cities at all distances.

d. Table 7-4 indicates also that there may be an element of displacement of one size of hinterland city by another size of hinterland city, not only within the sectors but between the sectors as well. Two given cities cannot occupy the same space, and each city can be of only one size at a given moment. If the conditions which measure accessibility also promote urban growth, one effect may be to cause the cities already present to grow to a greater than average size rather than to multiply the number of cities. As a consequence, the habitation ratios for the smaller sizes of cities will be low, unless other processes, such as suburbanization about the larger cities, enter to make up for the deficit caused by growth into other categories. The habitation ratio of 27,975 residents per 100 square miles for cities of 25,000 or more inhabitants in the 25-34 mile zone of the subdominant sectors of class B metropolitan communities, for example, may explain why the habitation ratio for this size of city, at the same distance, in the intermetropolitan sector is only 3,108, and why the habitation ratios are not higher for other sizes of cities at this distance. Obviously it is the total structure of city sizes, rather than the pattern for each individual size group of hinterland city, which is fostered or left undeveloped by accessibility.

7. These findings are not merely bits of interesting information about cities; together they make possible a most important conclusion concerning the metropolitan community. <u>Those areas which are most accessible to the metropolis have fostered to the greatest extent the growth of cities to all sizes,</u> and particularly the growth of centers which are now large cities. Those areas which are least accessible to the metropolis tend to be the least urbanized and to have a deficiency of large cities. The larger the metropolis, the more urban the hinterland tends to be, and the larger the individual hinterland cities become. Thus, the metropolitan center appears to have been a factor in the growth and development of urban places in the hinterland. There is no scarcity of <u>potential</u> urban communities, for there are thousands of villages and hamlets. There is no scarcity of potential major hinterland cities, since there are hundreds of small cities located at all distances in the hinterland.

Yet those hinterland cities which have attained the greatest size have tended to be located in positions which enabled them to enter into some functional relationship with the central city.

8. The tendency for habitation ratios to "level off," or even to increase, in the zones between 35 and 65 miles of the metropolis, persists for each size of hinterland city. While it is not possible here to verify a hypothesis in explanation of these variations in the intensity of urban land occupancy, the data behave as if the 35-44 mile zone is a preferred location for cities in class A and B metropolitan communities and that the 45-64 mile zone is a preferred location for hinterland cities in classes C and D, and that in these zones cities have multiplied and grown more rapidly than one would expect from the over all trend.

In the preceding sections a distance of 25 miles from the metropolis has been taken as being within easy commuting distance, and 35 miles as the outer limits of easy commuting to the central city from a point in the hinterland. Sixty-five miles is within a distance which permits rapid and frequent trucking service from the metropolis. Within this latter radius the metropolis should therefore be able to provide the residents with many goods and services on a daily basis, although at greater distances this becomes increasingly difficult. One may postulate, therefore, two major types of interaction between the metropolis and its hinterland on the basis of the predominant characteristic of the division of labor. Within a point between 35 and 45 miles one may postulate an area of "primary" or direct metropolitan dominance in which cities located within the primary zone may grow and expand as a result of the overflow of the metropolis and by virtue of being able to share in some of the locational advantages which the metropolis possesses. The populations residing within this zone are able to participate directly in the activities of the central city. Activities carried on within these near cities may reflect the locational assets which accrue from the presence of the metropolis itself, such as the convergence of rail and highway routes, nearness to a huge market, or plentiful supply of power and skilled manpower. Therefore, much of the settlement within the zone of primary dominance, or direct participation, may appear to be a direct product of the rise and growth of the metropolis. Growth of this type has been frequently termed "suburban" or "satellite" growth.

Outside the primary zone the hinterland populations must depend upon hinterland cities for many services, even though those services may be produced in the metropolis, or accumulated in the metropolis and distributed through the hinterland city. Such cities must then stand between the metropolis and the remainder of the hinterland. To the extent that there is this change from primary to secondary division of labor in the 35-64 mile zone, it is not surprising to find there a concentration of urban populations. Such cities could be regarded as "access cities" or cities which facilitate a division of labor between the hinterland and the metropolis. From each hinterland city a small "fan" of highway routes spreads out to provide access to more distant areas. While there is no absolute necessity that all such access cities be located at any one given distance from the metropolis, it could reasonably be anticipated that cities located just outside the ring of direct metropolitan influence, yet sufficiently close to the metropolis to benefit from its facilities, would prove to be favorable points for the distribution of needed services to the hinterland, for collecting the products of the hinterland, and for engaging in a division of labor with the metropolis. The exact location of such cities could depend upon several factors. The transportation era in which the central city rose to dominance may be one explanation of why these access cities lie closer to class A and B centers than to class C and D centers.

It may be that certain of the hinterland cities in the 35-44 and the 45-64 mile zones have sprung up solely for the purpose of acting as intermediaries, or interchangers, between the metropolis and the most distant parts of the hinterland, leaving the suburbanization movement to spread out from the metropolis later and fill in the vacancies between these outposts and the metropolis. The relatively smaller extent of this leveling off in the larger metropolitan communities may be due to the fact that the outward flow of population from these centers has not only reached the hinterland access cities, but has engulfed and passed beyond them. Such a pattern of development would adequately explain the "leveling off" of the habitation ratios at the intermediate distances.

9. Up to this point little has been said about the size of the hinterland city as a variable in metropolitan structure. The fact that the habitation ratios for the relatively few large hinterland cities of 10,000 or more inhabitants are higher than those for the more numerous smaller hinterland cities has led to the conclusion that the large hinterland cities play a more important role in the total structure. Yet within the framework of Table 7-4 few conclusions can be made about patterns of city size, for the reason that these tables do not take into account the fact that cities are interrelated. One of the basic principles of city study established in Chapter One was that studies of urbanism must recognize that cities are not isolated events of nature. In this section each size group of cities has

been examined as an independent set of observations. The next section will attempt to establish a research frame of reference for dealing with hinterland cities as interrelated events.

IV

The Scope of Subdominance of Hinterland Cities

As an aid to an understanding of the nucleation of the hinterland population about hinterland cities, and of the part which size of a hinterland city plays in the organizing of activities of the population within the metropolitan milieu, this section undertakes to measure the average amount of land area and population over which hinterland cities of each size exercise their subdominance, and to show how distance from the metropolis, sector type, and size of the metropolis alters the scope of this subdominance. Approximate answers to the following questions will be formulated:

Over how many square miles of land area and over how much population is a city of a given size subdominant? Does this amount vary with distance from the metropolis, sector type, and size of the metropolis?

These questions will be asked for each of four size groups of hinterland cities.

Precise answers to the above questions are beyond the scope of this study, since they would require that the functional boundaries between all hinterland cities be established, that the land area and population within those boundaries be measured, and that an average be taken for each size group of hinterland cities. Many indexes for areas about each individual city would have to be employed in the process of arriving at a precise determination of the boundaries of the area in which each city is the principal center for shopping, recreation, marketing, employment, education, finance, news, and other services and activities.

If such a precise study were undertaken, however, it soon would uncover the fact that no one center dominates all activities. Village centers would be found to supply a principal share of standard sustenance items to their residents and to residents in small adjacent areas, but would be found to provide a relatively small proportion of specialized goods and services. Larger hinterland cities, or in some cases even the metropolis, are the principal, and sometimes the only, sources of certain of the more specialized goods and services. Many market studies of consumer buying habits and of the trade structure of shopping centers and suburban centers have demonstrated this fact.[2] Stated in another way, each hinterland city may be expected to have not one area of subdominance, but several areas of subdominance, depending upon the type of function under examination. A small community could provide the residents in its immediate vicinity with groceries and work clothing; a larger place could provide the residents in its immediate vicinity with groceries and work clothing, and also furnish style clothing and household furnishings to residents of a much wider area. In this case the larger center would have two areas of subdominance — one corresponding to that of the smaller center, and another to provide for the specialized services which the smaller center lacked. An even larger place might have three, four, or even more areas of subdominance taking care of functions which centers smaller than itself also provide, and still have an added area for which it would be the sole or principal source in the area. Thus, two hinterland centers of unequal size may compete with each other for the privilege of providing the hinterland with services which they both offer. In the case of services which only one of them provides, the smaller center tends to be dependent upon the larger, and lies within its area of subdominance.

If it is assumed that the over-all size of the city, broadly construed, is an index of the number and degree of specialization of functions performed by the city and, consequently, that the entire hinterland area is blanketed with the subdominance of cities of each size class independently of those of other size classes, an approximate average area of subdominance may be computed for each size group of hinterland city by means of dividing the total hinterland area by the total number of cities of each size. Thus, if one metropolitan community contains 1,000 square miles of land area, and if there are 10 cities of a given size located within it, the above assumptions would lead to an estimate that each hinterland city claims one-tenth, or 100 square miles, of the land area as its area of subdominance. A similar procedure, using the total population rather than the land area, will yield an estimate of the average number of people under the subdominance of the hinterland city of a given size.[3]

In making such estimates concerning the average land area and population included in the area of subdominance of each size of hinterland city, recognition must be given to the principle, described earlier, that larger cities are subdominant over smaller ones only for the services which the smaller centers cannot provide. The average hinterland for the very largest cities will consist of the total area (or population) divided by the total number of cities of that class. The average hinterland for the next smaller class will consist of the total area (or population) minus the area (or population) of the largest cities, divided by the sum of both groups of cities. This procedure admits no potential subdominance by the smaller cities over the area and population of the larger cities, and recognizes the fact that the larger city provides, to a more restricted area, the same services as does the smaller city. The estimated area of subdominance for the very smallest size of city would consist therefore, of all the land area lying outside cities larger than itself divided by all the cities of all sizes in the hinterland. An estimate on any other basis would assume implicitly that cities of various sizes perform no duplicate functions and are completely independent of each other. The following charts and tables present the quasi-average amount of land area and population which is under the influence of hinterland cities of the different size classes. To illustrate the size of the area over which cities of each size are subdominant the land area, in square miles, is expressed as the estimated radius of influence which would be found if the area of subdominance of each hinterland city were circular.

A. The Land Area Under the Subdominance of Hinterland Cities of Each Size Group. (Table 7-5, Chart 7-2).

2. For example, see Richard P. Doherty, Trends in Retail Trade and Consumer Buying Habits in the Metropolitan Boston Retail Area, Boston University Bureau of Business Research (Boston College of Business Administration, 1941) and T. Lynn Smith, Farm Trade Centers in Louisiana 1901 to 1931, Louisiana State University Agricultural Experiment Station, Bulletin No. 234, 1933. See also the publications to which reference was made in Chapter Two.

3. As indicated above, such a procedure yields only an estimate of the "true" average size of hinterland which one would obtain if he actually divided the total hinterland into areas of subdominance of each of the hinterland cities and took an average of the actual areas. Neither the estimated average nor the true average is reliable except to the extent that the variation of the individual areas is relatively small. In the absence of better information, the estimates made here are useful chiefly for their ability to show the magnitude of the values which would be expected if the more refined process were carried out. The term "quasi-average" will be used in referring to the estimates of the true averages.

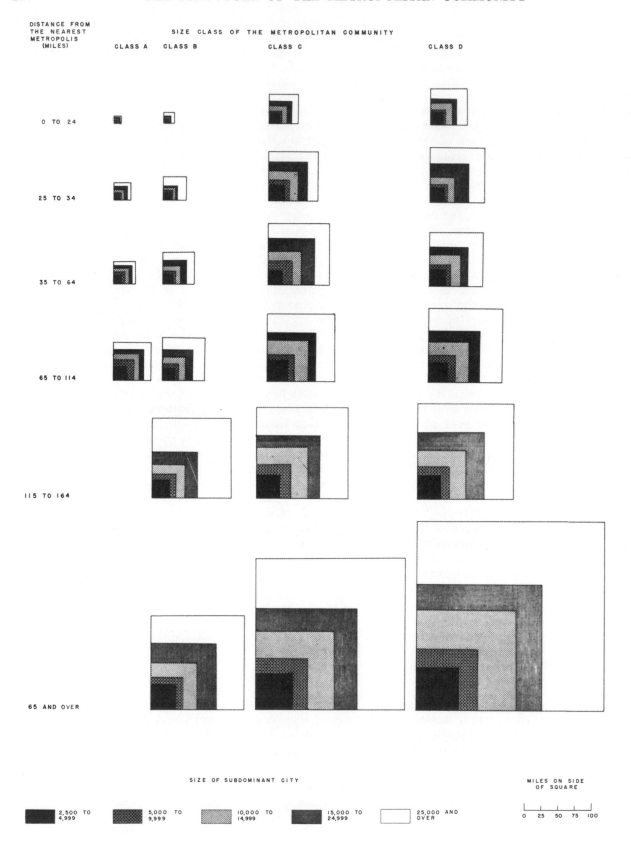

CHART 7-2 ESTIMATED LAND AREA UNDER THE SUBDOMINANCE OF HINTERLAND CITIES OF EACH SIZE BY SIZE CLASS OF THE METROPOLITAN COMMUNITY AND DISTANCE FROM THE NEAREST METROPOLIS

Table 7-5 reports the estimated radius, in miles, of influence of hinterland cities, according to their sizes, for each distance zone of each size of metropolitan center.[4] Chart 7-2 illustrates, in the form of a series of concentric squares, the actual area of estimated subdominance. This chart not only gives a visual impression of the total amount of area over which each size of city exerts its influence, but also indicates the proportion of that area which each city influences jointly with smaller cities.

1. The radius of influence of a hinterland city increases steadily with: (a) its own size, (b) its distance from the metropolis, and (c) the size of the metropolis. The minimum radius of influence for each size group of hinterland cities is found invariably in the 0-24 mile zone of the class A metropolitan communities. The maximum radii are found, in every case, in the outermost zone of the class D metropolitan communities. The following minimum and maximum values for hinterland cities of each size emphasize the fact that the hinterland city's scope of influence over its surrounding area varies greatly with its metropolitan location:

Size of hinterland city	Minimum radius (miles)	Maximum radius (miles)
2,500- 4,999	3	35
5,000- 9,999	3	50
10,000-14,999	4	81
15,000-24,999	5	102
25,000-49,999	6	154

In the inner zones of class A metropolitan communities, all hinterland cities of all sizes are almost devoid of an area of subdominance. In the class D communities all hinterland cities at all distances have considerable radii of influence.

2. The functional position of the rural population with respect to its hinterland cities may also be inferred from Table 7-5. In a class A metropolitan community, even the areas which are most inaccessible to the large hinterland cities are, on an average, only about 30 minutes distant from such centers via automobile, and a city of at least 2,500 population may be reached in less than half that time. In a class B metropolitan community the points which are most remote from urban influence are still only about 45 minutes journey from a hinterland city, and a city of 25,000 inhabitants may be reached within two hours. In the most inaccessible areas in the class D metropolitan communities, by way of contrast, a journey of more than an hour is required to reach any urban place, and four

and one-half hours are required to reach a city of 25,000 or more inhabitants. Thus, the pattern by which the hinterland is nucleated is far from being identical in all parts of the hinterland. The nearer one approaches to a central city, the more plentiful and easily accessible subdominant cities become. The further from the metropolis one goes, the more difficult it becomes to reach a hinterland city of any size, and the more access to a hinterland city of 25,000 or more inhabitants begins to assume the proportions of a full day's undertaking. It will be observed, however, that from no zone in the hinterland is the average distance to a major hinterland city greater than one day's travel (round trip), nor is it greater to a city of any size than one hour's travel. With the aid of present modes of transportation, the population of the United States can live at almost any point in the hinterland and commute to a city for work, or to obtain needed services, on an almost casual basis. Those specialized services which formerly were limited to the larger hinterland cities now may be enjoyed on an equal basis by residents of all except a very few areas. The number and distribution of hinterland cities is such that almost the entire population of the United States is able, on a daily basis, to reach and be reached by large urban centers.

3. From this evidence it may be inferred that the metropolitan location of hinterland cities, and of the rural population, will unavoidably influence their functioning. A city of 25,000 inhabitants, lying within 25 miles of a class A metropolitan center and dominating the area within 6 miles of itself, may be expected to differ both in internal organization and functioning from a city of the same size lying 400 miles from a class D metropolis and being the closest source of specialized goods and services for the population within a radius of 145 miles. The first instance is one of a compact unit organized within confined, and probably more homogeneous, circumstances. In the second, the hinterland unit is large and will involve, almost necessarily, a variety of external circumstances. Similarly, the integration of the activities of the dispersed rural populations with their nearest hinterland cities cannot be expected to be all of one pattern, since it will vary considerably with the degree of access and with the characteristics of those hinterland cities. The manner in which the populations, both urban and rural, of the individual hinterland areas, are organized and distributed to obtain a livelihood undoubtedly varies from one part of the metropolitan community to another according to the area which must be organized and

---

4. The "radius of influence" is obtained by expressing the area of subdominance, computed as described above, in the following form: Radius = $\sqrt{\dfrac{Area.}{\pi}}$

Table 7-5

Estimated radius of subdominance of hinterland cities of each size, classified by size class of metropolitan community and distance from nearest metropolis. United States, 1940.

Size class and distance zone (miles)	Size of hinterland city				
	2,500–4,999	5,000–9,999	10,000–14,999	15,000–24,999	25,000–49,999
	Estimated radius in miles[a]				
Class A					
0–24	3	3	4	5	6
25–34	5	6	9	11	14
35–64	7	10	13	15	18
65–114	11	17	21	26	31
115–164	b)	-	-	-	-
165–over	b)	b)	-	-	-
Class B					
0–24	4	4	5	6	9
25–34	6	8	10	12	19
35–64	9	11	15	20	26
65–114	10	14	19	26	35
115–164	15	20	27	38	65
165–over	21	27	38	54	77
Class C					
0–24	9	10	15	19	24
25–34	13	17	24	32	40
35–64	11	19	27	38	50
65–114	17	22	33	40	55
115–164	19	28	42	51	74
165–over	30	43	64	83	123
Class D					
0–24	10	13	18	21	30
25–34	12	15	20	31	44
35–64	14	18	25	31	43
65–114	16	22	32	42	60
115–164	19	26	39	54	78
165–over	35	50	81	102	154

a) Radius = $\sqrt{\dfrac{\text{Area}}{\pi}}$, area being as estimated in Table 7-9 of this study.

b) Area in eastern California and western Arizona and Nevada arbitrarily excluded as being unrepresentative of average hinterland area.

Source: Sixteenth Census of the United States. Compiled from Population, Vol.I, State tables 3 and 5; Areas of the United States, 1940, tables 2, 3, and 4.

integrated to support a hinterland city of a given size. A detailed description of some of these functional variations will constitute the subject matter of Part III of this study.

B. The Population Under the Subdominance of Hinterland Cities of Each Size Group. (Table 7-6)

1. Equally as important as the land area lying within the area of subdominance of a hinterland city, is the number of inhabitants to be found there. From Table 7-6 it is evident that the average number of people served by a given hinterland city is dependent upon the position of the city in the metropolitan community. A city of 2,500-4,999 inhabitants, lying within 25 miles of a class A metropolis, is in a position to serve only an estimated 4,200 people residing outside its borders, whereas the same size city, when located in a class D metropolitan community 165 or more miles from a metropolis, is able to serve an average of 22,200, or more than five times as many people. In the 0-24 mile zone of class A and B metropolitan communities, the hinterland city is subdominant over a population outside its own borders which is its own size or only slightly larger. With decreasing size of metropolis, and increasing distance, the hinterland city serves an increasingly large population which may be four, eight, or in some instances 10 or 11 times the population of the city itself.

2. Table 7-6 may be interpreted as a series of estimates concerning the actual size of the functional units of which the hinterland is composed. The presence of a city of 10,000 inhabitants appears to be much less of an "uncaused cause" when it is regarded as the focal point and source of services for an estimated 15,000-145,000 inhabitants in its immediate environs, and when it is recognized that the number of inhabitants potentially integrated with the activities of the city varies with the distance from a metropolis of a given size.

3. If the tabulations of Table 7-5 and Table 7-6 are examined together, the distribution of the hinterland population can be much more clearly envisaged. Thus, cities of 10,000-14,999 inhabitants, lying 35-64 miles from a class A metropolitan center, have, on the average, 56,600 hinterland inhabitants living within a radius of 13 miles, whereas a unit of the same city-size located at the same distance from a class C metropolitan community, has an average of 83,500 inhabitants within 27 miles of itself. Together, the two types of information characterize the functional base of hinterland cities in terms of the estimated radius of their influence, and in terms of the estimated population under that influence. This description may be carried even further by observing that, within the 27 mile radius of the average city noted above belong-

ing to the class C metropolitan communities, for example, there are two cities of 5,000-9,999 inhabitants, each serving an estimated 40,300 inhabitants, and about six cities of 2,500-4,999 inhabitants, each serving an estimated 12,700 inhabitants. The populations living in this area are within the radius simultaneously of three hinterland cities which are, at an average maximum, 27, 19, and 11 miles distant, respectively.

C. Sector Type and the Scope of Subdominance in Hinterland Cities. (Tables 7-7 and 7-8)

In Tables 7-7 and 7-8 the estimated radius of influence of hinterland cities of each size, and the estimated population lying within that radius, are reported for each type of sector. The procedure followed in computing these values is the same as that followed for Tables 7-5 and 7-6. These tables serve two useful functions: (a) They show that the previous estimates are fairly stable, in that estimates of the same general magnitude result when the data are submitted to this further subdivision, and (b) They show a consistent set of differences between sector types. It will be remembered that in Section IV, dealing with the habitation ratios, it was difficult to discern any consistent set of differences between the intermetropolitan and the local sectors in the intensity with which the hinterland was occupied by the smaller sizes of cities. It was noted there that such differences as existed tended to be hidden by the substitution of smaller for larger cities in the local sectors, and by the apparent mutual influence of cities.

1. Radius of Influence

a. Because of the greater frequency of their occurrence, the average radius of influence of all sizes of cities in the subdominant sectors is shorter than in either of the other sector types. The exceptions to this general rule occur at those points which have been described as zones of transition from direct to indirect metropolitan influence, and at the near areas in the metropolitan sectors which have been noted for their intense concentration.

b. While it is true that some local sectors have concentrations of very small cities which are equally as high as, or even higher than, those of the corresponding intermetropolitan sectors (evidenced here by a smaller quasi-average radius), the cumulative effect, with increasing size of city, is to overbalance this concentration in favor of intermetropolitan sectors. Thus, although intermetropolitan sectors may not have a consistently higher habitation ratio in every size group of smaller hinterland cities considered independently, the fact that these sectors contain major hinterland cities in addition to an equal or sometimes

Table 7-6

Estimated population under the subdominance of hinterland cities of each size, classified by size class of metropolitan community and distance from the nearest metropolis. United States, 1940.

Size class and distance zone (miles)	Size of hinterland city				
	2,500–4,999	5,000–9,999	10,000–14,999	15,000–24,999	25,000–49,999
	Estimated population in thousands of inhabitants				
Class A					
0-24[a]	4.2	6.7	15.8	31.6	56.2
25-34	7.7	16.8	37.6	67.4	125.7
35-64	12.5	27.1	56.6	82.3	118.0
65-114	13.4	34.9	60.8	93.3	149.4
115-164	b)	-	-	-	-
165-over	b)	b)	-	-	-
Class B					
0-24[a]	6.3	9.2	18.0	30.2	80.5
25-34	8.9	17.2	30.0	43.5	150.7
35-64	14.1	25.1	50.5	101.6	185.8
65-114	13.3	27.1	60.9	117.5	234.5
115-164	18.4	35.5	75.3	152.6	497.5
165-over	22.3	37.9	86.1	184.3	387.0
Class C					
0-24[a]	18.6	29.1	63.3	110.1	187.6
25-34	19.4	33.0	76.5	143.2	240.8
35-64	12.7	40.3	83.5	174.6	318.6
65-114	22.8	42.5	105.5	155.2	312.4
115-164	25.9	58.4	137.7	216.6	477.1
165-over	28.4	61.2	145.6	252.9	578.4
Class D					
0-24[a]	16.0	27.4	62.5	92.0	196.7
25-34	16.2	27.8	56.4	152.7	323.1
35-64	15.9	29.7	68.5	111.1	226.8
65-114	19.0	41.9	96.6	166.4	366.7
115-164	23.5	46.9	111.9	221.3	479.3
165-over	22.2	48.6	139.1	228.4	536.0

a) Includes population residing outside of metropolis in counties containing central cities.
b) Area in eastern California and western Nevada and Arizona arbitrarily excluded as being unrepresentative of average hinterland area.

Source: Sixteenth census of the United States. Compiled from Population, Vol.I, State tables 3 and 5.

Table 7-7

Estimated radius of subdominance of hinterland cities of each size, classified by type of sector, size class of metropolitan community, and distance from the nearest metropolis. United States, 1940. (Radius in miles)

SIZE CLASS OF METROPOLITAN COMMUNITY AND SIZE OF HINTERLAND CITY

Class A

Distance zone (miles)	2,500-4,999	5,000-9,999	10,000-14,999	15,000-24,999	25,000-over
Intermetropolitan					
25-34	4	5	7	10	11
35-64	6	9	13	14	15
65-114	12	15	19	23	31
115-164	a)	a)	a)	a)	a)
165-over	a)	a)	a)	a)	a)
Subdominant					
25-34	7	9	12	15	21
35-64	8	10	12	14	16
65-114	6	11	13	13	13
115-164	a)	a)	a)	a)	a)
165-over	a)	a)	a)	a)	a)
Local[b]					
25-34	7	10	11	14	-
35-64	7	11	16	24	-
65-114	12	29	-	-	-
115-164	a)	a)	a)	a)	a)
165-over	a)	a)	a)	a)	-

Class B

Distance zone (miles)	2,500-4,999	5,000-9,999	10,000-14,999	15,000-24,999	25,000-over
Intermetropolitan					
25-34	6	8	10	12	22
35-64	8	10	14	19	26
65-114	10	13	19	25	31
115-164	14	18	25	34	-
165-over	13	16	25	-	-
Subdominant					
25-34	5	6	8	8	11
35-64	9	11	13	16	17
65-114	8	9	11	16	24
115-164	14	18	26	35	40
165-over	22	27	38	49	69
Local[b]					
25-34	7	13	16	19	-
35-64	10	13	18	37	-
65-114	13	20	37	52	-
115-164	18	45	45	-	-
165-over	25	44	-	-	-

Class C

Distance zone (miles)	2,500-4,999	5,000-9,999	10,000-14,999	15,000-24,999	25,000-over
Intermetropolitan					
25-34	14	16	25	31	50
35-64	13	17	21	30	37
65-114	16	21	31	36	47
115-164	18	27	38	45	77
165-over	29	40	60	83	113
Subdominant					
25-34	9	9	11	12	12
35-64	13	23	52	52	52
65-114	13	19	28	29	41
115-164	19	26	36	41	45
165-over	20	29	36	36	54
Local[b]					
25-34	14	23	37	-	-
35-64	17	26	44	63	-
65-114	20	26	44	70	-
115-164	23	32	71	-	-
165-over	37	54	94	176	-

Class D

Distance zone (miles)	2,500-4,999	5,000-9,999	10,000-14,000	15,000-24,999	25,000-over
Intermetropolitan					
25-34	14	17	21	30	44
35-64	12	16	23	28	36
65-114	16	22	32	41	54
115-164	20	27	37	45	66
165-over	37	53	78	101	151
Subdominant					
25-34	10	11	13	25	25
35-64	14	19	21	22	27
65-114	14	20	29	29	34
115-164	16	22	28	40	56
165-over	21	27	44	44	49
Local[b]					
25-34	9	12	22	38	-
35-64	16	20	36	57	-
65-114	16	23	35	55	-
115-164	20	28	58	138	-
165-over	35	52	107	151	-

a) Area in eastern California and western Arizona and Nevada arbitrarily excluded as being unrepresentative of average hinterland area.

b) By definition there are no cities of 25,000 or more inhabitants at distances greater than 10 miles from the metropolis in local sectors.

Source: Sixteenth Census of the United States. Compiled from Population, Vol.I, State tables 3 and 5; Areas of the United States, 1940, tables 2, 3, and 4.

greater complement of smaller cities, means that the smaller hinterland city in the intermetropolitan sectors must be dominant over a much smaller area than is the case for the same size city in the local sector. In other words, the larger cities in the intermetropolitan sectors appropriate within their spheres of influence land area which, in a local sector, would be under the influence of a smaller size city. The net effect, of course, is to limit the scope of influence of the smaller size city in the intermetropolitan sector.

c. While the actual values reported in these tables for each size of city will not necessarily be an estimate for any single community, and since they implicitly assume that the distances and areas apply only within the sector type and distance zone (whereas in actual fact they frequently cut across both), such values must of necessity, nevertheless, approach the average values which would be obtained for a number of cities of equal size if functional boundaries were drawn between them, and hence also they must change with sector type in the same direction in which the averages obtained by actual functional delimitation would change. For this reason, the actual values of the tables may be of guidance to sociologists, market analysts, and others interested in trading and shopping areas and other aspects of urban influence. Their meaningfulness is also enhanced when it is remembered that they measure the average maximum distance which must be traveled along a given sector type to reach a town of the specified size or larger.

2. Population

The estimated average population lying within the radius of subdominance of each size of hinterland city follows the same general sector type pattern as does the land area.

a. The greater the frequency of occurrence of cities, the smaller is the average population which lies within the scope of influence of each. Thus, the cities in subdominant sectors have a smaller quasi-average population lying in their area of subdominance than have the cities in the other two types of sectors.

b. The total urban hierarchy in the intermetropolitan sectors permits a smaller-size city to have fewer inhabitants in its area of subdominance than is the case in the urban structure of local sectors. As with land area, the presence and functioning of the larger hinterland cities in the intermetropolitan sectors tend to overweigh the fact that the habitation ratios for cities of 2,500-4,999 are occasionally higher in the local than in the intermetropolitan sectors. Hence, the city of 5,000 to 25,000 inhabitants in the intermetropolitan sector not only has a smaller average radius of influence; it also

is subdominant over a smaller hinterland population than are cities of the same size in local sectors. A functional interpretation of this phenomenon could be that a larger population is required to support a city of this size in a local sector than in intermetropolitan or subdominant sectors.

c. The individual population values reported in these tables are, like the land area (radius) values, only estimated averages, and give at times numbers which seem impossibly high (particularly for the larger hinterland cities). If the precise meaning of these values is kept in mind — that one city of a stated size, or larger, is present in the indicated portion of the hinterland for each quantity of population stated — the inference that each and every hinterland city will approximate this "quasi-average" will be avoided. There are many hinterland areas which contain no cities at all of a certain size, and others which contain more than one such city. The judgment that these statements of probability are an estimate of the average amount of population contiguous to the hinterland city and within its sphere of influence is much more justified for the smaller sizes of hinterland cities, since one or more cities of this size is present in almost every distance zone and sector type of each metropolitan community, than it is for the larger hinterland cities where land area containing no city of a certain size is more frequently combined with land area which does contain such a city in order to compute the "quasi-average."

V

Summary

1. The metropolitan communities with central cities of 500,000 or more inhabitants have more hinterland cities and relatively larger hinterland cities in all zones and sector types than have the metropolitan communities with central cities of less than 500,000 inhabitants. There is a much more sparse distribution of cities in the metropolitan communities containing small central cities than in those containing large central cities.

2. A comparison of the frequencies with which the populations of various sizes of hinterland cities inhabit the various parts of the hinterland shows that, while the smaller cities are more numerous, they have fewer inhabitants per 100 square miles of hinterland than have the large sizes of hinterland cities. This tends to be true for all distances and for all sizes of metropolitan centers. It is interpreted as indicating the major importance of the larger outlying centers in the organization of

Table 7-8

Estimated population under the subdominance of cities of each size, classified by type of sector, size class of metropolitan community, and distance from the nearest metropolis. United States, 1940. (Population in thousands)

SIZE CLASS OF METROPOLITAN COMMUNITY AND SIZE OF HINTERLAND CITY

Class A [a]

Distance zone (miles)	2,500– 4,999	5,000– 9,999	10,000– 14,999	15,000– 24,999	25,000– over
Intermetropolitan					
25-34	5.5	12.7	30.5	61.4	91.2
35-64	11.0	25.0	55.4	67.3	86.2
65-114	14.6	27.1	42.9	74.6	144.7
115-164	a)	a)	a)	a)	a)
165-over	a)	a)	a)	a)	a)
Subdominant					
25-34	21.3	36.1	64.4	102.6	228.8
35-64	13.2	23.5	39.3	61.8	75.5
65-114	6.1	24.9	41.4	41.4	41.4
115-164	a)	a)	a)	a)	a)
165-over	a)	a)	a)	a)	a)
Local [b]					
25-34	12.6	28.8	64.9	64.9	–
35-64	15.7	36.2	85.0	215.2	–
65-114	16.1	112.2	-	-	a)
115-164	a)	a)	a)	a)	a)
165-over	a)	a)	a)	a)	a)

Class B

Distance zone (miles)	2,500– 4,999	5,000– 9,999	10,000– 14,999	15,000– 24,999	25,000– over
Intermetropolitan					
25-34	8.9	17.0	27.6	43.7	187.9
35-64	14.1	25.0	51.4	99.9	207.2
65-114	11.0	25.8	62.1	112.2	177.0
115-164	15.7	30.3	63.2	123.3	–
165-over	13.8	24.1	68.2	–	–
Subdominant					
25-34	10.8	13.8	29.8	35.6	78.0
35-64	13.7	22.9	38.9	58.5	70.0
65-114	10.8	15.6	26.2	60.0	160.0
115-164	20.3	32.9	78.2	145.0	199.9
165-over	24.1	38.8	80.2	142.1	302.6
Local [b]					
25-34	6.6	29.7	42.0	69.6	–
35-64	14.4	28.2	65.1	288.3	–
65-114	21.8	52.5	201.8	416.6	–
115-164	24.4	164.3	164.3	–	–
165-over	27.5	89.9	–	–	–

Class C

Distance zone (miles)	2,500– 4,999	5,000– 9,999	10,000– 14,999	15,000– 24,999	25,000– over
Intermetropolitan					
25-34	21.7	31.0	84.1	142.5	385.4
35-64	18.1	32.6	57.7	127.7	206.7
65-114	23.0	40.9	97.2	136.0	236.0
115-164	24.0	58.0	119.4	172.4	557.5
165-over	29.7	59.4	144.4	286.1	539.3
Subdominant					
25-34	7.4	9.7	14.4	22.8	22.8
35-64	19.6	66.6	358.3	358.3	358.3
65-114	16.9	37.2	86.6	99.0	214.9
115-164	30.4	62.2	123.2	168.8	206.7
165-over	31.1	72.7	116.8	116.8	285.8
Local [b]					
25-34	20.4	64.1	170.5	-	–
35-64	22.3	56.7	183.6	379.5	–
65-114	26.7	50.5	153.9	402.0	–
115-164	27.1	55.8	304.6	–	–
165-over	24.0	57.6	186.4	683.1	–

Class D

Distance zone (miles)	2,500– 4,999	5,000– 9,999	10,000– 14,999	15,000– 24,999	25,000– over
Intermetropolitan					
25-34	21.6	34.6	56.3	131.1	250.3
35-64	13.3	25.4	56.4	90.4	166.5
65-114	18.5	41.6	91.1	153.9	283.6
115-164	21.8	40.6	82.4	128.2	296.5
165-over	20.8	46.4	110.0	191.2	452.4
Subdominant					
25-34	11.7	17.7	23.8	132.0	132.0
35-64	20.2	43.8	52.3	58.3	103.0
65-114	18.6	44.6	100.2	100.2	144.8
115-164	24.4	48.1	85.1	182.0	380.4
165-over	30.8	52.0	146.6	146.6	187.4
Local [b]					
25-34	10.0	20.1	78.4	260.0	–
35-64	20.4	34.6	122.8	325.2	–
65-114	19.8	41.3	104.6	264.3	–
115-164	25.5	56.2	255.6	–	–
165-over	22.4	51.8	243.4	497.8	–

a) Area in eastern California and western Arizona and Nevada arbitrarily excluded as being unrepresentative of average hinterland area.

b) By definition there are no cities of 25,000 or more inhabitants at distances greater than 10 miles from the metropolis in local sectors.

Source: Sixteenth Census of the United States. Compiled from Population, Vol.I, State tables 3 and 5.

the hinterland. Each size class of city tends to follow the distance and sector type pattern which has been outlined in the preceding chapters.

3. The average land area and population lying within the estimated radius of influence of the hinterland city varies consistently with change in the size of the hinterland city itself, the size of the metropolis, and the distance from the metropolis by sector type. With each increase in size of hinterland city, when these last three variables are held constant, a larger land area and population is found to lie within the estimated radius of subdominance. For any given size of hinterland city the area of subdominance tends to decrease, and the population in that area tends to be smaller, as the size of the metropolis increases. For any given size of hinterland city, both the land area and the population lying within the estimated radius of subdominance tend to increase with increasing distance from all sizes of metropolises.

CHAPTER EIGHT

THE STRUCTURE OF THE RURAL-NONFARM AND OF THE RURAL-FARM POPULATIONS IN THE UNITED STATES

I

Introduction

The aim of this chapter is to determine:

a. The effect which the hinterland city of each size appears to have upon the distribution of the rural populations. Hence, the size of the subdominant unit becomes a major variable in the analysis of this chapter, supplementing the findings in Section IV of the preceding chapter.

b. Whether the metropolitan pattern, which has already been established for each of the rural populations, is due entirely to the effect of hinterland cities of varying sizes upon the rural populations, or whether the metropolitan pattern persists even when the effect of the hinterland cities is eliminated.

Since it is impossible to treat the aggregates of the rural-nonfarm and rural-farm populations in the same manner as cities were treated, that is, as individual units, the expedient of dealing with each of these types of rural populations in terms of county units has been adopted. The effect of the

ported separately for the purpose of comparison with all of the other variables. Except for this peculiarity of the data, the procedure is essentially the same as that which has been followed previously.

II

Description of the Land Area and Rural Population of the Hinterland. County Units Classified by Size of Largest City Contained.

A. The Number of County Units Containing Cities of Each Size, and Their Distribution Among the Sizes of Metropolitan Communities.
1. Of the 3,098 units of area in the United States which were defined as counties in 1940, only 3,061 contain rural populations. The remaining 37 units are considered to be completely urban, and have been included with the urban population. Of the units which contain rural population, 61 are counties which also contain central cities (central counties) and 3,000 are counties which do not contain a central city (hinterland counties).[2]
2. The great majority of the counties of the United States which contain rural populations do not contain sizeable hinterland cities:

41.0	percent contain no city or urban place							
20.7	"	"	a largest city of			2,500 to	4,999
16.6	"	"	"	"	"	"	5,000 to	9,999
12.1	"	"	"	"	"	"	10,000 to	24,999
4.4	"	"	"	"	"	"	25,000 to	49,999
3.2	"	"	"	"	"	"	50,000 or over	
2.0	"	"	"	central city				
100.0								

hinterland city upon these county units is studied by means of classifying the counties on the basis of the size of the largest city each contained.[1]

The majority of the central cities themselves are located within county units which also contain rural-nonfarm and rural-farm populations; therefore, one category of the "largest city contained" continuum will be "central counties," or counties containing central cities. Since units cannot have distance values or sector types, they must be re-

Thus, more than two-fifths of the hinterland county units are completely rural, and an additional one-fifth contain only cities of less than 5,000 inhabitants. About one county in 13 contains a major hinterland city of 25,000 or more inhabitants, and only one in 50 contains a central city.

B. The Distribution of Land Area and Rural Population by Size of Largest City Contained and Size Class of Metropolitan Community (Table 8-1).

---

1. For a description of the procedure, see Chapter Two, Section IV.
2. Some of the central cities are themselves counties. The counties surrounding such city-counties were not classified as "counties containing central cities."

1. The class A and B metropolitan communities have a much smaller proportion of land area which is classified as containing no city, or a very small city, than have the class C and D metropolitan communities. Almost two-thirds of the land area in the class C and D metropolitan communities falls in one or the other of these classifications. On the other hand, a much larger proportion of the land area is classified as containing a city of 10,000 or more inhabitants in the class A and B metropolitan communities than in the class C and D.

2. In all metropolitan communities, the areas which contain no cities also contain very small proportions of the rural-nonfarm and the rural-farm populations. The fact that both of the rural populations seem to shun county units which contain no

er proportion lies more than 165 miles from the metropolis. Hence, the smaller the size of the largest city contained in a county, the greater is the tendency for that county to be located at a considerable distance from the metropolis. The larger the size of the largest city contained, the greater the tendency becomes for the county in which it is contained to be located at a relatively short distance from the metropolis. Compare the distance distributions of the land area of counties which contain no city, for example, with the corresponding distribution of those whose largest city is only 2,500 to 4,999 inhabitants, and then compare both of these distributions with the distance distributions of counties whose largest city is 50,000 or more inhabitants:

| | Size of Largest City | | |
Distance	No city	2,500-4,999	50,000 & over
0- 64	6.9	14.7	35.6
65-164	29.5	39.1	33.7
165-over	63.6	46.3	30.5
Total	100.0	100.0	100.0

cities, or very small cities, can be verified by a comparison of the percentage distributions of land and population for counties classified according to size of largest city contained. The amount of this preference for a location in counties containing the larger centers can be summarized by a coefficient of dissimilarity between land area and each of the populations.

| | Coefficient of Dissimilarity | | | |
Population	A	B	C	D
Rural-nonfarm	46.6	24.7	22.1	25.4
Rural-farm	34.5	7.6	10.9	13.5

From the above coefficients of dissimilarity it may be inferred that the rural-nonfarm and the rural-farm populations do not occupy the hinterland without reference to near-by hinterland cities and to the sizes of those cities.

C. Distance from the Metropolis and Size of Largest City Contained (Table 8-2).
1. The county areas containing no hinterland cities tend to be located in the most remote portions of the hinterland. Only 6.9 percent of the land area of all such counties lies within 65 miles of a metropolis, and 63.6 percent of this type of area lies more than 165 miles from a metropolis.
2. As the size of the largest city contained increases, an increasing proportion of the land area lies within 65 miles of the metropolis, and a small-

D. Type of Sector and Size of Largest City Contained (Table 8-3)
A higher proportion of the land area of those counties which contain no urban place is located in local sectors than is the case in counties which contain a city. With increasing size of largest city contained, a decreasing proportion of land area lies in local sectors. Thus, the land areas of the United States which contain no city whatever tend to be located at great distances from metropolitan centers, in sectors which contain neither a major hinterland city nor an intermetropolitan thoroughfare. Conversely, the larger the size of the city which a county unit supports, the greater is the tendency for that county unit to be located near the metropolis, or at an intermediate distance, and to be either in an intermetropolitan or a subdominant sector.[3]

III

The Intensity with which the Rural-nonfarm
Population Occupies the Land,
by Subdominance Groups

A. Rural-nonfarm Population per 100 Square Miles of Rural Land Area. (Chart 8-1)
Chart 8-1 presents the rural-nonfarm habitation ratios for counties classified by the size of the largest city which they contain as well as by distance and size of metropolitan community. As in

---

3. See footnote on page 119.

Table 8-1

Percentage distribution of the rural land area and rural populations of counties classified by size of largest city contained and size class of metropolitan community.
United States, 1940.[a]

Size of largest city contained (thousand inhabitants)	All metropolitan communities	Size class of metropolitan community			
		A	B	C	D
Land Area					
Central counties	1.7	3.6	1.0	1.2	2.0
Hinterland counties					
No city	41.3	21.5	20.8	43.8	43.6
2.5-4.9	20.5	4.4	15.1	20.6	22.3
5.0-9.9	17.5	19.5	22.1	16.1	17.6
10.0-24.9	11.6	6.8	23.1	3.1	9.8
25.0-49.9	5.0	37.9	7.9	3.5	3.1
50.0-over	2.4	6.3	10.0	1.7	1.7
Total	100.0	100.0	100.0	100.0	100.0
Rural-nonfarm population					
Central counties	11.3	16.1	7.8	12.8	10.4
Hinterland counties					
No city	19.6	2.5	8.9	26.7	24.6
2.5-4.9	12.9	2.5	8.4	15.6	16.3
5.0-9.9	16.0	11.9	16.0	16.2	17.2
10.0-24.9	18.5	20.5	27.4	14.2	16.8
25.0-49.9	10.2	19.8	13.1	7.5	8.0
50.0-over	11.5	26.7	18.5	7.1	6.8
Total	100.0	100.0	100.0	100.0	100.0
Rural-farm population					
Central counties	3.3	6.4	2.1	2.7	3.9
Hinterland counties					
No city	29.0	3.6	18.2	32.9	30.0
2.5-4.9	22.0	10.4	13.4	24.0	23.0
5.0-9.9	19.6	17.6	18.8	19.8	19.8
10.0-24.9	15.6	17.1	24.8	13.7	15.0
25.0-49.9	6.0	23.2	10.3	4.1	5.3
50.0-over	4.6	21.7	12.4	2.8	3.0
Total	100.0	100.0	100.0	100.0	100.0

a) Counties containing no rural populations have been excluded. Independent cities
of Virginia were classified as lying in no county.

Source: Sixteenth Census of the United States. Compiled from Population, Vol. I,
State tables 3 and 5; Population, Vol. II, State tables 26 and 27; Areas of
the United States, 1940, Tables 2, 3, and 4.

Table 8-2

Percentage distribution of the rural land area and rural populations of hinterland counties classified by size of largest city contained and distance from the nearest metropolis. United States, 1940.[a)]

Distance zone (miles)	Size of largest city contained (thousand inhabitants)					
	No City	2.5-4.9	5.0-9.9	10.0-24.9	25.0-49.9	50.0-over
	Land area					
0-24	0.5	1.5	1.5	2.5	1.7	6.5
25-34	1.1	2.0	3.1	6.9	4.7	4.4
35-44	1.5	4.4	4.1	4.8	7.2	5.7
45-64	3.8	6.8	9.0	12.5	10.9	19.0
65-114	14.4	21.0	21.4	22.0	22.9	25.3
115-164	15.1	18.1	15.1	18.3	20.2	8.4
165-264	26.9	26.0	24.2	19.5	21.2	16.5
265-464	29.3	16.1	18.5	12.2	11.1	14.0
465-over	7.4	4.2	3.2	1.4	-	-
All zones	100.0	100.0	100.0	100.0	100.0	100.0
	Rural-nonfarm population					
0-24	2.0	6.1	6.4	11.9	12.3	16.8
25-34	4.0	5.4	5.0	13.7	9.9	10.6
35-44	3.7	7.6	5.9	8.7	12.6	10.8
45-64	9.3	11.9	18.2	17.4	13.8	22.3
65-114	26.2	26.0	28.2	25.4	28.4	23.8
115-164	20.8	20.7	14.7	12.2	12.7	6.1
165-264	23.1	17.7	16.7	8.2	6.6	7.5
265-464	9.0	4.1	4.5	2.2	3.8	2.1
465-over	2.0	0.6	0.4	0.2	-	-
All zones	100.0	100.0	100.0	100.0	100.0	100.0
	Rural-farm population					
0-24	1.6	3.1	3.5	5.0	4.1	8.6
25-34	2.5	4.2	5.8	10.1	7.7	5.8
35-44	4.0	5.9	3.9	6.8	10.6	5.6
45-64	8.5	12.9	14.6	16.2	18.4	26.0
65-114	29.7	25.6	32.1	27.3	29.7	27.4
115-164	23.4	25.4	20.4	21.3	19.3	9.1
165-264	22.0	19.3	15.8	10.4	7.0	14.4
265-464	6.4	3.0	3.2	2.4	3.1	3.1
465-over	1.7	0.5	0.6	0.4	-	-
All zones	100.0	100.0	100.0	100.0	100.0	100.0

a) Counties containing central cities and counties containing no rural population have been excluded. The independent cities of Virginia were classified as lying in no county.

Source: Sixteenth Census of the United States, compiled from Population, Vol.I, State tables 3 and 5; Population, Vol.II, State tables 26 and 27; Areas of the United States, 1940, Tables 2, 3, and 4.

Table 8-3

Percentage distributions of the rural land area and rural populations of hinterland counties classified by size of largest city contained and type of sector. United States, 1940.[a]

Type of sector	All sizes	Size of largest city contained (thousand inhabitants)					
		No city	2.5-4.9	5.0-9.9	10.0-24.9	25.0-49.9	50.0-over
		Land area					
Intermetropolitan	56.5	53.3	54.4	59.4	59.7	67.8	66.5
Subdominant	10.3	8.1	9.5	9.0	10.5	27.9	27.6
Local	33.2	38.5	36.1	31.6	29.8	4.3	5.9
All sectors	100.0	100.0	100.0	100.0	100.0	100.0	100.0
		Rural-nonfarm population					
Intermetropolitan	55.5	46.8	51.9	50.8	57.4	65.0	69.6
Subdominant	16.5	15.9	13.5	11.3	12.0	28.5	24.8
Local	28.0	37.3	34.6	37.9	30.6	6.4	5.7
All sectors	100.0	100.0	100.0	100.0	100.0	100.0	100.0
		Rural-farm population					
Intermetropolitan	53.4	47.0	52.2	54.0	59.6	61.4	66.4
Subdominant	17.1	17.6	16.4	12.7	14.4	31.1	27.0
Local	29.5	35.4	31.4	33.3	26.0	7.6	6.6
All sectors	100.0	100.0	100.0	100.0	100.0	100.0	100.0

a) Counties containing central cities and counties containing no rural populations have been excluded. The independent cities of Virginia were classified as lying in no county.

Source: Sixteenth Census of the United States. Compiled from Population, Vol.I, State tables 3 and 5; Population, Vol.II, State tables 26 and 27; Areas of the United States, 1940, Tables 2, 3, and 4.

previous chapters, these ratios are computed by dividing the actual nonfarm population residing in the counties of each type by the rural land area, in square miles (in hundreds), of those counties.

1. A study of the total columns for the class A, B, C, and D metropolitan communities makes it immediately apparent that "size of largest city contained" is a variable which is definitely associated with the intensity with which the land is occupied by the rural-nonfarm population. With each increase in size of largest city contained there is a consistently higher ratio of this population to land. The lowest intensities of land occupancy are found in those counties which contain no city whatsoever,

3. It will be noted that a small percentage of the land area of counties containing a city of 25,000 or more inhabitants lies in a local sector, even though local sectors are defined as containing no city of this size. The appearance of areas of this type in local sectors arises from the independent coding of county units by the location of their geographic centers. Thus, a few hinterland cities of 25,000 or more inhabitants lay sufficiently far from the geographic center of the counties containing them that they could be coded as lying in a different sector than that in which their county is located. In the tables which follow, this small group of counties will be included in the "all sector" totals, but will not be analyzed as a separate sector type.

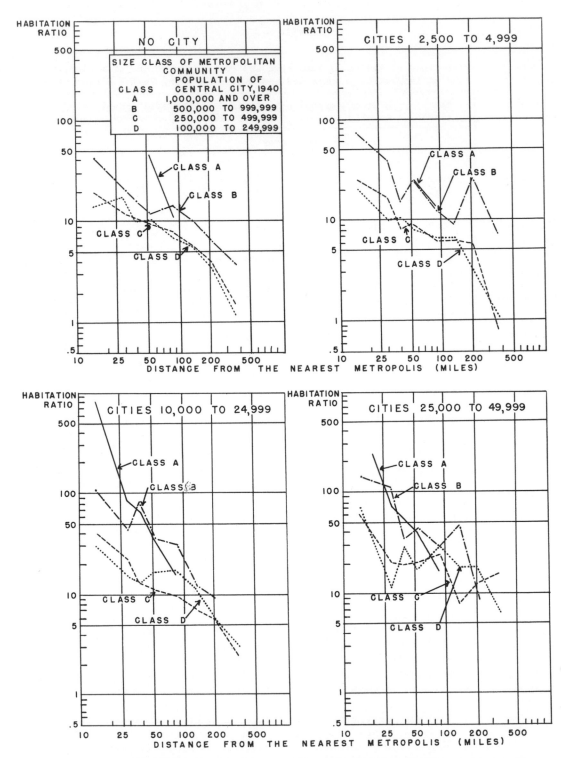

CHART 8-1   HABITATION RATIOS: RURAL-NONFARM POPULATION PER
SQUARE MILE OF HINTERLAND, BY SIZE OF LARGEST
HINTERLAND CITY CONTAINED IN THE COUNTY, SIZE
CLASS OF THE METROPOLITAN COMMUNITY, AND DISTANCE
FROM THE NEAREST METROPOLIS. UNITED STATES, 1940

and the highest intensities are found in those counties which contain the largest hinterland cities. This is true for all sizes of metropolitan communities. Thus, the degree to which the rural-nonfarm population inhabits the land is associated with the size of the nearby urban center. It appears either that the same set of circumstances which is conducive to the presence of larger hinterland cities is also conducive to the presence of rural-nonfarm populations, or that the presence of the hinterland city itself is conducive to the settlement of the land by this type of population. Whichever view is taken, it is apparent that the two populations are not distributed independently of each other.

2. The presence of the hinterland city, nevertheless, does not "explain," in its entirety the pattern of the distribution of the rural-nonfarm population. Even though the habitation ratios increase with increasing size of hinterland cities, the variables which have been used to study metropolitan patterns still persist. As the size of the metropolitan community changes, from class D through classes C, B, and A, each "size of largest city" group shows a rising average level of land occupancy. In a class D metropolitan community, an area whose largest city is 2,500 to 4,999 inhabitants has a habitation ratio which is less than one-third as large as the habitation ratio of the same type of area in a class A metropolitan community. Similar relationships hold for all of the other classes of counties and sizes of metropolitan communities. Thus, in spite of the fact that the local hinterland city appears to exercise an influence over the settlement of the land, the influence of the metropolis, in turn, seems to be superimposed upon it.

3. The influence of the metropolis upon the pattern of hinterland settlement by rural-nonfarm populations is also manifest in the habitation ratios for the various distance zones about the metropolis. The same pattern of declining ratios of people to land with increasing distance is present for each of the subdominance groups individually. Hence, the ability of a hinterland city of a given size to aggregate rural-nonfarm population about itself tends to wane with increasing distance from the metropolis. Even those areas containing the very largest sizes of hinterland cities, areas which, presumably, could throw off the influence of the metropolis most effectively follow the same general pattern as do the areas containing smaller hinterland cities; this condition exists in spite of the fact that the class D metropolitan centers appear to have much less control over the patterning of the large outlying centers than have the larger metropolises.

4. Those counties which contain no city whatever provide some interesting exceptions to the general pattern of distribution of the rural-nonfarm population. Except for the zone immediately surrounding the metropolis, the habitation ratio of the rural-nonfarm population in those counties which contain no city tends to be almost equal to or higher than the habitation ratio of counties which contain a largest city of less than 5,000. This situation exists in B, C, and D class metropolitan communities. (In the class A metropolitan communities there are too few counties which contain no city to permit a similar comparison.) It appears that the greater quantity of village populations compensates for the lack of a city. This phenomenon can be understood by reflecting upon the process by which an individual county area passes from one subdominance classification to another. If the sole village in a county which contains no cities begins to grow, and passes the 2,500 inhabitants requirement, the county passes from the lowest to the subdominance category above it. But in so doing it loses its only aggregation of rural-nonfarm population, since it must lose its village in order to obtain a city. Unless a new village of equal size is formed to replace the one which has been lost, the rural-nonfarm population will be smaller than it was formerly. Thus, embryonic cities (large villages) in counties which contain no city can raise effectively, by standing in place of the city, the rural-nonfarm habitation ratio to a position higher than that of the group above it, because the group above has recently lost units of village population in the process of obtaining cities. Stated in another way, the "no city" category is not, strictly speaking, a continuation of the "size of largest city contained" continuum.

B. Sector Type and the Distribution of the Rural-nonfarm Population by Subdominance Groups (Table 8-4)

In Table 8-4 the rural-nonfarm habitation ratios have been computed from data cross-classified by all four variables of distance, sector type, size of metropolis, and size of largest city contained. Although the number of county units contained in some cells, particularly in the large city sections and at the greatest distances, is extremely small, the general metropolitan pattern of distribution remains.

When the county units are given the full four-way classification all of the elements involved in the structure of the metropolitan community are found to be present. Present are:

a. The tendency for habitation ratios to rise with increasing size of metropolis.
b. The tendency for the intermetropolitan and the local sectors to follow a trend of gradual decrease in the intensity of land settlement with increasing distance from the metropolis.

Table 8-4

Habitation ratios: Rural-nonfarm population per 100 square miles of rural land area. County units classified by size of largest city contained, size class of metropolitan community, type of sector, and distance from the nearest metropolis. United States, 1940.[a]

SIZE OF LARGEST CITY CONTAINED AND TYPE OF SECTOR

Class D metropolitan community

Class of metropolitan community and distance zone (miles)	No city — Inter-metropolitan	No city — Subdominant	No city — Local	2,500–4,999 — Inter-metropolitan	2,500–4,999 — Subdominant	2,500–4,999 — Local	5,000–9,999 — Inter-metropolitan	5,000–9,999 — Subdominant	5,000–9,999 — Local	10,000–24,999 — Inter-metropolitan	10,000–24,999 — Subdominant	10,000–24,999 — Local	25,000–49,999 — Inter-metropolitan	25,000–49,999 — Subdominant	50,000–over — Inter-metropolitan	50,000–over — Subdominant
0–24 [b]	1443	1443	1443	1964	1964	1964	1852	1852	1852	2882	2882	2882	7182	7182	5977	5977
25–44	1609	282	944	1157	1230	807	915	1225	503	1332	1884	1735	1459	3045	8167	–
25–34	2103	354	1118	1029	927	1055	1073	–	1242	1469	1690	1667	707	2303	11353	–
35–44	1189	230	890	1198	1272	740	745	1225	302	1195	2098	1879	2107	3293	3405	–
45–64	979	789	1010	784	621	869	1072	1922	1278	1538	1302	1756	1745	1724	2474	1413
65–114	641	906	759	568	829	810	1302	1215	1226	1891	1796	1225	4273	1914	3471	–
115–164	430	1002	657	597	595	737	488	1061	1017	1053	1359	1005	1713	2187	3179	3602
165–264	309	606	337	303	898	236	420	1535	534	602	1732	374	726	6351	328	–
265–over	115	318	129	104	265	146	112	267	190	240	–	405	603	561	658	–

Class C metropolitan community

Class of metropolitan community and distance zone (miles)	No city — Inter-metropolitan	No city — Subdominant	No city — Local	2,500–4,999 — Inter-metropolitan	2,500–4,999 — Subdominant	2,500–4,999 — Local	5,000–9,999 — Inter-metropolitan	5,000–9,999 — Subdominant	5,000–9,999 — Local	10,000–24,999 — Inter-metropolitan	10,000–24,999 — Subdominant	10,000–24,999 — Local	25,000–49,999 — Inter-metropolitan	25,000–49,999 — Subdominant	50,000–over — Inter-metropolitan	50,000–over — Subdominant
0–24 [b]	1993	1993	1993	2446	2446	2446	2153	2153	2153	4040	4040	4040	6152	6152	8195	8195
25–44	1280	929	921	1182	1061	1090	986	–	1885	1964	–	2133	2902	–	–	2562
25–34	1647	886	889	1406	1074	1856	731	–	2207	2195	–	2448	2143	–	–	–
35–44	1062	971	963	983	1053	722	1461	–	1848	1433	–	621	4077	–	2122	2562
45–64	920	1570	605	845	1171	790	1083	1088	1747	1343	1222	676	1955	7239	1633	6624
65–114	827	768	709	680	643	481	775	686	787	1111	985	686	2283	735	3387	3721
115–164	556	871	470	695	583	463	819	572	515	724	1294	522	895	4632	1208	2044
165–264	420	716	280	638	1200	435	962	533	268	454	–	497	786	1540	–	–
265–over	175	517	122	112	–	47	166	–	310	215	–	261	–	–	–	–

Class B metropolitan community

Class of metropolitan community and distance zone (miles)	No city — Inter-metropolitan	No city — Subdominant	No city — Local	2,500–4,999 — Inter-metropolitan	2,500–4,999 — Subdominant	2,500–4,999 — Local	5,000–9,999 — Inter-metropolitan	5,000–9,999 — Subdominant	5,000–9,999 — Local	10,000–24,999 — Inter-metropolitan	10,000–24,999 — Subdominant	10,000–24,999 — Local	25,000–49,999 — Inter-metropolitan	25,000–49,999 — Subdominant	50,000–over — Inter-metropolitan	50,000–over — Subdominant
0–24 [b]	4192	4192	4192	7214	7214	7214	12215	12215	12215	10788	10788	10788	14172	14172	9490	9490
25–44	1667	–	2180	2950	3330	1561	5090	1537	1256	7032	–	–	5661	12132	3582	6368
25–34	–	–	2180	3950	3330	1561	3482	1537	1256	4326	–	–	9498	12132	5582	9936
35–44	1667	–	1286	2610	4498	1561	18805	4334	5041	8335	3490	1944	3437	1814	–	4554
45–64	1125	–	1585	1002	2659	1118	1670	1082	2424	4193	3873	3943	8450	2354	7055	1186
65–114	1108	2577	878	850	1029	1461	1542	1146	–	2206	991	4889	3192	3930	6485	3132
115–164	632	1739	381	2584	–	781	1974	783	784	1020	892	–	7225	1041	–	758
165–264	757	821	–	–	706	–	376	–	–	1100	–	–	–	–	–	–
265–over	–	359	–	–	–	–	–	–	–	–	–	–	–	–	–	–

Class A[c] metropolitan community

Class of metropolitan community and distance zone (miles)	No city — Inter-metropolitan	No city — Subdominant	No city — Local	2,500–4,999 — Inter-metropolitan	2,500–4,999 — Subdominant	2,500–4,999 — Local	5,000–9,999 — Inter-metropolitan	5,000–9,999 — Subdominant	5,000–9,999 — Local	10,000–24,999 — Inter-metropolitan	10,000–24,999 — Subdominant	10,000–24,999 — Local	25,000–49,999 — Inter-metropolitan	25,000–49,999 — Subdominant	50,000–over — Inter-metropolitan	50,000–over — Subdominant
0–24 [b]	*	–	–	–	–	–	10380	10380	10380	82872	82872	82872	22722	22722	40371	40371
25–44	–	–	–	–	–	–	28798	–	5513	8979	9191	6625	963	3372	14661	11030
25–34	–	–	–	–	–	–	–	–	5513	8969	9191	7532	7527	–	14661	11030
35–44	–	–	–	–	–	–	28798	–	–	9056	–	4721	6308	–	–	–
45–64	3510	–	5438	1186	–	4431	2144	1169	7447	1772	–	7918	5475	–	8719	6772
65–114	1386	–	935	516	–	1459	–	642	2364	1595	–	–	1641	–	21711	2744

a) Counties containing central cities and counties containing no rural population have been excluded. The independent cities of Virginia were classified as lying in no county.

b) At distances of less than 25 miles all sectors have been combined. The combined value is shown for each type of sector in this zone for purposes of comparison with values for other zones.

c) Distances of 115 miles or more have been excluded as being unrepresentative of the average hinterland of this class of metropolitan community.

Source: Sixteenth Census of the United States. Compiled from Population, Vol.I, State tables 3 and 5; Population, Vol.II, State table 26; Areas of the United States, 1940, Tables 2, 3, and 4.

c. The tendency for subdominant sectors to foster a more intense land settlement, and to maintain a high habitation ratio far into the hinterland.

d. The tendency for the intensity of land settlement to be higher with each increase in the size of the largest city contained, regardless of type of sector.

Thus, the characteristics of each variable remain, in modified form, in the presence of each of the other variables. Since three of these variables measure position with respect to the metropolis, and the fourth measures the degree of immediate subdominance of the hinterland city, it must be concluded that the rural-nonfarm population is distributed, and presumably organized, with respect both to the metropolis and to the hinterland city. The phenomena of dominance and of subdominance appear to coexist throughout the hinterland. Once it was demonstrated that the hinterland cities were distributed in a definite pattern about the metropolis, by distance, sector type, and size of metropolis, it could have been anticipated that the structure of the rural-nonfarm population would be comprised entirely of combinations of local communal units of population, consisting of a hinterland city and a standard complement of rural-nonfarm and rural-farm populations. In such a case, the differences between distance zones, sector types, and sizes of metropolises would disappear completely when the rural-nonfarm population is classified by size of largest subdominant. That the variables which have been used to isolate the patterns of both dominance and subdominance show their characteristic pattern is evidence that the distribution of population cannot be explained solely by relative location with respect to a central city, nor by location near a hinterland city. Both types of information are required.

IV

The Intensity with which the Rural-farm Population Occupies the Land, by Subdominance Groups

A. Rural-farm Population per 100 Square Miles of Rural Land Area. (Chart 8-2)

The rural-farm habitation ratios for each distance zone of each size of metropolitan community, for counties classified by size of largest city contained, are presented in Chart 8-2.

1. In class B, C, and D metropolitan communities, the units containing the larger hinterland cities in general also have higher ratios of rural-farm population to land. Very intense urban and metropolitan influence appears to discourage the settlement of the rural-farm population, as is indicated by the absence of this tendency in the near distance zones of class A metropolitan communities and in counties containing cities of 50,000 or more inhabitants when located in class B metropolitan communities.

2. The apparent tendency of rural-farm populations to be discouraged by intense urban and metropolitan influence is further indicated by the tendency of the habitation ratios to level off in the 0-24 mile zone, or even to decline, as the size of the largest city contained increases beyond 25,000 inhabitants. Cities of 50,000 or more inhabitants seem to foster a rural-farm settlement which is only a very little more intense at any distance, and in any size of metropolitan community, than that fostered by cities of 25,000 to 50,000 inhabitants. There is a persistent rise in the average rural-farm population per 100 square miles as the size of the city contained in the county rises from 2,500 to 50,000 inhabitants.

3. Containing a city of 2,500, or containing no city at all, appears to be almost a matter of unimportance at distances of less than 115 miles from the metropolis. It is only at distances greater than this, where cities occur much less frequently, that the habitation ratios in counties containing a small city are consistently higher than in those which contain no city.

4. Yet, through this pattern of local aggregation, the variables measuring metropolitan pattern still exhibit their influence.

a. The effect of the size of the metropolis is in evidence, as witnessed by a steadily rising habitation ratio with increasing size of metropolis in the B, C, and D groups. Class A metropolitan communities show tendencies both toward attracting the rural-farm population very intensively, and also toward repelling it. The general pattern, in most distance zones, is one of an intense attraction equal to or higher than that of the class B or C metropolitan communities.

b. The influence of the metropolis is further evidenced by the decline in rural-farm habitation ratios with increasing distance. This decline is more sharp among the counties containing small cities than among those containing cities of 10,000 or more inhabitants. The combined effect of metropolitan and of subdominant influence upon the rural-farm population appears to be, then, to sustain an intense settlement of rural-farm population far into the hinterland, and to crowd out the rural-farm population, either with rural-nonfarm residence or other activities, from those areas of the maximum metropolitan and urban settlement.

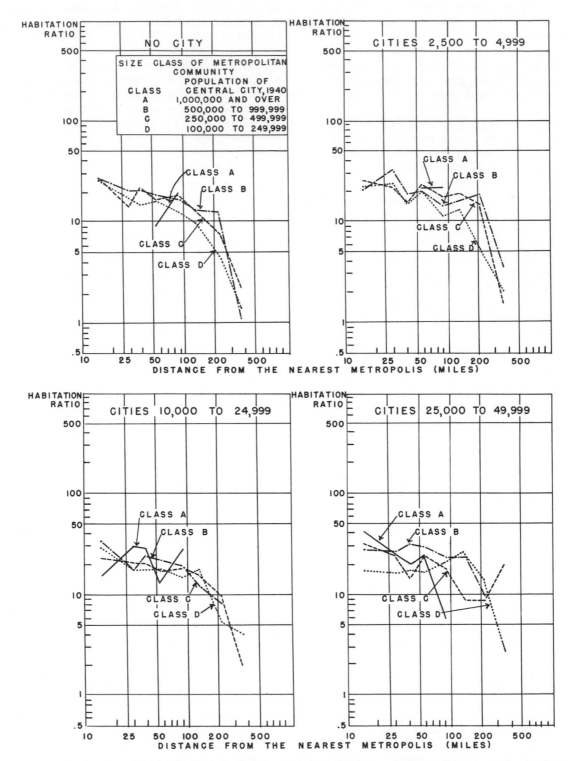

CHART 8-2 HABITATION RATIOS: RURAL-FARM POPULATION PER SQUARE MILE OF HINTERLAND, BY SIZE OF LARGEST HINTERLAND CITY CONTAINED IN THE COUNTY, SIZE CLASS OF THE METROPOLITAN COMMUNITY, AND DISTANCE FROM THE NEAREST METROPOLIS. UNITED STATES, 1940

B. Sector Type and the Distribution of the Rural-farm Population by Subdominance Groups. (Table 8-5)

Habitation ratios based upon simultaneous cross-classifications of sector type, distance, size of metropolis, and size of largest city contained are presented in Table 8-5.

1. All elements of the metropolitan rural-farm population structure coexist, although with numerous fluctuations and apparent interactions. The characteristic patterns associated with distance, size of metropolis, sector type, and size of largest city contained are present. It must be concluded that the rural-farm population is distributed, and presumably organized, with respect both to the metropolis and to the hinterland city. Thus, the elements of dominance and of subdominance appear to be present together in all parts of the hinterland. Just as no single variable was able to account completely for the distribution of the other hinterland populations, so now all four variables are necessary for an adequate description of the metropolitan structure of the rural-farm population. From the variations present in these data it must be admitted that still other factors — the quality of the land, the climate, and similar variables — are also operative. Yet the conclusion is almost inescapable that the distribution of the rural-farm population is related to the position of that population with respect to the metropolis and to the hinterland city.[4]

2. The ability of the subdominant sectors to foster an intense settlement of rural-farm population at all distances is evident in all of the locations except those involving the most intense concentration of urban populations. In counties whose largest city has less than 25,000 inhabitants and lies in class B, C, and D metropolitan communities this tendency is unmistakably present. In class A metropolitan communities, and in all counties containing a city of 25,000 or more inhabitants, the habitation ratios are very high, but they appear to be limited (as has been noted in other instances) by the intense urbanization and suburbanization in these areas. Thus, the major hinterland city appears to foster a very intense rural-farm occupancy of the land in the distance between itself and the central city.

3. The local sectors appear to promote very intense settlements of the rural-farm population at shorter distances, but they seem to be more affected by distance from the metropolis than do the inter-metropolitan sectors. The habitation ratios of local sectors decline more rapidly outside the 45 mile zone than do those of the intermetropolitan sectors. This tendency is much more marked in the class B and C metropolitan communities than in the class A.

V

The Relationship of Rural-nonfarm
to Rural-farm Population (Table 8-6)

The rural-nonfarm population occupies a unique position in the total population structure of the metropolitan community, in that it tends to conform at some points to the pattern of the urban populations and at other points to the pattern of the rural-farm population. It has already been observed that in the vicinity of the metropolis and of the large hinterland cities the rural-nonfarm residents are highly concentrated, but that in the remote areas they tend to follow the distributional pattern of the rural-farm population. The rural-nonfarm population is less independent of the land than is the urban population, but more independent of the land than the rural-farm population, lying almost midway between the two extremes in this respect. Populations of this type are expressive apparently, not of one, but of two functional positions in the metropolitan organization: that of a local trade center for other rural populations, and that of a suburban residence for groups which gain their livelihood in cities.

If the first type of function were the only one which rural-nonfarm populations exercise, it would be logical to expect to find a fairly constant ratio between the numbers of rural-nonfarm and rural-farm populations. Each 100 farm residents would require a given number of village residents to provide them with needed goods and services, and to participate in the collection, processing, and marketing of rural products. Given the pattern of city distribution which has been found for the hinterland, and still assuming that rural-nonfarm populations function only as local service populations, one would

---

4. Because the rural-farm population is the least patterned of the hinterland populations, the populations present in each cell were compared with the numbers which would be expected in that cell if there were no differences associated with each variable, and if all differences were due to the other three variables. In each case, the sum of the differences between the actual and the expected numbers was large and highly significant by the Chi Square test, and was in the direction indicated by the preceding analysis. The irregularities of Table 8-5 are understandable when it is recognized that the average number of counties per cell in the 10,000-24,999 category, for example, is only 4.5, and that many cells are represented by only one or two counties.

Table 8-5

Habitation ratios: Rural-farm population per 100 square miles of rural land area. County units classified by size of largest city contained, type of sector, and distance from the nearest metropolis. United States, 1940.a)

Class of metropolitan community and distance zone (miles)	SIZE OF LARGEST CITY CONTAINED AND TYPE OF SECTOR																
	No city			2,500 – 4,999			5,000 – 9,999			10,000 – 24,999			25,000 – 49,999			50,000 – over	
	Inter-metro-politan	Subdom-inant	Local	Inter-metro-politan	Subdom-inant	Local	Inter-metro-politan	Subdom-inant	Local	Inter-metro-politan	Subdom-inant	Local	Inter-metro-politan	Subdom-inant	Local	Inter-metro-politan	Subdom-inant
Class D	Class D			Class D			Class D			Class D			Class D			Class D	
0-24 b)	2502	2502	2502	2226	2226	2226	2578	2578	2578	2848	2848	2848	1705	1705	1705	1771	1771
25-44	1435	1932	1593	1583	2232	1527	1443	4951	1019	1641	1887	2119	1387	2430	2430	2005	–
25-34	1957	1762	1187	2026	4150	2530	1771	–	3208	1525	2060	2313	1224	3159	3159	2169	–
35-44	1009	2091	1719	1438	1970	1254	1092	4951	1115	1756	1697	1710	1528	2187	2187	1761	–
45-64	1540	1709	1566	1681	2592	2177	1812	1507	2150	1712	2199	1602	1488	1834	1834	2174	2021
65-114	1143	1866	1264	939	1598	1364	1691	611	1804	1341	2394	1422	2940	1535	1535	2544	–
115-164	671	2116	1042	1133	1763	1281	1046	1796	541	1710	1997	1662	2583	1253	1253	2395	909
165-264	399	1056	416	506	2507	368	411	1518	121	513	1385	509	1371	1118	1118	152	2582
265-over	121	525	167	162	540	330	132	537		449		315	220	1290	1290	416	1669
Class C	Class C			Class C			Class C			Class C			Class C			Class C	
0-24 b)	2665	2665	2665	2494	2494	2494	2776	2776	2776	2313	2313	2313	3068	3068	3068	3397	3397
25-44	2017	2558	1420	2174	2566	1409	2084	–	1923	2252	–	1558	2651	2651	2651	–	913
25-34	1508	2033	1138	2079	3192	2357	2390	–	2152	2306	–	1617	2392	2392	2392	–	–
35-44	2321	2675	1791	2257	2218	955	1513	–	1908	2129	–	1276	3051	3051	3051	2513	913
45-64	1940	2313	1078	2865	2029	1807	2604	–	2646	2033	–	1021	2376	2376	2376	1198	2371
65-114	1986	1588	1516	1806	1894	1615	1549	2001	1494	2148	3287	1209	1759	3562	3562	3325	909
115-164	1322	1915	1056	2073	2233	1214	2100	2096	1312	1333	3294	1319	1088	647	647	3141	2582
165-264	729	1366	547	1260	2183	1283	1591	2055	536	795	2094	815	862	1050	1050		
265-over	279	1794	147	227	1411	102	342	3278	297	230		128		2005	2005		
Class B	Class B			Class B			Class B			Class B			Class B			Class B	
0-24 b)	2651	2651	2651	2050	2050	2050	3044	3044	3044	3432	3432	3432	2655	2655	2655	2264	2264
25-44	2120	–	–	3219	3082	1792	2318	2949	1589	2145	–	–	3040	2486	2486	3301	2519
25-34	–	–	–	3219	3082		2264		1589	1689		–	2912	2486	2486	3301	4097
35-44	2120	–	2266	1874	2408	1793	2784	2949	2668	2362	–	1876	3114	2867	2867	–	1716
45-64	1386	2426	1731	1254	2583	1885	1738	2926	1536	2319	1747	1747	2906	1990	1990	2696	2182
65-114	1581	1463	1356	1671	2476	1572	1612	1223		2065	1843	1429	2643	2597	2597	2308	
115-164	1187	1201	1148	1796	–	845	1475	1030		1234	1064		1493	1035	1035	–	1505
165-264	1869	109		–	347		1659	500	378	1758	734		–			–	950
265-over																	
Class A c)	Class A			Class A			Class A			Class A			Class A			Class A	
0-24 b)	–	–	–	–	–	–	3365	3365	3365	1528	1528	1528	4179	4179	4179	3126	3126
25-44	–	–	–	–	–	–	1926	–	2329	3227	2922	2051	2117	2128	2128	2010	2323
25-34	–	–	–	–	–	–	–	–	2339	3309	3953	1583	2521	2128	2128	–	2323
35-44	–	–	–	–	–	–	–	–		2620		2889	1649			–	4097
45-64	1474	–	463	1827	–	2744	1926	1673	2091	911		2112	2274	2128	2128	2010	3156
65-114	1223	–	2198	1481	–	2215	1608	1897	2192	2855			584	2519	2519	4507	3233
																2181	

a) Counties containing central cities and counties containing no rural population have been excluded. The independent cities of Virginia were classified as lying in no county. No counties with largest cities of 25,000 inhabitants were classified as local.

b) At distances of less than 25 miles all sectors have been combined. The combined value is shown for each type of sector in this zone for purposes of comparison with values for other zones.

c) Distances of 115 miles or more have been excluded as being unrepresentative of the average hinterland of this class of metropolitan community.

Sources: Sixteenth Census of the United States. Compiled from Population, Vol.I, State tables 3 and 5; Population, Vol.II, State table 26; Areas of the United States, 1940, tables 2, 3, and 4.

expect to find a decrease in the number of rural-nonfarm residents per 100 rural-farm residents as he approaches the central city, since the greater accessibility of hinterland cities and of the metropolis itself would make the presence of village service centers less necessary. As the number of hinterland cities per 1000 square miles increases, an increasing proportion of the rural-farm population would reside in the immediate vicinity of a city and would make use of city services rather than village services. For this reason, one would expect the ratio of village service center population to rural-nonfarm population to be highest in the most distant and least urbanized parts of the metropolitan community and to be lowest in those areas where the metropolis and hinterland cities are most accessible. At the shorter distances and in particular, in the subdominant sectors, one would anticipate a very low ratio of rural-nonfarm to rural-farm population.

On the other hand, if suburban residence were the sole criterion used in classifying residents as rural-nonfarm, an entirely different type of distribution would be expected. In county areas containing no cities, one would expect almost no rural-nonfarm population. With increasing size of the largest city contained in the county area, a higher level of rural-nonfarm land occupancy would be expected. Since suburban residence is completely associated with the presence and size of cities, and since many other factors must operate to promote farm residence, one would anticipate a consistent rise in the ratio of rural-nonfarm to rural-farm population with increasing size of largest city contained or decreasing distance from the metropolis. For the same reason, one would anticipate that, in subdominant sectors, the number of rural-nonfarm residents per 100 rural-farm residents would be greater than in local sectors, since the relative absence of large cities would make the latter unlikely places of suburban residence. Because of their ready access to the metropolis, intermetropolitan sectors should be favored places for the location of suburban populations. Obviously, all of the shorter distance zones would also be so favored, regardless of sector type.

Depending upon which of the two functional roles of the rural-nonfarm population one considers, therefore, two separate and opposing patterns of population distribution can be expected. The village service center function calls for high ratios of rural-nonfarm to rural-farm populations at those points which are most remote from the metropolis and from hinterland cities. The suburban residence function calls for high ratios of rural-nonfarm populations to rural-farm populations at the points which are most accessible to the metropolis and

hinterland cities. By cross-classifying the county units according to the dominance-subdominance variables, and by examining the ratios of the rural-nonfarm to the rural-farm population in each of the resulting accessibility areas, a clearer understanding can be reached concerning the bipartite distribution and the dual functional position of the rural-nonfarm population. Table 8-6 presents these ratios for county areas classified by size of largest city contained, sector type, size class of metropolitan community, and distance from the nearest metropolis.

Every element involved in the anticipated relationship of rural-nonfarm to rural-farm population, under both sets of assumptions concerning the functional role of the rural-nonfarm population, can be tested from the data of Table 8-6.

1. In the counties which contain no cities and lie in class D metropolitan communities and, hence, in which suburban residence is at a minimum, the highest ratios of rural-nonfarm to rural-farm populations are found in the most distant zones and the lowest ratios at the inner zones, indicating the greater dependency of the rural-farm population upon village service centers in those areas where cities are least frequent, and the lesser dependency upon such centers in the inner zones, where there is a greater likelihood of a city being present in an adjacent county. In the local sectors of such areas the rural-farm population outnumbers the rural-nonfarm population in the ratio of about 3 to 2 at all distances, and in the ratio of almost 4 to 3 in the zone beyond 165 miles from the central city.

2. At the other extreme, in counties whose largest city contains 25,000 or more inhabitants and is located within 25 miles of a class A central city, the rural-nonfarm population outnumbers the rural-farm populations by ratios which are as high as 10 to 1. In all areas in which large cities are known to be present, or very near, the rural-nonfarm population tends to be present in great numbers in comparison with the rural-farm population. At short distances, in metropolitan communities with large central cities, in intermetropolitan sectors, and in all county areas whose largest city is 10,000 or more inhabitants, this situation tends to exist. The ratios of rural-nonfarm to rural-farm population are raised to values well in excess of those which would be required by the hypothesis of village service centers. Yet these same areas, because of the greater accessibility and frequency per 100 square miles of their urban centers, would necessitate the very lowest concentrations of rural-nonfarm populations as service centers. Clearly, the functional position of the rural-nonfarm population is a dual one.

Table 8-6

Ratio of rural -nonfarm to rural-farm population. County units classified by size of largest city contained, size class of metropolitan community, type of sector, and distance from the nearest metropolis. United States, 1940.a)

Size of central city and distance zone (miles)	No city			2,500 - 4,999			5,000 - 9,999			10,000 - 24,999			25,000 - over	
	Inter-metro-politan	Subdom-inant	Local	Inter-metro-politan	Subdom-inant	Local	Inter-metro-politan	Subdom-inant	Local	Inter-metro-politan	Subdom-inant	Local	Inter-metro-politan	Subdom-inant
Class D	**Class D**			**Class D**			**Class D**			**Class D**			**Class D**	
0-24 b)	0.57	-	0.59	0.84	0.89	0.93	0.74	-	0.60	1.18	-	0.86	3.06	4.21
25-44	1.12	0.14	0.59	0.73	0.55	0.53	0.63	0.25	0.49	0.81	1.00	0.82	2.25	1.25
45-64	0.64	0.46	0.65	0.47	0.24	0.40	0.59	1.28	0.90	0.90	0.59	1.10	1.16	0.94
65-114	0.56	0.49	0.60	0.60	0.52	0.59	0.77	0.47	0.57	1.41	0.75	0.86	1.40	1.19
115-164	0.64	0.41	0.63	0.53	0.34	0.58	0.47	0.59	0.56	0.62	0.68	0.60	0.87	1.75
165-264	0.77	0.57	0.81	0.60	0.36	0.64	1.02	1.01	0.99	1.17	1.25	0.73	0.71	2.46
265-over	0.95	0.61	0.77	0.64	0.49	0.44	0.85	0.50	1.57	0.53	-	1.28	2.09	0.43
Total	0.71	0.48	0.66	0.59	0.41	0.58	0.70	0.63	0.70	0.95	0.74	0.87	1.48	1.31
Class C	**Class C**			**Class C**			**Class C**			**Class C**			**Class C**	
0-24 b)	0.35	1.21	1.00	0.66	-	1.99	0.81	0.78	0.52	1.16	-	2.05	2.66	2.42
25-44	0.63	0.39	0.65	0.54	0.41	0.77	0.47	-	0.98	0.87	-	1.37	1.09	2.81
45-64	0.47	0.68	0.56	0.29	0.58	0.44	0.42	-	0.66	0.66	-	0.66	0.82	-
65-114	0.42	0.48	0.47	0.38	0.37	0.30	0.50	0.54	0.53	0.53	0.37	0.57	1.32	2.49
115-164	0.42	0.46	0.44	0.34	0.29	0.38	0.39	0.33	0.39	0.54	0.30	0.40	0.89	1.81
165-264	0.58	0.52	0.51	0.51	0.27	0.34	0.60	0.28	0.50	0.57	0.62	0.61	1.22	1.57
265-over	0.63	0.29	0.84	0.49	0.85	0.46	0.48	0.16	1.04	0.93	-	2.05	-	0.77
Total	0.49	0.52	0.54	0.41	0.33	0.46	0.51	0.41	0.58	0.63	0.42	0.81	1.16	1.91
Class B	**Class B**			**Class B**			**Class B**			**Class B**			**Class B**	
0-24 b)	-	-	1.58	-	-	3.52	4.41	-	3.65	2.99	-	3.67	5.68	5.62
25-44	0.79	-	1.06	1.23	1.08	0.87	2.20	0.52	0.79	3.28	-	-	1.68	3.60
45-64	0.81	-	0.57	1.39	1.87	0.75	0.96	-	1.89	1.81	2.00	1.04	2.70	1.43
65-114	0.70	1.06	0.92	0.80	1.02	0.93	0.96	1.48	1.58	1.07	2.10	2.26	2.24	1.18
115-164	0.53	1.19	0.64	0.51	0.42	0.92	1.34	0.88	-	0.83	0.93	3.42	4.84	1.66
165-264	0.41	0.68	0.33	1.44	-	-	0.23	1.11	-	0.63	1.22	-	-	0.90
265-over	-	3.29	-	-	2.04	-	-	1.57	2.08	-	-	-	-	-
Total	0.66	0.99	0.75	0.92	1.12	1.05	1.29	1.07	1.86	1.74	1.62	2.10	2.92	1.62
Class A c)	**Class A**			**Class A**			**Class A**			**Class A**			**Class A**	
0-24 b)	-	-	-	-	-	-	-	-	3.08	-	-	54.25	7.84	10.04
25-44	-	-	-	-	-	-	14.95	-	2.36	2.78	2.33	3.18	5.07	3.37
45-64	2.38	-	11.74	0.65	-	1.51	1.33	0.70	3.56	1.88	-	3.75	2.03	1.82
65-114	1.13	-	0.43	0.35	-	0.66	-	0.34	1.08	0.56	-	-	4.01	0.86
Total	2.22	-	2.06	0.52	-	0.77	1.52	0.58	2.99	2.32	2.33	7.09	3.92	2.08

a) Counties containing central cities and counties containing no rural populations have been excluded. The independent cities of Virginia were classified as lying in no county.

b) At distances of less than 25 miles sector types have been reported because both populations were drawn from the same areas. However, values for sector types at this distance are not reliable, and are presented here for comparison with other distance zones rather than with each other.

c) Distances of 115 miles or more have been excluded as being unrepresentative of the average hinterland of this class of metropolitan community.

Source: Sixteenth Census of the United States. Compiled from Population, Vol.I, State tables 3 and 5; Population, Vol.II, State tables 26 and 27.

3. Returning to the counties containing no city or a city of less than 5,000 inhabitants, the inference may be made, through a comparison of sector types, that in the relative absence of suburban residence the ratio of village service population to farm population declines as soon as a city of some size is present. In the completely rural counties, with their minimum of suburban residence, the ratio of rural-nonfarm to rural-farm residents is lower in the subdominant sectors at all distances than in the local or the intermetropolitan sectors. The single distinguishing trait of the subdominant sectors is, of course, the presence of a major hinterland city. An average loss of about 18 villagers per 100 farm residents is occasioned by the proximity of a major hinterland city.

Additional evidence that, in the absence of suburban residence, the ratio of village to farm population declines when urban services are available may be drawn from the counties whose largest city is less than 5,000 inhabitants. Such a city is not large enough to promote extensive suburban residence, but its presence in the county can effectively replace a certain portion of the village service centers. In the zones beyond 115 miles from the metropolis, the ratio of rural-nonfarm to rural-farm population is lower in the counties containing such a small city than it is in counties which contain no city. This is true distance zone by distance zone and sector type by sector type, as well as being present also in the class C as well as in the class D metropolitan communities. The presence of a single city reduces the number of rural-nonfarm residents per 100 rural-farm residents by an average of about 8 per 100.

4. From the above it can be concluded that the "normal" village service center population is present in the ratio of about 66-75 villagers for every 100 farm residents, when cities are completely absent from the immediate locality. As the accessibility of cities increases, the relative importance of the village as a service center declines rapidly. The presence of a single small city in the county area reduces the number of village residents by about 8 per 100 farm residents, and the presence of a major hinterland city in a nearby county reduces the number of villagers by about 18 per 100 farm residents. As soon as the county contains a city of 5,000 or more inhabitants, the suburbanization phenomenon enters, because the ratios in such areas rise above the values found for areas

with no cities, in spite of the fact that the probability of two or more cities being present in the county has increased, and has brought with it a decrease in the necessity for village service population. In areas where the size of the hinterland city is even larger than 5,000 the extent of suburbanization becomes greater. There is no way of tracing further the decline in the relative importance of village service populations in the areas of greater urban concentration, but it must be well above the 18 per hundred which was noted in the case of the presence of a major hinterland city in a nearby county. With large cities actually present in the county, and numerous smaller cities likely also to be present, the ratio of village service population to farm population may be expected to decline to a very low value, and to reach almost zero in counties which contain major hinterland cities and lie within 25 miles of the metropolis.[5]

5. Two further observations are worthy of considerable emphasis:

a. A very small proportion of the rural-farm population is served exclusively by village service centers. Not only the rural-nonfarm but the rural-farm population as well is intimately associated with the urban population.

b. Suburbanization is a widespread phenomenon, and occurs in the vicinity of cities as small as 5,000 inhabitants. This is a fact which should be explored thoroughly in studies of decentralization and urban growth.

VI

Summary

1. Both the rural-nonfarm and the rural-farm populations occupy more intensively those counties which contain a large hinterland city than they occupy counties which contain a small city. With each increase in the size of the largest city contained, the average level of land occupancy tends to rise.

2. In spite of these marked and uniform differences, which are attributable only to the influence of the local hinterland cities, the elements of the metropolitan population pattern remain in each of the distributions. It is concluded that, to the extent that population distribution is related to population organization, the rural-nonfarm and the rural-farm populations are organized with respect both to the metropolis and to the hinterland city.

---

5. By a more detailed study of the changes in the ratios of Table 8-6 with changes in distance and size class of metropolitan community, a crude estimate is made, in the original manuscript, of the proportion of the total rural-nonfarm population which is engaged in serving rural populations and the proportion which is suburban. It is estimated there that not less than 44.1 per cent, and perhaps as much as 50 per cent, of the rural-nonfarm population in the United States was suburban in 1940.

CHAPTER NINE

THE PHYSICAL ENVIRONMENT AND THE METROPOLITAN COMMUNITY

This chapter attempts to study the metropolitan community in its environmental setting. Following the conceptual framework laid down in Chapter Two, it adopts the view that the metropolitan community and the distribution of population in it have developed as one form of adaptation to conditions which exist in the natural environment. Data showing the relation of population distribution to various measures of environmental conditions will be presented and, by way of summary, a few tentative conclusions will be mentioned concerning the relationship between the metropolitan community and the physical environment.

I

Natural Resources and Population Distribution

It is well known that not all parts of the surface of the earth, or even of one nation, are equally endowed with all of the resources which are used to support life and to maintain human communities. In fact, resources are so unequally distributed and the patterns for any two resources are so unlike that a description of the geographic location within which events occur has frequently been mistaken for a scientific explanation or theory of the events. It is within the realm of possibility that every element involved in the population patterns which have been characterized could have arisen solely from the pattern of resource distribution. To reach this conclusion, however, it is necessary to assume that populations inhabit most intensively those areas with the richest and most varied resources for the sustaining of life and that the population patterns which have been found are in reality patterns of resource distribution. That the present distribution of population in the United States does not arise solely from such resource patterns may be shown easily by pointing to the fact that many small areas have much richer combinations of natural resources than have New York, Chicago, Detroit and other areas of intense settlement, and yet have only a very small fraction of the population which is concentrated in and about these cities. On the other hand, one cannot deny categorically the influence of the physical environment in population distribution, for it can be demonstrated just as easily that in the deserts, in the mountainous waste lands, and on eroded prairies there is a relative scarcity not only of rural-farm population, but also of urban population and even of metropolitan centers. Somewhere between the characteristics of the physical environment, and the abilities of man to make use of that environment and to alter it, lies an explanation of the distribution of population. To interpret the structure of the metropolitan community in terms of either extreme is to fail to use all of the facts.

The demonstration that a pattern of population distribution exists with respect to the metropolitan variables can lead only to the inference that:

a. Natural resources are distributed by a metropolitan pattern, or

b. The combining procedure has tended to eliminate differences in resources by averaging areas of rich and poor resources, leaving a residue which may be called metropolitan dominance, or

c. Population is distributed as it is by factors involved both in inference (a) and inference (b)

This chapter will attempt to examine these three alternatives and to arrive at a conclusion as to which most adequately summarizes the known facts.

A. The Pattern of Distribution of Natural Resources

Students of industrial location and of natural resources have provided many worth-while clues for interpreting the distribution of population over the land. That the resources of the physical environment are useful at the present stage of technological development only if there is a complex organization of population they freely acknowledge. These patterns and specialized areas must arise, of necessity, in the process of extracting, transporting, and assembling useful resources, and in the producing and marketing of goods and services from those resources.

"... Even in the absence of any geographic differentiation at all (that is, if natural resources were distributed in a perfectly uniform fashion over the globe) certain patterns of specialization and concentration of activities would have to arise in accordance with economic, social, and political principles. There would be cities, towns, trade routes, specialized areas, and doubtless many of the problems of 'locational pathology' even if we removed altogether from the picture the factor of differences in distribution of natural resources...."[1]

Hence, in organizing itself for self-sustenance, the population must become concentrated, specialized, and diversified, in order to employ effectively modern technological methods. It may be inferred that the patterns of population distribution must reflect this necessity for organization.

In the process of utilizing the resources of the environment, however, and of specializing and concentrating in certain areas for the purpose of producing useful syntheses of these resources, there is great latitude for human preference. Those resources of the environment which are required to sustain life are not all equally permanent and incapable of human manipulation. A large class of resources are permanent only insofar as they are sustained or replaced as they are used. Only such irrecoverable resources as minerals, and such ubiquitous resources as air, are fixed and thus not subject to having their pattern of distribution altered through replacement by human activity.[2] In fact, the major man-made modifications of the environment are almost as permanent and immovable in their distribution as are the replaceable resources.

"The sustainable type of semi-natural resources then appears to be in about the same category of mobility, as the bulkier sort of capital goods: that is, unlikely to be bodily transferred, but capable of gradual change in geographic distribution through allocation of replacements."[3]

The possibility of exercising choice concerning replacements and location of replacements means that the resource pattern of any area may be altered.

Under present conditions of technology only a very small portion of the total population is forced to live at the point of extraction of natural resources, since only a small proportion of the total population is engaged in the extractive processes. In 1940, only 2.0 percent of the employed population of the United States was engaged in extracting nonreplaceable resources, and an additional 18.8 percent was engaged in extracting agricultural and forest products from sustainable resources. The remaining 79.2 percent of the employed population was engaged at tasks which permitted a greater latitude of choice in location.[4] Hence, in the distribution and organization of the population, actual resource extraction required a fixed location for about one-fiftieth of the working population and a semifixed location for an additional 18.8 percent. About four-fifths of the working population was free to be located completely independently so far as the source of raw materials was involved, except as considerations of cost, economy, and efficiency enter in the form of organizational factors, into resource use. Apparently, the pattern belonging to the 98.0 percent of the population which is free to organize itself, with at least partial independence from the direct obtaining of resources, is the metropolitan pattern which has been described in the preceding four chapters.

While the above evidence does not prove effectively that population is not distributed with respect to resources, it does disprove any theory of population distribution which relates population solely and directly to resources and which omits the principle that population must organize in order to utilize resources.

B. The Distribution of Population and Agricultural Resources. (Table 9-1)

The second inference, that the population patterns brought out by this study are to be interpreted as being completely the result of control emanating from metropolitan and other urban centers, is also false, as may be seen readily in Table 9-1. Coefficients of dissimilarity have been computed between the distribution of the hinterland population and the distribution of the various grades of land according to their suitability for agricultural purposes. These coefficients measure the linkage of population distribution to an index of agricultural resources.

To construct this table the land areas of the United States have been classified according to the agricultural productivity which they would have without benefit of irrigation, additional drainage, or the use of chemical fertilizers.

"Grade 1, roughly, is excellent for staple crops climatically adapted to the region; grade 2 is good; grade 3 is fair; grade 4 is

1. E. M. Hoover, Introduction to Geographic Economics, Manuscript prepared for Fondo de Cultura Economics, Mexico City, 1942, p. 2.

2. Ibid., p. 7.

3. Ibid., p. 12.

4. National Resources Planning Board. Industrial Location and National Resources, Chapter 3, "Major Groups of Economic Activity," by Sargent Florence and Ruth Friedson (Washington, D.C., United States Government Printing Office, 1942) p. 66.

Table 9-1

Coefficients of dissimilarity between the distributions of land, agricultural activities, and population. United States, 1940.[a]

| | Land suitable for agriculture[b] | Measures of agricultural activity | | Population, 1940 | | |
		Number of farms	Cash farm income	Urban	Rural-nonfarm	Rural-farm
Land:						
Total land area	35.8	37.7	32.6	51.3	38.8	39.5
Available for crops	12.9	25.5	23.9	48.2	36.0	28.6
Suitable for agriculture[b]	-	22.7	24.7	49.0	35.4	25.9
Quality of land:						
Excellent (grade 1)	48.4	57.9	48.0	64.8	64.7	61.2
Good (grade 2)	15.2	29.4	32.8	51.2	42.1	32.0
Fair (grade 3)	18.0	23.9	33.7	52.1	34.1	24.7
Poor (grade 4)	30.8	31.4	36.0	54.9	35.5	33.0
Nontillable (grade 5)	67.8	64.8	56.0	66.6	61.2	65.9
Agricultural activity:						
Harvested land	13.4	25.3	22.1	48.2	37.2	27.8
Number of farms	22.7	-	24.8	44.2	24.8	5.3
Cash farm income	24.7	24.8	-	33.7	24.8	28.8
Population, 1940:						
Urban	49.0	44.2	33.7	-	24.9	45.5
Rural-nonfarm	35.4	24.8	24.8	24.9	-	26.3
Rural-farm	25.9	5.3	28.8	45.5	26.3	-

a) Coefficients of dissimilarity were computed from percentage distributions of the various items by states.

b) Land suitable for agriculture consists of grades 1, 2, and 3.

Source: Population information compiled from Sixteenth Census of the United States, Population, Vol. II, Table 21. Information for land and agricultural activities compiled from data reported in National Resources Planning Board, Industrial Location and National Resources, Chapter 2, Tables 3 and 4, p. 37-38, 1942.

poor; and grade 5 is essentially incapable of tillage. Grade 4 . . . is distinctly low in physical productivity and is undesirable for standard arable farming except where uncommonly favored by compensating economic advantages such as nearness to urban markets."[5]

The series of coefficients of dissimilarity which have been computed compare the percentage distributions among the 48 states and the District of Columbia for population, quality of agricultural land, amount of available and harvestable crop land, number of farms, and amount of cash farm income.[6]

A very high proportion of the land area of the United States is ill-suited to agriculture, 65.5 percent being either untillable or of low grade. Only 34.6 percent is of standard quality or better. Land suitable for agriculture is not distributed evenly among the states, as is indicated by the coefficient of dissimilarity of 35.8 between total land area and land suitable for agriculture. The proportion of land classified as "excellent" is not only small, but is also very localized. The West North Central States contain 61.0 percent, and the East North Central States 29.0 percent, of this land.[7]

5. Ibid., p. 39.

6. All of the data pertaining to farm land and farming activities were taken from tables 3 and 4, Chapter Two, "Non-mineral Resources" in Industrial Location and National Resources, National Resources Planning Board, 1942, p. 37 and 38.

7. Ibid.

Table 9-1 should be read as follows: Each cell represents the total amount of difference between the percentage distribution, by states, of the item heading the column and a similar distribution of the item heading that row of the stub. Each column or row reports the amount of dissimilarity between one measure and several other measures. Ranking the coefficients of any row or column in ascending order makes it possible to determine with which factors each is most closely and least closely associated.

1. All populations show a marked degree of association with the quality of the land. The distributions of the urban, the rural-nonfarm, and the rural-farm population show much higher coefficients of dissimilarity with the distribution of nontillable land than with the distribution of land suitable for agriculture. The coefficients for the comparisons of population distribution with land quality decline consistently through each grade of land from grade 5 through grade 3, inclusive. (Seemingly the very best grades of land cover too small an area to contain even the farm population, since the coefficients of dissimilarity between population and "excellent" land are almost as high or higher than those between population and "nontillable" land. Note also the high coefficient of dissimilarity (48.4) between "excellent" land and the land suitable for agriculture. Similarly, the coefficients between population and "good" land are only slightly lower than those between population and "poor" land.) That all populations are attracted to the better land can be demonstrated most clearly by making a comparison between their distribution with grades 1 to 3 combined ("excellent," "good," "fair") and their distribution with grade "nontillable." For the urban population there is a drop of 17.6 percentage-points in the coefficient of dissimilarity, and there are even larger drops for the rural populations (25.8 percentage-points for the rural-nonfarm and 40.0 percentage-points for the rural-farm). Hence the inference that the metropolis "causes" urban and rural populations to be aggregated as they are is untenable, since the distribution of all populations is related unmistakably to the quality of land as well as to metropolitan factors. Even the urban population, of which only a very small fraction is engaged in resource extraction, is positively associated in its distribution with the better quality of land. A similar analysis for other types of resources very probably would support this conclusion.

2. Even though it is positively associated with quality of land, the distribution of the urban population shows the greatest total amount of independence from land quality, while the rural-farm

population shows the least degree of independence. Thus it would be necessary to move 49.0 percent of the urban, 35.4 percent of the rural-nonfarm, and 25.9 percent of the rural-farm population across state boundaries, before states which contain a given percentage of land suitable for agriculture could be expected also to contain the same percentage of each of these populations.

3. Though the rural-farm population has the lowest coefficient of dissimilarity with quality of land, the very fact that it is only 23 percentage-points lower than the same coefficient for the urban population indicates that factors other than quality of resources are operative in the distribution of the rural-farm population. Other of the coefficients also strongly indicate that this is the case:

a. The large difference between the coefficients of dissimilarity for grades 4 and 5 indicates that there is considerable concentration of the rural-farm population on poor and submarginal land.

b. There is more similarity between the distribution of cash farm income and the distribution of urban population than there is between the distributions of the rural-farm and the urban populations. Likewise, the distribution of the number of farms resembles the distribution of the urban population more than the distribution of the rural-farm population does. On the other hand, there is less correspondence between the distribution of the fair or better farm land and the urban population than there is between the distributions of the rural-farm and the urban populations. Observation of similar combinations of the coefficients for other variables makes it evident that the tendency of the indexes relating to agriculture have a pattern of increasing similarity to the distribution of urban population as their logical relation to urban markets becomes more direct.

	Coefficient of dissimilarity with urban population
Suitable for agriculture	49.0
Harvested crop land	48.2
Rural-farm population	45.5
Number of farms	44.2
Cash farm income	33.7

The above information makes it appear that in areas with urban concentrations one will find concentrations of rural-farm populations and more numerous farms, as well as greater farm income than would be expected if the suitability of the land for farming were the only criterion.

c. The absolute size of the coefficients of dissimilarity between the indexes of farm activity and the quality of the land is itself evidence that factors other than quality of land are operative in the distribution of farming activities. The low coefficient of dissimilarity between the number of farms and the size of the farm population shows that these two indexes measure almost the same thing: many farms mean many farm people. That high quality farm land is not synonymous with intensive farm operations is shown by coefficients of dissimilarity between the distribution of rural-farm population and the measures of land quality and farm activity, which are four or more times as great as the amount of dissimilarity between the distribution of farms and farm population.

Therefore, the variables of this study — distance from the metropolis, sector type, size of metropolis, the size of city — cannot be declared independent of the quality of agricultural resources. Even though there is no necessary direct relationship between resources and metropolitan pattern, they appear to be linked. Land suitable for agriculture is conducive to the presence of cities; the presence of cities is conducive to more intensive agricultural operations. Since, in areas of intensive farming, soil fertility and other elements of land quality must constantly be sustained by replacement, it can only be inferred that location with respect to cities is one element in the pattern of land maintenance for agricultural purposes. One must conclude that the third inference made above, that the population patterns which have been described in this study are an expression both of metropolitan organization and of the distribution of resources, is the proper view of the metropolitan community in its natural setting. Since the pattern of population distribution is related both to the metropolis

and to the physical environment, and neither of these factors compels that pattern, one is led to the conclusion that the metropolitan community is a pattern of population organization, an adaptation, to the physical environment. This view is amplified in the next section by a comparison of the metropolitan community with the geographic region.

II

Geographic Regions and Metropolitan Dominance

The fact that not all areas are alike in resources and activity has led to the delimiting and study of geographic regions. Within recent years it has been shown that there are differences between broad geographic areas not only in soil, climate, minerals, and other resources, but also in population composition, level of technological development, employment opportunities, levels of living, and many other elements of social organization.[8]

The region is commonly regarded as an area of alikeness or unity based upon conditions common to the constituent parts.

"A region . . . is a territory which possesses enough of the measure of sameness to distinguish it fundamentally from its neighbors."[9]

There may be many types of regions — climatic, economic, demographic, ethnic, racial, or even ideological — depending upon the particular element under consideration. That such geographic differentials are not isolated events is also evident. Areas involving poor soil, subsistence farming, low level of living, and absence of industrial cities tend to coincide, the net effect of which is to give to vast areas of land and to large numbers of people a similar mode of life.[10] Because of these observable differences in groups of traits, the United States has been divided into various divisions or major regions. Implicit in this procedure is the assumption that life within each region is fairly homogeneous, and different from that in

8. National Resources Committee. "Regional Distribution of Economic Opportunity." Ch. 2 in Problems of a Changing Population. (Washington, D.C.: Government Printing Office, 1938). A. R. Mangus. Rural Regions of the United States. (Washington, D.C.: United States Government Printing Office, 1940). Warren S. Thompson and P. K. Whelpton. Population Trends in the United States (New York: McGraw-Hill Book Company, 1933) Regional tables presented in the chapter for each population characteristic. Howard W. Odum. American Regionalism. (Chapel Hill: University of North Carolina Press, 1940). National Resources Committee. Regional Factors in National Planning and Development (Washington, D.C.: United States Government Printing Office, 1935). National Resources Planning Board. "Natural Resources and Location" Chapters 1 and 2 in Industrial Location and National Resources. (Washington, D.C.: United States Government Printing Office, 1942).

9. N.S.B. Gras. "Regionalism and Nationalism." Foreign Affairs, April 1929, p. 465.

10. Howard W. Odum. American Social Problems (New York: Henry Holt and Company, 1945) p. 120-121.

other regions. Howard W. Odum explains his six-fold regional division of the United States as follows:

"These are major regions approximating a greater degree of homogeneity measured by a larger number of indices for a larger number of purposes and classifications than any other regional framework that has been utilized or than any other that, on the basis of our data and premises, would appear possible."[11]

The problem of geographic division is of particular importance for this study for two reasons:

a. To the extent that regional distributions of populations imply regional differences in resources and a regional organization of population, the regional hypothesis becomes either an alternative to the metropolitan hypothesis or a hypothesis of population distribution which is supplementary to the metropolitan hypothesis.

b. To the extent that metropolitan communities, as here defined, do not coincide with geographic regions, the differences which have been found to be associated with metropolitan locations may be, in reality, reflections of regional differences.

While the evidence presented here must be brief, and admittedly incomplete, it does throw considerable light both on the metropolitan and on the regional view of population distribution.

The simplest, and of course the most direct, test which could be performed upon the data of this study for the purpose of learning the relationships between the metropolitan and the regional interpretation of population distribution would be a further tabulation of the data by geographic regions. Unfortunately, such a tabulation cannot be performed in full. The small number of cities and counties make it impossible to obtain sufficient cases for such a detailed analysis. A next best procedure, and the one which has been adopted, is to cross-classify the data for population and land area by only a few of the variables. The regional classification which has been used is the standard "geographic division," or combinations of such divisions as used by the United States Census.

A. The Regional Composition of Land Area and Population, by Distance from the Nearest Metropolis. (Chart 9-1)

1. There is a very strong regional bias in the distribution of population and land area by distance from metropolitan centers.

a. Each of the following divisions comprises an increasingly smaller percentage of the land area as the distance from the central city increases.

    New England states
    Middle Atlantic states
    East North Central states

b. Each of the following divisions comprises an increasingly larger percentage of the land area as the distance from the central city increases.

    West North Central states
    Mountain states
    Pacific states

c. With increasing distance there is considerable fluctuation among the proportions which the following geographic divisions comprise each zone:

    West North Central states
    South Atlantic states
    East South Central states

Thus, a higher than average proportion of the industrial East is contained in the short distance zones and a higher than average proportion of the Central and Mountain states is contained in the more distant zones. Almost two-thirds of the land area 265 or more miles from the metropolis, for example, is accounted for by the Mountain states.

3. The regional compositions of the urban, the rural-nonfarm, and the rural-farm populations also vary greatly with distance from the metropolis. In general, the Northeast predominates in the shorter zones and the Mountain and West Central divisions constitute an unduly large share of the more distant zones. Since it is a matter of common knowledge that the Northeast is more densely inhabited than are the Western and Central states, at least some of the metropolitan pattern may be attributable to changes in regional composition with increasing distance from the metropolis.

B. Habitation Ratios for Geographic Divisions, by Distance from the Nearest Metropolis. (Chart 9-2)

The extent to which the distance pattern of land occupancy may be attributed to regional differences can be envisaged by computing habitation ratios for each distance zone, by geographic regions. Such ratios are reported, in Chart 9-2, for four broad regional groupings. In studying these patterns it must be remembered that the marked differences which have been found to exist between sector types, size of metropolis, and size of local community are not held constant here, but appear as a part of the regional variations. To the extent

---

11. Ibid., p. 122. (Italics are mine.)

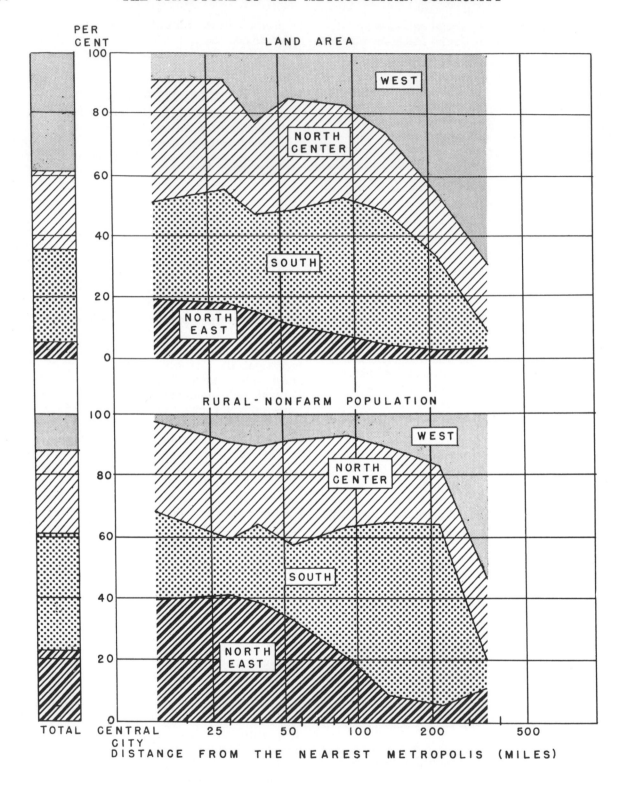

PER
CENT

LAND AREA

WEST

NORTH
CENTER

SOUTH

NORTH
EAST

RURAL-NONFARM POPULATION

WEST

NORTH
CENTER

SOUTH

NORTH
EAST

TOTAL   CENTRAL
        CITY
DISTANCE FROM THE NEAREST METROPOLIS (MILES)

CHART 9-1 REGIONAL COMPOSITION OF THE LAND
           DISTANCE FROM THE NEAREST METROPOLIS.

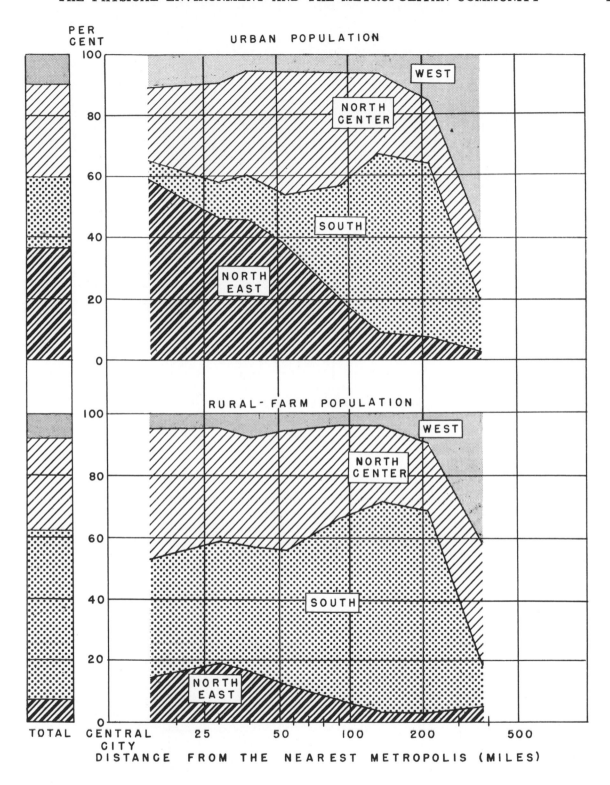

AREA AND POPULATION OF THE HINTERLAND, BY
UNITED STATES, 1940

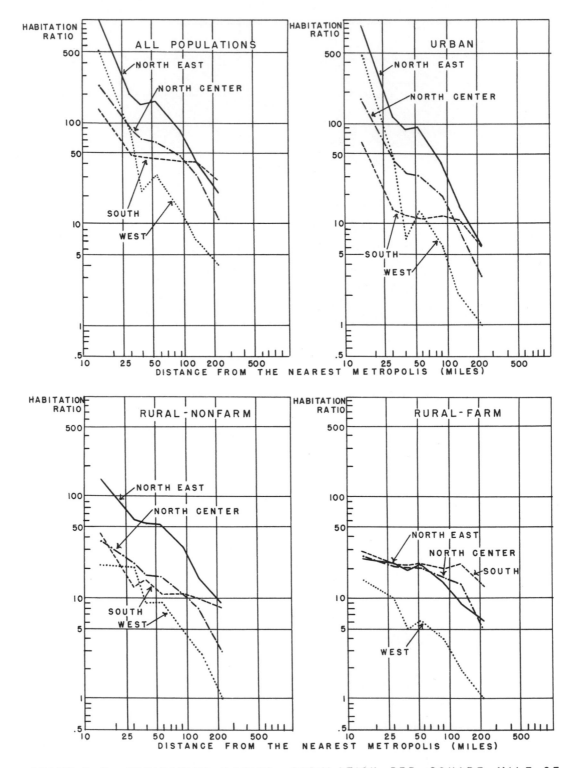

CHART 9-2 HABITATION RATIOS: POPULATION PER SQUARE MILE OF
HINTERLAND, BY GEOGRAPHIC REGION AND DISTANCE
FROM THE NEAREST METROPOLIS. UNITED STATES, 1940

that regions differ in their composition according to type of sector, size of metropolitan center, and size of hinterland cities, the regional differences shown represent both regional and metropolitan differences. Thus, the high values for the Northeast may be due to the greater size of metropolitan centers located there, as well as to differences in natural resources or other elements of the physical environment.

1. For every geographic region there are at least some evidences of a declining habitation ratio with increasing distance from the metropolis. The urban population in particular exhibits this pattern, but it is unmistakably present for all populations.

2. The regions which show the smallest change per unit of distance, and also exhibit the most variation, are primarily southern areas which only recently have begun to experience the rise of metropolitan centers.

3. Within any one region the range of differences with distance is greater, on the whole, than the level of differences between regions. The differentiation of land area according to its metropolitan position appears to be more pronounced than the regional differentiation of areas. Thus, <u>even though the major differences in land settlement between geographic regions may be associated with resource differences, within each region there are even greater differences which are associated with metropolitan organization.</u> Had the size of the central cities been held constant, the settlement differences between regions would have tended to become even smaller. Such a procedure would have transferred the concentrative effects of huge centers of 500,000 or more inhabitants from the category of regional differences to that of metropolitan differences, and undoubtedly would have made the above intra-regional differences even more striking in comparison to inter-regional differences.

III

Geographic Regions and Subdominance
(Tables 9-2, 9-3, 9-4)

Just as it has been demonstrated that population within each geographic region tends to be distributed by the metropolitan dominance pattern, so it may be shown that the metropolitan pattern of subdominance tends to be present in each region. Table 9-2 presents, for each geographic division, the habitation ratios for each size group of hinterland cities by distance from the nearest metropolis. Tables 9-3 and 9-4 present the same information for the rural-nonfarm and the rural-farm popula-

tions, by size of largest city contained. Two of the metropolitan variables, size class of the central city and type of sector, are not held constant. The effects which they have upon the distribution of population are allowed to appear as interdivisional differences.

1. In each geographic division the level of land occupancy tends to decline with distance from the metropolis, (even when "size of city" or "size of largest city contained" is held constant). The major deviations occur in the South, and for the larger rather than the smaller sizes of cities. In all geographic divisions, the areas which are most remote from the metropolis have either very low habitation ratios, or a complete absence of cities of a given size.

2. For both of the rural populations, as the size of the largest city contained increases the level of land occupancy also increases. The phenomenon of subdominance is therefore present in each geographic division, and, together with metropolitan dominance, gives to each region a metropolitan structure.

3. Even though the patterns of dominance and subdominance are present, there are, nevertheless, characteristic differences in these patterns between regions. The South particularly exhibits such divergent patterns as concentrations of rural-farm and rural-nonfarm populations which are higher in remote areas than in near areas, high rural-farm habitation ratios at all distances, and a relative scarcity of urban centers of the larger sizes. In the Northeast, the North Center, and the West the ability of a hinterland city to aggregate rural populations in its immediate vicinity appears to be conditioned by its metropolitan position. In the South, however, the hinterland city shows much more independence in its ability to aggregate population. Even though the cities are distributed with a decreasing frequency with distance from the metropolitan center, the level of aggregation of rural populations within that distribution tends to be independent of distance from the metropolis. It cannot be argued that this difference between the South and other regions results from the fact that size of metropolis is uncontrolled. Only in the large metropolitan communities have such large rural habitation ratios been found to exist at the greater distances. Since metropolitan communities in the South are primarily in the class C and D groupings, their high habitation ratios for rural populations are attained in spite of, not because of, the size of the metropolis. Southern metropolitan centers appear, on all counts, to modify the activities of their hinterland cities to a much smaller degree than do such centers in the remainder of the United States.

Table 9-2

Habitation ratios: Urban population per square mile of land area, by geographic division, size of hinterland city and distance from the nearest metropolis. United States, 1940.

Geographic Division	DISTANCE FROM THE NEAREST METROPOLIS (miles)							
	0-24 [a]	25 - 34	35 - 44	45 - 64	65 - 114	115 - 164	165 - 264	265 - over
Cities of 2500 - 4999 inhabitants								
New England	1	6	6	4	1	1	2	0
Middle Atlantic	76	11	9	9	8	3	2	-
East North Central	16	6	5	4	3	2	1	2
West North Central	18	3	2	2	2	2	1	0
South Atlantic [b]	8	4	6	2	2	2	2	-
East South Central	3	4	3	3	2	2	1	-
West South Central	14	1	3	2	2	2	1	1
Mountain	21	2	1	1	1	0	0	0
Pacific	25	11	5	1	1	1	0	0
Cities of 5000 - 9999 inhabitants								
New England	38	47	14	6	8	4	4	1
Middle Atlantic	180	15	11	9	8	5	3	-
East North Central	28	7	6	6	5	2	2	1
West North Central	17	2	2	3	2	2	1	0
South Atlantic [b]	13	2	3	2	2	2	2	-
East South Central	9	5	1	3	2	2	1	-
West South Central	13	3	3	3	2	2	1	1
Mountain	26	3	1	1	0	0	0	0
Pacific	73	9	2	3	2	0	1	0
Cities of 10,000 - 24,999 inhabitants								
New England	136	49	35	48	21	6	4	-
Middle Atlantic	334	29	16	18	9	4	6	-
East North Central	38	14	7	7	6	3	3	7
West North Central	40	4	4	4	3	3	0	1
South Atlantic [b]	23	4	8	3	4	3	2	9
East South Central	11	3	3	1	3	3	2	-
West South Central	37	3	3	3	2	2	1	1
Mountain	-	5	1	1	1	0	0	0
Pacific	100	37	2	2	2	2	0	1
Cities of 25,000 - 49,999 inhabitants								
New England	198	32	73	18	4	8	2	-
Middle Atlantic	159	20	3	12	6	-	-	-
East North Central	36	6	25	10	5	4	1	-
West North Central	22	-	3	1	1	1	1	-
South Atlantic [b]	14	4	-	1	4	2	1	-
East South Central	5	-	3	3	2	2	-	-
West South Central	-	-	-	1	1	2	0	2
Mountain	-	-	3	-	1	-	-	0
Pacific	105	25	-	5	2	0	-	-
Cities of 50,000 - over inhabitants								
New England	237	221	108	49	11	-	-	-
Middle Atlantic	585	10	-	32	7	-	-	-
East North Central	50	31	-	8	8	-	-	-
West North Central	120	-	-	6	3	-	1	-
South Atlantic [b]	26	12	-	2	4	4	5	-
East South Central	11	-	-	-	1	2	2	-
West South Central	-	-	-	2	2	2	1	-
Mountain	-	-	-	-	1	-	-	0
Pacific	313	43	-	6	-	-	1	-

a) Includes land area and population of counties containing the central cities, but excludes the land area and population of central cities.

b) Independent cities of Virginia were classified as lying in no county.

Source: Sixteenth Census of the United States. Compiled from Population, Vol.I, State tables 3 and 5; Population, Vol.II, State tables 26 and 27; Areas of the United States, 1940, tables 2, 3, and 4.

Table 9-3

Habitation ratios: Rural-nonfarm population per square mile of rural area, by geographic division, size of largest city contained, and distance from the nearest metropolis. United States, 1940.

Geographic Division	DISTANCE FROM THE NEAREST METROPOLIS (miles)							
	0 - 24 a)	25 - 34	35 - 44	45 - 64	65 - 114	115 - 164	165 - 264	265 - over
Largest place less than 2500 inhabitants								
New England	-	-	-	47	-	13	9	4
Middle Atlantic	-	23	10	56	8	22	-	-
East North Central	34	18	15	15	11	9	6	-
West North Central	19	22	12	11	8	7	4	2
South Atlantic b)	22	15	10	11	10	11	11	9
East South Central	13	24	8	11	9	9	10	-
West South Central	-	12	9	6	6	4	4	2
Mountain	-	4	4	1	2	2	1	1
Pacific	-	-	13	4	3	3	2	1
Largest city 2500 - 4999 inhabitants								
New England	-	-	-	-	-	-	10	8
Middle Atlantic	-	29	16	43	18	11	-	-
East North Central	18	21	12	13	12	7	7	4
West North Central	25	7	6	8	6	7	3	2
South Atlantic b)	45	25	20	14	12	11	15	-
East South Central	14	14	16	8	10	7	10	-
West South Central	10	8	8	6	5	6	3	2
Mountain	25	9	2	1	2	2	1	1
Pacific	11	25	4	7	4	3	2	0
Largest city 5000 - 9999 inhabitants								
New England	27	-	-	16	26	16	14	8
Middle Atlantic	104	31	45	57	23	17	7	-
East North Central	19	18	13	15	14	8	9	2
West North Central	7	11	12	8	7	7	3	2
South Atlantic b)	94	8	35	13	18	12	33	-
East South Central	21	8	18	19	17	13	10	-
West South Central	-	6	-	8	7	7	7	3
Mountain	-	-	2	-	5	2	1	1
Pacific	-	53	16	9	6	-	4	2
Largest city 10,000 - 24,999 inhabitants								
New England	19	50	-	26	27	18	13	-
Middle Atlantic	829	46	64	53	35	15	17	-
East North Central	33	34	17	21	19	13	6	3
West North Central	-	13	8	7	8	8	5	2
South Atlantic b)	128	25	29	18	21	21	31	11
East South Central	9	20	11	26	19	8	9	-
West South Central	42	8	9	14	11	10	8	-
Mountain	-	7	5	5	3	1	2	2
Pacific	28	67	54	15	13	5	1	4
Largest city 25,000 - 49,999 inhabitants								
New England	80	-	46	-	22	24	11	-
Middle Atlantic	227	87	31	43	34	-	-	-
East North Central	40	12	39	28	25	19	9	-
West North Central	296	10	-	8	11	13	5	-
South Atlantic b)	-	-	-	13	54	41	50	-
East South Central	52	-	12	15	34	15	-	-
West South Central	-	-	-	17	25	8	10	10
Mountain	-	-	9	-	6	-	-	6
Pacific	-	51	15	-	10	6	2	-
Largest city 50,000 - over inhabitants								
New England	129	174	86	53	217	31	-	-
Middle Atlantic	131	115	108	73	82	-	-	-
East North Central	61	80	48	71	38	-	-	-
West North Central	125	-	-	13	17	10	17	-
South Atlantic b)	75	-	109	98	53	43	52	-
East South Central	101	-	-	-	15	37	14	-
West South Central	-	-	26	-	20	25	15	0
Mountain	-	-	-	-	4	-	-	7
Pacific	-	-	46	27	-	-	8	-

a) Includes land area and population of counties containing the central cities, but excludes the land area and population of central cities.

b) Independent cities of Virginia were classified as lying in no county.

Source: Sixteenth Census of the United States. Compiled from Population, Vol.I, State tables 3 and 5; Population, Vol.II, State tables 25 and 27; Areas of the United States, 1940, tables 2, 3, and 4.

Habitation ratios: Rural-farm population per square mile of rural area, by geographic division, size of largest city contained, and distance from the nearest metropolis. United States, 1940.

Geographic Division	DISTANCE FROM THE NEAREST METROPOLIS (miles)							
	0 - 24 a)	25 - 34	35 - 44	45 - 64	65 - 114	115 - 164	165 - 264	265 - over
Largest place less than 2500 inhabitants								
New England	-	-	-	7	-	10	5	1
Middle Atlantic	-	19	4	6	6	18	-	-
East North Central	28	20	20	20	17	11	6	-
West North Central	20	25	19	15	11	12	6	3
South Atlantic b)	24	21	18	21	18	23	17	11
East South Central	27	19	34	25	27	28	22	-
West South Central	-	9	8	11	11	7	7	3
Mountain	-	2	2	2	2	1	1	1
Pacific	-	-	2	2	3	1	1	1
Largest city 2500 - 4999 inhabitants								
New England	-	-	-	-	-	-	14	4
Middle Atlantic	-	18	18	26	13	8	-	-
East North Central	25	24	24	20	18	14	9	2
West North Central	18	16	13	17	12	14	8	3
South Atlantic b)	18	36	23	32	19	25	23	-
East South Central	35	30	28	30	31	37	31	-
West South Central	53	21	9	19	14	13	9	5
Mountain	10	10	1	1	1	1	1	1
Pacific	9	25	4	7	4	2	2	1
Largest city 5000 - 9999 inhabitants								
New England	24	-	-	6	10	8	10	5
Middle Atlantic	34	15	24	18	17	7	8	-
East North Central	26	26	25	21	20	15	9	2
West North Central	17	14	17	15	16	15	8	4
South Atlantic b)	35	43	17	23	27	29	22	-
East South Central	31	31	35	33	30	32	30	-
West South Central	-	21	-	15	15	15	18	8
Mountain	-	-	2	-	4	2	1	1
Pacific	-	6	11	4	5	-	5	2
Largest city 10,000 - 24,999 inhabitants								
New England	22	16	-	16	9	12	7	-
Middle Atlantic	15	24	23	17	15	9	14	-
East North Central	30	25	18	23	20	17	8	4
West North Central	-	17	13	15	15	16	14	4
South Atlantic b)	38	20	32	19	16	35	29	1
East South Central	23	31	31	31	35	36	26	-
West South Central	12	17	20	23	22	23	11	-
Mountain	-	7	4	7	4	2	2	3
Pacific	26	21	15	9	12	5	1	2
Largest city 25,000 - 49,999 inhabitants								
New England	17	-	14	-	10	17	5	-
Middle Atlantic	42	26	21	24	17	-	-	-
East North Central	24	16	22	24	22	28	21	-
West North Central	36	17	-	12	19	21	9	-
South Atlantic b)	-	-	-	8	31	40	11	-
East South Central	42	-	36	25	37	25	-	-
West South Central	-	-	-	25	21	6	10	16
Mountain	-	-	15	-	2	-	-	2
Pacific	-	23	11	-	5	5	1	-
Largest city 50,000 - over inhabitants								
New England	22	24	29	15	22	15	-	-
Middle Atlantic	26	16	18	38	22	-	-	-
East North Central	23	29	22	34	24	-	-	-
West North Central	45	-	-	17	19	16	27	-
South Atlantic b)	15	-	23	26	32	32	23	-
East South Central	39	-	-	-	32	9	38	-
West South Central	-	-	9	-	17	23	17	3
Mountain	-	-	-	-	3	-	-	4
Pacific	-	-	17	19	-	-	10	-

a) Includes land area and population of counties containing the central cities, but excludes the land area and population of central cities.

b) Independent cities of Virginia were classified as lying in no county.

Source: Sixteenth Census of the United States. Compiled from Population, Vol.I, State tables 3 and 5; Population, Vol.II, State tables 25 and 27; Areas of the United States, 1940, tables 2, 3, and 4.

IV

Summary

1. Since only a very small proportion of the labor force of the United States is actively engaged in extractive industries, the metropolitan patterns of population distribution which have been found in the preceding chapters are not a direct result of the pattern of resource distribution.

2. Yet it can be demonstrated that some areas with rich resources contain a higher proportion of population, both rural and urban, than do equal areas with poor resources. The distribution of the urban and rural populations, for example, is unmistakably related to the suitability of the land for agriculture. This relationship, even though it is expressive of human organization rather than of resource patterns directly, does imply that, to some undetermined extent, the structure of the metropolitan community is conditioned by the distribution of natural resources.

3. Therefore, metropolitan dominance is not a pattern arbitrarily imposed by great cities, nor is it a pattern imposed by the physical environment. Rather, it appears to be a working arrangement and an organization of population over the land for the purpose of making use of the environment. The metropolitan structure of population in the United States can be characterized most simply and consistently as a pattern of human adaptation to the physical environment which uses modern commercial and industrial techniques.

4. This form of adaptation appears to have become almost universal in the United States and, since the patterns of dominance and subdominance are present in each of the major geographic regions it is employed to adapt to a wide variety of environmental conditions.

PART III

THE STRUCTURE OF SUSTENANCE ACTIVITIES IN METROPOLITAN COMMUNITIES

Introduction to Part III*

After having observed the tendency for the intensity of land settlement to vary with the variables which indicate position with respect to the metropolis and to hinterland cities, it is pertinent to ask:

Is this metropolis-centered pattern related to the activities by which the individual local communities sustain themselves?

Other studies of communal organization have found that some of the forces which are most powerful in making for structure within the individual community are those which are related to the gaining of a livelihood, or those activities which sustain the population and, consequently, the community. It is for this reason that attention is now turned to sustenance activities in an attempt to explain the existence and operation of this apparent metropolitan dominance.

Within each local community the individual inhabitant must find sustenance or perish. Individuals do not seek a livelihood without reference to their fellows, but through participation in an established system of production and exchange. This system antedates each person and, presumably, will exist long after he has ceased to participate. In any community the total sustenance activities (the composite of the established system) must either be such that the community is completely self-sufficient, or such that goods and services which cannot be provided locally will be caused to flow into the community from outside areas. The latter alternative, the only course which the great majority of communities can follow in the modern commercial-industrial society, can be accomplished only by local production of surpluses of some commodities to be exchanged for those items which cannot be obtained locally. Thus, there must be an intercommunity division of labor and an intercommunity exchange. Such exchanges are not made directly, or by barter, but through the market. Since the market relates intercommunity needs to each other, the producers and consumers of each commodity or service may orient themselves to market centers rather than to the direct consumer.

It is well known that great cities are the principal market centers of the nation. Though the marketing system is a complex mechanism composed of many scattered units, most marketing activities are integrated into key units located in metropolitan centers. It is well known that the great industrial system of the nation is also metropolis oriented. This tendency may be a partial result of the desire to be near markets, to enjoy greater access to the variety of raw materials which are assembled there, to employ a varied labor force, or to benefit from the productive efforts of other industries.

The hypothesis of this section of the study is that the population patterns are accompanied by definite sustenance patterns, that in each portion of the hinterland in other words, populations have adapted themselves to the metropolitan market and to metropolitan industries, even while adapting to their own local environments, and have thereby established a pattern of sustenance activities which is related to, and helps to explain, the total population pattern. The subject matter, therefore, is <u>community specialization</u> and apparent <u>territorial division of labor.</u>

Four broad categories of sustenance activity have been taken for study. They are, as defined by the United States Bureau of the Census, retail trade, services, wholesale trade, and manufactures. Each is measured by three indexes: "number of establishments per 1,000 inhabitants," "number of wage earners per 1,000 inhabitants," and "dollar value per inhabitant."

The chapters of this section are arranged as follows: Chapter Ten describes briefly the general pattern of concentration of all four activities. Chapters Eleven, Twelve, Thirteen, and Fourteen each take up one of the sustenance activities and analyze it in terms of specialization and exchange.

---

*In this section of the study considerable reliance is placed upon the use of data for wholesale trade and manufacture. I am greatly indebted to the United States Bureau of the Census for providing tabulations of the total number of wage earners, and the dollar value, of these activities for groups of counties and cities for which it had been necessary for the Census to withhold the information in published reports. These groups totals were provided for units combined in accordance with the variables of the study. Sufficient numbers of places were included in each group to avoid violating the rules concerning disclosure.

CHAPTER TEN

A DESCRIPTION OF THE DISTRIBUTION OF FOUR OF THE MAJOR
SUSTENANCE ACTIVITIES IN THE METROPOLITAN COMMUNITY

I

How Are the Sustenance Activities Distributed
by Size Class of Metropolitan Community?
(Table 10-1)

With a few exceptions, the four size classes of
metropolitan communities contain proportions of
retail trade, services, wholesale trade, and manufactures which are roughly proportional to their

populations. This means that, although there are
undoubtedly a great many interdependences in regard to specific items between the various size
classes of metropolitan communities, there is no
great deficit of any one broad type of activity. The
largest differences are in manufactures and wholesale trade; the smallest differences are in retail
trade and services. But no class of metropolitan
community is so deficient in one type of activity
that it must depend completely upon other sizes of

Table 10-1

Distribution of land area, population, and selected sustenance activities, by size class of metropolitan community.
United States, 1939-40.

Size class of metro-politan commu-nity[a]	NUMBER								PERCENT					
	Land Area (thousand square miles)	Popu-lation	Sustenance activities				Land area	Popu-lation	Sustenance activities			
			Retail trade	Services	Whole-sale trade	Manu-facture			Retail trade	Services	Whole-sale trade	Manu-facture
			Number of establishments (thousands)						Number of establishments			
Class A	124	29,456	444	190	56	65	4.2	22.4	25.1	29.4	27.9	35.3
Class B	202	24,171	330	122	34	38	6.8	18.4	18.6	18.9	16.9	20.7
Class C	992	35,314	433	150	50	38	33.3	26.8	24.5	23.2	24.9	20.7
Class D	1,658	47,727	563	184	61	43	55.7	32.5	31.8	28.4	30.3	23.4
All classes	2,976	131,668	1,770	646	201	184	100.0	100.0	100.0	100.0	100.0	100.0
			Number of wage earners (thousands)						Number of wage earners			
Class A	-	-	1,278	386	560	2,512	4.2	22.4	27.8	35.0	35.9	31.8
Class B	-	-	956	202	303	1,876	6.8	18.4	20.8	18.3	19.4	23.8
Class C	-	-	1,080	263	345	1,496	33.3	26.8	23.5	23.9	22.1	19.0
Class D	-	-	1,286	251	354	2,002	55.7	32.5	28.0	22.8	22.7	25.4
All classes	-	-	4,600	1,102	1,562	7,887	100.0	100.0	100.0	100.0	100.0	100.0
			Dollar value (millions of dollars)[b]						Dollar value			
Class A	-	-	12,011	1,353	24,083	8,864	4.2	22.4	28.6	39.6	43.6	35.9
Class B	-	-	8,697	664	10,401	5,981	6.8	18.4	20.7	19.4	18.8	24.2
Class C	-	-	9,543	682	11,216	4,335	33.3	26.8	22.7	19.9	20.3	17.6
Class D	-	-	11,791	722	9,566	5,503	55.7	32.5	28.0	21.1	17.3	22.3
All classes	-	-	42,042	3,420	55,266	24,683	100.0	100.0	100.0	100.0	100.0	100.0

a) Includes central cities and counties containing central cities.

b) Dollar value for manufacturing is "value added by manufacture". Dollar value of other activities is total
sales or receipts.

Source: Sixteenth Census of the United States. Compiled from Population, Vol.I, State tables 3 and 5; Retail Trade,
1939, Vol.I, table 16; Service Establishments, 1939, table 2; Wholesale Trade, 1939, Vol.II, table 13.
Manufactures, 1939, Vol.III, State table 2.

metropolitan communities. Table 10-1 indicates that each size class of metropolitan community provides its own inhabitants with approximately the proportions of retail and service activities which they require, although the class C and D metropolitan communities are dependent to some extent upon the class A and B metropolitan communities for wholesale and manufacturing activities. Undoubtedly, the surplus resulting from the wholesaling and manufacturing activities of these larger metropolitan communities is exchanged for a portion of the agricultural surpluses of the class C and D communities.

II

How Are the Sustenance Activities
Distributed by Distance
from the Nearest Metropolis?
(Table 10-2)

All four of the sustenance activities tend to be concentrated heavily in the central cities. Whereas central cities contain only 25.7 percent of the population, they contain:

37.9 percent of the retail sales
54.8 percent of the receipts from services
71.8 percent of the wholesale sales
39.0 percent of the value added by manufacture

The other indexes of the sustenance activities show similar concentrations in central cities.

That there is a definite concentration of sustenance activities at the inner distances can be verified by a comparison of their percentage distributions with population, and with the percentage distributions for land, as presented in Chapter Four. The total amount of difference between these distributions is indicated by the coefficients of dissimilarity reported in Table 10-2. It is evident that the general nature of this distance pattern will consist of relative concentration in the inner distance zones, and relative deficit in the outer zones, with respect both to land area and to population. Thus, although the sustenance activities are patterned, with respect to land, in the same general manner as population, they differ sufficiently in their distributions to indicate definitely that differences in specialization exist with distance from the metropolis. The details of this distance pattern will be studied in the chapters which follow. It is evident that the most marked differences in specialization with distance will be found for wholesale trade and for manufacture, and that smaller differences will be found for retail trade and services.

The percentages of Table 10-2 indicate that the central city produces a considerable surplus of all four of the goods and services which result from these sustenance activities, and that at least a portion of the hinterland is dependent to some extent upon the metropolis for the satisfaction of some of its needs. The amount of the excess at the center and of the deficit in the hinterland is much greater, in every case, than the amounts of excess and deficit found between the various size classes of metropolitan communities. There is evidence within the metropolitan community, therefore, of extensive interdependency among the composite local communities, and of a definite locational pattern in regard to the areas of surplus and deficit of each activity. It should be noted, particularly, however, that in no instance is any distance zone completely devoid of any one of the four sustenance activities. In other words, at no distance is an area completely dependent upon the metropolis for the performance of one type of function. On the other hand, at no distance does any area appear to be completely self-sufficient in all activities, although this situation may be very nearly approached, if not actually attained, for retail trade alone in the outer distance zones. The dependences appear to be selective. There is greater reliance upon the metropolis for some types of sustenance activities than for others, and, within each type, some items appear to be provided locally and others to be obtained from the central city. While data in support of this latter point have not been marshalled here, it is generally assumed that the most specialized types of retailing, services, wholesaling, and manufacture are located in or very near the metropolis. Those items for which there is a small per capita demand, those for which many different components and many skills are required, or those which must be brought from great distances are the ones which are presumed to be centered in the metropolis.[1]

It should be noted that the number of establishments in each zone more nearly approaches the proportion of the population residing there than does the number of wage earners or the dollar value of the activity. A greater proportion of the large, and presumably the more influential, units of each activity are located at the center

1. See R. D. McKenzie, The Metropolitan Community, pp. 73-74, and 323-324, for data in support of this hypothesis.

Table 10-2

Percentage distributions of measures of retail trade, services, wholesale trade, and manufacturing activities for central cities and hinterland areas classified by distance from the nearest metropolis. United States, 1939

Distance zone (miles)	SUSTENANCE ACTIVITIES MEASURED IN TERMS OF DOLLAR VOLUME							
	DOLLAR VOLUME				WAGE EARNERS			
	Retail trade	Services	Whole-sale trade	Manu-facture	Retail trade	Services	Whole-sale trade	Manu-facture
Central city	37.9	54.8	71.8	39.0	41.5	54.7	62.0	33.6
0-14	9.4	8.4	4.2	14.7	8.8	7.6	5.4	13.1
15-24	4.9	3.9	2.0	7.3	4.4	3.3	2.1	7.0
25-34	5.2	3.7	1.9	6.7	4.9	3.2	2.5	7.2
35-44	4.3	2.9	1.6	5.4	4.0	2.7	2.1	5.7
45-64	9.3	6.5	3.9	9.6	8.8	6.4	5.6	11.4
65-114	13.5	9.3	6.4	10.0	13.2	9.8	8.7	12.4
115-164	6.9	4.9	4.0	4.0	6.8	6.1	5.7	5.5
165-264	5.8	3.8	3.0	2.6	5.4	4.6	4.2	3.5
265-464	2.4	1.5	1.1	0.8	2.1	1.5	1.4	0.7
465-over	0.3	0.2	0.2	0.1	0.3	0.1	0.2	-
All distances	100.0	100.0	100.0	100.0	100.0	100.0	100.0	100.0
Coefficient of dissimilarity with land area	55.0	65.1	74.8	66.5	56.2	63.0	66.4	61.9
Coefficient of dissimilarity with population	12.3	29.2	46.1	22.1	15.7	29.0	36.4	17.0

Distance zone (miles)	NUMBER OF ESTABLISHMENTS			
	Retail	Services	Wholesale	Manufacture
Central city	28.2	39.8	44.8	44.6
0-14	9.3	6.7	4.5	8.7
15-24	5.1	4.4	2.5	4.4
25-34	5.7	4.9	3.4	4.5
35-44	4.8	4.0	3.1	4.0
45-64	10.7	9.3	7.8	8.7
65-114	16.4	14.1	13.8	12.0
115-164	9.5	8.1	8.6	6.7
165-264	7.5	6.2	7.2	4.8
265-464	2.6	2.2	3.4	1.5
465-over	0.4	0.3	0.8	0.2
All distances	100.0	100.0	100.0	100.0
Coefficient of dissimilarity with land area	47.6	53.0	50.3	58.8
Coefficient of dissimilarity with population	3.5	14.1	20.5	18.9

Source: Sixteenth Census of the United States. Compiled from Population, Vol.I, State tables 3 and 5; Retail Trade, 1939, Vol.I, table 16; Service Establishments, 1939, table 2; Wholesale Trade, 1939, Vol.II, table 13; Manufactures, 1939, Vol.III, state table 2.

and in the inner zones. A larger than proportional share of the smaller units is located in the more distant zones.[2]

III

How are the Sustenance Activities Distributed Between the Types of Sectors? (Table 10-3)

The intermetropolitan and the subdominant sectors contain definite concentrations of all four sustenance activities. The local sectors have a deficit of all sustenance activities, with respect both to land area and to population. Thus, those sectors which contain an intermetropolitan thoroughfare or a major hinterland city tend to be more specialized in retail trade, services, wholesale trade, and manufacture than the local sectors. Since a surplus of these sustenance activities is provided by the high mobility sectors, it can only be inferred that the local sectors satisfy a considerable proportion of their needs through these

Table 10-3

Percentage distributions of land area, population, and selected sustenance activities by type of sector. United States, 1939-40.

Type of sector[a]	Land area	Population	SUSTENANCE ACTIVITIES			
			Retail trade	Services	Wholesale trade	Manufacture
			Number of establishments			
Intermetropolitan	56.4	58.0	58.2	59.4	60.7	59.5
Subdominant	10.4	18.5	18.0	18.1	15.9	19.4
Local	33.2	23.5	23.8	22.4	23.4	21.1
All sectors	100.0	100.0	100.0	100.0	100.0	100.0
			Number of wage earners			
Intermetropolitan	56.4	58.0	61.2	61.9	63.2	59.8
Subdominant	10.4	18.5	19.5	21.3	19.8	22.4
Local	33.2	23.5	19.3	16.9	17.1	17.8
All sectors	100.0	100.0	100.0	100.0	100.0	100.0
			Dollar value[b]			
Intermetropolitan	56.4	58.0	60.6	63.6	65.2	62.9
Subdominant	10.4	18.5	18.7	18.9	18.8	20.6
Local	33.2	23.5	20.7	17.6	16.0	16.5
All sectors	100.0	100.0	100.0	100.0	100.0	100.0

a) Data for central cities and counties containing central cities have been excluded.

b) Dollar value for manufacturing is "value added by manufacture." Dollar value for other activities is total sales or receipts.

Source: Sixteenth Census of the United States. Compiled from Population, Vol. I, State tables 3 and 5; Retail Trade, 1939, Vol. I, table 16; Service Establishments, 1939, table 2; Wholesale trade, 1939, table 13; Manufactures, 1939, Vol. III, State table 2.

---

2. In 1939 the Census of Manufactures did not obtain reports for establishments whose product was valued at less than $5,000. Other very small business units frequently cannot be identified. For these reasons the data of this study may underestimate the specialization of small communities and remote areas. The amount of this underestimation could not be large enough to alter the conclusions.

other types of sectors. This dependence of the local sectors, while not as marked as that between the metropolis and its zones, is of a consistency which indicates a functional integration of parts in the hinterland.

The local sectors are not greatly deficient in number of establishments. As was true concerning the differences in specialization between the metropolis and its zones, the differences between the sectors are primarily a matter of average size of individual establishments rather than of number of enterprises as such.

IV

How Are the Sustenance Activities Distributed Among the Metropolis, the Principal Hinterland Cities, and the Other Hinterland Areas?
(Table 10-4)

The preceding tables have dealt with distance zones and sector types as such, without attempting to distinguish between hinterland cities and other areas. An analysis of the specialization of smaller hinterland cities of less than 10,000 inhabitants, by size, has not been made in this study because of certain limitations of the available data. The United States Census of Manufactures does not publish data for cities which are smaller than 10,000 inhabitants. Although data for wholesale trade are available for cities as small as 5,000 inhabitants, and for retail trade and services for all cities,[3] it is necessary, in order that full comparability may be obtained between the four types of functions to restrict the analysis to cities for which manufacture data are available.[4] The hinterland areas which are used in the study of sustenance patterns are not urban and rural areas, therefore, but cities of 10,000 inhabitants or more and "other areas," the latter comprising the rural area and all cities of less than 10,000 inhabitants. In the chapters which follow, hinterland cities of 10,000 or more inhabitants are termed "principal

Table 10-4

Percentage distributions of land area, population, and the dollar value of selected sustenance activities. Hinterland units classified by size. United States, 1939-40.

Type of unit	Land area	Population	Retail sales	Services	Wholesale sales	Value added by manufacture
Central cities	0.1	25.7	37.9	34.8	71.8	39.0
Hinterland cities	0.3	21.9	32.0	27.4	17.3	34.8
25,000 and over	0.1	14.4	21.3	19.5	12.8	25.2
10,000 to 24,999	0.1	7.5	10.8	8.0	4.5	9.6
Other hinterland areas	99.6	52.4	30.0	17.8	10.9	26.3
Central counties [a)	1.7	3.9	2.2	1.4	0.9	4.2
50,000 – over	2.4	4.3	2.4	1.5	0.9	4.4
25,000 – 49,999	5.0	4.2	2.3	1.3	0.9	3.6
10,000 – 24,999	11.6	8.6	4.3	2.5	1.3	5.3
5,000 – 9,999	17.4	11.1	8.2	5.1	3.1	5.0
2,500 – 4,999	20.4	9.6	5.7	3.4	2.2	2.4
No city	41.1	10.7	4.8	2.6	1.6	1.4
All units	100.0	100.0	100.0	100.0	100.0	100.0

a) Counties containing central cities. Other counties classified by size of largest city contained

Source: Sixteenth Census of the United States. Compiled from Population, Vol.I, State tables 3 and 5; Retail Trade, 1939, Vol.I, table 16; Service Establishments, 1939, table 2; Wholesale Trade, 1939, Vol.II, table 13; Manufactures, 1939, Vol.III, State table 2.

See footnotes on page 152.

hinterland cities,"[5] and the part of each county which remains after these cities have been deducted from the total of the county is termed "other area." The fact that hinterland cities of less than 10,000 cannot be studied places no restriction upon the classification of other areas by "size of largest city contained." Since the "other areas" in each case are county units, the same classification that of "size of largest city contained," which was employed in the population analysis can be used to study the concentration of sustenance activities in these "other areas" in which the largest city is of a known size.

Excepting wholesale trade, which is so heavily concentrated in central cities that only a small proportion is available for distribution throughout the hinterland, the principal hinterland cities are areas of considerable total concentration of the sustenance activities. While the "other area" of the hinterland contains more than half of the total population, it contains only:

30.0 percent of the retail trade
17.8 percent of the receipts from services
10.9 percent of the wholesale trade
26.3 percent of the value added by manufacture

Principal hinterland cities contain a larger proportion than their share of the population would indicate of that amount of each sustenance activity which is performed in the hinterland. The hinterland cities of 25,000 or more inhabitants are more specialized than are those containing 10,000 to 24,999 inhabitants. The "other areas" containing no cities are the least specialized in the four sustenance activities. Although these latter areas constitute 41.1 percent of the total land area and contain 10.7 percent of the population, they contain only 1.4 to 4.8 percent of the sustenance activities. The larger the size of the city, apparently, the greater the degree of specialization, since, with increasing size of largest city contained up to 10,000 inhabitants, the disparity between the percentage of population and the percentage of sustenance activities gradually decreases.

---

3. With the occasional exception of some places classified as "urban under special rule."

4. Had the data for cities of less than 10,000 been tabulated, where available, it would have been necessary to abandon the "size of largest city" tabulations for the "other areas," or else to be content with tabulations for rural areas and small cities which were not comparable to each other.

5. It will be recalled that in determining whether or not a given sector were to be classified as subdominant the term "major hinterland city" was employed to designate hinterland cities of 25,000 or more inhabitants. It should not be confused with the term "principal hinterland city."

CHAPTER ELEVEN

THE STRUCTURE OF RETAIL TRADE IN THE METROPOLITAN COMMUNITY

I

Introduction

The objective of this chapter is to show that there is a metropolitan pattern of retail activity with respect to the population, and that this pattern

II

Standards for Measuring Retail Specialization — Regional Indexes

In 1940 the indexes of retail specialization for the nation as a whole, and for each geographic division, were as follows:

Geographic division	Establishments per thousand population	Wage earners per thousand population	Retail sales per inhabitant
New England	14.4	34.5	$ 393
Middle Atlantic	15.0	32.3	374
East North Central	13.7	30.7	347
West North Central	14.6	27.0	306
South Atlantic	11.2	23.8	245
East South Central	9.4	16.0	171
West South Central	12.2	23.4	237
Mountain	13.8	28.4	344
Pacific	16.0	35.9	442
United States	13.4	28.3	319

is related logically to the pattern of population distribution. Are the residents of some parts of the hinterland more specialized in retail trade than are the residents of other parts? If so, is there any relationship between the degree of this specialization and metropolitan location? Providing such a relationship is found to exist, what plausible hypotheses can be developed concerning the reasons for it? Such are the questions which will be asked. The measure of specialization used will be the ratio of retail activity to population. If one of two neighboring areas has a ratio of retail activity to population which is so low that it cannot possibly meet the needs of the population residing there, and the other area has a ratio which is so high that it is obviously in excess of the needs of the resident population, it is presumed that the two areas are participating in a division of labor, the first depending upon the second for the performance of a considerable share of its retail functions. Since it is the division of labor, — the degree of specialization, — which is being measured, the units of measurement must be expressed in terms both of population and retail activity: "x retail trade per unit of population." Such measures will be called "per capita retail indexes."

It is evident that the geographic differences in retail activity are considerable. A portion of this difference undoubtedly represents regional differences in volume of consumption, in degree of family self-sufficiency, and in level of living. A portion of it may be associated also with the metropolitan communities themselves, and is due to regional differences in size of metropolitan centers, distance, sector type, and number and size of hinterland cities per unit of area. Unfortunately, it is impossible to separate the regional differences in level of retail consumption from the regional level of metropolitan development. We can use the differences between regions only as a reference point in making comparisons between various parts of the metropolitan community or between size classes of metropolitan communities. In any event, it is not difficult to show that differences in retail consumption are as great within metropolitan communities as they are between geographic regions, and sometimes greater, and that it is impossible for regional differences to account for the apparent specialization within the metropolitan community.

Each of the three indexes of retail specialization has a tendency to emphasize a different aspect of community organization and specialization.

a. "Number of establishments per 1000 inhabitants" measures the relative number of retail units which a given population supports, without specifying the size of the units. This index states the frequency, relative to the population, with which enterprises of the retail type are undertaken in a given area.

b. "Number of employees per 1000 inhabitants" is primarily a measure of employment specialization, although it is also a measure of the volume of activity. An area with a high ratio of retail workers to total population gains its livelihood through serving other populations in retail activity. In this sense the index is a measure of community employment, or measure of the type of activity by which the community sustains itself. "Number of employees per 1000 inhabitants" does not include the self-employment of proprietors in their own establishments or the employment of unpaid workers from the proprietor's family. Both of these factors can vary considerably from one part of the metropolitan community to another, as can the proportion of the wage earners which is composed of part-time employees. For these reasons the index is used to measure the degree of community employment in retail trade rather than to measure the volume of retail activity.

c. "Receipts per person" is a more suitable measure of the volume of retail activity than is either of the other two indexes. It is stated in the units by which the volume of business is usually measured, and is not subject to some of the limitations to which the other indexes, as measures of volume, are subject. The volume of sales is not an exact measure of the comparative size of retail establishments nor of the physical volume of goods retailed. In one respect, however, this fact improves its utility as an index of specialization. Costly items tend to be specialized items. Those areas which attain high indexes of dollar receipts per person by retailing costly items must be, of necessity, those areas which retail specialized items. Thus, although greater emphasis is placed in this study upon the dollar value index as a measure of community specialization, the other two indexes of retail activity emphasize other important aspects of intercommunity division of labor. Data concerning all three indexes are reported for all except the most detailed tables.

In examining the tables which follow, it should be borne in mind that retail activity is not one kind of activity, but many kinds. The data presented below combine all of these diverse types of business into one total for each city or each county. Nothing can be said concerning the specialization of any part of the metropolitan community in one general type of retail activity. It should be kept in mind, however, that low values of the indexes of retail specialization denote the absence of some types of retail activity as well as indicating a small amount of each type of activity. Just which types of activity are most highly developed and which are absent from each type of sector, distance zone, and size of hinterland city cannot be determined by this study. It is generally assumed that those commodities, such as food, which constitute the most constant and frequently purchased necessities of life, are the most widely distributed, and that those purchases are the most concentrated which involve major outlays of income for specialized and durable goods. Hence, it is assumed that low indexes of retail specialization indicate the presence of establishments which retail relatively unspecialized and frequently purchased items, and the absence of establishments which retail costly, specialized, and infrequently purchased items.

Another factor to be kept in mind is that the rural-farm, rural-nonfarm, and urban populations differ in the average amount of their expenditures. It has been shown that the proportions of these three types of populations in the total hinterland population change considerably with distance from the metropolis, size of metropolis, sector type, and size of hinterland city or size of largest city contained. Some of the differences between areas, therefore, may be presumed to arise from the urban-rural composition of the population rather than from differences in the volume of cash expenditure made by each of these groups. The National Resources Planning Board estimated that the average per capita expenditures, in 1935-36, of members of farm, rural-nonfarm, and urban families in the United States were as follows:[1]

Urban	$477
Rural-nonfarm	338
Farm	175
All types	$371

While the level of expenditures for all types of families may have risen or declined between 1935 and 1940, the probability is very small that these sharp differences between expenditures and population

1. National Resources Planning Board. Family Expenditures in the United States (Washington, D. C.: U. S. Government Printing Office, 1941) Table 40, p. 13.

type were erased.[2] Differences in urban-rural composition, therefore, may be expected to form one element in the pattern of retail specialization in various parts of the metropolitan community.

III

Retail Specialization and Distance from the Metropolitan Center of Each Size Class (Chart 11-1)

1. Central cities, taken as a whole, are more specialized in retail trade than is any one of the distance zones.

2. In the hinterland, retail trade tends to be widely dispersed among the populations of the various distance zones. In the inner zones, embracing the suburbs of the city, retail trade declines to a relatively low point, indicating that suburban residents depend upon the specialized establishments of the central city for many purchases. Beyond the 45 mile zone there is little indication that the metropolis functions directly as a retail center for the hinterland, as far as any significant proportion of hinterland purchases are concerned. At the intermediate distances (65-114 miles) the indexes of specialization gradually decrease. This may be explained as a result of the gradual increase in total self-sufficiency caused by the greater proportion at such distances of the rural population to the total. (See Chart 6-3).

3. The general level of consumption is higher in metropolitan communities presided over by large central cities (500,000 or more habitants) than in those with small central cities. This, again, seems to be a function of the high percentage of the hinterland population, in the hinterland of these larger metropolitan centers, which is classed as urban. The pattern of differences between the various sizes of metropolitan communities is very similar to the pattern noted in Chapter Six, of differences in urban-rural composition.

IV

Retail Specialization in Each Type of Sector and Size Class of Metropolitan Community (Table 11-1)

1. Intermetropolitan sectors are more specialized in retailing than are subdominant and local sectors.

The subdominant are more specialized than are the local sectors. The preceding statements are true in spite of the fact that the urban-rural ratio has been found to be higher in subdominant than in intermetropolitan sectors. The retail specialization of intermetropolitan sectors may be considered a logical consequence of the location of such sectors between two central cities, with the result that establishments located there have a superior ability to obtain merchandise from the metropolitan centers with minimum delay and transportation cost.

2. The number of retail establishments per 1000 residents reflects none of the above differences. This index of the presence or absence of retail establishments indicates that even in local sectors, with few cities, the frequency of occurrence of retailing enterprises is as high as it is in the other types of sectors. The smaller cities of the local sectors therefore supply the standard needs of the local population with numerous stores which are smaller, on the average, than are the stores in other sectors.

3. A portion of the relatively high per capita receipts found for intermetropolitan sectors could be a result also of services rendered to the transient population which flows along major intermetropolitan thoroughfares. Such populations would not have been included in the base used to compute the per capita retail indexes. The lower than average values for local sectors, however, would indicate that the populations of such sectors make some use of the shopping centers located in intermetropolitan sectors.

V

The Retail Specialization of Principal Hinterland Cities and of Other Hinterland Areas (Table 11-2)

The foregoing does not imply that all hinterland areas outside the 45 mile zone are about equally specialized in retail trade, and that retail establishments are completely dispersed over the land. Such is certainly not the case. Each principal hinterland city (10,000 or more inhabitants) appears to have its surrounding trade territory. Within this territory the residents depend upon the principal city for much of their retail service. In other words, the retail structure of the hinterland is a structure of local trade territories.

---

2. That differences of this type were present in 1939-40 has been demonstrated in a recent study by the Bureau of Agricultural Economics of the United States Department of Agriculture: "Differences Between Rural and Urban Levels of Living," prepared by Walter C. McKain and Grace L. Flagg, January, 1948 (mimeographed).

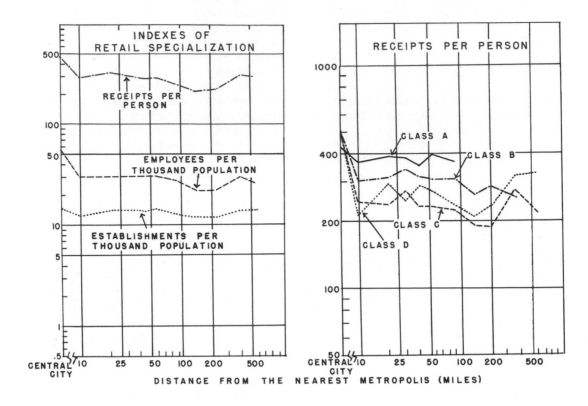

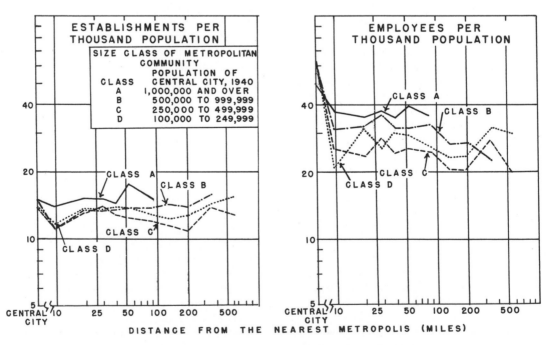

CHART 11-1 SPECIALIZATION IN RETAIL TRADE——DISTANCE. RETAIL
ESTABLISHMENTS, RETAIL EMPLOYEES, AND RETAIL
SALES PER UNIT OF POPULATION. ALL AREAS OF THE
UNITED STATES CLASSIFIED BY SIZE CLASS OF THE
METROPOLITAN COMMUNITY AND DISTANCE FROM THE
NEAREST METROPOLIS. UNITED STATES, 1939-40

Table 11-1

Specialization in retail trade - sector type: Number of retail establishments, number of retail employees, and retail sales per unit of population, by type of sector and size class of metropolitan community. United States, 1939-40.[a]

Type of sector	SIZE CLASS OF METROPOLITAN COMMUNITY				
	All metropolitan communities	Class A	Class B	Class C	Class D
Retail sales per person (dollars)					
Intermetropolitan	283	391	319	234	261
Subdominant	276	372	319	209	253
Local	239	372	258	203	231
Number of employees per thousand inhabitants					
Intermetropolitan	29.7	38.3	33.0	25.2	28.0
Subdominant	29.7	38.1	33.1	24.1	28.0
Local	23.1	32.7	25.3	19.8	22.8
Number of establishments per thousand inhabitants					
Intermetropolitan	13.2	15.4	13.2	12.0	13.1
Subdominant	12.8	14.0	13.8	11.6	12.4
Local	13.3	16.7	12.7	12.3	13.5

a) Excludes central cities and counties containing central cities

Source: Sixteenth Census of the United States. Compiled from Population, Vol.I, State tables s and 5; Retail Trade, 1939, Vol.II, table 16.

1. Principal hinterland cities, in all sizes of metropolitan communities and at all distances greater than 25 miles from the metropolis, are highly specialized in retail trade. This is shown by their higher than average indexes of retail activity. Conversely, the remaining portion of the hinterland (the rural areas and cities of less than 10,000 considered together) have a considerable deficit of retail trade. Thus, cities of 10,000 or more inhabitants appear to be highly specialized sub-centers of retail activity in the hinterland, and rural areas and minor communities depend upon them for a considerable proportion of their consumption needs.

2. The farther one progresses from the metropolis, the more specialized in retail trade he finds the principal cities to be. At distances of 65 miles from the metropolis, the principal hinterland cities enjoy a degree of retail specialization equal to that of the central city itself. Beyond 65 miles the principal cities become even more intensively specialized in retail trade than is the central city. All indexes demonstrate these facts, which form, together, the most outstanding characteristic of the retail structure of hinterland cities.

3. While the principal cities become even more specialized at greater distances, the remaining area of the hinterland tends to remain relatively unchanged, or to have an even greater deficit of retail trade, with increasing distance. (The single exception is the 265 mile zone, where outlying "other areas" have a higher index of retail specialization than elsewhere. Perhaps at these distances the sparsity of cities requires that smaller cities take over a major share of retailing.) The increasing specialization of such cities with increasing distance is due not so much to the greater dependence of the "other areas" upon the principal cities as to the fact that the radius of influence of hinterland cities increases with distance and that their trade territories, therefore, are larger and include more people. This enlargement of trade territory is created by a decreasing frequency of cities of all sizes as the distance from the metropolis increases. (See Chapter Seven for proof of this generalization.) There is no reason whatsoever to infer that, at distances greater than 45 miles, this increased retail specialization is related, to any great extent, to the retail activities of the metropolis. It is incorrect to infer that the pattern is a result of an increasing independence in regard to the specialized institutions of the central city, since that independence appears already to have been achieved at about 45 miles. The

retail pattern beyond 45 miles may be regarded, for all practical purposes, as an adjustment of hinterland cities to the size and urban-rural composition of their trade territories. The fact that, beyond 65 miles, the hinterland cities are as specialized in retail trade as are their central cities, and that the sales per capita to the total population change very little from zone to zone (Chart 11-1), indicates that factors other than competition with the metropolis have entered.[3] It must be concluded that the retail sales of central cities are confined to a relatively small area in the immediate environs of such cities.

One corollary of the tendency of retail trade to follow population, therefore, is the fact that central cities have a retail specialization sufficient only to satisfy the needs of their own residents, and some of the needs of the residents of their suburbs and other areas lying within 45 miles. Undoubtedly, they also retail highly specialized items to residents living at greater distances, but the proportion of the outlying population which affords such specialties is so small that the volume of sales is almost insignificant in the total purchases of these zones. Only minor traces of such extended buying appear in the 35-44 mile zone, and then only in the vicinity of the larger centers whose suburban areas may extend to such a distance into the hinterland.

4. The greater retail specialization of intermetropolitan sectors appears to arise from a greater specialization both of cities and of the other areas located in sectors of this type.

5. Some of the most specialized retail cities in the United States occur in local sectors at the greatest distances, although on the whole, cities in such sectors tend to be less specialized than cities in other sectors. Local sectors in class A and B metropolitan communities tend to contain particularly specialized cities at the greater distances.

VI

Size of Hinterland City and Retail Specialization
(Chart 11-2)

1. Cities of 10,000-24,999 tend to be slightly less specialized than cities of 25,000-49,999. This is particularly true in intermetropolitan sectors and at distances greater than 65 miles. Cities of 50,000 or more inhabitants tend to be no more specialized than cities of 25,000-49,999 inhabitants.

2. The somewhat greater specialization of cities lying in intermetropolitan, compared to the specialization of those located in the local, sectors

_____

3. For further proof see the comparison of estimated retail needs with actual retail sales, Chapter Three, Section I.

Table 11-2

Specialization in retail trade - principal cities and other areas. Number of retail establishments, number of retail employees, and retail sales, per unit of population, of cities of 10,000 or more inhabitants and of other hinterland areas, by size class of metropolitan community, type of sector, and distance from the nearest metropolis. United States, 1939-40.

RETAIL SALES PER PERSON (DOLLARS)

Type of sector and distance zone (miles)	Cities of 10,000 or more inhabitants				Cities of less than 10,000 and rural areas			
	Class A	Class B	Class C	Class D	Class A	Class B	Class C	Class D
All sectors	466	440	464	493	270	205	154	180
0-9	431	301	309	341	246	195	154	168
10-14	393	444	555	393	195	197	123	151
15-24	412	422	401	435	284	210	189	198
25-34	503	443	456	457	233	219	192	175
35-44	550	456	498	488	273	221	192	188
45-64	526	507	485	515	293	399	152	190
65-114	561	519	493	513	266	208	154	167
115-164	-	515	459	487	-	198	138	160
165-264	-	596	498	545	-	189	137	193
265-over	-	-	619	650	-	254	200	242
Intermetropolitan	462	462	485	492	264	202	154	177
0-9	428	318	339	363	269	188	119	151
10-14	406	449	555	386	195	225	188	182
15-24	423	426	496	423	265	249	178	174
25-34	550	508	486	440	235	184	166	180
35-44	552	482	489	485	277	205	146	191
45-64	508	551	485	508	262	208	155	161
65-114	608	523	497	488	261	197	144	149
115-164	-	491	471	483	-	185	142	187
165-264	-	558	534	596	-	197	197	239
265-over	-	-	612	656	-	-	-	-
Subdominant	486	421	420	498	218	208	126	155
0-9	526	286	263	293	-	-	-	-
10-14	381	296	210	-	-	-	160	-
15-24	492	419	368	489	233	279	191	219
25-34	503	420	405	481	198	166	128	160
35-44	566	413	-	500	161	293	202	200
45-64	524	470	407	565	225	215	158	145
65-114	441	497	477	543	206	186	136	157
115-164	-	523	423	492	-	216	117	149
165-264	-	599	419	471	-	195	102	112
265-over	-	-	601	662	-	257	124	198
Local	462	377	433	491	333	213	172	196
0-9	365	285	259	757	-	-	-	-
10-14	204	297	309	407	-	225	48	216
15-24	564	421	663	422	319	139	190	179
25-34	517	287	553	529	278	200	231	200
35-44	478	375	618	494	294	304	223	202
45-64	707	478	538	475	378	216	162	202
65-114	-	572	497	563	291	223	161	181
115-164	-	673	572	502	-	177	144	177
165-264	-	-	610	516	-	105	159	226
265-over	-	-	601	635	-	239	228	254

NUMBER OF WAGE EARNERS PER THOUSAND INHABITANTS

Type of sector and distance zone (miles)	Cities of 10,000 or more inhabitants				Cities of less than 10,000 and rural areas			
	Class A	Class B	Class C	Class D	Class A	Class B	Class C	Class D
All sectors	47.5	48.6	55.4	58.4	23.6	18.4	14.8	17.0
0-9	44.6	32.8	32.5	37.2	23.7	16.8	14.0	15.0
10-14	38.0	49.4	56.2	43.6	19.0	18.3	10.9	17.9
15-24	43.0	44.1	42.4	49.6	24.2	20.3	18.2	18.5
25-34	55.5	50.0	58.5	51.6	20.4	19.5	18.3	16.5
35-44	60.5	57.6	58.3	55.5	23.9	18.7	18.9	17.2
45-64	58.2	60.2	60.2	60.2	24.7	17.7	14.6	18.4
65-114	60.2	59.5	60.9	64.0	22.5	19.0	15.1	16.0
115-164	-	59.1	57.1	62.2	-	18.2	13.4	15.6
165-264	-	63.3	63.9	64.1	-	15.7	13.1	18.0
265-over	-	-	68.8	69.9	-	22.2	18.0	21.5
Intermetropolitan	46.9	47.6	58.0	58.6	23.0	18.4	14.8	16.8
0-9	44.4	33.4	36.6	39.1	20.1	-	10.5	17.9
10-14	39.4	49.4	46.3	43.5	19.0	17.5	18.5	17.6
15-24	39.7	42.6	45.3	48.5	19.8	21.8	16.7	16.7
25-34	56.4	53.2	52.6	50.7	21.2	22.2	15.3	17.0
35-44	60.7	53.7	58.1	58.7	24.0	15.3	14.5	18.7
45-64	56.1	60.4	58.1	62.4	22.0	16.6	15.2	18.4
65-114	65.4	60.7	57.2	64.4	21.2	18.9	14.0	14.7
115-164	-	58.2	57.9	67.2	-	17.9	13.4	16.9
165-264	-	50.6	66.2	71.2	-	19.2	17.7	21.2
Subdominant	51.8	47.6	52.5	60.6	19.4	17.8	12.9	15.0
0-9	55.0	32.8	25.6	33.2	21.6	30.2	-	-
10-14	37.3	30.0	18.9	-	16.3	-	11.8	18.1
15-24	48.2	45.6	40.3	57.4	13.9	21.9	17.5	12.6
25-34	53.4	48.2	54.4	50.1	20.0	18.4	14.9	18.9
35-44	63.4	17.0	54.3	56.8	23.5	16.3	20.9	18.9
45-64	58.9	53.7	60.1	68.4	-	19.8	55.5	13.5
65-114	50.8	55.2	55.4	67.3	-	19.2	11.9	14.6
115-164	-	58.1	55.4	65.0	-	10.4	10.4	14.3
165-264	-	64.5	79.4	61.2	-	12.6	20.1	-
265-over	-	-	-	72.9	-	22.5	-	-
Local	44.1	40.6	46.8	55.2	27.7	19.6	16.2	18.4
0-9	36.6	30.6	25.4	38.4	-	-	-	-
10-14	19.1	42.3	31.8	47.6	21.0	18.1	3.2	19.9
15-24	47.1	12.3	58.1	44.1	25.5	20.4	16.9	17.6
25-34	46.0	30.6	67.9	57.2	23.5	22.4	15.3	19.6
35-44	49.2	37.3	64.0	54.3	27.2	18.7	15.1	16.7
45-64	75.6	31.8	64.5	55.6	31.2	20.7	13.6	17.0
65-114	-	66.6	55.3	65.4	24.8	19.8	15.6	17.2
115-164	-	99.0	65.2	55.2	-	15.6	15.3	21.1
165-264	-	-	67.7	62.5	-	8.0	19.9	22.2

NUMBER OF ESTABLISHMENTS PER THOUSAND INHABITANTS

Type of sector and distance zone (miles)	Cities of 10,000 or more inhabitants				Cities of less than 10,000 and rural areas			
	Class A	Class B	Class C	Class D	Class A	Class B	Class C	Class D
All sectors	16.0	14.1	15.7	16.4	14.2	12.5	10.9	12.1
0-9	16.0	10.2	13.2	14.4	12.6	10.5	9.6	10.8
10-14	13.1	14.1	13.1	15.1	9.6	10.4	10.6	8.5
15-24	15.8	14.6	15.6	16.2	14.0	12.3	12.6	12.0
25-34	17.9	14.6	16.6	17.0	12.9	12.0	12.8	12.5
35-44	17.5	14.6	17.3	16.6	13.4	12.7	12.2	12.5
45-64	16.7	16.5	16.7	16.6	17.2	12.9	11.1	12.8
65-114	18.0	16.0	16.0	16.5	13.5	13.5	11.0	12.7
115-164	-	15.8	16.0	16.5	-	13.5	10.5	11.9
165-264	-	17.3	17.8	16.7	-	12.8	9.8	11.3
265-over	-	-	-	-	-	15.6	12.8	12.1
Intermetropolitan	16.4	14.4	15.6	16.3	13.8	12.3	10.9	11.9
0-9	16.6	10.6	13.9	14.6	17.9	11.2	10.7	8.5
10-14	13.9	14.1	13.1	15.1	9.6	12.3	12.6	11.2
15-24	15.7	14.4	15.0	16.2	13.9	12.8	11.4	12.5
25-34	17.9	15.7	17.1	16.5	13.2	11.1	11.3	12.2
35-44	16.4	17.1	16.5	16.5	16.3	12.1	10.8	12.7
45-64	18.0	15.3	15.7	16.0	12.3	12.6	11.0	11.7
65-114	19.7	15.5	15.1	17.0	-	14.3	10.5	11.6
115-164	-	-	15.1	18.1	-	-	9.8	13.0
165-264	-	-	17.1	-	-	-	13.1	-
Subdominant	14.4	12.1	15.6	15.9	13.4	13.4	10.0	11.0
0-9	12.5	10.6	10.9	11.4	12.0	-	11.1	-
10-14	11.1	12.2	13.1	-	-	-	12.7	12.2
15-24	16.9	15.1	15.0	15.1	20.2	20.2	10.7	11.3
25-34	14.5	15.2	15.6	19.2	10.0	10.0	11.3	11.2
35-44	17.0	15.7	-	18.0	10.3	15.2	11.3	11.4
45-64	16.8	15.4	17.3	16.6	15.5	12.9	10.8	10.9
65-114	13.8	15.8	16.2	15.9	11.0	13.6	10.0	10.6
115-164	-	15.8	15.4	15.9	-	14.1	9.7	10.5
165-264	-	17.5	17.1	14.5	-	12.7	8.7	13.1
265-over	-	-	-	18.1	-	15.1	7.6	-
Local	16.1	12.1	16.1	17.4	17.0	12.9	11.7	13.0
0-9	15.4	8.0	12.3	16.0	-	-	-	-
10-14	8.4	12.3	14.1	15.9	-	7.9	8.2	-
15-24	15.4	12.8	20.9	17.6	14.8	10.1	12.5	13.0
25-34	18.6	12.6	19.4	19.1	14.8	18.4	13.8	12.5
35-44	17.4	16.2	19.0	18.1	15.2	12.9	11.4	13.7
45-64	23.4	16.8	17.7	17.7	16.6	13.6	12.9	13.5
65-114	-	17.0	18.1	17.7	-	14.1	11.3	12.4
115-164	-	23.5	18.7	18.1	-	12.7	11.2	12.2
165-264	-	-	19.4	17.6	-	15.1	11.1	13.7
265-over	-	-	19.3	16.7	-	18.5	13.8	15.4

a) Excludes central cities. Counties containing central cities appear in all sectors total but are excluded from the individual sector types.

Source: Sixteenth Census of the United States. Compiled from Population, Vol.I, State tables 3 and 5; Retail Trade, 1939, Vol.II, table 16.

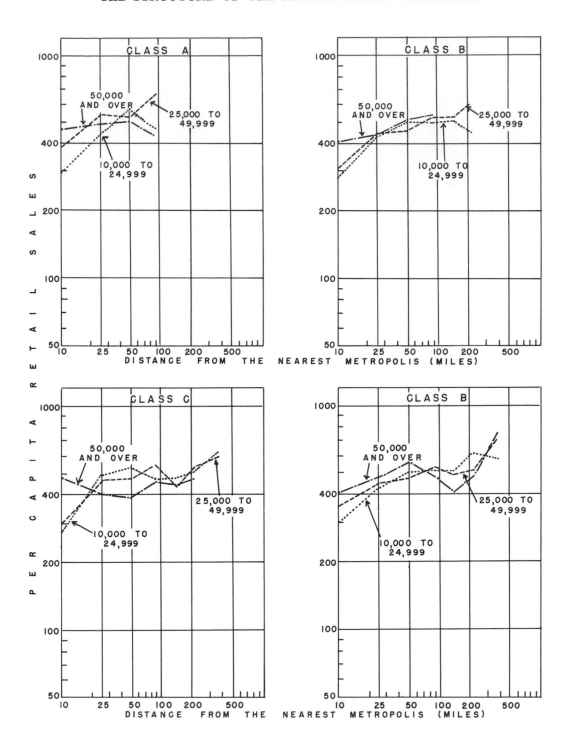

CHART 11-2   SPECIALIZATION IN RETAIL TRADE————————PRINCIPAL
HINTERLAND CITIES CLASSIFIED BY SIZE. PER
CAPITA RETAIL SALES OF THREE SIZES OF HIN-
TERLAND CITIES CLASSIFIED BY SIZE CLASS OF
THE METROPOLITAN COMMUNITY AND DISTANCE
FROM THE NEAREST METROPOLIS. UNITED STATES,
1939-40.

cannot be attributed to any one particular size of hinterland city. (See appendix table VII). It tends to arise primarily as a result of the greater specialization, at the greater distances, of those cities of all sizes which lie in intermetropolitan sectors.

3. Thus, among cities of more than 10,000 inhabitants, size alone appears to be only one of several factors which tend to be associated with the degree of a city's retail specialization. Metropolitan position, distance from the metropolis, and (to a smaller extent) available means of access to the metropolis tend to be of equal or greater importance. This could be expected, since hinterland cities of all sizes, at distances greater than 65 miles, are more specialized in retail trade than are the metropolitan centers themselves. Such differences as do exist as a result of the increased size of the hinterland city, can be attributed to the greater radius of influence which such cities possess compared to the smaller cities.

VII

Size of Largest City Contained and Retail Specialization in Small Cities and Rural Areas (Chart 11-3)

An examination of the degree of retail specialization of county units, classified by size of largest city contained, gives two useful insights into the retail structure of the metropolitan community. First, it permits some understanding of how completely the function of retailing is diffused over the countryside. Second, it permits some insight into the part which small cities play in retailing activity.

1. County areas containing no city and located in a local sector 265 miles or more from a central city have a level of retail activity which is about $227 per capita per year. This is well below the national average of $319 per year. Because at this distance the nearest urban place is, on the average, a maximum of 35 miles away (Table 7-10), it may be presumed that a large proportion of the total shopping is done locally, and that the average level of consumption of this completely rural population is well below the national average. In any event, the need of the population for retail services appears to be so constant and so frequent that, in the complete absence of cities, retail establishments follow the population into villages and other rural areas. Not less than two-thirds, and perhaps as much as three-fourths or more, of the retail needs of such relatively isolated populations are satisfied locally by hamlet and village shopping centers.

2. Counties which do contain a city, no matter how small it may be, have a higher index of retail specialization than have counties containing no city. This indicates that hinterland cities of all sizes are, to some degree at least, specialized centers of retailing. Counties containing a city of 5,000-9,999 inhabitants have higher indexes of specialization than counties containing a city of 2,500-4,999 inhabitants. This would lead to the inference that as the city population increases to 5,000 or more inhabitants it draws trade from areas outside the county which contains it. The counties containing a city of 5,000 inhabitants have a higher index of specialization, in local sectors, than the national average, lending additional plausibility to the above inference.

3. The concentration of retail activity in larger cities, when such cities are present in the county, is made manifest by the sharp drop in the index of specialization for small cities and rural areas in those counties which contain a city of 10,000 or more inhabitants. Such indexes, in fact, are lower than those for rural areas containing no city. Plainly, the outlying residents of counties containing principal cities depend upon these cities as shopping centers, when they are available.

4. In spite of the presence of principal hinterland cities, however, more than half of the retail needs of the rural and small city population continue to be satisfied by outlying establishments. This is another indication that the tendency for retail activity to be located as near as possible to the ultimate consumer is a very pervasive one.

5. The "other areas" portion of the local sectors tends to have a higher per capita index of retail specialization, than either the intermetropolitan or the subdominant sectors, (see Appendix Table VIII). It would appear, therefore, that, in the absence of principal highway routes or major hinterland cities, the residents of rural areas and of counties containing small cities tend to provide their own retail functions rather than to travel longer distances to shop. The indexes for the subdominant sectors are so much lower than the indexes for either of the other two sector types that one can only infer that people living in such sectors travel to the major hinterland city to shop. It seems to be true also that people living in intermetropolitan sectors make considerable use of intermetropolitan highways for the purpose of shopping in larger cities which are located along such routes.

6. Sector differences persist, even when each county involved in the comparison contains a city of 10,000-24,999 inhabitants (Appendix Table VIII). In class C and D metropolitan communities the outlying areas of intermetropolitan sectors are persistently more specialized than subdominant sectors which would indicate the rendering either of more intensive service to the local population

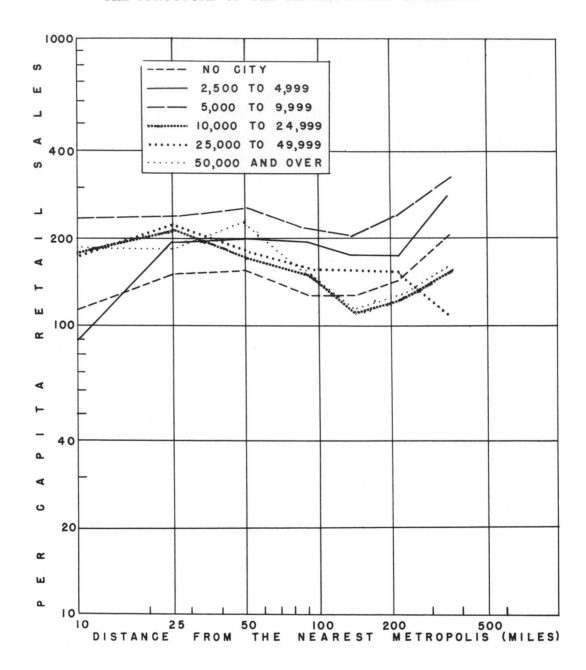

CHART II-3 SPECIALIZATION IN RETAIL TRADE————
RURAL AREAS AND CITIES OF LESS THAN
10,000 INHABITANTS. PER CAPITA RETAIL
SALES OF COUNTIES, WITH CITIES OF 10,000
OR MORE INHABITANTS EXCLUDED, CLASSIFIED
BY SIZE OF LARGEST CITY CONTAINED AND
DISTANCE FROM THE NEAREST METROPOLIS.
UNITED STATES, 1939-40

or of service to transient populations. The local sectors are more specialized than either of the other two types, indicating the presence of greater retail self-sufficiency under conditions of less accessibility to major hinterland cities.

7. The differences between large (class A and B) and small (class C and D) metropolitan centers persist among the small cities and rural areas. The ratio of sales to resident population is higher for the larger than for the smaller size classes of metropolitan communities. This is probably due, in large part, to the higher proportion of urban and rural-nonfarm populations residing in the class A and B metropolitan communities. It may also indicate a higher level of expenditure in the larger metropolitan communities, resulting from the tendency for a higher proportion of the rural populations, including the farm population, to participate in the cash-economy which is usually associated with metropolitan and urban life.

VIII

Summary

1. The function of retailing is widely dispersed throughout the hinterland. Each distance zone and sector type contains the bulk of whatever retail establishments are required to sustain its populations in their given types of residence, urban or rural. The central city functions primarily as a major shopping center for its own population and suburbs, and as a source of specialized goods for a limited trade territory. There is evidence that, to a distance of about 45 miles, the retail establishments of the central city are used as sources of supply to satisfy at least some portion of the total needs of the population. Beyond this point the hinterland appears independent, to a large extent, of the retail activities of the central city.

2. Intermetropolitan sectors tend to be more specialized, at all distances, than other sectors, which may result from a retailer preference for locations which provide ready access to two or more central cities.

3. The metropolitan position of a hinterland city seems to be a more important factor than its size in determining the intensity of retail specialization.

4. Rural areas and minor cities provide the bulk of their retail requirements locally, but become heavily dependent upon an urban center if one is present.

5. From whatever angle the retail structure of the metropolitan community is viewed, the metropolis plays only an indirect role, that of acting as a factor in the size and location of principal hinterland cities. This indirect influence of the metropolis seems to be identified with those factors which make for decreasing frequency of urban places with increasing distance, in the presence or absence of a major intermetropolitan route, and in the general accessibility of one part of the hinterland to another.

CHAPTER TWELVE

THE STRUCTURE OF SERVICES IN THE METROPOLITAN COMMUNITY

I

Introduction

In addition to obvious differences in the type of commodity which they offer for exchange, service establishments differ from retail establishments in two principal ways. First, services embrace a great many activities which are consumed primarily by other business organizations, which is not true of retail trade. The United States Census of Business classifies services into seven major groups:[1]

Personal services — bakeshops, laundries, etc.
Business services — advertising agencies, etc.
Services allied to transportation — warehousing, etc.
Automotive repair services — repair shops, parking lots, etc.
Other repair services — radio, typewriter, electrical, etc.
Custom industries — welding, cabinetmaking, bookbinding, etc.
Miscellaneous services — interior decorating, etc.

These major groupings are subdivided into 71 kinds of businesses. The services which fall in the first group are similar to retail trade establishments in their primary orientation toward individual consumers. Those in the second group represent a marked departure from this orientation, since other businesses, rather than individuals, are the consumers. The remaining services are required both by individual consumers and by business units.

A second difference between the service and retail activities lies in the behavior of consumers: The consumption of services which are purchased by some consumers may be postponed by other consumers, or the consumer may by performing particular services for himself, avoid altogether patronage of some service establishments. The individual consumer may, if he desires, redecorate his own home, do his own laundry, provide his own beauty care, and make his own repairs. Some of these services he may postpone indefinitely. The business establishment may provide many of its needed services as a minor part of its own operations. One may expect, therefore, that service establishments will be located in those areas in which commercially provided services are regularly consumed as a normal part of the culture of the population. With these differences in mind, the service structure of the metropolitan community will now be examined.

II

Standards for Measuring Service Specialization — Regional Indexes

In 1940 the indexes of specialization in services for the United States and for each geographic division were as follows:

Geographic division	Establishments per thousand population	Wage earners per thousand population	Receipts per person
New England	5.4	8.2	$27.9
Middle Atlantic	5.8	10.1	36.4
East North Central	4.9	8.0	27.4
West North Central	5.3	6.6	20.9
South Atlantic	3.5	7.7	17.3
East South Central	3.2	5.9	12.1
West South Central	4.3	7.8	17.8
Mountain	4.5	6.2	20.0
Pacific	7.0	12.9	42.7
United States	4.9	8.4	$26.0

See footnote on Page 165.

Establishments of the service type occur only about one-third as frequently as do retail sales establishments, and they provide employment only one-third as frequently and involve only one-twelfth the expenditure.

There are also greater regional differences in the consumption of services than in the consumption of retail sales. Whereas the range of retail sales, from the geographic division with the highest to the division with the lowest per capita index, is about two-thirds of the national average, for services the range of receipts is 118 percent of the national average. This greater deviation is caused not only by a low index for southern areas, but also by an extremely high index for the industrialized Middle Atlantic states and for the Pacific states.

III

Service Specialization:
Distance from the Metropolis
and Size of the Metropolis. (Chart 12-1)

1. The population of central cities is far more specialized in regard to services than is that of any single distance zone. All central cities considered together have an index of specialization which on the basis of employment and receipts, is more than three times that of the index for all hinterland areas, and an index almost twice that of the hinterland on the basis of number of establishments.
2. The larger the size of the metropolis, the higher is its index of service specialization. Class A metropolises are almost 50 percent more specialized than class D metropolitan centers, with class B and C centers occupying intermediate positions in the order of their sizes.
3. Unlike specialization in retail trade, specialization in services tends to decline fairly uniformly with increasing distance from the metropolis. This is true for all classes of metropolitan communities, and for all indexes of service specialization. The differences which exist between large and small metropolitan centers (those of 500,000 or more inhabitants as compared to those of fewer inhabitants) tend to be carried over into the hinterland and to be present in each distance zone. Distance zones of the class A metropolitan communities tend to be more specialized than the dis-

tance zones of the class B metropolitan communities, both of which are more specialized than either class C or D. Size of metropolis appears to have but little effect upon the degree of specialization of class C, as compared with class D, hinterland cities.
4. It was noted that since the 0-14 mile suburban zone was a zone of deficiency as far as retail trade was concerned, the residents of this zone appeared to make extensive use of the retail establishments in the central city. No similar phenomenon exists in regard to services. The index of service specialization in the 0-14 mile zone is second only to the index of the central city itself, and is higher, on the average, than that of any other distance zone. Only in the class D metropolitan communities does the pattern of suburban deficiency appear. Thus, suburban populations are, on the whole, more specialized in services than is the remainder of the hinterland. If they are dependent upon the metropolis for services, it appears that they are much less dependent, rather than more dependent (as in the case of retail trade) than are other areas of the hinterland. The fact that the 0-14 mile zone is below the national per capita service index suggests that this highly urbanized zone is dependent to some extent upon the central city.
5. Specialization in service functions has a pattern of distribution which leads to the conclusion either that the central cities and their immediate environs consume services in large quantities while the remainder of the hinterland areas forego, postpone, or perform these same services for themselves, or that the entire hinterland is extremely dependent upon the metropolis as a source of supply for those activities performed by service establishments.

IV

Service Specialization and Type of Sector.
(Table 12-1)

1. The intermetropolitan sectors are, on the whole, slightly more specialized in services than are the subdominant sectors. These latter sectors are, in turn, considerably more specialized than are the local sectors. This pattern is manifest in all three indexes of service specialization, and the tendency appears to exist for all classes of metropolitan communities considered together, although in the

---

1. Sixteenth Census of the United States, Service Establishments, 1939, pp. 1-3. The Census of Service Establishments does not include the activities of doctors, lawyers, dentists and others engaged in professional or scientific service. Enterprises in the fields of education, real estate, insurance, transportation and finance are not included. Also excluded are religious and charitable institutions, hospitals, sanitariums, public utilities, and government-operated enterprises.

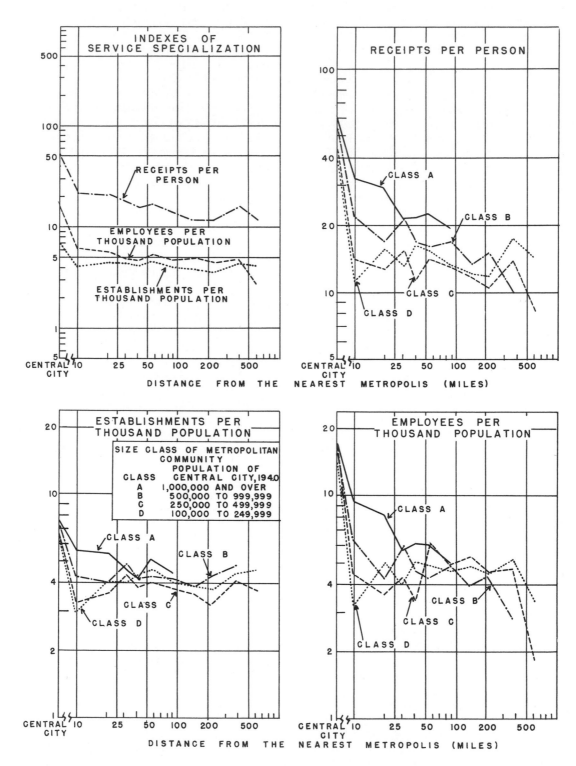

CHART 12-1 SERVICE SPECIALIZATION——DISTANCE. SERVICE ESTAB-
LISHMENTS, SERVICE EMPLOYEES, AND RECEIPTS FROM
SERVICES PER UNIT OF POPULATION. ALL AREAS OF
THE UNITED STATES CLASSIFIED BY SIZE CLASS OF
THE METROPOLITAN COMMUNITY AND DISTANCE FROM
THE NEAREST METROPOLIS. UNITED STATES, 1939-40

Table 12-1

Service specialization - sector type: Number of service establishments, number of service employees, and receipts from services, per unit of population, by type of sector and size class of metropolitan community, United States, 1939-40.[a]

Type of sector	SIZE CLASS OF METROPOLITAN COMMUNITY				
	All metropolitan communities	Class A	Class B	Class C	Class D
	Receipts per person (dollars)				
Intermetropolitan	17.7	29.5	19.1	13.7	15.2
Subdominant	16.5	21.6	19.2	13.8	14.2
Local	12.1	20.1	13.1	10.3	11.5
	Number of employees per thousand inhabitants				
Intermetropolitan	5.6	8.3	5.3	4.9	5.2
Subdominant	6.1	6.0	5.6	7.3	5.4
Local	3.8	5.4	3.5	3.5	3.7
	Number of establishments per thousand inhabitants				
Intermetropolitan	4.3	5.4	4.4	3.8	4.2
Subdominant	4.1	4.6	4.7	3.6	3.9
Local	4.0	4.7	3.7	3.8	4.1

a) Excludes central cities and counties containing central cities.

Source: Sixteenth Census of the United States. Compiled from Population, Vol.I, State tables 3 and 5; Service Establishments, 1939, table 2.

B and C classes there appear to be no differences between the intermetropolitan and the subdominant sectors.

2. The number of establishments per thousand residents is about the same for all sector types. Sector differences, therefore, are due primarily to differences in the average size of establishments, as measured by average receipts and average number of employees per establishment.

V

The Service Specialization of Principal Hinterland Cities and Other Hinterland Areas. (Table 12-2)

When a division is made between the principal hinterland cities and the other hinterland areas, the over-all pattern of service specialization becomes much clearer.

1. With increasing distance from the metropolis there is a gradual rise in the service specialization of principal hinterland cities, as was true for retail trade.

2. There is evidence that cities within the suburban zone, under the direct influence of the metropolis, depend upon the metropolis to supply a share of their services, since cities in the innermost zone tend to be less specialized than those in the zone surrounding them.

3. The rural areas have a very low index of service specialization. Whereas at no point outside the suburban zone does the retail trade in the dispersed areas sink to a ratio of less than one-third the index of the principal cities, the outlying areas frequently have only one-fourth or even one-sixth the degree of specialization for services which the principal hinterland cities have. With increasing distance, moreover, the index for the outlying areas tends to decline slowly. It is this tendency which gives to the distribution of services among the total population the pattern of gradual decline with distance. With increasing distance the populations of outlying areas are either more dependent upon the principal cities, or they forego a great many more services than do the populations of the inner zones.

4. There is considerable reason to believe that the metropolis performs services which are consumed by hinterland populations lying at great distances. Only in the outer zones do the hinterland cities even approach the intensity of specialization attained by the centers. This fact can mean that some services needed by the populations lying at even considerable distances are obtained directly from the central city. The alternative point of view may be taken, of course, that the existence of other businesses in central cities is what creates the demand there for a large volume of service establishments. This hypothesis will be examined in the next section.

5. The cities of local sectors are less specialized than the cities of other types of sectors, but this difference does not exist between the "other areas" of the various types of sectors. Whereas principal cities in local sectors are much less specialized than are the principal cities of the subdominant sectors, their other areas tend to compensate to some extent by exhibiting a slightly greater degree of specialization than can be found in the "other areas" of the other sector types at the same distances.

6. In local sectors, service establishments occur as frequently per 1,000 residents at all distances, in all size classes of metropolitan communities, and in both principal cities and other areas, as they do at these same locations in other types of sectors. Service enterprises in local sectors are not scarce but are merely smaller than average in size.

7. Employment in service enterprises tends to rise in the principal hinterland cities with increasing distance. It remains almost constant in the other areas under these conditions. In rural areas and minor cities service is a very infrequent source of employment, it averaging only about 2.5 per thousand residents.

VI

Service Specialization and Size of Hinterland City (Appendix Table IX, Chart 12-2)

1. There is a marked difference between the degree of service specialization of large and of small hinterland cities: the larger the city, the more specialized it tends to be.

2. The pattern of increasing specialization with increasing distance tends to be present within each size group of cities. It is most clearly manifested in the intermetropolitan and local sectors, and is less evident in the subdominant sectors.

3. The cities in the intermetropolitan sectors are more specialized than those in subdominant or local sectors, this is the case for each size of metropolitan community. Superior access to the central city appears to be positively associated with a high degree of service specialization in hinterland cities. (Appendix Table IX).

4. The degree of specialization which a hinterland city attains is not related in any uniform way to the size of the metropolitan center. Cities of each size in class A and class B metropolitan communities have service specialization indexes which are markedly similar. The B and C metropolitan communities have indexes which are both higher and

Table 12-2

Service specialization - principal cities and other areas: Number of service establishments, number of service employees, and receipts from services, per unit of population, or cities of 10,000 or more inhabitants and of other hinterland areas, by size class of metropolitan community, type of sector, and distance from the nearest metropolis. United States, 1939-40[a]

RECEIPTS PER PERSON (DOLLARS)

Type of sector and distance zone (miles)	Cities of 10,000 or more inhabitants				Cities of less than 10,000 and rural areas			
	Class A	Class B	Class C	Class D	Class A	Class B	Class C	Class D
All sectors	36.3	29.4	32.2	32.3	14.4	9.4	7.5	8.5
0-9	42.6	25.3	20.4	24.4	18.7	8.4	7.1	7.0
10-14	30.4	33.2	31.5	24.6	11.5	9.4	4.5	6.6
15-24	36.4	24.6	29.0	25.9	16.9	9.9	8.2	9.1
25-34	34.2	28.6	30.8	26.9	9.5	13.1	9.0	8.0
35-44	35.5	27.2	24.8	32.7	16.2	9.8	9.1	8.1
45-64	34.9	29.7	33.3	33.1	13.2	8.8	8.1	9.7
65-114	33.5	32.8	33.4	33.1	12.0	9.4	7.9	8.2
115-164	-	33.9	36.7	35.8	-	8.4	7.0	8.1
165-264	-	36.3	36.6	38.9	-	8.8	6.4	8.7
265-over	-	-	36.8	46.1	-	10.1	8.5	10.2
Intermetropolitan	38.3	30.9	33.3	33.8	11.0	9.7	7.5	8.4
0-9	46.2	26.8	24.1	28.1	27.6	8.8	3.5	-
10-14	33.8	35.8	38.5	24.6	-	10.3	9.2	6.6
15-24	36.6	26.1	69.3	25.5	11.9	5.0	5.7	7.8
25-34	35.1	29.8	32.5	25.2	5.1	10.2	7.4	7.8
35-44	36.9	29.7	32.5	34.5	6.6	10.5	7.4	8.2
45-64	34.2	30.0	29.4	31.6	10.1	7.6	7.8	10.0
65-114	39.8	34.0	33.6	34.4	7.9	8.4	9.4	8.0
115-164	-	33.0	35.8	36.5	-	9.4	7.0	7.9
165-264	-	20.0	40.6	36.5	-	8.2	7.0	8.2
265-over	-	-	35.9	47.4	-	7.4	8.0	9.7
Subdominant	30.8	28.8	33.2	31.0	9.1	9.1	6.2	7.5
0-9	38.1	24.1	44.0	18.1	-	-	8.0	-
10-14	20.9	22.1	7.7	-	-	-	7.1	10.7
15-24	36.0	24.9	22.5	29.2	11.9	16.1	5.7	6.2
25-34	32.0	29.8	28.5	25.1	5.1	5.0	5.7	7.1
35-44	37.8	30.6	-	29.7	6.6	10.2	6.9	7.6
45-64	32.8	30.7	77.0	34.9	10.1	15.5	6.6	7.6
65-114	22.1	34.5	34.2	34.9	7.9	10.2	6.2	8.5
115-164	-	-	38.5	28.9	-	7.9	5.5	9.4
165-264	-	37.9	30.2	36.3	-	8.5	5.8	10.1
265-over	-	-	42.0	52.7	-	10.1	5.8	13.4
Local	28.8	23.0	24.3	27.7	16.3	9.5	8.5	9.3
0-9	23.5	23.5	14.0	25.1	-	11.3	1.4	-
10-14	12.8	26.0	13.9	25.0	22.3	6.9	7.6	10.6
15-24	35.3	18.7	35.6	23.2	9.3	7.5	9.9	8.9
25-34	25.8	16.6	30.9	28.4	11.1	13.9	11.6	8.2
35-44	18.3	17.0	31.6	25.6	16.6	8.5	9.0	9.9
45-64	49.3	21.0	30.4	30.4	11.5	10.2	8.3	8.6
65-114	-	28.5	30.3	30.4	-	-	8.1	8.5
115-164	-	37.0	37.4	26.9	-	37.0	8.4	10.4
165-264	-	-	35.0	24.8	-	-	7.1	10.4
265-over	-	-	35.7	37.1	-	-	10.0	11.1

NUMBER OF WAGE EARNERS PER THOUSAND INHABITANTS

Type of sector and distance zone (miles)	Cities of 10,000 or more inhabitants				Cities of less than 10,000 and rural areas			
	Class A	Class B	Class C	Class D	Class A	Class B	Class C	Class D
All sectors	10.5	8.7	13.2	11.5	3.4	2.2	2.6	2.7
0-9	13.4	8.0	6.2	7.3	4.1	1.6	2.1	1.8
10-14	8.3	8.7	11.7	7.2	2.7	2.7	1.2	3.0
15-24	10.1	6.3	8.4	6.5	4.3	2.5	2.1	2.7
25-34	10.4	8.2	8.2	8.4	2.7	3.0	2.4	2.3
35-44	10.4	8.9	8.7	10.5	4.3	2.0	2.6	3.0
45-64	9.9	8.9	17.4	12.4	3.1	1.9	2.5	2.6
65-114	9.3	10.8	13.4	12.8	2.8	2.2	2.8	2.7
115-164	-	10.2	17.2	14.4	-	2.2	2.9	3.0
165-264	-	10.5	16.5	15.6	-	2.6	2.6	3.1
265-over	-	-	14.9	14.9	-	2.8	2.3	2.7
Intermetropolitan	11.1	9.1	12.2	12.0	3.3	2.3	2.6	2.7
0-9	14.7	8.4	7.5	8.2	7.9	2.5	0.7	-
10-14	9.2	9.4	14.6	8.3	2.1	2.5	2.4	3.0
15-24	10.3	6.8	17.3	8.3	3.1	4.5	2.5	2.2
25-34	10.0	7.7	8.9	9.4	4.6	1.5	2.2	2.1
35-44	10.7	9.0	8.8	11.0	2.6	1.7	2.3	2.4
45-64	9.6	8.6	10.1	11.0	2.9	2.2	2.7	3.1
65-114	11.0	10.6	13.0	12.8	-	2.1	2.5	2.6
115-164	-	11.4	13.8	15.7	-	2.1	2.7	3.0
165-264	-	5.4	16.9	14.3	-	2.8	2.5	2.8
265-over	-	-	11.8	15.0	-	-	1.9	2.4
Subdominant	9.0	8.8	18.9	11.9	2.0	2.2	2.8	2.8
0-9	11.4	7.8	3.1	6.7	3.8	-	-	-
10-14	6.2	5.3	1.4	-	0.8	-	2.7	4.0
15-24	9.4	6.5	7.0	10.0	-	4.3	1.6	1.4
25-34	8.8	8.9	8.4	5.7	3.8	0.7	3.1	3.1
35-44	11.0	8.1	-	10.3	0.8	3.5	3.1	3.0
45-64	9.9	10.0	96.5	10.2	1.2	2.5	2.7	2.6
65-114	6.2	9.7	16.3	12.4	2.1	1.7	2.5	2.5
115-164	-	10.3	24.2	11.6	1.2	2.1	3.1	3.1
165-264	-	11.0	16.8	18.9	-	2.5	2.8	3.1
265-over	-	-	22.2	21.9	-	2.5	2.6	4.2
Local	8.1	6.5	8.1	9.2	4.2	2.5	2.9	3.0
0-9	7.3	7.5	4.0	7.2	-	3.4	0.2	-
10-14	3.1	7.2	2.8	7.1	-	1.8	2.2	3.1
15-24	9.6	4.4	9.9	6.9	5.7	1.7	2.2	3.0
25-34	5.6	4.4	7.5	8.8	2.4	2.9	3.1	1.9
35-44	6.4	4.1	7.5	7.8	3.7	2.0	2.7	2.9
45-64	13.4	5.8	11.1	8.8	4.3	2.5	2.5	2.8
65-114	-	9.3	10.7	11.0	2.9	3.0	3.3	3.1
115-164	-	-	14.2	10.6	-	-	3.3	3.4
165-264	-	-	12.0	9.7	-	2.5	2.6	3.1
265-over	-	-	14.8	11.1	-	4.6	2.9	3.1

NUMBER OF ESTABLISHMENTS PER THOUSAND INHABITANTS

Type of sector and distance zone (miles)	Cities of 10,000 or more inhabitants				Cities of less than 10,000 and rural areas			
	Class A	Class B	Class C	Class D	Class A	Class B	Class C	Class D
All sectors	6.25	5.72	5.87	6.14	3.68	3.23	3.11	3.45
0-9	6.67	4.51	4.79	4.56	3.90	2.52	2.15	2.40
10-14	5.20	6.11	5.57	5.34	3.28	2.62	2.03	1.99
15-24	6.09	5.31	5.64	5.71	4.05	2.71	3.04	2.97
25-34	6.52	5.61	6.49	6.13	2.84	3.09	3.56	3.26
35-44	6.34	6.56	6.57	6.43	3.17	3.23	3.52	3.85
45-64	6.69	5.80	6.30	6.68	4.00	3.12	3.33	3.87
65-114	6.28	6.17	5.88	6.16	3.47	3.46	3.27	3.52
115-164	-	-	5.95	6.19	-	3.32	3.44	3.44
165-264	-	6.84	5.79	5.91	-	3.59	2.82	3.55
265-over	-	-	6.86	6.95	-	4.82	3.53	3.87
Intermetropolitan	6.45	5.78	6.00	6.19	3.52	3.23	3.15	3.43
0-9	6.88	4.53	5.20	4.70	5.41	2.73	1.82	1.99
10-14	5.73	5.28	6.00	5.09	3.28	2.95	3.36	2.95
15-24	6.04	5.38	5.64	5.83	3.75	3.67	3.57	3.17
25-34	6.75	5.66	6.83	6.03	3.05	2.78	3.38	3.39
35-44	6.18	6.76	6.51	6.44	3.42	3.06	3.22	3.84
45-64	6.70	6.18	6.29	6.83	3.86	3.47	3.24	3.42
65-114	7.48	4.54	5.92	6.08	3.17	3.34	3.06	3.34
115-164	-	-	5.94	6.43	-	3.79	3.45	3.45
165-264	-	-	5.85	7.01	-	-	2.80	3.54
265-over	-	-	7.03	-	-	-	3.61	-
Subdominant	5.67	5.94	5.59	6.02	3.08	3.29	2.75	3.09
0-9	6.75	4.88	3.79	3.60	3.15	4.07	2.69	-
10-14	3.59	5.78	4.29	-	2.00	2.10	2.77	2.73
15-24	7.55	5.48	5.56	5.44	2.80	3.82	3.02	2.53
25-34	5.39	7.11	5.93	6.55	3.61	3.13	3.12	2.94
35-44	7.42	5.89	-	5.85	2.59	2.99	3.43	3.15
45-64	6.08	5.23	6.17	6.19	-	3.12	2.66	3.25
65-114	4.10	5.47	5.11	6.95	-	3.56	3.01	3.09
115-164	-	-	5.86	6.51	-	3.12	2.41	2.82
165-264	-	7.07	5.31	5.12	-	4.75	1.82	4.58
265-over	-	-	6.47	8.06	-	-	-	-
Local	5.51	4.58	5.65	6.09	4.32	3.42	3.51	3.84
0-9	5.29	3.51	4.13	5.04	-	2.22	1.65	-
10-14	3.12	4.92	4.42	5.95	-	1.51	2.80	3.02
15-24	5.48	4.50	6.69	5.41	4.63	2.69	3.63	3.69
25-34	5.48	3.95	7.35	6.38	3.33	4.36	3.71	3.47
35-44	3.80	4.83	7.23	6.88	3.95	3.29	3.51	4.13
45-64	8.99	6.47	6.44	6.36	4.17	3.69	3.65	3.78
65-114	-	5.60	6.44	6.22	4.29	3.96	3.51	3.71
115-164	-	9.38	6.81	6.22	-	3.48	3.28	3.97
165-264	-	-	7.82	5.85	-	5.16	3.89	4.64
265-over	-	-	6.76	6.13	-	-	-	-

a) Excludes central cities. Counties containing central cities appear in all sectors total but are excluded from the individual sector types.

Source: Sixteenth Census of the United States. Compiled from Population, Vol.I, State tables 3 and 5; Service Establishments, 1939, table 2.

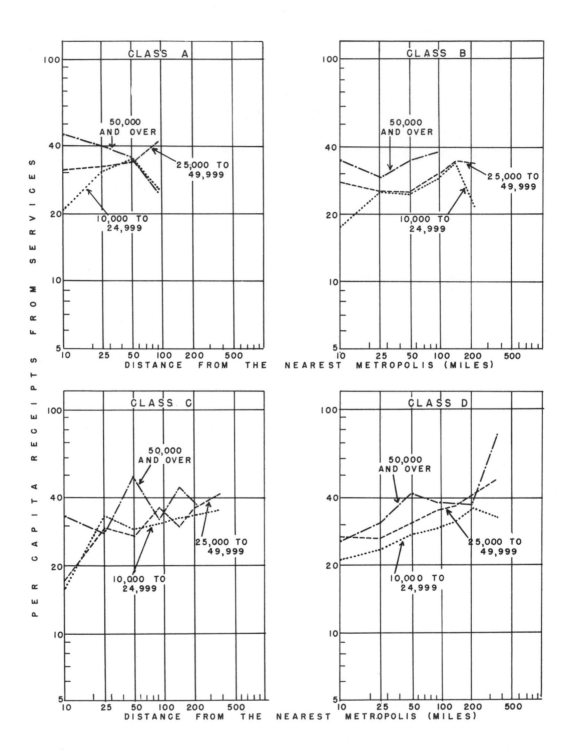

CHART 12-2   SERVICE   SPECIALIZATION————PRINCIPAL   HINTER-
LAND CITIES CLASSIFIED BY SIZE. PER ·CAPITA
RECEIPTS FROM SERVICES OF THREE SIZES OF
HINTERLAND CITIES CLASSIFIED BY SIZE CLASS
OF THE METROPOLITAN COMMUNITY AND DISTANCE
FROM THE NEAREST METROPOLIS. UNITED STATES,
1939-40

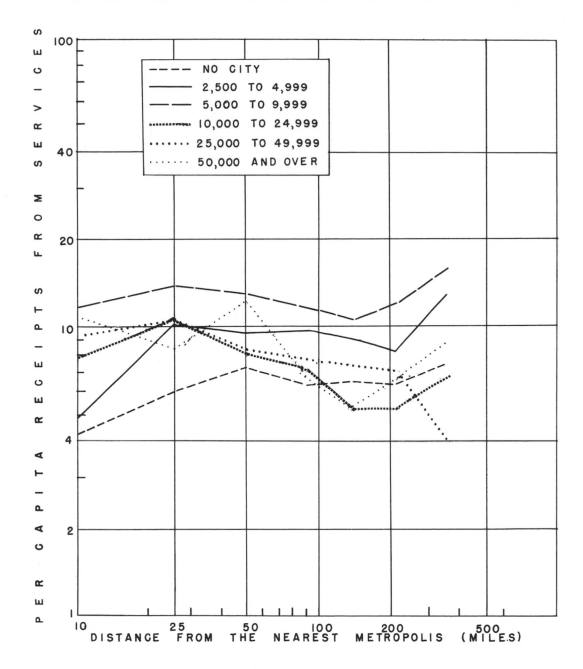

CHART 12-3 SERVICE SPECIALIZATION————RURAL AREAS
            AND CITIES OF LESS THAN 10,000 INHAB-
            ITANTS. PER CAPITA RECEIPTS FROM SER-
            VICES OF COUNTIES, WITH CITIES OF 10,000
            OR MORE INHABITANTS EXCLUDED, CLASSIFIED
            BY SIZE OF LARGEST CITY CONTAINED AND
            DISTANCE FROM THE NEAREST METROPOLIS.
            UNITED STATES, 1939-40

lower than those of the metropolitan communities at each end of the size range.

VII

Size of Largest City Contained and the Service Specialization of Small Cities and Rural Areas (Appendix Table X, Chart 12-3)

1. County areas which contain no city and are located in local sectors of class D metropolitan communities have a level of service activity which is $6.90 per capita per year. This is about one-fourth the specialization index for the nation as a whole. In this same type of area, the index of retail specialization has been found to be more than two-thirds as great as the national index. Even in the most remote portions of the metropolitan community, where urban centers are most sparsely distributed, the rural areas provide only a small amount of service. It has been found that in these areas there is considerable specialization in retail trade, in an apparent effort to compensate for a lack of larger urban retail centers. Instead of providing needed services locally, these isolated areas appear either to forego services or to rely upon the service establishments of the larger hinterland cities. County units which contain a city have a considerably higher ratio of receipts from services to population than have completely rural counties. Counties which contain a city of 5,000 to 9,999 inhabitants have a service specialization index which is almost twice that of the completely rural counties.

2. The local sectors tend to make up for their inaccessibility to the service institutions of major hinterland cities by means of a higher degree of local specialization. As for retail trade, at greater distances the local sectors tend to be more specialized than the other sectors.

3. The dependence of the small cities and rural areas upon the principal cities is indicated also by the low degree of specialization in such areas when the county in which they lie contains a city of 10,000 or more inhabitants. With increasing size of hinterland city contained, the index of specialization tends to decline to a value equal to or below that of the "no city" areas. Rural areas and small cities in the vicinity of larger hinterland cities, therefore, have a less developed service structure than have similar areas which are located at a distance from large hinterland cities.

4. Those rural areas and small cities which lie in class A and B metropolitan communities tend to be more specialized than are these same types of areas and cities when they lie in the smaller metropolitan communities. This is particularly evident in those county areas which contain a city of 10,000 or more inhabitants. A portion of this difference may be due to a greater diffusion of establishments outward from the larger cities located in the hinterlands of class A and B metropolises.

5. The degree of specialization of the rural areas in each size group tends to remain relatively unchanged, or even to increase slightly, with increasing distance from the metropolis. Cities of all sizes tend to become more specialized with distance, and hinterland areas of all sizes tend to remain at about the same level of specialization or even to increase with distance; the findings from Chart 12-1, therefore, which indicate there is a gradual decrease in over-all service specialization, may appear to be an inconsistency between the whole and its parts. This apparent inconsistency arises from the fact that smaller hinterland cities and rural areas occur much more frequently in outlying areas, and hence tend to lower the total level of specialization with distance.

VIII

Summary

1. Service establishments tend to cling to urban centers to a much greater degree than do retail trade establishments. Compared to the areas surrounding them, both central cities and principal hinterland cities are more specialized in services than in retail trade. The degree of specialization is related to the size of the hinterland city and to the size of the central city.

2. With increasing distance from the metropolis there is a gradual decrease in service specialization, in each zone as a whole. With increasing distance from the metropolis, however, the hinterland cities tend to become more specialized in service functions. The other areas tend to maintain or to increase slightly the degree of their specialization with increasing distance.

3. Cities lying in intermetropolitan sectors tend to be more specialized than cities lying in other types of sectors.

4. Rural areas and small cities either depend heavily upon the principal hinterland cities for a large proportion of their services, or consume far fewer services per capita than do residents of larger cities. The dependence of the outlying areas upon urban places is confirmed by a steady increase in service specialization with increasing size of largest city contained, and a rise in per capita values for cities whose radii of trade territory become larger with increasing distance.

CHAPTER THIRTEEN

THE STRUCTURE OF WHOLESALE TRADE IN THE METROPOLITAN COMMUNITY

I

Introduction

As defined by the United States Census, wholesale establishments are those enterprises engaged primarily in selling merchandise to distributors for resale or to purchasers who buy for business use. Whereas the activities of retail trade are completely oriented toward, and culminate in, sales to the individual consumer, the activities of wholesale trade enterprises are oriented completely toward other businesses. The United States Census has divided wholesale activities into 28 major business groups and 172 different types of business.[1]

II

Standards for Measuring Wholesale Specialization

In 1940, the indexes of wholesale specialization for the nation as a whole, and for each of the principal geographic divisions, were as follows:

Geographic division	Establishments per thousand population	Wage earners per thousand population	Wholesale sales per person
New England	1.2	11.2	$ 376
Middle Atlantic	1.6	15.6	687
East North Central	1.5	11.5	422
West North Central	2.5	12.3	430
South Atlantic	1.0	9.7	256
East South Central	0.8	5.9	182
West South Central	1.4	8.6	265
Mountain	1.8	9.0	262
Pacific	2.0	18.6	519
United States	1.5	11.9	$ 420

Although the number of establishments per 1,000 inhabitants is much lower in the case of wholesale trade than in the case of either retail trade or services, the dollar value of sales per capita for wholesale trade is about 16 times that for services and about one and one-third times that for retail trade. There are more retail workers, but fewer service workers, per thousand inhabitants than there are workers in wholesale trade. Wholesale establishments are larger, on the average, and have higher dollar receipts per wage earner, than

have the other two types of commercial activities. As was found in the case of retail trade and services, the lowest dollar values per capita are found in the South and the highest values in the Northeast and West. The range of these differences is greater than the range for either retail trade or services, being more than 120 percent of the national average per capita sales. Wholesale trade is, therefore, distributed even more unevenly between regions than is retail trade or services. The large variation arises both from relatively lower values for the South and from the higher specialization of the Northeast and the West.

III

Wholesale Specialization by Distance from the Metropolis and by Size Class of Metropolitan Community   (Chart 13-1)

1. Central cities as centers of wholesale trade, are extremely specialized compared to the remainder of the metropolitan community. The metropolis has seven times the per capita sales, four and one-half times the employment per thousand residents, and two and one-half times the number of wholesale establishments per thousand residents that the hinterland has.

2. The general distance pattern of wholesale specialization among the hinterland populations has a fairly constant per capita dollar value throughout all distances, the values tending to decline somewhat between 35 and 165 miles and to return to their

See Footnote on Page 175.

173

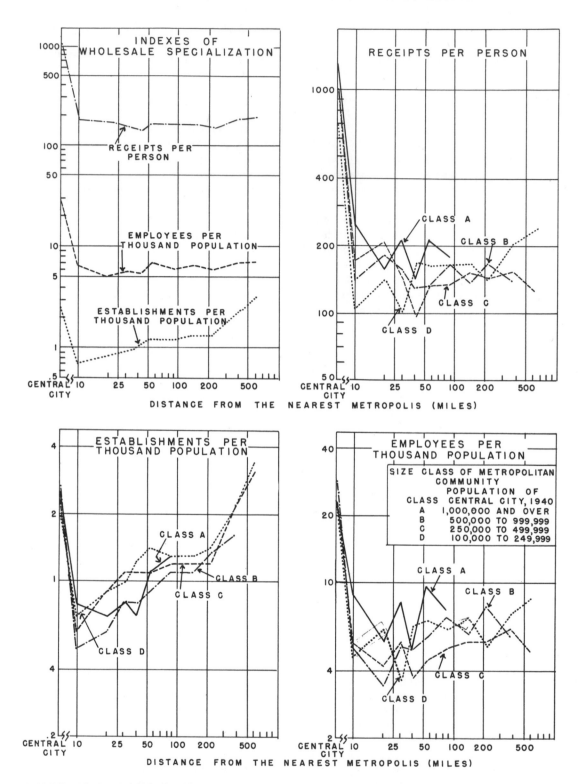

CHART 13-1 SPECIALIZATION IN WHOLESALE TRADE————DISTANCE. WHOLESALE ESTABLISHMENTS, WHOLESALE EMPLOYEES, AND WHOLESALE SALES PER UNIT OF POPULATION. ALL AREAS OF THE UNITED STATES CLASSIFIED BY SIZE CLASS OF THE METROPOLITAN COMMUNITY AND DISTANCE FROM THE NEAREST METROPOLIS. UNITED STATES, 1939-40

former levels at more distant areas. The number of employees per thousand residents tends to remain fairly steady or to increase slightly with distance. The number of establishments per thousand residents rises steadily from the central city to the periphery. This latter phenomenon is peculiar to wholesale trade, not being found in any of the other three functions studied. Although the frequency of the occurrence of wholesale establishments actually increases among the hinterland population with greater distance, specialization in terms of wage earners and dollar value remains comparatively unchanged, as in the case of services. Because of these two tendencies there is a gradual decrease, from the central city to the periphery, in the average number of people employed per establishment.

3. The larger the central city, the more specialized it is in wholesale trade. Class A central cities have an index of wholesale specialization which, by all standards, is much greater than that of the smaller central cities.

4. In the hinterland, the size of the central city is only slightly related to the degree of wholesale specialization. Aside from the central city differences, there is no uniform difference in the degree of specialization between size classes of metropolitan communities. Throughout most distances beyond 45 miles, the class D metropolitan communities are more specialized than the class B. The hinterlands of the class A metropolitan communities tend to show a greater degree of specialization at distances beyond 45 miles than do the other three size classes.

5. The tendency for wage earners per thousand to increase slightly with greater distance is exhibited by all four classes of metropolitan communities. The number of establishments per thousand inhabitants also increases steadily with increasing distance. The gradual decrease in average size of wholesale establishments with increasing distance from the metropolis is a part of the pattern of each of the four sizes of metropolitan communities.

6. There is evidence that retail establishments in the suburban zone behave toward their wholesale sources of materials in the same fashion as individual consumers behave with respect to retail establishments: they make use of the central city. The suburban zone of all four metropolitan communities contains a deficit of wholesale trade, compared to the zone immediately surrounding it.

7. The distance pattern of wholesale trade in all four size classes of metropolitan communities is one which involves a very great specialization at the center, a slight deficit of wholesale trade in the suburban zones, and a fairly constant low level of specialization in the vast outlying territory. There is some evidence of a concentration of wholesale specialization in the 35-64 mile area, where the direct dominance of the central city changes to indirect dominance. The specialization in wholesale trade at the center is so much greater than that in retail trade as to make it inconceivable that the wholesale activities of metropolitan centers exist solely for the purpose of supplying the metropolis and its suburbs. The degree of specialization is so great, in fact, that the dependence of the hinterland upon the metropolis must be presumed to be much greater for wholesale activities than for services.

IV

Wholesale Specialization by Type of Sector
(Table 13-1)

1. Except for the class B metropolitan communities, the intermetropolitan sectors are considerably more specialized than the subdominant sectors. Both of these types of sectors are much more specialized in wholesale trade than are the local sectors. It has been noted before that the class B metropolitan communities seem to have a tendency to place greater emphasis upon their subdominant connections than upon their intermetropolitan ones, and that the class A metropolitan communities seem to exhibit an extremely great dependence upon intermetropolitan sectors. The greater specialization of the intermetropolitan sectors in the A, C, and D metropolitan communities is indicated by all of the indexes of specialization. Not only are there higher per capita sales in such areas, but wholesale establishments also occur more frequently and employ a larger share of the resident population than they do in the local sectors.

2. While the higher per capita retail sales of the intermetropolitan sectors may be interpreted as being due, in part, to the serving of transient population, no such explanation is warranted in the case of wholesale trade. A position along a major highway appears to constitute a superior location for the distribution of commodities to other establishments. Sectors containing no major hinterland cities appear to be the least desirable locations for wholesale enterprises.

---

1. Included in the category of wholesale trade enterprises are manufacturer-owned sales outlets, petroleum bulk stations, agents, brokers, and assemblers of farm products. Sixteenth Census of the United States, Wholesale Trade, 1939, Vol. II, pp. 1-52.

Table 13-1

Specialization in wholesale trade - sector type: Number of wholesale establishments, number of wholesale employees, and wholesale sales, per unit of population, by type of sector and size class of metropolitan community. United States, 1939-40.[a]

Type of sector	SIZE CLASS OF METROPOLITAN COMMUNITY				
	All metropolitan communities	Class A	Class B	Class C	Class D
	Wholesale sales per person (dollars)				
Intermetropolitan	183	229	167	168	183
Subdominant	166	173	172	157	163
Local	111	144	84	102	117
	Number of employees per thousand inhabitants				
Intermetropolitan	6.7	8.9	6.3	5.7	6.9
Subdominant	6.6	7.5	6.8	5.8	6.9
Local	4.5	5.5	3.4	4.1	4.8
	Number of establishments per thousand inhabitants				
Intermetropolitan	1.2	0.9	1.0	1.3	1.4
Subdominant	1.0	0.8	1.0	1.0	1.1
Local	1.2	0.9	0.7	1.1	1.4

a) Excludes central cities and counties containing central cities.

Source: Sixteenth Census of the United States. Compiled from Population, Vol.I, State tables 3 and 5; Wholesale Trade, 1939, Vol.II, Table 13.

V

The Wholesale Specialization of Hinterland Cities and of Other Areas (Table 13-2)

1. Wholesale trade in the hinterland tends to be centered to a much greater extent in cities of 10,000 or more inhabitants than it does in rural areas and cities of less than 10,000 inhabitants. The principal cities of all zones beyond 25 miles from the metropolis are more specialized in wholesale trade than is the hinterland as a whole. This specialization is much greater than is retail specialization in such cities. Rural areas and small centers are very dependent upon hinterland cities.
2. The relationship of the wholesale specialization of hinterland cities to distance is a very consistent one. From the central city outward through the hinterland, the hinterland cities become progressively more specialized until, at the periphery, their index of specialization is more than double that of the inner zones, and well above the hinterland average. Yet in no case does the index of specialization of any single group of hinterland cities attain the level of the index of the central city.
3. Though the principal hinterland cities become even more specialized with distance, the remaining area of the hinterland tends to remain relatively unchanged. The 265 mile and over zone constitutes an outstanding exception; here the "other areas" attain a very high index of wholesale trade. In these remote areas, where principal cities are far apart, wholesale enterprises tend to locate in smaller communities.
4. The rising level of specialization in wholesale trade with increasing distance is undoubtedly due in part to the familiar fact that the trade territories of distant cities are larger than those of cities nearer the metropolis, and contain more population. This rising index is not an indication that the distant areas are less dependent upon the metropolis. The level of wholesale specialization of the central city is so great that if the hinterland areas were to become entirely self-sufficient, and if they required wholesale trade at the same average rate as does the metropolitan community, they would find it necessary to raise their per capita sales by $260, or 162 percent. There can be little doubt that the wholesale enterprises of the central cities serve an extremely broad expanse of hinterland. Their activities are one of the most important elements for which outlying areas are dependent upon the metropolis.
5. From the foregoing it must not be concluded that small cities and other areas do not play a sizeable part in the wholesale servicing of the hinterland population. Between one-fifth and one-fourth of the per capita requirements of the class A, B, C, and D metropolitan communities are provided by such areas. Since wholesale establishments serve business enterprises primarily, and since it has been shown that the rate of retail and service specialization is lower in these areas than in the principal hinterland cities, small cities and outlying areas may be expected to have a lower rate of wholesale specialization. In other words, there is no need for a wholesale establishment to be located nearer to the ultimate consumer than are the retail or service establishments which it serves. It is evident that location in the central city and in the largest hinterland cities means that the wholesale function is much more removed from the consumer than is retail trade; wholesale establishments, however, are not as far removed from their customers as the per capita indexes might seem to indicate. The dependence of business establishments in small cities and outlying areas upon the wholesale establishments of the principal hinterland cities is undoubtedly not as great as might be inferred from the direct comparison of wholesale trade with population.
6. Although the per capita dollar value of wholesale activity attains the level of the central city in no group of hinterland cities, the number of wholesale establishments per 1,000 residents in distant cities of class C and D metropolitan communities is even higher, in some instances, than it is in the central city. This denotes a much smaller average size of establishment in the outlying areas. The number of establishments per thousand inhabitants tends to increase with distance, whereas the volume of sales remains about constant. Hence, wholesale enterprises do not decrease in frequency, either in hinterland cities or in outlying areas, as the distance from the metropolis increases. They merely become smaller in average volume of sales.

VI

Wholesale Specialization and Size of Hinterland City (Chart 13-2, Appendix Table XI)

1. The larger the size of the hinterland city, the greater is the degree of wholesale specialization. This tendency is most noticeably present at distances of more than 65 miles in all classes of metropolitan communities.
2. The wholesale specialization of some of the largest hinterland cities is as high or higher than that of the central city itself in the class D metropolitan communities. A city of 50,000 or more inhabitants, lying 65 miles or more from the central city, tends to be highly specialized. Undoubtedly,

Table 13-2

Specialization and wholesale trade – principal cities and other areas: Number of wholesale establishment, number of wholesale employees, and wholesale sales, per unit of population, of cities of 10,000 or more inhabitants and of other hinterland areas, by size class of metropolitan community, type of sector, and distance from the nearest metropolis. United States, 1939–40.

Type of sector and distance zone (miles)	WHOLESALE SALES PER PERSON (DOLLARS) Cities of 10,000 or more inhabitants A	B	C	D	Cities of less than 10,000 rural areas A	B	C	D	NUMBER OF WAGE EARNERS PER THOUSAND INHABITANTS Cities of 10,000 or more inhabitants A	B	C	D	Cities of less than 10,000 rural areas A	B	C	D	NUMBER OF ESTABLISHMENTS PER THOUSAND INHABITANTS Cities of 10,000 or more inhabitants A	B	C	D	Cities of less than 10,000 rural areas A	B	C	D
All sectors	278	250	405	400	128	79	77	90	10.1	9.8	14.5	15.6	6.1	2.8	2.7	3.5	1.06	1.19	1.80	1.89	0.70	0.70	0.96	1.16
0-9	386	167	182	175	237	55	59	84	13.0	5.8	5.6	7.7	9.7	1.9	1.7	3.4	1.07	0.53	0.69	0.80	0.76	0.29	0.35	0.57
10-14	113	216	553	195	38	35	115	55	3.7	8.1	18.3	8.8	1.3	1.5	2.8	8.6	0.49	0.90	1.62	1.11	0.20	0.29	0.34	0.54
15-24	185	128	691	252	111	235	72	68	6.9	4.4	10.2	11.4	3.0	2.6	2.8	2.7	0.91	0.79	1.49	1.20	0.37	0.50	0.71	0.72
25-34	369	225	256	177	71	74	98	72	12.2	8.2	9.9	7.0	4.9	1.8	3.5	2.3	1.21	1.09	1.38	1.35	0.40	0.56	0.99	0.92
35-44	249	228	210	355	98	64	78	80	10.1	8.9	7.9	13.3	3.0	2.3	3.1	3.0	1.43	1.17	1.37	1.78	0.45	0.50	1.02	0.99
45-64	340	292	301	752	126	53	82	84	14.6	12.6	11.7	13.8	6.1	2.1	2.2	4.5	1.48	1.58	1.77	1.92	0.81	0.60	0.91	1.23
65-114	305	353	373	486	104	76	76	91	13.1	15.2	14.7	17.0	4.7	3.1	2.7	3.6	1.70	1.73	1.88	2.11	1.11	0.86	0.98	1.09
115-164	-	353	534	556	-	76	76	84	-	15.2	19.6	25.1	-	3.4	2.7	3.6	-	2.07	2.33	2.32	-	0.88	0.94	1.16
165-264	-	384	568	546	-	74	76	89	-	15.4	21.7	19.6	-	4.7	2.8	3.4	-	2.50	2.49	2.50	-	0.92	0.96	1.30
265-over	-	-	423	535	-	139	100	127	-	18.3	19.0	20.1	-	5.7	3.7	4.3	-	-	2.42	2.46	1.55	2.31	-	2.22
Intermetropolitan	294	262	437	434	114	90	82	90	10.5	10.4	15.3	16.4	6.1	2.8	2.7	3.3	1.09	1.29	1.86	1.93	0.62	0.74	1.10	1.21
0-9	149	192	192	299	96	-	79	-	15.0	6.5	6.2	10.4	3.2	1.7	2.7	8.6	1.17	0.60	0.77	1.11	0.44	0.20	0.31	0.54
10-14	117	256	712	158	38	79	293	91	4.2	9.6	24.0	7.6	-	2.6	2.6	2.2	0.56	1.07	2.02	1.07	0.20	0.31	0.96	0.68
15-24	193	123	480	297	128	21	74	72	7.0	3.4	26.0	13.0	2.7	2.1	2.6	2.3	0.91	0.79	3.17	1.31	0.11	0.59	1.01	0.90
25-34	396	180	327	168	87	48	98	91	12.7	7.0	11.9	6.9	7.1	1.2	2.6	3.6	1.24	1.11	1.68	1.27	0.42	0.61	1.68	1.10
35-44	278	275	224	401	100	70	62	77	10.2	10.4	8.4	14.0	2.4	1.9	2.5	4.0	1.40	1.34	1.44	1.77	0.36	0.38	1.44	1.31
45-64	309	309	288	355	158	38	58	79	13.8	13.5	11.7	14.5	2.6	3.4	2.6	2.9	1.53	1.72	1.76	1.90	0.86	0.62	1.02	1.07
65-114	284	360	345	557	60	73	60	111	10.8	15.6	13.8	18.3	-	4.3	2.8	3.3	1.75	1.80	1.82	2.09	0.68	0.91	1.08	1.13
115-164	-	279	546	579	-	89	77	-	-	13.3	19.1	25.0	-	10.6	2.4	3.5	-	2.22	2.32	2.79	-	0.99	1.01	1.31
165-264	-	247	656	599	-	-	79	-	-	8.5	24.5	21.3	-	-	4.3	3.5	-	2.06	2.54	2.84	-	1.86	1.03	1.31
265-over	-	-	425	501	-	-	107	126	-	-	18.7	20.1	-	-	4.3	4.5	-	-	2.55	2.33	-	-	3.02	2.11
Subdominant	246	269	408	371	75	70	58	81	9.8	10.4	15.4	15.2	4.4	2.9	2.0	3.6	0.97	1.19	1.78	1.80	0.61	0.72	0.67	0.88
0-9	107	165	537	80	-	-	40	-	4.3	6.0	12.2	3.9	-	-	3.8	-	0.60	0.56	0.43	0.56	-	-	0.27	-
10-14	119	43	8	-	-	-	52	55	2.4	1.8	0.4	-	-	-	1.6	1.7	0.29	0.21	0.27	-	-	-	0.44	0.30
15-24	123	147	208	150	35	75	38	40	4.8	5.6	8.0	7.4	1.2	3.6	1.0	1.2	0.89	0.86	1.22	0.94	0.18	0.43	0.70	0.49
25-34	281	267	181	153	21	44	55	57	11.9	9.3	7.8	5.1	1.0	1.3	1.4	2.0	1.09	1.11	0.96	1.22	0.28	0.38	1.09	0.68
35-44	208	152	-	216	62	220	48	66	10.5	6.9	14.2	12.4	2.4	8.7	2.5	2.5	1.59	0.97	1.90	1.64	0.67	1.03	0.73	0.87
45-64	419	293	546	360	100	70	76	92	16.9	12.2	20.0	12.0	5.5	1.3	2.1	3.9	1.26	1.37	1.97	1.89	1.00	0.47	0.85	0.91
65-114	398	339	514	402	73	38	60	87	17.3	14.9	19.3	16.9	4.4	2.3	1.7	5.2	1.61	1.54	2.20	2.13	-	0.51	0.70	0.85
115-164	-	490	496	535	-	58	48	76	-	17.8	17.2	26.7	-	3.8	1.7	2.5	-	1.91	2.21	2.21	-	0.30	0.51	0.91
165-264	-	507	461	519	-	70	65	108	-	19.2	28.1	18.8	-	6.3	2.2	3.0	-	2.54	2.30	2.01	-	0.76	0.34	2.64
265-over	-	-	613	1026	-	140	-	-	-	-	-	20.8	-	-	-	-	-	-	2.26	3.57	-	1.62	-	-
Local	196	115	227	291	121	72	85	94	7.5	4.5	9.1	12.4	4.7	3.0	3.5	3.8	0.94	0.62	1.51	1.79	0.89	0.74	1.02	1.31
0-9	226	93	110	156	-	-	-	-	7.7	3.0	3.3	8.2	-	-	-	-	0.85	0.25	0.57	0.77	-	-	-	-
10-14	20	109	117	284	-	22	42	77	0.5	4.1	3.4	11.7	-	0.9	1.6	-	0.11	0.42	0.61	1.21	-	0.21	0.72	-
15-24	162	76	196	153	112	112	87	40	7.2	4.3	8.2	8.6	3.7	2.9	3.0	3.6	0.85	0.99	1.79	1.00	0.36	0.25	0.52	0.84
25-34	149	66	129	241	82	48	155	89	5.8	3.1	5.3	9.1	2.1	1.7	5.8	2.6	1.05	0.53	1.51	1.88	0.49	0.74	0.98	1.07
35-44	204	76	30	289	101	53	88	67	8.6	5.7	1.6	10.9	6.2	2.2	3.9	2.3	1.07	0.52	0.45	1.96	0.84	0.53	0.91	0.89
45-64	382	117	206	306	107	77	65	97	13.2	13.0	9.3	10.8	8.7	2.8	2.0	5.6	1.91	1.23	1.80	2.16	0.86	0.67	0.91	1.25
65-114	-	386	323	333	198	91	73	83	-	9.5	11.8	13.1	-	3.4	2.9	3.4	1.97	1.91	2.16	2.15	-	0.94	0.94	1.21
115-164	-	199	646	455	-	85	91	105	-	-	29.8	22.3	-	4.7	3.0	3.8	-	2.46	3.54	2.08	-	0.82	1.00	1.34
165-264	-	-	360	306	-	-	95	94	-	-	21.7	12.1	-	0.7	5.2	3.6	-	-	3.11	2.38	-	0.43	1.20	1.47
265-over	-	-	316	480	-	133	98	131	-	-	14.7	20.0	-	2.7	3.2	4.0	-	-	2.27	2.58	-	1.22	1.72	2.46

Source: Sixteenth Census of the United States. Compiled from Population, Vol.I, State tables 3 and 5; Wholesale Trade, 1939, Vol.II, Table 13.

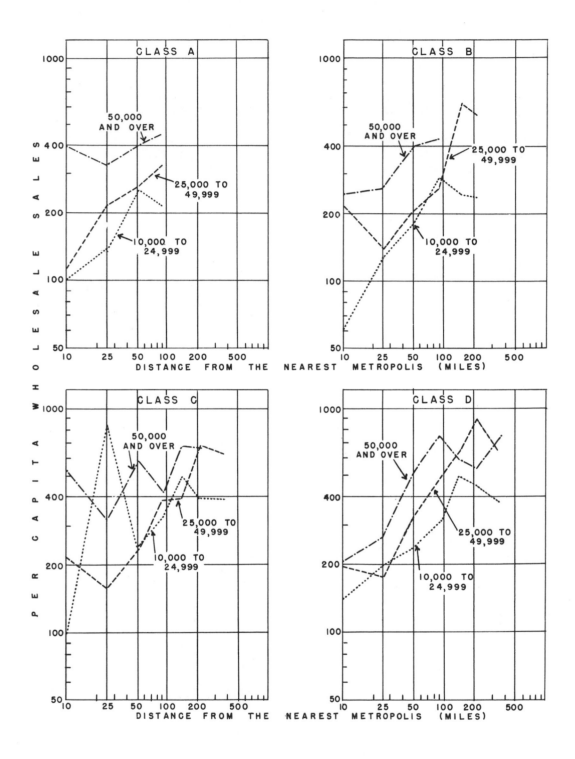

CHART 13-2   SPECIALIZATION IN WHOLESALE TRADE————PRIN-
CIPAL HINTERLAND CITIES CLASSIFIED BY
SIZE. PER CAPITA WHOLESALE SALES OF THREE
SIZES OF HINTERLAND CITIES CLASSIFIED BY
SIZE CLASS OF THE METROPOLITAN COMMUNITY
AND DISTANCE FROM THE NEAREST METROPOLIS.
UNITED STATES, 1939-40

there are many individual hinterland cities of 25,000 or more inhabitants which are as specialized as is their central city.

3. The wholesale specialization of all sizes of hinterland cities tends to increase with distance. Those cities lying within the suburban area of central cities tend to have very low indexes of specialization.

4. Since the hinterland cities lying at the greater distances have a larger trade territory than those lying within 65 miles of the metropolis, a portion of the rising level of specialization with increasing distance represents a wider area of service rather than an increasing independence of the central city. The fact that some individual hinterland cities attain a level of specialization in wholesale trade which is even greater than the level attained by their central cities indicates, that at the most distant areas, the principal cities either perform a very high proportion of all of the wholesale functions, or have a very large trade territory.

VII

Wholesale Specialization in "Other Areas," Classified by Size of Largest City Contained (Chart 13-3, Appendix Table XII)

1. The presence of a hinterland city, and the size of such a city, modify considerably the extent of wholesaling in rural areas. Counties which contain no city have very low indexes of wholesale specialization, compared to counties which do contain cities, and compared to cities themselves. The index of specialization of counties containing a city of 2,500-4,999 is about 60 percent higher than the index of counties with no city. A similar, but smaller, difference exists between counties containing a city of 5,000-9,999 and those containing a city of less than 5,000 inhabitants. An increase in specialization with increasing size of city occurs at all distances and in all sizes of metropolitan communities.

2. There can be little doubt that when wholesale establishments are present in the hinterland cities, great dependence is placed upon them. The outlying areas in counties containing cities of 10,000 or more inhabitants are no more specialized in wholesale trade than are areas containing no cities, although the outlying areas contain smaller cities and considerably greater concentrations of population. Those counties which lack a city of 5,000 or more inhabitants, and which lie in subdominant sectors, have a much lower index of specialization than similar counties in the intermetropolitan and local sectors.

3. In the absence of major hinterland cities and of intermetropolitan transportation routes, "other areas" of the local sectors tend to develop their own wholesale structure. Under such conditions the index of wholesale specialization tends to be higher than for other sector types. This same tendency is present in all sectors, at all distances greater than 115 miles from the metropolis. At these distances, the sparsity of the principal hinterland cities and the inaccessibility of the metropolis itself seem to foster such a development.

VIII

Summary

1. The central city is several times more specialized in wholesale trade than is any hinterland area. It is also more specialized than are most hinterland cities. In fact, a very high degree of specialization in wholesale activities, when accompanied by greater than average specialization in the other activities, appears to be one mark of the metropolis.

2. The larger central cities are more specialized than the smaller classes of central cities. Large hinterland cities are more specialized than small ones. Counties containing cities are more specialized than counties containing no cities. From all angles, there is evidence that an urban location is preferred. The dispersing of wholesale trade into small cities and rural areas seems to be practiced only when service to the more dispersed retail and service establishments appears to require it.

3. With increasing distance from the metropolis, the principal hinterland cities become progressively more specialized. At the greatest distances the "other areas" are also more specialized. Some of this specialization is due, undoubtedly, to the larger average trade area of hinterland cities with increasing distance. Yet the extreme specialization of the central city indicates that the metropolis performs wholesale functions for a wide area. Retail and service establishments over a very wide area appear to depend upon the wholesale establishments of the metropolis as a source of supply. The scope of this dependence appears to decrease with distance. For some wholesale activities, however, almost complete dependence upon the wholesale establishments of the metropolis is necessary throughout the entire metropolitan community.

4. Cities in intermetropolitan sectors tend to be more specialized in wholesale trade than do cities in other types of sectors. Local sectors are much less specialized than are other types of sector.

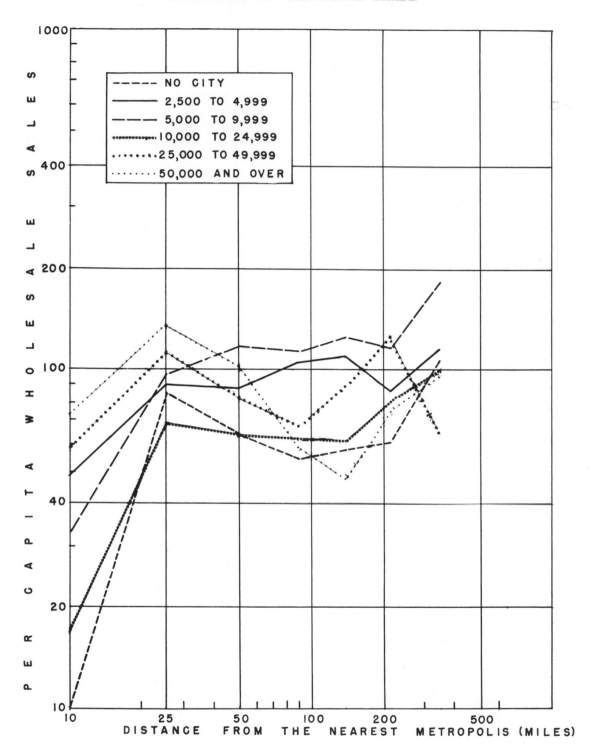

CHART 13-3   SPECIALIZATION IN WHOLESALE TRADE——
RURAL AREAS AND CITIES OF LESS THAN
10,000 INHABITANTS. PER CAPITA WHOLESALE
SALES OF COUNTIES, WITH CITIES OF 10,000
OR MORE INHABITANTS EXCLUDED, CLASSIFIED
BY SIZE OF LARGEST CITY CONTAINED AND
DISTANCE FROM THE NEAREST METROPOLIS.
UNITED STATES, 1939-40

CHAPTER FOURTEEN

THE STRUCTURE OF MANUFACTURES IN THE METROPOLITAN COMMUNITY

I

Introduction

Considerable attention has been given in recent years to the economic factors of industrial location.[1] These studies have demonstrated that the functioning and survival of industry at any given location are influenced by many variables, among which are sources of materials, power and fuel, water, transportation, markets, labor supply, capital, and management. Because the problem of industrial location does contain so many different variables, there is a surprisingly wide latitude for choice. The combinations of circumstances under which industry can prosper and thrive are many. The possible combinations also vary with the type of industry. Since most manufactured products contain not one but several different types of raw materials or other components, the location must be one which will permit their economical assemblage, though it need not always be at the actual source of supply of any one raw material. Hence, although the manufacturing industry, like agriculture, cannot ignore resource patterns completely, its distribution is not determined solely by resource considerations. The other factors are of such importance that:

There are relatively few industries in which one location factor far outweighs any other. More commonly, several factors play an important part in the determination of a location.[2]

Because the functions whose distribution has been studied thus far are primarily consumer oriented, one may anticipate that the pattern of manufacturing specialization will differ considerably from the patterns of the other functions, because of the operation of factors which are unique to manufacturing enterprises.

In 1939 the United States Census of Manufactures classified all manufacturing activities into 20 major industry groups.[3] These major categories are subdivided into 446 different types of manufacturing industries. From the point of view of the variety of products and the processes of work involved, the operation of a manufacturing industry is a much more specialized task than is the operation of a retail, wholesale, or service business. The greater number of categories which the Census has found necessary in the classification of industries by type is indicative of this fact.

II

Standards for Measuring Manufacturing Specialization.

The indexes of manufacturing specialization for the United States and for each geographic division in 1940 were as follows:

Geographic division	Establishments per thousand population	Wage earners per thousand population	Value added by manufacture per resident	Value of products per resident
New England	1.9	113.0	$288	$580
Middle Atlantic	2.0	81.7	267	582
E. N. Central	1.5	82.5	292	660
W. N. Central	1.1	28.3	101	282
South Atlantic	1.0	55.4	125	302
E. S. Central	0.7	33.2	77	182
W. S. Central	0.8	20.1	63	196
Mountain	1.0	16.7	66	198
Pacific	1.8	44.1	164	390
United States	1.4	59.9	$188	$432

See Footnotes on Page 183.

An average of $188 for each person in the nation was added to the value of products through the process of manufacture. The total value of manufactured products was $432 per person, or about midway between the per capita value index for retail trade and that for wholesale trade. The number of manufacturing establishments per 1,000 inhabitants is 1.4. This is a frequency of occurrence which is about equal to that of wholesale establishments, less than one-third that of service establishments, and less than one-ninth that of retail establishments. These comparisons, however, do not show completely the relative importance of the position manufacturing holds among the sustenance activities. Since the basic process is one not of transferring ownership, but of transforming materials, the number of people employed is necessarily high in relation to the value of the product. Although the value per person of manufactured products is equal, roughly, to the average of wholesale and retail trade, the number of people employed in manufacturing in the United States is 60 per thousand — more than twice that of retailing, seven times that of service, and five times that of wholesale trade. Manufacturing provides employment more frequently than do all of these other activities combined.

Manufacturing specialization varies among regions by about the same amount as does wholesale trade. The range in per capita value added between the most concentrated and the least concentrated region is about 122 percent of the national average. This great variation is created by the very low degree of specialization of the South Central and Mountain divisions and the very high degree of specialization of the northeastern divisions.

III

Manufacturing Specialization and Distance
from Metropolitan Centers for Each Size Class.
(Chart 14-1)

1. The population of central cities is no more specialized in manufacturing, on the whole, than are the residents of the areas lying within 25 to 35 miles of the central city. In fact, the residents of the class A, B, and D central cities are less specialized than are the residents of at least one of these inner zones. This situation differs greatly

from that which exists for retail trade, services, and wholesale trade, in all of which the central city is more specialized than any one of the outlying zones.

2. Nevertheless, a high degree of specialization in manufacturing is most definitely associated with proximity to, or location in, the central city. Beyond a given distance from the metropolis the level of manufacturing activity per unit of population tends to decline very rapidly, and to reach a relatively low point at the greater distances. For class A and B metropolitan communities this point appears to be as far as 65 miles from the central city. For class C and D metropolitan communities it appears to be between 25 and 35 miles from the central city. Out to these points the index of manufacturing may fluctuate at a high level or decrease gradually; beyond these points it declines at a very rapid rate with relative increase in distance. At the greatest distances the index has only a small fraction of the value it has in the inner zones. Though the entire hinterland does not appear to be dependent upon the central cities for manufactures, as it does in the case of wholesale trade, the outer portions of the metropolitan community must rely upon the inner portion, including the central cities, for manufactured products.

3. The degree to which a central city is specialized in manufacturing varies with size; those which are larger than 500,000 inhabitants tend to be more specialized than those which are smaller.

4. A similar difference exists between the hinterlands of metropolitan communities with large central cities and those with smaller ones. The value added by manufacture, the number of wage earners, and the number of establishments per unit of population are all larger in class A and B metropolitan communities, at all distances from the central city, than in class C and D metropolitan communities.

5. The area of positive concentration, or of specialization in manufacturing in excess of the index for the metropolitan community as a whole, lies entirely within 45 miles of the central city. Hinterland areas lying at greater distances than this tend to add less value, to employ fewer people, and to contain fewer establishments per unit of population than does the average metropolitan community.

6. Any distance zone, as a whole, seems able to achieve a level of manufacturing higher than the national average of $187 value added per person,

1. Outstanding examples are: E. M. Hoover, Location Theory and the Shoe and Leather Industries, (Cambridge: Harvard University Press, 1939); Daniel Creamer, Is Industry Decentralizing? (Philadelphia: University of Pennsylvania Press, 1935); National Resources Planning Board, Industrial Location and National Resources, (Washington, D. C.: Government Printing Office, 1942).

2. National Resources Planning Board, op. cit., p. 3.

3. Sixteenth Census of the United States. Manufactures, 1939, Vol. IV, p. 2.

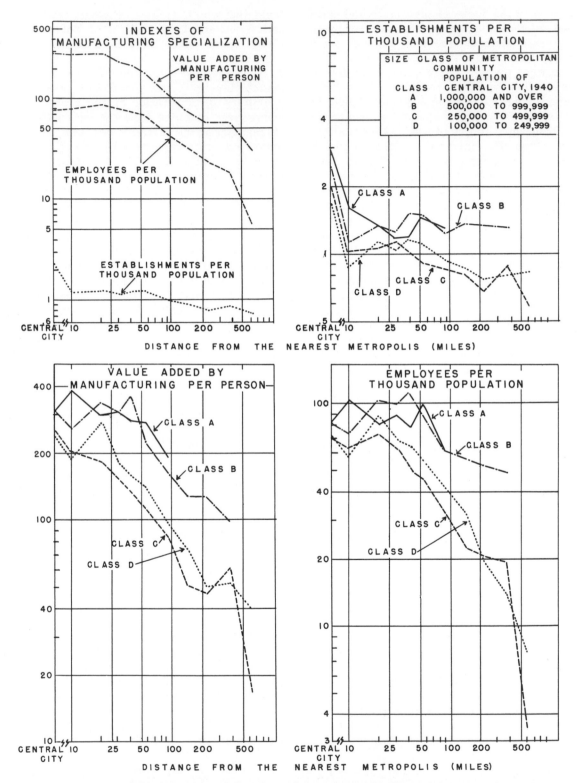

CHART 14-1   SPECIALIZATION IN MANUFACTURING———DISTANCE. MANU-
FACTURING ESTABLISHMENTS, MANUFACTURING EMPLOYEES,
AND VALUE ADDED BY MANUFACTURING PER UNIT OF
POPULATION. ALL AREAS OF THE UNITED STATES
CLASSIFIED BY SIZE CLASS OF THE METROPOLITAN
COMMUNITY AND DISTANCE FROM THE NEAREST
METROPOLIS. UNITED STATES, 1939-40

if it lies within 115 miles of a class A central city, within 65 miles of a class B metropolitan community, or within about 25 miles of a class C or D metropolitan community.

7. Whereas the indexes for value added and for employment sink to very low levels in the outer zones, the number of establishments does not undergo a correspondingly sharp decline. The relative decrease in the number of establishments with increase in relative distance is much more gradual. From this it must be concluded that, with increasing distance, the average size of the individual establishment decreases at a faster rate than does the number of establishments. It will be remembered that this same phenomenon exists for all of the other three sustenance activities.

IV

Manufacturing Specialization in Each Type of Sector of Each Size Class of Metropolitan Community.
(Table 14-1)

1. As has been the tendency when the other sustenance activities have been examined, the intermetropolitan and the subdominant sectors tend to be more specialized in manufacturing than the local sectors, whether the measurement is in terms of number of establishments, employment, or dollar value. Those sectors which possess neither intermetropolitan routes nor a principal hinterland city are deficient in manufacturing specialization.

2. Contrary to the tendencies of the other functions, manufacturing is somewhat more concentrated in subdominant sectors than in intermetropolitan sectors. In terms of value added and of number of establishments, the intermetropolitan sectors are more specialized than the subdominant sectors in only two of the four classes of metropolitan communities. In terms of wage earners, the subdominant sectors of all size classes of metropolitan communities are more specialized than are the intermetropolitan sectors. Since it is the only one of the sustenance functions which has shown this tendency to concentrate in subdominant sectors, the conclusion must be drawn that specialization in manufacturing is one of the principal factors in the development of hinterland cities which are "off the beaten path" between metropolitan centers.

V

The Manufacturing Specialization of Principal Hinterland Cities and of Other Hinterland Areas.
(Table 14-2)

It has been found in the three preceding chapters that, outside of the immediate suburban zone, the structure of the hinterland is composed of trade areas, or of a subdivision of the total hinterland into smaller areas in which the hinterland city provides the great bulk of goods and services consumed. Does this same pattern extend to manufacturing? The data indicate that it does not. There is very little evidence to indicate that, as the distance from the central city increases and, consequently, as competition with the central city decreases, local manufacturing springs up to replace the activities of the metropolis.

1. Manufacturing which occurs in the hinterland tends to be centralized in the principal hinterland cities of 10,000 or more inhabitants rather than in the small towns and open country. Yet, in this respect, it is considerably less concentrated than are hinterland services and wholesale trade. A comparison of Tables 11-2, 12-2, 13-2, and 14-2 will show, in fact, that the extent of this concentration is almost midway between the extensive dispersion of retail trade and the market concentration of wholesale establishments. For each dollar's worth of value added by manufacture in the small city and open country areas, between 2.2 and 3.6 dollars are added by manufacture in the principal cities, depending upon the size class of each metropolitan community. Thus, manufacturing activities are much more widely dispersed than is generally recognized. Not only are they distributed over a fairly extensive zone surrounding the central city, but, compared to wholesale trade and services, they are also much more prone to be located in small cities and the open country.

2. The pattern of manufacturing specialization for hinterland cities of 10,000 or more inhabitants is essentially the same as that for the hinterland as a whole. Immediately surrounding the metropolis there is, as has been seen, a broad zone several miles deep which appears to favor manufacturing. Cities which lie inside this zone may become quite specialized in manufactures; the group of cities which lie outside it have a very low degree of specialization. For cities, the outer limits of this zone are somewhat broader than those indicated for hinterland areas as a whole. Cities located in a class A metropolitan community can become about as specialized at any one distance as at any other. In other words, distance from the metropolis does not seem to act as a brake upon manufacturing specialization within the 115 miles radius over which class A central cities are supposed to be dominant. In the other size classes of metropolitan communities the zones of hinterland city specialization in manufacturing do not extend beyond 65 miles. At distances greater than those named above, the specialization of hinterland cities of all sizes decreases consistently with increasing

Table 14-1

Specialization in manufacturing - sector type: Number of manufacturing establishments, number of manufacturing wage earners, and value added by manufacture, per unit of population, by type of sector and size class of metropolitan community.   United States, 1939-40.[a]

	SIZE CLASS OF METROPOLITAN COMMUNITY				
Type of sector	All metropolitan communities	Class A	Class B	Class C	Class D
	Value added per person (dollars)				
Intermetropolitan	164	313	241	94	121
Subdominant	171	359	225	87	125
Local	107	242	158	80	86
	Number of employees per thousand inhabitants				
Intermetropolitan	55.0	91.6	78.0	33.5	46.0
Subdominant	65.0	107.2	82.6	42.9	50.6
Local	40.7	70.0	55.5	33.5	36.0
	Number of establishments per thousand inhabitants				
Intermetropolitan	1.08	1.59	1.29	0.87	0.95
Subdominant	1.12	1.02	1.54	0.86	0.96
Local	0.96	1.08	1.04	0.92	0.94

a) Excludes central cities and counties containing central cities

Source: Sixteenth Census of the United States.   Compiled from Population, Vol. I, State tables 3 and 5; Manufacture, 1939, Vol. II, State table 2.

Table 14-2

Specialization in manufacturing – principal cities and other areas: Number of manufacturing establishments, number of manufacturing wage earners, and value added by manufacture per unit of population, of cities of 10,000 or more inhabitants and of other hinterland areas, by size class of metropolitan community, type of sector, and distance from the nearest metropolis. United States, 1939-40.

Type of sector and distance zone (miles)	VALUE ADDED BY MANUFACTURING PER PERSON (DOLLARS)								NUMBER OF WAGE EARNERS PER THOUSAND INHABITANTS								NUMBER OF ESTABLISHMENTS PER THOUSAND INHABITANTS							
	Cities of 10,000 or more inhabitants				Cities of less than 10,000 and rural areas				Cities of 10,000 or more inhabitants				Cities of less than 10,000 and rural areas				Cities of 10,000 or more inhabitants				Cities of less than 10,000 and rural areas			
	A	B	C	D	A	B	C	D	A	B	C	D	A	B	C	D	A	B	C	D	A	B	C	D
All sectors	412	331	202	260	186	152	66	73	121.1	108.2	73.1	89.5	53.8	53.2	26.4	31.4	1.71	1.60	1.50	1.56	1.06	1.08	0.70	0.77
0-9	472	241	229	265	210	301	175	157	122.4	67.7	76.5	88.1	55.0	83.8	52.2	45.4	2.29	1.23	1.29	1.18	1.25	0.74	0.68	0.71
10-14	445	236	295	387	173	279	88	9	129.0	69.7	90.0	138.5	49.7	84.8	79.8	2.9	1.17	1.50	2.00	1.82	0.61	0.55	0.55	0.41
15-24	363	502	362	352	204	192	131	220	98.5	143.2	112.6	115.5	55.4	84.7	11.3	70.2	1.51	1.75	1.86	1.43	1.11	0.99	0.84	0.94
25-34	375	411	358	454	232	179	108	84	126.6	137.0	112.3	158.7	55.3	54.0	40.3	37.3	1.48	1.49	1.86	1.79	0.92	0.98	0.85	0.77
35-44	353	486	530	284	250	280	74	96	113.2	158.7	166.8	103.8	62.6	78.4	32.4	44.9	1.83	2.15	1.69	1.81	0.92	1.09	0.92	0.83
45-64	428	360	168	321	166	155	67	97	111.7	132.5	91.9	109.8	68.9	99.6	30.4	36.1	1.75	2.02	1.49	1.81	1.22	1.21	0.72	0.87
65-114	326	336	129	243	118	81	63	79	116.0	116.0	59.9	87.6	32.3	34.3	25.7	30.5	1.77	1.57	1.44	1.52	1.03	1.09	0.71	0.77
115-164	-	251	129	176	82	96	35	60	-	113.6	46.4	54.4	18.3	29.0	25.2	28.5	-	1.71	1.35	1.49	0.85	1.25	0.70	0.74
165-264	-	196	99	105	68	106	39	56	-	78.3	32.7	35.6	14.5	44.5	18.8	18.2	-	1.71	1.30	1.23	0.86	1.19	0.58	0.74
265-over	-	-	75	68	22	97	49	46	-	-	23.8	18.8	7.1	49.1	15.5	11.8	-	1.76	1.47	1.38	0.56	1.30	0.72	0.67
Intermetropolitan	390	344	218	273	201	159	54	65	113.1	107.4	70.5	92.5	60.0	54.3	21.8	29.2	1.90	1.58	1.53	1.55	1.12	1.05	0.66	0.73
0-9	450	299	268	314	421	-	-	-	110.1	83.7	85.4	90.2	146.8	-	18.3	2.9	2.64	1.24	1.37	1.22	4.20	0.61	-	-
10-14	310	299	276	384	173	353	64	9	80.5	68.3	63.2	130.2	49.7	107.0	26.3	85.5	1.29	1.52	1.92	1.40	0.61	0.61	0.40	0.11
15-24	401	523	831	419	287	245	84	289	110.2	145.1	258.3	135.7	81.4	80.7	36.6	38.0	1.66	1.46	1.55	1.43	1.46	1.18	0.75	0.87
25-34	357	432	264	455	168	220	100	89	122.2	116.6	96.1	152.9	56.1	67.6	25.0	41.9	1.54	1.58	2.02	1.58	1.08	1.22	0.79	0.74
35-44	353	474	557	320	253	287	45	94	107.8	144.9	171.9	116.1	61.0	79.5	31.3	33.5	1.74	2.14	1.71	1.88	0.86	0.75	0.70	0.82
45-64	304	339	290	319	198	130	74	73	158.7	122.0	104.4	111.2	81.3	55.9	22.0	29.1	2.11	2.06	1.55	1.79	1.32	1.19	0.68	0.87
65-114	-	359	170	252	149	80	63	51	109.3	90.5	56.3	92.3	34.4	29.0	18.9	28.4	1.90	1.42	1.44	1.54	0.91	1.03	0.65	0.73
115-164	-	197	132	167	82	107	31	55	-	109.1	49.8	44.7	14.6	40.0	16.9	12.7	-	1.70	1.48	1.34	1.07	0.99	0.72	0.68
165-264	-	324	108	86	69	58	43	55	-	-	27.9	26.2	14.5	29.1	7.5	11.2	-	1.97	1.31	1.29	0.84	1.36	0.56	0.68
265-over	-	-	67	54	22	-	26	43	-	-	44.0	12.2	7.1	-	-	-	-	-	1.44	1.32	0.56	-	0.61	0.64
Subdominant	480	317	173	253	174	128	53	73	145.9	113.0	80.7	83.6	56.3	50.6	28.0	37.5	1.07	1.73	1.38	1.52	0.94	1.34	0.66	0.74
0-9	173	189	58	222	-	-	-	-	51.4	57.5	21.0	80.4	-	-	-	-	1.10	1.54	0.93	0.98	-	-	-	-
10-14	1070	109	333	-	-	-	178	186	351.0	39.5	177.6	-	-	-	106.5	102.3	0.71	1.45	1.79	-	-	-	0.80	1.26
15-24	259	498	317	250	100	118	78	66	64.1	146.0	177.2	76.9	23.6	59.3	37.7	23.5	0.95	2.13	1.98	1.47	0.64	0.95	0.56	0.92
25-34	486	424	270	476	179	103	67	89	166.1	153.1	141.4	159.9	21.7	33.0	59.5	59.3	0.99	1.11	1.66	1.74	0.41	0.64	0.52	0.78
35-44	333	386	-	166	236	449	99	98	109.1	189.9	-	62.2	20.0	99.4	22.9	49.9	1.88	2.81	-	1.53	0.95	2.50	0.67	0.74
45-64	469	374	126	408	236	191	91	75	116.2	131.3	30.8	109.6	101.8	92.6	22.6	34.5	0.90	1.84	0.99	1.96	1.38	1.49	0.66	0.79
65-114	366	282	143	291	99	109	58	68	128.2	105.5	63.5	96.5	27.0	59.6	31.8	35.0	1.54	1.87	1.26	1.52	0.81	1.45	0.67	0.66
115-164	-	315	130	180	96	76	52	52	-	111.5	40.1	77.5	19.6	34.2	26.1	29.7	-	1.78	1.08	1.73	0.77	1.47	0.63	0.71
165-264	-	183	96	128	-	124	35	68	-	-	44.8	41.0	-	50.9	22.3	4.4	-	1.74	1.30	1.07	-	1.20	0.61	0.61
265-over	-	-	75	68	-	94	106	15	-	75.3	35.9	18.3	-	45.7	38.4	-	-	-	1.45	1.72	-	1.18	-	-
Local	483	309	171	216	145	104	68	68	144.8	95.0	72.8	84.2	40.1	44.3	28.5	29.4	1.28	1.22	1.55	1.67	1.00	0.97	0.83	0.84
0-9	855	184	171	260	-	-	-	-	253.1	44.6	66.4	91.4	-	-	-	-	1.33	0.42	1.17	1.28	-	-	-	-
10-14	3	274	348	393	-	11	8	132	1.3	87.8	158.7	158.7	-	3.1	6.4	-	0.20	1.42	2.24	2.84	-	0.35	0.39	-
15-24	143	451	18	154	95	46	217	73	33.6	127.7	4.2	44.3	20.8	15.4	61.8	44.3	0.74	1.35	0.99	1.42	0.66	0.65	0.98	0.97
25-34	397	116	107	435	556	164	132	106	162.5	84.6	53.2	64.9	107.0	39.5	44.8	37.9	1.66	1.83	1.76	2.94	1.02	1.34	1.03	0.83
35-44	411	715	175	205	301	143	106	80	160.9	189.5	99.9	99.1	85.4	63.7	43.6	44.6	2.21	1.17	1.43	1.71	1.25	1.00	1.27	0.89
45-64	176	490	108	162	80	192	60	67	79.0	232.6	45.5	78.4	31.3	31.1	31.6	35.2	1.89	2.66	1.47	1.67	1.01	1.01	0.82	0.90
65-114	-	320	192	169	61	69	64	67	-	92.9	79.6	97.4	29.4	69.8	31.7	31.1	-	1.98	1.71	1.46	1.33	1.36	0.88	0.85
115-164	-	33	75	218	-	125	28	52	-	44.5	43.3	65.9	13.4	9.1	13.4	25.6	-	1.00	1.59	1.93	-	0.64	0.66	0.85
165-264	-	-	57	129	50	13	31	57	-	-	67.0	67.0	-	-	14.8	20.4	-	-	1.16	1.50	1.58	1.96	0.59	0.77
265-over	-	-	91	143	-	117	69	58	-	-	35.3	51.2	-	6.6	22.2	14.3	-	-	1.53	1.50	-	-	0.92	0.76

Source: Sixteenth Census of the United States. Compiled from Population, Vol.I, State tables 3 and 5; Manufactures, 1939, Vol.II, State table 2.

distance from the central city. It will be remembered that cities in these outer zones are more sparsely distributed over the land and that the populations of these zones are more rural in character. It will be remembered also that the wholesale facilities through which the majority of manufactured products are marketed are concentrated in the central city. Because a location in the vicinity of a large city provides accessibility to many diverse sources of materials and to employment of the varied skills required to fabricate complex products, and because such a location also provides easy access to the primary wholesale customers, it is not surprising that few hinterland cities would attain a high level of manufacturing specialization.

In this connection, it should be noted that the manufacturer need not be located right at the doorstep of his customers, even in those cases in which his market is entirely local. Since his customers are numerous, and are themselves distributed throughout a given area, the locational pull of any one customer is relatively small. The total size of the market within an area may be a very effective force in drawing a manufacturer into an area, but the particular pattern by which that market is distributed within the area is of lesser importance.[4] It is possible, for this reason, that specialization is not confined to the central city proper, but may be diffused over the broader inner zone, in response to other factors.

3. Small cities and rural areas, out to about 45 miles from the class A and B central cities, are able to enjoy a high degree of manufacturing specialization. The total population of these areas is more specialized in manufacturing than is the total population of all metropolitan communities. Even in the small cities and rural areas of at least one inner zone of class C and D metropolitan communities, the level of specialization approaches that of the nation. Outside the inner zone, which has been found to favor manufacturing activities, specialization of rural areas and small cities in manufacturing declines swiftly with increasing distance. At the outer zones of such areas manufacturing reaches its lowest level. Since their indexes of specialization are as low as one-fourth of the national average, and one-sixth of the level at the center or at least one of the intermediate zones, it is very evident that these peripheral areas are extremely dependent upon the core of the metropolitan community. There is no evidence, at these distances, of any attempt by the small towns and rural areas to compensate for the relative scarcity of manufacturing in larger cities. All evidence points

to the conclusion that hinterland conditions beyond 35-64 miles from the metropolis become increasingly discouraging to specialization in manufacture with increasing distance. The exact distance at which the point of diminishing specialization begins varies with the size class of the metropolitan community. Metropolitan centers of more than 500,000 inhabitants appear to be able to encourage small-city and open-country manufacturing at much greater distances into the hinterland than do central cities of smaller size.

4. These differences, noted above, in specialization among the three types of sectors cannot be attributed solely to the principal hinterland cities or to the other hinterland areas. The greater specialization of the subdominant sectors compared to that of the intermetropolitan sectors seems to arise from two sources: i.e., the specialization of principal hinterland cities located in the subdominant sectors of class A and B metropolitan communities, and the specialization of small hinterland cities and rural areas in class C and D metropolitan communities. The lower index of specialization in local sectors must be attributed both to the principal hinterland cities and to the other areas. Within the zone of manufacturing which has been described above there tends to be little difference between one sector type and another. Outside this zone, however, the principal cities and rural areas show unusually low indexes compared to other sectors, and those indexes decline at a more rapid rate with increasing distance.

V

Manufacturing Specialization and Size of Hinterland City (Chart 14-2, Appendix Table XIII)

1. In general, the larger the hinterland city the greater is its degree of manufacturing specialization. While this tendency is present for the cities of all classes of metropolitan communities considered together, there are important major exceptions in individual classes of metropolitan communities. A great many large hinterland cities have very low manufacturing indexes, and a great many small cities have high manufacturing indexes. There is no simple and consistent relationship, between size of hinterland city and degree of specialization in manufacturing, analogous to that found for wholesale trade, for services, and (to a lesser extent) for retail trade. This reemphasizes the fact that market factors, or the trade territory, are of less importance in the distribution of manufacturing activities than in the distribution of these

---

4. National Resources Planning Board, Industrial Location and National Resources, p. 204.

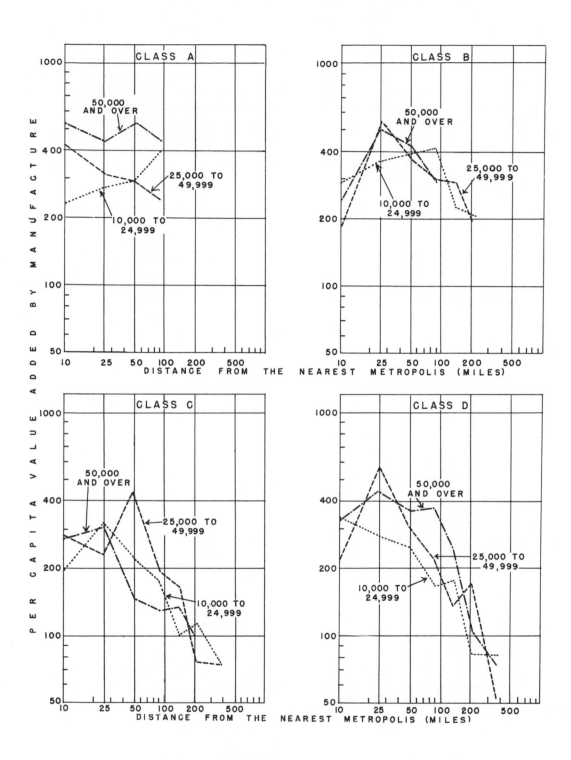

CHART 14-2   SPECIALIZATION IN MANUFACTURING————PRINCIPAL
HINTERLAND CITIES CLASSIFIED BY SIZE. PER
CAPITA VALUE ADDED BY MANUFACTURING OF
THREE SIZES OF HINTERLAND CITIES CLASSIFIED
BY SIZE CLASS OF THE METROPOLITAN COMMUNITY
AND DISTANCE FROM THE NEAREST METROPOLIS.
UNITED STATES, 1939-40

other activities. It is only when all hinterland cities of each size, regardless of the size of the metropolitan community in which they are located, are considered together that the very general relationship between size of city and specialization in manufacturing emerges with any clarity. Only in the class A metropolitan communities does this principle seem to operate with any great consistency.

2. All sizes of principal hinterland cities are subject to the apparent effect of distance upon manufacturing specialization. Although there are fluctuations with distance in the inner zones, the general level of specialization remains high. Beyond 65 miles, each size class of hinterland city participates in the general pattern of a rapid decrease in specialization with increasing distance, save in class A metropolitan communities, where distance does not appear to be a very significant factor in the degree of specialization of principal hinterland cities.

3. It has already been noted that, in the metropolitan communities whose central city is large (class A and B), the principal hinterland cities tend to be more specialized in manufacturing than they do in metropolitan communities with smaller central cities (class C and D). This differential exists for each size of hinterland city in each sector type. The effect of the larger central cities seems to be to increase the manufacturing specialization of the cities of 10,000-24,999 inhabitants more than the specialization of the two larger sizes of hinterland cities. This size of city enjoys a greater relative specialization in the larger metropolitan communities than do cities of more than 25,000 inhabitants.

5. The lower manufacturing specialization of the local sectors is due not only to the fact that they contain no major cities. A comparison of the sector differences for the 10,000-24,999 class of hinterland cities indicates that, beyond 65 miles from the metropolis, the cities of the local sectors have a considerably lower index of specialization than have the cities of the same size in other sectors. Once again it appears that isolation from the metropolis and absence of near major hinterland cities, are effective deterrents to manufacturing, even in those sizeable hinterland cites which, in other locations, would exhibit a high index of industrial specialization.

VI

Manufacturing Specialization in "Other Areas," Classified by Size of Largest City Contained (Chart 14-3, Appendix Table XIV)

An examination of the manufacturing specialization of county units after cities of 10,000 or more

have been subtracted, and with the counties classified by size of largest city contained, makes it possible to gain a great deal of information about the circumstances under which manufacturing "disperses" into the countryside.

1. Those counties which contain no city have very little manufacturing activity. Such areas produce, on the average, only $25 value added by manufacture per resident, which is only 13 percent of the national per capita level of manufacturing. In the area immediately surrounding the central city (0-14 miles), manufacturing in counties containing no cities is almost non-existent. Such areas seem to be set aside for residential purposes only, or to have such unusual topographic characteristics that no intensive manufacturing use is feasible. Between 15 and 34 miles from the central city these completely rural areas enjoy some of the manufacturing specialization which is characteristic of the zone, but only to a very modest degree ($38-$101). At distances greater than this, manufacturing activities drop to an index level of approximately $20 per capita and remain at about this point for all distances. No area, regardless of its metropolitan position, attains great specialization in manufacturing in the absence of an urban center. Only in the vicinity of the metropolis can this requirement be lifted, and then but partially. To those extreme decentralists who wish to make of industry a completely rural phenomenon, this evidence must seem very discouraging. It would appear that those factors upon which manufacturing activities must depend — access to sources of supply, labor force, markets, and transportation — are not present in sufficient quantities in completely rural areas to warrant any extensive manufacturing specialization.

2. Not only the presence of a city, but the presence of a fairly sizeable city, is associated with intensive specialization in manufacture. Though the presence of a hinterland city of 2,500-4,999 inhabitants almost doubles the intensity of manufacturing activity, the level of specialization still remains low. The greatest gains are, as would be expected, at the greatest distances. In the presence of a city of the smallest class, the level of manufacturing trebles at distances greater than 265 miles. The level of specialization, however, remains well below the national average, and the averages for all small city and hinterland areas.

3. Principal hinterland cities greatly encourage manufacturing activities in small cities and rural areas. For all of the other sustenance activities it has been observed that, if a city of 10,000 or more inhabitants is present in a county, the other areas do not develop in these activities, but depend upon the larger city for a sizeable proportion of

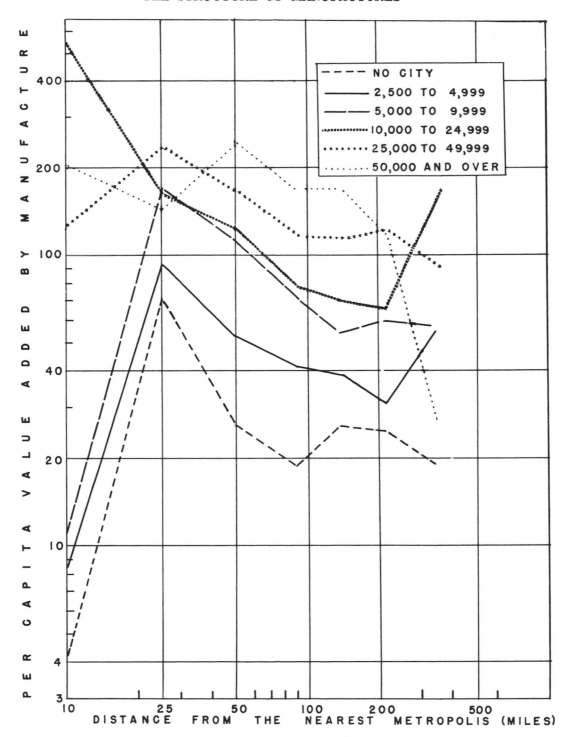

CHART 14-3   SPECIALIZATION IN MANUFACTURING——
RURAL AREAS AND CITIES OF LESS THAN
10,000 INHABITANTS. PER CAPITA VALUE
ADDED BY MANUFACTURING OF COUNTIES,
WITH CITIES OF 10,000 OR MORE INHAB-
ITANTS EXCLUDED, CLASSIFIED BY SIZE
OF LARGEST CITY CONTAINED AND DISTANCE
FROM THE NEAREST METROPOLIS. UNITED
STATES, 1939-40

goods and services. The specialization index for the "other area" in regard to these functions is well below that for counties containing largest cities of 5,000-9,999 inhabitants, or even containing largest cities of 2,500-4,999. Such is not the case with manufacturing. The presence of a principal hinterland city is conducive to manufacturing activities in the small cities and rural areas. The larger the hinterland city contained, the greater the specialization of the outlying communities tends to be. Viewed in another way, the diffusion of manufacturing into the countryside appears to be possible only when there is a nearby city of 10,000 or more inhabitants. The relative gain for the countryside increases with distance from the metropolis. Those who hope for some decentralization of industry, should place their greatest expectations for the future not upon the industrial development of completely rural areas, but upon the growth of smaller hinterland cities to a size which will permit them to support manufacturing activities themselves and to foster the spread of such activities into smaller communities in their immediate vicinity. If the number of cities of 10,000-24,999 inhabitants was doubled through a promotion of the growth of about 600 cities from the 5,000-9,999 group into the larger size classification, the dispersive and diffusive effect of decentralization would be much greater potentially than an attempt to "seed" completely rural areas with manufacturing establishments which could survive only with difficulty.

4. In all of the above distributions, the influence of the metropolis is greatly in evidence. Regardless of the size of the largest city contained, the level of specialization in manufacturing tends to decline as the distance from the metropolitan center increases. The decline is most precipitous for those areas which contain no city, and is most gradual for those areas which contain a city of 50,000 or more inhabitants. In all cases, the combined effect of distance from the metropolis and of presence of a local center is observable.

5. At distances greater than 165 miles, small cities and rural areas in counties containing cities of less than 25,000 inhabitants show evidences of attempting to cast off the influence of the central city and to develop a level of specialization comparable to that of the inner manufacturing zone about the metropolis. The fact that the rate of decline with distance gradually decreases and is eventually reversed may constitute evidence that those cities which lie at the greatest distances from the metropolitan center and are, therefore,

most able to exploit local resources in competition with the metropolis, are fostering small local centers of industrial development through the use of the motor truck, electrical energy, and a local market. It is interesting to note that the greatest specialization is in the local and subdominant sectors, rather than in the intermetropolitan sectors with their direct routes to the central cities. Evidence indicating this manufacturing specialization about large and distant hinterland cities is present in all four size classes of metropolitan communities.

VII

Summary

Although manufacturing specialization is no less patterned with respect to the metropolis than are retail trade, wholesale trade, and services, the elements of the pattern differ considerably from those of the other sustenance activities.

1. At the core of the metropolitan community there is a zone which is 25-64 miles in radius, within which high levels of manufacturing specialization can be attained by individual principal hinterland cities and even by small cities and rural areas. Outside this zone, specialization in manufacturing decreases very rapidly with increasing distance.

2. Although the metropolis itself is highly specialized in manufacturing, it is little more specialized, if any, than are the individual city and county units within the inner zones. This is true in spite of the fact that these zones include large concentrations of rural-farm populations, which are combined with the other populations for the purpose of computing many of the per capita indexes.

3. The level of manufacturing specialization is higher in class A and B metropolitan centers, and at all distances into their hinterlands, than is the level in class C and D central cities and their hinterlands.

4. Intermetropolitan sectors are no more specialized than are subdominant sectors, and both are much more specialized than are local sectors.

5. The larger hinterland city tends to be more specialized in manufacturing than do the smaller hinterland cities, but there is no great consistency in this tendency. A location inside or outside the inner zone of manufacturing specialization seems to be of much greater relative importance.

6. Manufacturing in small cities and rural areas occurs on an extensive scale only in the vicinity of cities of 10,000 or more inhabitants.

APPENDIX TABLE I

Number of Sectors of each type in each metropolitan community.

Metropolitan community	Total number of sectors	Inter-metropolitan	Sub-dominant	Local
New York	9	7	0	2
Chicago	8	5	1	2
Philadelphia	11	5	2	4
Detroit	5	1	3	1
Los Angeles	8	6	1	1
Total	41	24	7	10
Percentage distribution	100.0	58.5	17.1	24.4
Cleveland	7	4	1	2
Baltimore	10	5	0	5
St Louis	12	8	0	4
Boston	7	2	3	2
Pittsburgh	12	8	2	2
Washington, D.C.	8	3	0	5
San Francisco	6	4	1	1
Milwaukee	7	4	2	1
Buffalo	4	0	0	4
Total	73	38	9	26
Percentage distribution	100.0	52.1	12.3	35.6
New Orleans	10	4	2	4
Minneapolis	12	9	0	3
Cincinnati	10	4	2	4
Kansas City, Mo.	12	7	2	3
Indianapolis	12	9	1	2
Houston	11	4	2	5
Seattle	11	3	1	7
Rochester	6	2	0	4
Denver	12	7	0	5
Louisville	12	5	1	6
Columbus	11	9	1	1
Portland	11	3	0	8
Atlanta	12	6	3	3
Dallas	8	6	0	2
Memphis	12	7	1	4
Toledo	9	7	0	2
Birmingham	12	6	1	5
San Antonio	12	5	2	5
Providence	5	1	2	2
Total	200	104	21	75
Percentage distribution	100.0	52.0	10.5	37.5

Metropolitan community	Total number of sectors	Inter-metropolitan	Sub-dominant	Local
Omaha	12	5	0	7
Dayton	8	4	0	4
Syracuse	8	3	2	3
Oklahoma City	12	4	2	6
San Diego	2	1	0	1
Richmond	11	5	1	5
Fort Worth	7	5	2	0
Jacksonville	8	5	0	3
Miami	3	2	0	1
Nashville	12	6	0	6
Hartford	5	2	2	1
Grand Rapids	11	2	1	7
Des Moines	12	5	1	6
Salt Lake City	12	8	0	4
Springfield	2	0	0	2
Tulsa	10	7	0	3
Scranton	10	6	1	3
Albany	11	5	1	5
Chattanooga	12	5	1	6
Spokane	12	5	0	7
Fort Wayne	11	6	0	5
Erie	4	1	1	2
Wichita	11	4	1	6
Knoxville	12	6	1	5
Tampa	8	3	1	4
Sacramento	9	4	0	5
Peoria	9	4	1	4
South Bend	8	2	1	5
Duluth	9	5	0	4
Charlotte	12	6	3	3
Norfolk	10	4	1	5
Davenport, Moline, Rock Island	11	5	1	5
El Paso	8	7	0	1
Evansville	12	7	1	4
Total	314	150	26	138
Percentage distribution	100.0	47.8	8.3	43.9
Grand total	628	316	63	249
Percentage distribution	100.0	50.3	10.0	39.7

Appendix Table II

Number of hinterland cities of each size group classified by size class of metropolitan community, sector type, and distance from the nearest metropolis. United States, 1940. a)

S I Z E   G R O U P   O F   H I N T E R L A N D   C I T Y

2,500 – 4,999

Distance zone (miles)	All metropolitan communities	Size class of metropolitan community			
		A	B	C	D
All sectors					
All distances	1422	201	242	385½	593½
0–24	206	67	46	36	57
25–34	222	62	43	45	72
35–44	109	26	25	25	33
45–64	113	18	18	28	41
65–114	189	36	37	43	73
115–164	376	27	75	97	177
165–264	205½	4	26	79	97½
265–over	165½	1	12	71	78½
	57		3	14½	39½
Intermetropolitan					
All distances	812½	126	147½	216	323
0–24	126	43	35	22	28
25–34	135	43	25	21	43
35–44	64	29	13	7	15
45–64	69	15	12	14	28
65–114	111	22	22	23	44
115–164	211½	11	49½	56	95
165–264	60½	3	3	51	43
265–over	29½	1		8	14½
	3			2	25½
Subdominant					
All distances	203½	28	40½	108	72
0–24	18	10	2	4	6
25–34	21	6	5	6	2
35–44	7	3	1	3	4
45–64	12	3	3	5	2
45–64	30	6	7	11	10
65–114	60½	1	8½	23	27
115–164	39		8	13	17
165–264	32		2	17	1
265–over	3				
Local					
All distances	406	47	54	106½	198½
0–24	62	16	9	12	25
25–34	68	12	13	20	23
35–44	38	7	7	11	13
45–64	32	8	8	9	7
45–64	48	8	8	13	19
65–114	104½	10	17	22	55
115–164	57½	1	4	24	37½
165–264	45		1	17	27
265–over	21½			8½	12

5,000 – 9,999

Distance zone (miles)	All metropolitan communities	Size class of metropolitan community			
		A	B	C	D
All sectors					
All distances	965	153	183½	247½	381
0–24	229	85	57	37	50
25–34	133	36	30	24	43½
35–44	75	21	15	15	24
45–64	60	15	17	9	19
65–114	131½	17	22	28½	64
115–164	218½	8	45½	73	92
165–264	117	6	16	79	62
165–264	98	1	11	35	46
265–over	38		2	11	24
Intermetropolitan					
All distances	550	99	108½	146½	202
0–24	140	51	33	22	34
25–34	83	27	18	15	23
35–44	44	17	10	11	10½
45–64	39	10	12	4	13
65–114	75½	9	13	17½	36
115–164	123½	5	27½	45	46
165–264	55		8	20	27
165–264	46	6	3	20	17
265–over	27	1	1	7	19
Subdominant					
All distances	141	28	45	34	34
0–24	38	20	8	7	3
25–34	16	2	8	3	2
35–44	10	2	6	1	1
45–64	6		1	2	1
65–114	11	4	4	2	1
115–164	31	1	8	10	12
115–164	23		8	7	8
165–264	18		1	7	7
265–over	4			1	1
Local					
All distances	274	26	36	67	145
0–24	51	14	16	8	13
25–34	34	6	4	6	18
35–44	21	2	1	5	13
45–64	15	4	2	3	5
45–64	45	4	5	9	27
65–114	64	2	10	18	34
115–164	39			12	27
165–264	34			12	22
265–over	7		1	2	12

10,000 – 24,999

Distance zone (miles)	All metropolitan communities	Size class of metropolitan community			
		A	B	C	D
All sectors					
All distances	665	112	174	147	232
0–24	196	73	68	24	31
25–34	109	21	27	16	45
25–34	95	11	18	7	23
35–44	44	6	9	7	22
45–64	86	11	24	22	29
65–114	133	7	32	36	58
115–164	74		11	22	38
165–264	45		9	17	19
265–over	22			10	12
Intermetropolitan					
All distances	389	69	93	91	136
0–24	109	45	35	10	19
25–34	68	13	15	12	28
25–34	52½	11	18	6	11½
35–44	26	2	4	6	14
45–64	55	4	17	17	17
65–114	72	7	15	21	29
115–164	46		9	16	21
165–264	24		2	8	14
265–over	15			7	8
Subdominant					
All distances	104	17	50	15	22
0–24	51	11	18	11	11
25–34	24	4	8	1	4
35–44	10½	2	4½	1	7
45–64	9	2	1	1	1
45–64	21	2	3	5	3
65–114	16		13	5	9
115–164	13		4	5	1
165–264			7		1
Local					
All distances	172	26	31	41	74
0–24	56	17	15	13	11
25–34	27	4	7	3	13
35–44	17½	2	5	2	5
45–64	14	5	4	1	6
45–64	22	5	4	5	8
65–114	40	1	4	10	26
115–164	12		1	4	8
165–264	8			3	4
265–over	7			4	3

25,000 – over

Distance zone (miles)	All metropolitan communities	Size class of metropolitan community			
		A	B	C	D
All sectors					
All distances	343	90	80	73	100
0–24	125	55	37	15	18
25–34	51	15	12	7	17
25–34	27	5	7	7	6
35–44	24	6	5	2	11
45–64	51	14	11	10	16
65–114	65	6	13	21	24
115–164	26		3	10	13
165–264	17		3	9	5
265–over	8			1	7
Intermetropolitan					
All distances	226½	69	43	48	64½
0–24	79	43	21	7	8
25–34	35	12	9	4	13
25–34	17	4	3	2	5
35–44	17	4	3	2	8
45–64	37	10	6	9	12
65–114	14½	4	10	17	16
115–164	8			5	9½
165–264	8			6	2
265–over	6				6
Subdominant					
All distances	102	19	33	21	29
0–24	32	10	12	4	6
25–34	9	3	4½	3	4
35–44	7	1	2	2	1
45–64	7	2	2	1	3
45–64	14	4	5	1	4
65–114	18	2	3	5	8
115–164	11		3	3	3
165–264	9		1	3	3
265–over	2				1
Local b)					
All distances	14½	2	4	4	4½
0–24	14	2	4	4	4
25–34					
165–264	½ c)				½ c)

a) Those cities which lie in two counties between which a metropolitan community boundary passes have been coded as one-half city in each metropolitan community.

b) By definition there are no cities of 25,000 or more inhabitants at distances greater than 10 miles from the metropolis in local sectors.

c) One-half of Rocky Mount, North Carolina.

Source: Sixteenth Census of the United States. Compiled from Population, Vol.I, State tables 3 and 5; Areas of the United States, 1940, tables, 2, 3, and 4.

Appendix Table III

Number of hinterland cities of each size group per 1000 square miles, classified by size class of metropolitan community, sector type, and distance from the nearest metropolis. United States, 1940.

SIZE GROUP OF HINTERLAND CITY

All sectors

Distance zone (miles)	2500–4999 All metro.	A	B	C	D	5000–9999 All metro.	A	B	C	D	10,000–24,999 All metro.	A	B	C	D	25,000–over All metro.	A	B	C	D
All distances	0.48	1.63	1.20	0.39	0.36	0.32	1.24	0.91	0.25	0.23	0.22	0.91	0.86	0.15	0.14	0.12	0.73	0.40	0.07	0.06
0–24 a)	2.20	9.55	4.78	1.36	1.13	2.45	12.11	5.92	1.40	0.99	2.09	10.40	7.07	0.91	0.61	1.34	7.84	3.85	0.57	0.36
25–44	1.26	5.87	2.78	0.81	0.76	0.75	3.41	1.94	0.43	0.45	0.62	1.99	1.75	0.29	0.47	0.29	1.42	0.78	0.13	0.18
25–34	1.11	6.06	2.99	0.87	0.83	0.95	5.54	2.40	0.59	0.64	0.81	2.53	2.15	0.35	0.62	0.35	1.52	0.81	0.20	0.16
35–44	1.11	5.63	2.54	0.93	0.71	0.60	3.25	2.10	0.30	0.33	0.44	1.30	1.27	0.23	0.38	0.24	1.30	0.70	0.07	0.19
45–64	0.91	2.26	1.39	0.67	0.72	0.63	1.07	0.83	0.45	0.63	0.24	0.49	0.90	0.34	0.28	0.25	0.88	0.41	0.16	0.16
65–114	0.69	1.46	1.39	0.49	0.65	0.40	0.43	0.40	0.37	0.34	0.16	0.36	0.59	0.18	0.21	0.12	0.32	0.26	0.11	0.09
115–164	0.44	b)	0.65	0.46	0.39	0.25	b)	0.31	0.22	0.25	0.06	–	0.35	0.13	0.15	0.06	–	0.11	0.06	0.05
165–264	0.23	b)	0.33	0.28	0.20	0.14	b)	0.14	0.14	0.12	0.03	–	0.25	0.07	0.05	0.02	–	0.08	0.04	0.01
265–over	0.08	b)	0.15	0.07	0.08	0.05	b)	0.10	0.05	0.05	–	–	–	0.05	0.02	0.01	–	–	0.00	0.01

Intermetropolitan

Distance zone (miles)	2500–4999 All metro.	A	B	C	D	5000–9999 All metro.	A	B	C	D	10,000–24,999 All metro.	A	B	C	D	25,000–over All metro.	A	B	C	D
All distances	0.50	1.56	1.84	0.41	0.33	0.34	1.23	1.28	0.28	0.21	0.24	0.85	1.16	0.17	0.14	0.14	0.85	0.54	0.09	0.07
0–24 a)	2.20	9.55	4.78	1.36	1.13	2.45	12.11	5.92	1.40	0.99	2.09	10.40	7.07	0.91	0.61	1.34	7.84	3.85	0.57	0.36
25–44	1.29	6.96	2.87	0.72	0.74	0.81	4.27	2.06	0.51	0.39	0.66	2.06	1.72	0.41	0.48	0.34	1.90	0.96	0.14	0.22
25–34	1.27	8.56	2.96	0.81	0.77	0.89	5.02	2.51	0.71	0.55	0.85	3.25	2.51	0.49	0.55	0.36	2.36	1.04	0.13	0.19
35–44	1.30	5.12	2.77	1.01	0.87	0.73	2.77	2.77	0.29	0.41	0.49	0.68	0.92	0.43	0.44	0.32	1.36	0.69	0.11	0.25
45–64	1.04	3.01	1.52	0.66	0.87	0.71	1.23	0.90	0.51	0.71	0.51	0.55	1.17	0.49	0.34	0.35	1.37	0.41	0.26	0.24
65–114	0.70	0.91	1.67	0.48	0.66	0.41	0.41	0.93	0.39	0.32	0.24	0.58	0.50	0.18	0.20	0.16	0.33	0.34	0.15	0.11
115–164	0.45	b)	0.71	0.54	0.33	0.23	b)	0.44	0.21	0.21	0.19	–	0.49	0.17	0.16	0.06	–	–	0.05	0.07
165–264	0.23	b)	0.75	0.28	0.21	0.12	b)	0.75	0.15	0.08	0.06	–	0.50	0.06	0.09	0.02	–	–	0.04	0.01
265–over	0.07	b)	–	0.06	0.07	0.06	b)	–	0.07	0.05	0.03	–	–	0.07	0.02	0.01	–	–	–	0.02

Subdominant

Distance zone (miles)	2500–4999 All metro.	A	B	C	D	5000–9999 All metro.	A	B	C	D	10,000–24,999 All metro.	A	B	C	D	25,000–over All metro.	A	B	C	D
All distances	0.68	1.85	0.53	0.61	0.66	0.47	1.85	0.59	0.33	0.31	0.35	1.12	0.65	0.15	0.20	0.34	1.25	0.43	0.20	0.27
0–24 a)	2.20	9.55	4.78	1.36	1.13	2.45	12.11	5.92	1.40	0.99	2.09	10.40	7.07	0.91	0.61	1.34	7.84	3.85	0.57	0.36
25–44	1.33	2.83	1.75	1.12	0.85	1.02	1.44	2.80	0.84	0.28	0.89	1.89	1.75	0.28	0.56	1.02	1.41	2.10	0.84	0.56
25–34	1.27	2.20	1.85	0.85	0.96	1.52	1.45	2.67	0.66	0.08	1.52	1.75	2.04	0.26	1.05	1.77	0.75	2.01	1.99	1.08
35–44	1.31	3.97	1.65	1.45	0.78	0.65	1.32	1.65	0.97	0.20	0.44	1.46	0.82	0.07	0.20	0.76	2.65	1.63	0.69	0.59
45–64	1.12	1.58	1.34	1.11	0.92	0.41	1.01	0.76	0.32	0.09	0.34	2.65	0.57	–	0.36	0.52	1.01	0.96	0.41	0.36
65–114	1.02	5.27	1.17	0.88	0.92	0.52	0.88	1.10	0.46	0.41	0.35	0.51	0.30	0.23	0.10	0.30	1.76	0.55	0.18	0.27
115–164	0.46	–	0.52	0.43	0.57	0.27	–	0.52	0.22	0.27	0.19	–	0.26	0.09	0.30	0.13	–	0.20	0.20	0.10
165–264	0.36	–	0.28	0.49	0.28	0.20	–	0.28	0.09	0.28	0.15	–	0.25	0.11	0.04	0.10	–	0.11	0.11	0.12
265–over	0.12	–	0.12	–	0.19	0.16	–	0.06	0.77	0.19	–	–	–	–	–	0.08	–	–	0.39	0.19

Local

Distance zone (miles)	2500–4999 All metro.	A	B	C	D	5000–9999 All metro.	A	B	C	D	10,000–24,999 All metro.	A	B	C	D	25,000–over Local c)
All distances	0.43	2.05	1.26	0.30	0.36	0.29	1.14	0.84	0.19	0.19	0.18	1.14	0.73	0.12	0.13	·
0–24 a)	2.20	9.55	4.78	1.36	1.13	2.45	12.11	5.92	1.40	0.99	2.09	10.40	7.07	0.91	0.61	·
25–44	1.17	5.67	3.35	0.88	0.78	0.59	2.83	1.03	0.26	0.61	0.46	1.89	1.80	0.13	0.44	·
25–34	1.73	5.38	3.84	1.06	1.58	0.91	1.69	0.43	0.35	1.17	0.62	1.69	1.28	0.24	0.68	·
35–44	0.86	8.56	2.60	0.77	0.44	0.40	4.28	1.95	0.21	0.24	0.38	2.14	2.60	0.07	0.34	·
45–64	0.65	1.72	1.16	0.57	0.48	0.61	0.86	0.72	0.39	0.68	0.30	1.07	0.58	0.22	0.20	·
65–114	0.57	2.09	1.00	0.36	0.56	0.35	0.38	0.59	0.29	0.35	0.22	–	0.23	0.16	0.27	·
115–164	0.40	–	0.77	0.30	0.42	0.27	–	–	0.25	0.30	0.08	–	0.15	0.06	0.09	·
165–264	0.18	–	0.28	0.21	0.17	0.14	–	0.25	0.15	0.14	0.03	–	–	0.05	0.03	·
265–over	0.09	–	0.39	0.08	0.09	0.03	–	0.39	0.02	0.03	0.03	–	–	0.03	0.03	·

a) No sector types shown separately for distances of less than 25 miles. A combined value for all sectors is reported for each sector type at this distance zone for purposes of comparison with other zones. Zone 0-24 miles includes land area and cities of counties containing central cities.

b) Area in eastern California and western Nevada and Arizona arbitrarily excluded as being unrepresentative of average hinterland area.

c) By definition there are no cities of 25,000 or more inhabitants at distances greater than 10 miles from the metropolis in local sectors.

Source: Sixteenth Census of the United States. Compiled from Population, Vol.I, State tables 3 and 5; Areas of the United States, 1940, tables 2, 3, and 4.

Appendix Table IV

Number of hinterland counties, classified by size class of metropolitan community, type of sector, distance from the nearest metropolis, and size of largest city contained, United States, 1940.

Size class of metropolitan community and distance (miles)	SUMMARY—BY SECTOR TYPE				Intermetropolitan						Subdominant						Local					
	All Sectors	Inter-metro-politan	Subdom-inant	Local	No City	2,500-4,999	5,000-9,999	10,000-24,999	25,000-49,999	50,000-over	No City	2,500-4,999	5,000-9,999	10,000-24,999	25,000-49,999	50,000-over	No City	2,500-4,999	5,000-9,999	10,000-24,999	25,000-49,999	50,000-over

TYPE OF SECTOR BY SIZE OF LARGEST CITY CONTAINED

a) The independent cities of Virginia were considered to lie in no county. Counties containing central cities have been excluded.

Source: Sixteenth Census of the United States. Compiled from Population, Vol.I, State tables 2 and 5.

Appendix Table V

Habitation ratios: Rural-nonfarm population per 100 square miles of rural land area. County units classified by size of largest city contained, size class of metropolitan community, and distance from nearest metropolis. United States, 1940.[a])

Class of metro-politan community and distance zone (miles)	Size of largest city contained (thousand inhabitants)					
	No city	2.5-4.9	5.0-9.9	10.0-24.9	25.0-49.9	50.0 - over
Class D, total	379	491	657	1,152	1,734	2,749
0-24	1,443	1,964	1,852	2,882	7,182	5,977
25-34	1,683	1,029	1,115	1,530	1,102	11,353
35-44	980	1,068	504	1,351	3,062	3,405
45-64	976	789	1,202	1,602	1,698	2,474
65-114	721	659	1,266	1,644	2,796	3,302
115-164	568	656	757	1,107	1,791	3,179
165-264	345	295	516	572	1,788	2,014
265-over	121	114	126	302	600	658
Class C, total	470	584	779	838	1,643	3,136
0-24	1,993	2,446	2,153	4,040	6,152	8,195
25-34	1,231	1,596	876	2,275	2,143	-
35-44	1,026	832	1,707	1,284	1,977	2,562
45-64	921	888	1,365	1,104	1,955	2,622
65-114	780	617	810	975	2,352	2,109
115-164	574	629	705	715	812	3,059
165-264	411	577	643	567	1,265	3,695
265-over	150	81	203	230	1,540	-
Class B, total	1,079	1,402	1,833	3,012	4,227	4,670
0-24	4,192	7,214	12,215	10,788	14,172	9,490
25-34	2,180	3,823	2,775	4,326	11,240	6,788
35-44	1,667	1,561	6,409	8,335	3,437	6,072
45-64	1,203	2,418	2,919	3,651	4,371	5,543
65-114	1,451	1,242	1,919	3,145	2,778	6,485
115-164	1,040	867	1,422	1,179	4,679	3,132
165-264	661	2,584	942	913	1,041	758
265-over	359	706	783	-	-	-
Class A,[b]) total	321	1,549	1,673	8,310	1,434	11,614
0-24	-	-	10,380	82,872	22,722	40,371
25-34	-	-	5,513	8,652	7,527	11,030
35-44	-	-	28,798	6,391	5,614	14,661
45-64	4,542	2,458	4,904	3,847	3,943	7,649
65-114	1,071	1,335	1,811	1,595	1,641	10,377
115-164	-	-	-	-	-	-
165-264	70	-	-	-	-	-
265-over	54	-	-	-	-	-

a) Counties containing central cities and counties containing no rural population have been excluded. The independent cities of Virginia were classified as lying in no county.

b) Distances of 115 miles or more have been excluded as being unrepresentative of the average hinterland of this class of metropolitan community.

Source: Sixteenth Census of the United States. Compiled from Population, Vol.I, State tables 3 and 5; Population, Vol.II, State tables 26; Areas of the United States, 1940, tables 2, 3, and 4.

Appendix Table VI

Habitation ratios: Rural-farm population per 100 square miles of rural land area. Counties classified by size of largest city contained, size class of metropolitan community, and distance from nearest metropolis. United States, 1940.[a]

Size of metropolis and distance zone (miles)	Size of largest city contained (thousand inhabitants)					
	No. city	2.5 - 4.9	5.0 - 9.9	10.0 - 24.9	25.0 - 49.9	50.0 - over
Class D total	579	870	947	1295	1439	1508
0-24	2502	2226	2578	2848	1705	1771
25-34	1682	2331	2124	1744	1633	2169
35-44	1456	1461	763	1746	1764	1761
45-64	1566	1893	1598	1754	1627	2174
65-114	1264	1113	1953	1466	2061	2501
115-164	970	1274	1423	1760	2647	2395
165-264	463	518	512	539	1380	948
265-over	139	199	134	399	280	416
Class C total	920	1436	1511	1286	1436	1980
0-24	2625	2494	2776	2313	3068	3397
25-34	1437	2252	2367	2086	2392	-
35-44	2232	1484	1764	1972	1463	913
45-64	1689	2335	2622	1672	2376	1488
65-114	1772	1751	1576	1847	1825	1310
115-164	1318	1895	1859	1551	858	1947
165-264	752	1454	1176	953	885	3009
265-over	220	154	407	196	2005	-
Class B total	1382	1393	1347	1698	2076	1948
0-24	2651	2050	3044	3432	2655	2264
25-34	2062	3191	2049	1689	2630	3703
35-44	2120	1793	2903	2362	3114	2174
45-64	1812	1967	2083	2181	2882	2487
65-114	1724	1428	1602	1915	2321	2308
115-164	1328	1569	1319	1204	2346	1505
165-264	1229	1796	1197	840	1035	950
265-over	109	347	466	-	-	-
Class A[b] total	152	2139	805	2244	547	3058
0-24	-	-	3365	1528	4179	3126
25-34	-	-	2339	2979	2521	2323
35-44	-	-	1926	2785	1916	2010
45-64	933	2223	1881	1336	2421	3765
65-114	1905	2119	2097	2835	584	2810

a) Counties containing central cities and counties containing no rural population have been excluded. The independent cities of Virginia were classified as lying in no county.

b) Distances of 115 miles or more have been excluded as being unrepresentative of the average hinterland of this class of metropolitan community.

Source: Sixteenth Census of the United States. Compiled from Population, Vol.I, State tables 3 and 5; Population, Vol.II, State table 27; Areas of the United States, 1940, tables 2, 3 and 4.

Appendix Table VII

Specialization in retail trade - principal hinterland cities classified by size: Per capita retail sales of hinterland cities of 10,000 or more inhabitants, classified by size, type of sector, size class of metropolitan community, and distance from the nearest metropolis. United States, 1939-40.

Size class of metropolitan community and distance (miles)	PER CAPITA RETAIL SALES (DOLLARS) BY SIZE OF HINTERLAND CITY AND TYPE OF SECTOR									
	10,000-24,999				25,000 - 49,999 [a]			50,000 - over [a]		
	All sectors	Inter-metropolitan	Subdom-inant	Local	All sectors	Inter-metropolitan	Subdom-inant	All sectors	Inter-metropolitan	Subdom-inant
Class D										
0-14	300	368	235	221	359	378	286	405	381	325
15-34	424	388	534	478	441	445	431	478	467	537
35-64	493	471	615	485	479	462	514	548	548	-
65-114	518	478	516	563	528	510	548	491	485	549
115-164	510	520	478	517	498	500	506	411	411	-
165-264	603	623	599	516	512	571	440	477	512	464
265-over	581	599	-	615	688	693	662	733	733	-
All distances	491	480	518	503	496	499	500	493	500	470
Class C										
0-14	271	279	210	270	299	341	263	476	476	-
15-34	483	478	135	595	464	466	463	406	503	368
35-64	526	519	-	548	479	479	-	393	382	407
65-114	473	501	314	497	556	543	619	458	448	494
115-164	479	474	437	572	445	522	363	446	433	461
165-264	508	530	429	610	529	562	453	481	525	402
265-over	622	612	-	640	601	-	601	-	-	-
All distances	472	491	369	471	471	502	462	452	469	415
Class B										
0-14	260	300	261	260	303	309	242	416	468	325
15-34	431	508	203	369	443	417	486	435	401	439
35-64	494	516	503	425	461	482	434	507	528	463
65-114	499	527	444	572	521	533	506	532	520	624
115-164	504	491	499	673	534	-	534	-	-	-
165-264	455	558	434	-	608	-	608	879	-	879
265-over	-	-	-	-	-	-	-	-	-	-
All distances	420	459	375	377	420	403	441	468	495	446
Class A										
0-14	296	328	267	233	383	353	481	461	460	499
15-34	437	383	478	554	538	538	-	484	481	514
35-64	551	504	468	641	553	553	555	508	494	540
65-114	473	473	-	-	673	753	452	434	-	434
All distances	415	387	403	487	490	491	505	476	473	508

a) By definition local sectors can contain cities of 25,000 or more inhabitants only at distances of less than 10 miles. Cities of this size lying in local sectors are included in the "all sectors" total

Source: Sixteenth Census of the United States. Compiled from Population, Vol.I, State tables 3 and 5; Retail Trade, 1939, Vol.II, table 16.

Appendix Table VIII

Specialization in retail trade - Rural areas and cities of less than 10,000 inhabitants: Per capita retail sales of counties, with cities of 10,000 or more inhabitants excluded, classified by size of largest city contained, type of sector, size class of metropolitan community, and distance from the nearest metropolis. United States. 1939-40.

Size class of metropolitan community and distance (miles)	SUMMARY-ALL SECTORS BY SIZE OF LARGEST CITY CONTAINED						PER CAPITA RETAIL SALES BY SIZE OF LARGEST CITY CONTAINED AND TYPE OF SECTOR a)(DOLLARS)																
							NO CITY			2,500 - 4,999			5,000 - 9,999			10,000 - 24,999			25,000-49,999		50,000-over	
	No city	2,500-4,999	5,000-9,999	10,000-24,999	25,000-49,999	50,000-over	Inter-metropolitan	Subdominant	Local	Inter-metropolitan	Subdominant	Local	Inter-metropolitan	Subdominant	Local	Inter-metropolitan	Subdominant	Local	Inter-metropolitan	Subdominant	Inter-metropolitan	Subdominant
Class D																						
0-14	126	90	740	63	-	-	126	-	-	90	-	-	740	-	-	63	-	-	-	-	-	-
15-34	134	172	223	178	218	163	141	89	121	156	110	204	228	-	211	160	196	202	188	251	162	-
35-64	140	201	243	143	195	161	148	105	138	209	156	206	232	227	256	127	128	167	187	200	161	-
65-114	129	204	211	133	151	116	129	118	132	193	201	222	208	193	221	133	60	159	135	167	107	237
115-164	136	182	213	117	122	89	138	100	151	178	170	189	207	223	215	107	124	134	111	200	89	-
165-264	160	198	266	121	130	76	155	127	182	210	129	207	248	204	307	107	151	149	167	87	92	75
265-over	223	282	355	168	110	159	224	171	227	283	190	289	351	413	464	148	-	202	112	102	159	-
All distances	149	198	237	140	162	138	154	114	155	199	162	210	235	211	246	129	117	168	147	184	137	133
Class C																						
0-14	106	-	60	242	48	121	106	-	-	-	-	-	-	60	-	-	242	-	-	-	121	-
15-34	145	208	220	186	191	176	138	171	133	175	160	248	212	-	270	174	-	201	144	250	-	171
35-64	144	184	208	112	116	178	145	157	129	162	157	229	223	-	194	110	-	122	101	-	90	286
65-114	119	167	210	123	112	68	117	114	127	178	171	144	213	183	215	132	70	111	114	36	65	78
115-164	110	164	182	84	129	92	127	82	104	160	151	197	189	167	177	91	66	84	142	111	60	93
165-264	129	145	180	104	82	96	140	100	135	157	120	148	169	133	239	89	51	148	93	57	99	84
265-over	167	279	283	133	109	-	162	90	181	288	163	302	281	142	364	124	-	154	-	109	-	-
All distances	128	171	203	123	118	110	133	112	131	168	143	198	204	166	213	121	71	143	113	101	86	129
Class B																						
0-14	-	-	225	188	189	-	-	-	-	-	-	-	-	-	225	188	-	-	189	-	-	-
15-34	211	212	292	208	177	204	-	-	211	237	327	115	306	-	199	244	-	105	194	155	209	204
35-64	171	233	221	195	173	219	170	-	171	198	173	285	223	284	204	186	275	237	149	226	187	229
65-114	144	203	274	205	205	175	127	159	154	207	152	207	245	164	316	233	185	190	198	215	175	-
115-164	163	223	249	149	154	270	155	192	134	196	216	276	245	254	-	143	206	103	140	160	-	270
165-264	125	244	243	175	178	213	151	131	103	244	-	-	217	253	-	105	187	-	-	178	-	213
265-over	232	277	243	-	-	-	-	232	-	-	277	-	-	244	239	-	-	-	-	-	-	-
All distances	156	223	256	193	180	205	146	164	158	211	231	233	256	249	262	195	196	184	179	181	188	224
Class A b)																						
0-14	-	-	-	-	-	201	-	-	-	-	-	-	-	-	-	-	-	-	-	-	201	-
15-34	-	-	272	271	257	207	-	-	-	-	-	-	-	-	272	237	219	319	257	-	221	205
35-64	443	299	393	286	230	243	361	-	504	290	-	305	325	372	430	306	-	270	222	206	256	205
65-114	241	268	338	166	222	303	283	-	227	262	-	291	-	318	348	166	-	-	222	-	353	170
115-164	-	-	-	-	-	-	-	-	-	-	-	-	-	-	-	-	-	-	-	-	-	-
165-264	-	-	-	-	-	-	-	-	-	-	-	-	-	-	-	-	-	-	-	-	-	-
265-over	-	-	-	-	-	-	-	-	-	-	-	-	-	-	-	-	-	-	-	-	-	-
All distances	385	291	370	273	243	238	367	-	397	279	-	294	356	355	383	253	219	302	244	225	256	202

a) The independent cities of Virginia were considered as lying in no county. Counties containing central cities have been excluded.

b) In Class A metropolitan communities counties lying at distances greater than 115 miles have been excluded from the distance breakdown, but are included in the totals.

Source: Sixteenth Census of the United States. Compiled from Population, Vol.I, State tables 3 and 5; Retail Trade, 1939, Vol.II, table 16.

Appendix Table IX

Service specialization - principal hinterland cities classified by size: Per capita receipts from services of hinterland cities of 10,000 or more inhabitants classified by size, type of sector, size class of metropolitan community, and distance from the nearest metropolis. United States, 1939-40.

| Size of metropolitan community and distance (miles) | PER CAPITA RECEIPTS FROM SERVICES (DOLLARS) BY SIZE OF HINTERLAND CITY AND TYPE OF SECTOR | | | | | | | | | |
| | 10,000 - 24,999 | | | | 25,000 - 49,999[a] | | | 50,000 - over[a] | | |
	All sectors	Inter-metropolitan	Subdominant	Local	All sectors	Inter-metropolitan	Subdominant	All sectors	Inter-metropolitan	Subdominant
Class D										
0-14	21.0	24.2	29.6	11.5	26.6	31.4	14.4	25.2	23.7	17.6
15-34	23.5	21.7	29.6	25.9	26.4	28.1	22.5	30.4	29.7	34.3
35-64	27.2	27.3	30.6	25.7	30.2	30.2	30.0	43.3	43.3	-
65-114	28.8	27.3	30.2	30.4	34.5	33.1	36.0	38.1	38.5	34.2
115-164	30.8	34.7	23.8	27.2	36.5	38.3	34.3	37.0	37.0	-
165-264	35.4	38.3	27.8	24.8	40.6	37.6	44.2	37.3	42.5	35.5
265-over	32.9	30.3	-	37.1	48.6	47.8	52.7	76.6	76.6	-
All distances	28.1	28.5	27.9	27.3	33.2	34.0	32.0	37.7	39.2	32.0
Class C										
0-14	16.1	21.7	7.7	13.4	17.0	22.1	14.0	33.3	33.3	-
15-34	33.7	36.0	9.9	32.8	29.4	24.3	31.0	28.8	41.0	23.9
35-64	29.5	29.1	-	30.6	27.3	27.3	-	51.0	30.1	77.0
65-114	31.1	31.3	32.0	30.3	36.3	35.1	42.5	33.1	33.9	30.1
115-164	33.0	32.6	32.3	37.4	36.4	41.6	18.4	45.5	37.6	55.3
165-264	34.0	36.5	30.7	35.0	36.8	39.1	31.5	38.2	43.1	29.5
265-over	35.8	35.9	-	35.7	42.0	-	42.0	-	-	-
All distances	30.0	31.5	29.4	26.8	29.8	32.1	29.5	36.0	35.8	36.4
Class B										
0-14	17.5	15.9	19.5	18.3	27.4	25.2	23.6	34.4	40.6	26.9
15-34	25.1	30.9	17.9	17.9	25.0	22.3	29.6	29.5	20.5	30.6
35-64	24.8	26.4	27.4	18.9	25.2	25.0	25.6	34.9	35.6	33.5
65-114	28.5	32.9	23.5	28.5	29.4	28.2	30.9	37.3	35.7	49.6
115-164	33.7	33.0	34.8	37.0	34.4	-	34.4	-	-	-
165-264	22.0	20.0	22.4	-	34.1	-	34.1	68.3	-	68.3
265-over	-	-	-	-	-	-	-	-	-	-
All distances	24.2	26.6	22.3	20.2	27.5	25.0	28.6	34.7	37.2	33.1
Class A										
0-14	20.4	24.1	17.1	12.9	31.6	33.1	30.7	45.0	47.5	32.1
15-34	31.2	30.3	31.4	33.2	32.3	32.3	-	39.5	39.8	36.4
35-64	35.2	31.4	32.3	40.3	34.3	33.1	37.4	35.4	36.8	32.4
65-114	26.4	26.4	-	-	41.2	50.6	15.5	25.9	-	25.9
All distances	28.2	28.1	26.7	29.4	33.4	34.5	31.2	41.1	43.2	32.2

a) By definition local sectors can contain cities of 25,000 or more inhabitants only at distances of less than 10 miles. Cities of this size lying in local sectors are included in the "all sectors" total.

Source: Sixteenth Census of the United States. Compiled from Population, Vol.I, State tables 3 and 5; Service Establishments, 1939, table 2.

Appendix Table X

Service specialization – Rural areas and cities of less than 10,000 inhabitants: Per capita receipts from services of counties, with cities of 10,000 or more inhabitants excluded, classified by size of largest city contained, type of sector, size class of metropolitan community, and distance from the nearest metropolis. United States, 1939-40.

PER CAPITA RECEIPTS FROM SERVICES — SUMMARY-ALL SECTORS, BY SIZE OF LARGEST CITY CONTAINED

Size class of metropolitan community and distance (miles)	No city	2,500-4,999	5,000-9,999	10,000-24,999	25,000-49,999	50,000-over
Class D						
0-14	3.8	—	34.7	0.9	7.9	7.0
15-34	5.0	9.7	10.6	7.1	8.9	6.6
35-64	6.8	9.7	11.9	7.7	6.9	6.8
65-114	6.3	9.7	10.9	6.5	6.9	6.4
115-164	6.3	9.6	10.9	5.6	6.1	6.4
165-264	7.1	9.2	12.3	4.8	5.7	3.3
265-over	8.2	12.2	16.9	6.7	4.3	8.6
All distances	6.7	9.7	11.7	6.5	7.3	6.2
Class C						
0-14	4.6	—	2.6	12.4	1.4	3.3
15-34	6.3	10.3	11.1	7.7	6.7	6.1
35-64	6.6	8.7	12.2	5.4	5.3	11.9
65-114	5.9	9.1	10.7	5.9	6.0	2.8
115-164	5.5	8.2	9.5	3.8	6.0	3.1
165-264	5.7	7.0	9.2	5.0	3.8	2.7
265-over	5.7	13.6	14.2	6.0	3.5	—
All distances	5.9	8.6	10.6	5.6	5.6	4.3
Class B						
0-14	7.0	10.2	11.3	8.0	9.6	10.0
15-34	7.6	10.9	24.4	10.2	6.7	10.1
35-64	7.0	8.8	8.9	8.5	7.5	6.4
65-114	8.2	8.0	13.9	8.8	9.2	10.0
115-164	5.3	5.7	10.5	6.8	4.8	10.0
165-264	10.6	10.5	10.8	6.1	6.7	16.6
265-over	—	—	9.7	—	—	—
All distances	7.1	9.7	13.1	8.4	7.5	9.6
Class A [b]						
0-14	—	—	—	—	—	12.9
15-34	14.7	6.8	12.6	14.4	13.4	8.1
35-64	9.0	10.9	18.5	13.2	9.9	14.5
65-114	—	—	16.6	6.5	10.2	15.7
All distances	12.8	9.8	18.3	13.9	11.9	13.4

PER CAPITA RECEIPTS FROM SERVICES, BY SIZE OF LARGEST CITY CONTAINED AND TYPE OF SECTOR [a] (DOLLARS)

Size class and distance	No city Inter-metro	No city Subdom	No city Local	2,500-4,999 Inter-metro	2,500-4,999 Subdom	2,500-4,999 Local	5,000-9,999 Inter-metro	5,000-9,999 Subdom	5,000-9,999 Local	10,000-24,999 Inter-metro	10,000-24,999 Metro	10,000-24,999 Subdom	10,000-24,999 Local	25,000-49,999 Inter-metro	25,000-49,999 Metro	25,000-49,999 Subdom	25,000-49,999 Local	50,000-over Inter-metro	50,000-over Metro	50,000-over Subdom
Class D																				
0-14	3.8	6.5	4.8	4.8	6.9	12.2	34.7	—	11.5	0.9	—	7.1	8.4	6.4	—	9.7	—	6.8	—	—
15-34	5.0	7.9	6.6	8.1	6.8	9.4	10.3	10.9	12.1	7.3	—	6.4	8.0	10.1	—	5.3	7.0	6.6	—	—
35-64	6.8	5.9	6.3	10.6	8.3	9.9	11.7	9.3	11.1	6.4	—	5.0	7.6	5.9	—	6.3	7.9	4.4	—	9.3
65-114	6.3	4.4	6.9	9.3	9.2	10.0	11.5	12.9	11.9	5.6	—	4.9	6.4	8.6	—	7.7	7.2	6.4	—	—
115-164	6.8	5.7	6.9	9.4	5.6	10.4	10.7	12.0	14.0	4.1	—	4.5	6.6	3.4	—	3.1	6.9	11.9	—	2.6
165-264	7.0	14.6	7.8	10.7	6.9	16.3	16.3	22.7	18.6	6.5	—	4.5	7.1	3.4	—	9.5	—	8.6	—	—
265-over	7.8	—	8.5	—	—	—	—	—	—	—	—	—	—	—	—	—	—	—	—	2.6
All distances	6.8	5.6	6.9	9.7	7.6	10.4	11.6	11.4	11.8	6.0	—	5.6	6.4	7.0	—	7.9	7.6	6.2	—	5.0
Class C																				
0-14	4.6	7.2	5.7	9.6	8.0	11.2	10.9	2.6	12.2	7.9	12.4	—	7.5	5.3	3.3	3.6	—	3.3	—	6.6
15-34	6.1	6.7	6.3	7.9	7.6	10.5	11.3	—	13.1	5.6	—	—	4.4	4.6	—	—	7.1	31.7	—	7.1
35-64	6.7	4.9	6.4	9.3	10.5	8.3	10.8	9.1	11.2	6.6	1.6	—	5.3	6.3	—	3.8	2.6	3.3
65-114	6.0	5.0	6.4	7.9	7.1	9.0	9.7	9.1	9.3	3.3	3.0	—	7.2	7.7	—	3.1	1.5	2.8
115-164	6.0	4.8	5.8	6.8	8.0	7.5	9.2	7.4	10.1	4.5	2.4	—	6.9	4.1	—	3.5	2.6	3.4
165-264	5.9	3.7	5.5	13.8	6.8	15.0	12.4	9.6	21.4	5.8	—	—	6.6	—	—	—	—	—
265-over	5.6	—	5.9	—	10.5	—	—	—	—	—	—	—	—	—	—	—	—	—
All distances	6.0	5.3	6.0	8.2	8.1	9.6	10.4	8.8	11.6	5.7	3.0	—	6.4	5.8	—	3.3	3.5	—	4.6
Class B																				
0-14	—	—	7.0	14.2	9.3	3.4	26.8	—	11.3	8.0	—	—	11.3	9.6	—	4.9	5.0	—	—	9.6
15-34	7.8	—	7.4	10.7	6.9	—	9.7	10.1	8.4	12.1	14.0	—	8.4	8.2	—	10.5	9.1	9.6	—	11.9
35-64	6.3	—	7.5	9.7	7.1	8.1	12.7	9.1	7.5	8.2	6.5	—	15.8	6.2	—	10.8	7.9	7.6
65-114	7.4	7.0	8.0	8.7	8.0	11.1	10.7	10.4	—	11.5	8.2	—	—	8.1	—	10.8	4.4	6.4
115-164	4.9	9.0	5.1	9.7	—	—	8.2	11.7	—	6.8	6.6	—	—	4.5	—	4.9	—	10.0
165-264	—	5.4	—	—	10.5	—	—	9.7	—	3.2	—	—	9.7	—	—	6.7	—	16.6
265-over	—	10.6	—	9.7	—	—	—	9.7	—	—	—	—	9.7	—	—	—	—	—
All distances	6.9	7.3	7.2	10.5	8.6	9.5	14.8	10.6	12.3	9.0	7.4	—	12.3	7.8	—	7.0	7.7	—	12.4
Class A [b]																				
0-14	—	—	—	—	—	—	—	—	—	—	—	—	—	—	—	—	—	12.9	10.5	16.6
15-34	7.9	—	19.8	11.1	—	4.3	14.6	17.5	12.6	10.4	5.7	—	20.7	13.4	—	—	7.8	8.8
35-64	12.0	—	7.9	8.5	—	11.1	—	16.3	20.6	14.6	—	12.1	8.6	—	9.7	5.2
65-114	—	—	—	—	—	—	—	—	16.7	6.5	—	—	10.2	—	—	—
All distances	10.5	—	14.3	10.1	—	9.8	18.6	17.2	18.2	11.4	5.7	—	17.7	12.0	—	11.0	16.0	—	8.1

a) The independent cities of Virginia were considered to lie in no county. Counties containing central cities have been excluded.

b) In Class A a metropolitan communities counties lying at distances greater than 115 miles have been excluded from the distance breakdown but are included in the totals.

Source: Sixteenth Census of the United States. Compiled from *Population, Vol.I*, State tables 3 and 5; *Service Establishments, 1939*, table 2.

Appendix Table XI

Specialization in wholesale trade - principal hinterland cities classified by size: Per capita wholesale sales of hinterland cities of 10,000 or more inhabitants, classified by size, type of sector, size class of metropolitan community, and distance from the nearest metropolis. United States, 1939-40.

| Size of metropolitan community and distance (miles) | PER CAPITA WHOLESALE SALES (DOLLARS) BY SIZE OF HINTERLAND CITY AND TYPE OF SECTOR | | | | | | | | | |
| | 10,000-24,999 | | | | 25,000-49,999[a] | | | 50,000-over[a] | | |
	All sectors	Inter-metropolitan	Subdominant	Local	All sectors	Inter-metropolitan	Subdominant	All sectors	Inter-metropolitan	Subdominant
Class D										
0-14	141	189	98	85	197	418	65	203	96	89
15-34	198	200	175	200	176	181	162	268	294	121
35-64	238	211	272	275	329	329	328	529	529	-
65-114	304	279	288	333	496	559	429	748	783	389
115-164	497	503	661	285	625	673	403	591	591	-
165-264	451	489	374	306	896	1045	714	540	678	489
265-over	371	304	-	480	617	538	1026	757	757	-
All distances	305	301	393	285	421	452	376	518	562	332
Class C										
0-14	89	67	8	110	216	232	537	516	516	-
15-34	825	1098	10	155	155	122	166	309	549	213
35-64	236	250	-	184	225	225	-	580	607	546
65-114	323	295	441	323	385	314	743	415	417	408
115-164	498	497	388	646	393	463	318	672	679	663
165-264	391	319	493	360	670	823	322	655	753	479
265-over	387	425	-	316	613	-	613	-	-	-
All distances	357	394	411	250	329	328	409	504	550	406
Class B										
0-14	60	78	29	61	216	151	396	242	324	122
15-34	129	163	102	72	140	115	182	258	200	265
35-64	178	209	164	96	203	204	202	399	424	349
65-114	287	354	200	326	266	288	238	433	379	835
115-164	246	279	182	199	629	-	629	-	-	-
165-264	237	247	235	-	556	-	556	933	-	933
265-over	-	-	-	-	-	-	-	-	-	-
All distances	161	194	136	110	250	177	348	324	358	308
Class A										
0-14	100	104	131	68	110	92	97	393	436	122
15-34	138	125	155	159	218	218	-	329	340	230
35-64	251	127	391	288	257	261	249	389	369	433
65-114	214	214	-	-	330	341	300	456	-	456
All distances	149	129	205	167	194	192	181	373	392	302

a) By definition local sectors contain cities of 25,000 or more inhabitants only at distances of less than 10 miles. Cities of this size lying in local sectors are included in the "all sectors" total.

Source: Sixteenth Census of the United States. Compiled from Population, Vol.I, State tables 3 and 5; Wholesale Trade, 1939, Vol.II, table 13.

Appendix Table XII

Specialization in wholesale trade – Rural areas and cities of less than 10,000 inhabitants: Per capita wholesale sales of counties, with cities of 10,000 or more inhabitants excluded, classified by size of largest city contained, type of sector, size class of metropolitan community, and distance from the nearest metropolis. United States, 1939-40.

Size class of metropolitan community and distance (miles)	SUMMARY—ALL SECTORS, BY SIZE OF LARGEST CITY: No city	2,500-4,999	5,000-9,999	10,000-24,999	25,000-49,999	50,000-over	No City Inter-metro	No City Subdom	No City Local	2,500-4,999 Inter-metro	2,500-4,999 Subdom	2,500-4,999 Local	5,000-9,999 Inter-metro	5,000-9,999 Subdom	5,000-9,999 Local	10,000-24,999 Inter-metro	10,000-24,999 Subdom	10,000-24,999 Local	25,000-49,999 Inter-metro	25,000-49,999 Subdom	25,000-49,999 Local	50,000-over Inter-metro	50,000-over Subdom
Class D																							
0-14	8	48	244	28	–	49	8	–	–	48	–	–	244	–	–	28	–	–	–	–	–	–	–
15-34	71	67	104	62	51	82	68	–	85	58	28	87	102	–	107	59	64	65	57	56	56	43	–
35-64	73	93	128	66	81	65	97	22	59	101	63	90	111	97	114	48	66	87	105	60	60	82	63
65-114	558	108	101	68	83	80	69	47	52	102	137	110	96	110	105	68	45	77	56	112	112	65	–
115-164	56	114	148	72	77	143	69	31	57	107	92	129	137	190	143	65	64	64	76	123	123	80	–
165-264	64	93	120	74	72	–	64	59	66	107	84	73	112	84	140	61	97	103	85	58	58	663	98
265-over	122	125	177	118	68	95	116	121	132	120	89	139	182	221	150	131	–	96	73	35	35	95	–
All distances	68	102	124	70	77	70	78	44	65	101	90	106	123	128	123	64	31	107	78	87	60	67	86
Class C																							
0-14	12	–	16	60	42	184	12	–	–	–	–	–	–	16	–	–	60	–	–	–	–	184	–
15-34	107	114	94	54	38	68	89	36	269	67	52	170	97	–	74	63	–	43	52	24	53	–	57
35-64	53	75	100	51	45	397	60	49	41	76	52	84	107	142	94	50	16	52	50	31	171	205	31
65-114	49	82	120	45	54	27	53	37	46	95	76	57	118	88	115	52	36	34	52	52	51	24	35
115-164	53	101	97	36	82	31	66	36	45	97	96	119	100	80	98	31	29	57	122	51	26	9	10
165-264	60	77	94	95	171	35	69	40	63	82	58	88	92	108	109	65	–	161	226	–	41	36	30
265-over	77	118	167	76	51	–	84	78	67	113	13	123	165	–	204	73	–	82	–	–	–	–	–
All distances	59	88	108	55	67	87	62	40	65	89	70	100	108	112	107	51	31	70	78	39	60	116	38
Class B																							
0-14	–	–	22	11	59	–	–	–	–	–	–	–	–	–	–	11	–	–	59	–	–	–	–
15-34	32	81	75	133	78	303	75	–	32	120	61	19	76	83	22	90	60	72	99	53	53	430	23
35-64	58	95	65	37	65	59	34	61	36	83	29	130	66	47	72	36	25	59	18	171	171	32	101
65-114	49	71	113	69	58	70	102	37	58	64	53	81	106	77	59	124	78	46	63	51	51	70	–
115-164	76	95	91	76	32	22	96	25	100	97	96	92	105	86	126	77	55	67	45	26	26	–	22
165-264	32	152	95	50	41	144	–	64	25	152	–	–	121	228	–	24	–	–	–	41	–	–	144
265-over	64	53	201	–	–	–	–	–	–	–	53	–	–	–	133	–	–	–	–	–	–	–	–
All distances	52	85	96	59	60	126	64	38	53	92	64	91	93	110	109	61	43	90	60	60	60	164	90
Class A b)																							
0-14	–	–	–	–	–	43	–	–	–	–	–	–	–	–	–	–	–	–	–	–	–	43	–
15-34	–	–	91	66	159	26	–	–	–	–	–	–	–	–	91	34	28	108	159	–	–	35	24
35-64	97	135	121	150	117	102	90	–	168	76	–	168	112	261	109	212	–	99	106	154	154	122	46
65-114	122	219	125	62	61	49	137	–	223	180	–	223	–	49	159	62	–	159	61	81	81	37	81
All distances	109	198	134	90	136	76	101	–	212	118	–	212	158	196	109	84	28	105	138	147	147	94	40

a) The independent cities of Virginia were considered to lie in no county. Counties containing central cities have been excluded.

b) In Class A metropolitan communities counties lying at distances greater than 115 miles have been excluded from the distance breakdown, but are included in the totals.

Source: Sixteenth Census of the United States. Compiled from Population, Vol.I, State tables 3 and 5; Wholesale Trade, 1939, Vol.II, Table 13.

Appendix Table XIII

Manufacturing specialization - principal hinterland cities classified by size: Per capita value added by manufacture, of hinterland cities of 10,000 or more inhabitants classified by size, type of sector, size class of metropolitan community, and distance from the nearest metropolis. United States, 1939-40.

Size of metro-politan community and distance (miles)	PER CAPITA RECEIPTS FROM MANUFACTURING (DOLLARS) BY SIZE OF HINTERLAND CITY AND TYPE OF SECTOR										
	10,000 - 24,999				25,000 - 49,999 [a]			50,000 - over [a]		
	All Sectors	Inter-metro-politan	Subdom-inant	Local	All Sectors	Inter-metro-politan	Subdom-inant	All sectors	Inter-metro-politan	Subdom-inant
Class D										
0-14	341	435	316	216	209	49	314	332	527	70
15-34	282	270	293	303	568	577	547	439	510	35
35-64	253	304	175	185	312	275	388	365	365	-
65-114	168	162	211	169	222	225	219	374	339	738
115-164	177	142	203	250	136	131	155	239	239	-
165-264	84	65	192	129	173	236	97	106	48	128
265-over	83	45	-	143	53	51	62	74	74	-
All distances	207	210	213	200	263	249	289	336	357	203
Class C										
0-14	192	134	333	220	285	422	58	272	272	-
15-34	322	411	166	72	231	303	208	304	237	331
35-64	227	259	-	116	456	456	-	149	168	126
65-114	177	201	56	192	196	222	71	131	97	252
115-164	102	103	118	75	167	186	146	136	146	123
165-264	114	171	86	37	76	70	90	97	92	105
265-over	75	67	-	91	75	-	75	-	-	-
All distances	173	197	98	149	257	303	128	192	178	221
Class B										
0-14	290	365	71	389	179	196	187	240	267	243
15-34	360	368	348	353	545	690	302	503	529	500
35-64	390	334	285	606	383	424	332	426	415	450
65-114	406	479	354	320	301	353	234	294	313	154
115-164	227	197	358	33	296	-	296	-	-	-
165-264	208	324	184	-	193	-	193	174	-	174
265-over	-	-	-	-	-	-	-	-	-	-
All distances	338	358	253	412	311	363	265	336	323	387
Class A										
0-14	231	224	91	405	421	395	155	525	417	1234
15-34	272	319	204	199	313	313	-	439	433	498
35-64	292	399	219	251	291	316	228	533	491	626
65-114	403	403	-	-	237	224	273	420	-	420
All distances	274	311	169	255	339	333	203	496	434	755

a) By definition local sectors can contain cities of 25,000 or more inhabitants only at distances of less than 10 miles. Cities of this size lying in local sectors are included in the "all sectors" total.

Source: Sixteenth Census of the United States. Compiled from Population, Vol.I, State Tables 3 and 5; Manufactures, 1939, Vol.II, State table 2.

Appendix Table XIV

Specialization in manufacturing – Rural areas and cities of less than 10,000 inhabitants: Per capita value added by manufacture of counties, with cities of 10,000 or more inhabitants excluded, classified by size of largest city contained, type of sector, size class of metropolitan community, and distance from the nearest metropolis. United States, 1939-40.

SUMMARY—ALL SECTORS BY SIZE OF LARGEST CITY CONTAINED

Size class of metropolitan community and distance (miles)	No City	2,500-4,999	5,000-9,999	10,000-24,999	25,000-49,999	50,000-over
Class D						
0-14	6	8	-	11	-	-
15-34	101	79	125	238	66	55
35-64	29	55	92	93	153	181
65-114	18	46	81	94	127	40
115-164	33	46	68	77	40	263
165-264	30	30	67	47	193	127
265-over	20	28	74	127	81	28
All distances	29	45	82	111	114	87
Class C						
0-14	2	-	10	315	8	76
15-34	60	117	107	167	135	115
35-64	23	44	88	95	110	233
65-114	15	35	65	48	113	413
115-164	16	28	33	40	120	130
165-264	18	31	47	49	50	135
265-over	15	67	20	189	148	-
All distances	20	42	61	81	120	204
Class B						
0-14	-	-	11	592	135	-
15-34	38	73	130	160	292	211
35-64	12	53	280	157	154	289
65-114	36	59	58	92	108	127
115-164	29	57	69	119	284	75
165-264	51	45	99	171	176	71
265-over	111	139	70	-	-	-
All distances	35	64	107	159	200	208
Class A [b]						
0-14	-	-	-	-	-	220
15-34	-	-	729	106	259	232
35-64	39	152	117	182	240	234
65-114	19	60	128	33	65	261
All distances	31	83	184	127	200	234

PER CAPITA VALUE ADDED BY MANUFACTURING BY SIZE OF LARGEST CITY CONTAINED AND TYPE OF SECTOR [a] (DOLLARS)

Size class and distance (miles)	No City Inter-metropolitan	No City Subdominant	No City Local	2,500-4,999 Inter-metropolitan	2,500-4,999 Subdominant	2,500-4,999 Local	5,000-9,999 Inter-metropolitan	5,000-9,999 Subdominant	5,000-9,999 Local	10,000-24,999 Inter-metropolitan	10,000-24,999 Subdominant	10,000-24,999 Local	25,000-49,999 Inter-metropolitan	25,000-49,999 Subdominant	50,000-over Inter-metropolitan	50,000-over Subdominant
Class D																
0-14	6	-	-	8	-	-	-	-	-	11	84	114	-	-	-	-
15-34	124	21	46	44	124	107	149	-	62	315	71	110	9	135	57	-
35-64	35	49	21	49	69	60	80	105	103	85	135	157	134	148	181	-
65-114	16	83	21	48	57	98	47	75	106	80	94	52	140	112	38	61
115-164	18	27	23	48	49	48	33	84	94	50	24	48	33	76	265	-
165-264	29	2	32	35	21	48	56	19	96	85	-	196	10	407	536	106
265-over	21	-	20	-	21	11	-	-	157	-	-	-	91	23	28	-
All distances	28	45	24	39	54	50	71	67	99	111	91	121	98	127	88	90
Class C																
0-14	2	-	-	-	-	-	-	10	-	-	315	-	-	-	76	118
15-34	76	23	68	67	147	167	99	-	156	122	-	24	56	24	403	297
35-64	25	26	16	29	56	63	87	74	88	106	11	51	88	89	477	227
65-114	11	25	13	27	16	59	44	24	99	79	17	83	156	231	94	154
115-164	11	17	19	29	24	27	32	45	22	50	68	32	32	56	149	57
165-264	18	20	17	30	35	26	51	21	32	18	-	66	48	148	-	-
265-over	6	13	30	13	262	65	20	-	20	118	-	358	-	-	-	-
All distances	19	22	21	32	79	66	54	58	76	70	49	119	106	148	242	152
Class B																
0-14	-	-	-	-	-	-	-	-	11	592	-	-	135	109	-	-
15-34	-	-	-	75	173	24	82	-	451	202	150	40	436	250	272	86
35-64	17	56	38	34	6	86	363	229	183	162	125	121	109	124	250	298
65-114	42	27	5	57	68	61	57	28	62	59	88	100	97	141	127	-
115-164	18	75	26	50	59	97	71	-	-	79	166	401	624	176	-	75
165-264	9	111	40	45	139	-	22	126	117	198	-	-	-	-	-	71
265-over	-	-	13	-	-	-	-	51	-	-	-	117	-	-	-	-
All distances	28	57	26	49	85	70	115	89	109	178	136	116	238	151	202	189
Class A [b]																
0-14	-	-	-	-	-	-	-	-	-	-	-	-	-	-	220	100
15-34	-	-	-	-	-	-	-	-	729	136	179	57	259	-	369	201
35-64	28	-	47	71	-	197	212	227	56	258	-	123	173	253	246	54
65-114	13	-	21	6	-	65	-	240	79	33	-	-	65	-	327	-
All distances	21	-	37	45	-	90	116	231	231	164	179	81	193	184	256	160

a) The independent cities of Virginia were considered to lie in no county. Counties containing central cities have been excluded.

b) In Class A metropolitan communities counties lying at distances greater than 115 miles have been excluded from the distance breakdown, but are included in the totals.

Source: Sixteenth Census of the United States. Compiled from Population, Vol.I, State tables 3 and 5; Manufactures, 1939, Vol.II, State table 2.

INDEX